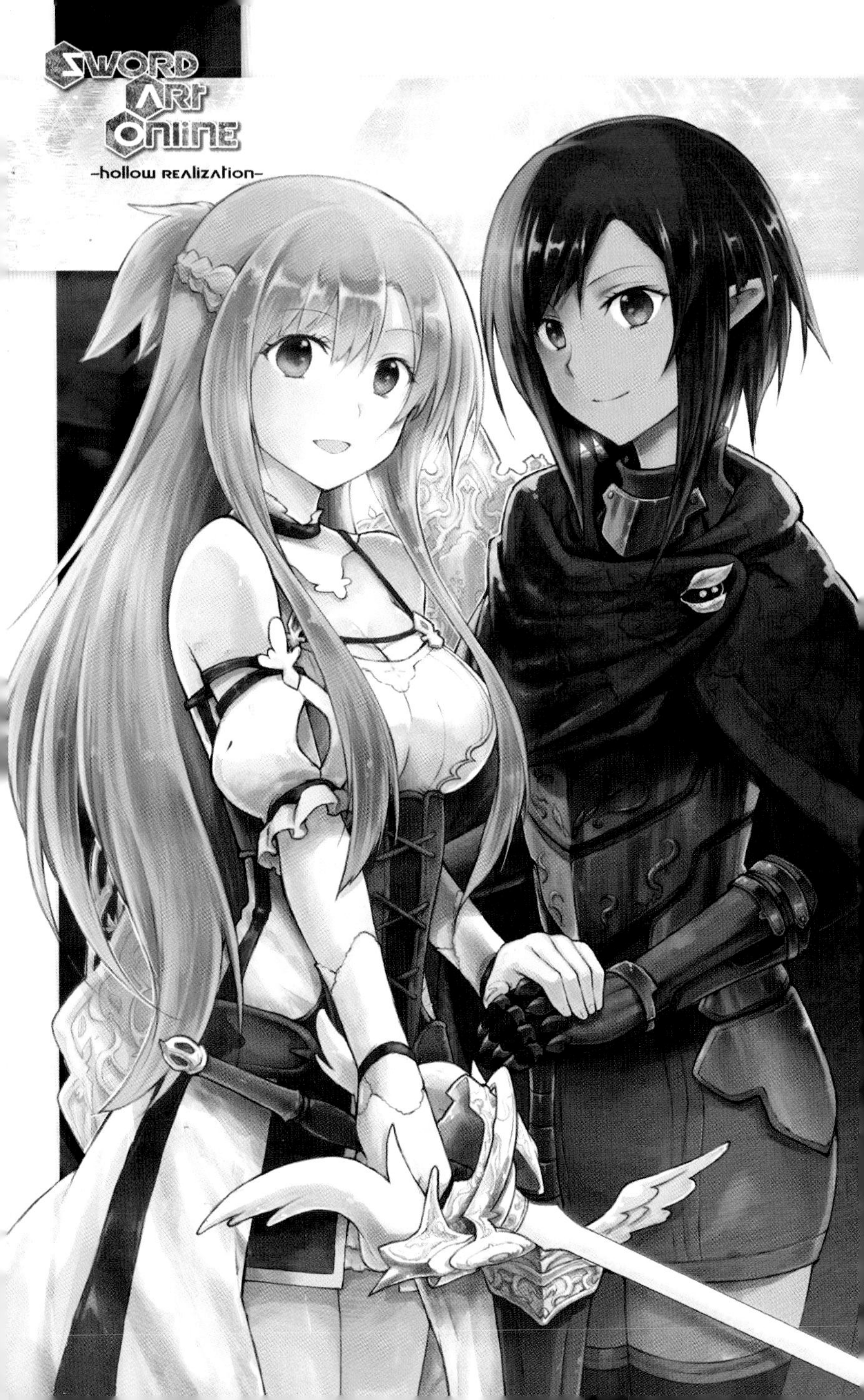
SWORD ART ONLINE
-hollow realization-

SWORD ART ONLINE
—HOLLOW REALIZATION—

003

CONTENTS

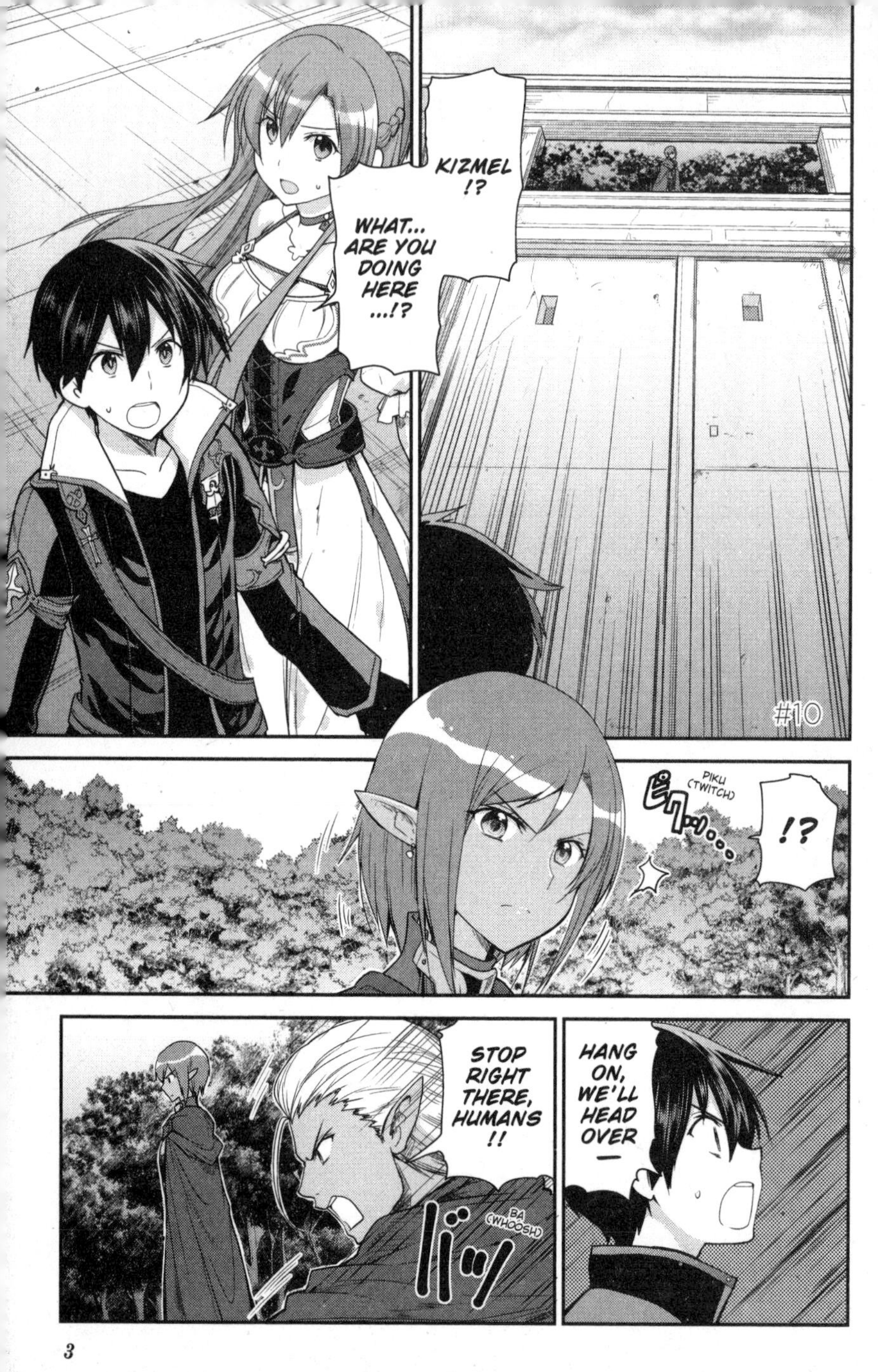
KIZMEL !?
WHAT... ARE YOU DOING HERE ...!?
#10
PIKU (TWITCH)
!?
HANG ON, WE'LL HEAD OVER —
STOP RIGHT THERE, HUMANS !!
BA (WHOOSH)

#10: The Dark Elf

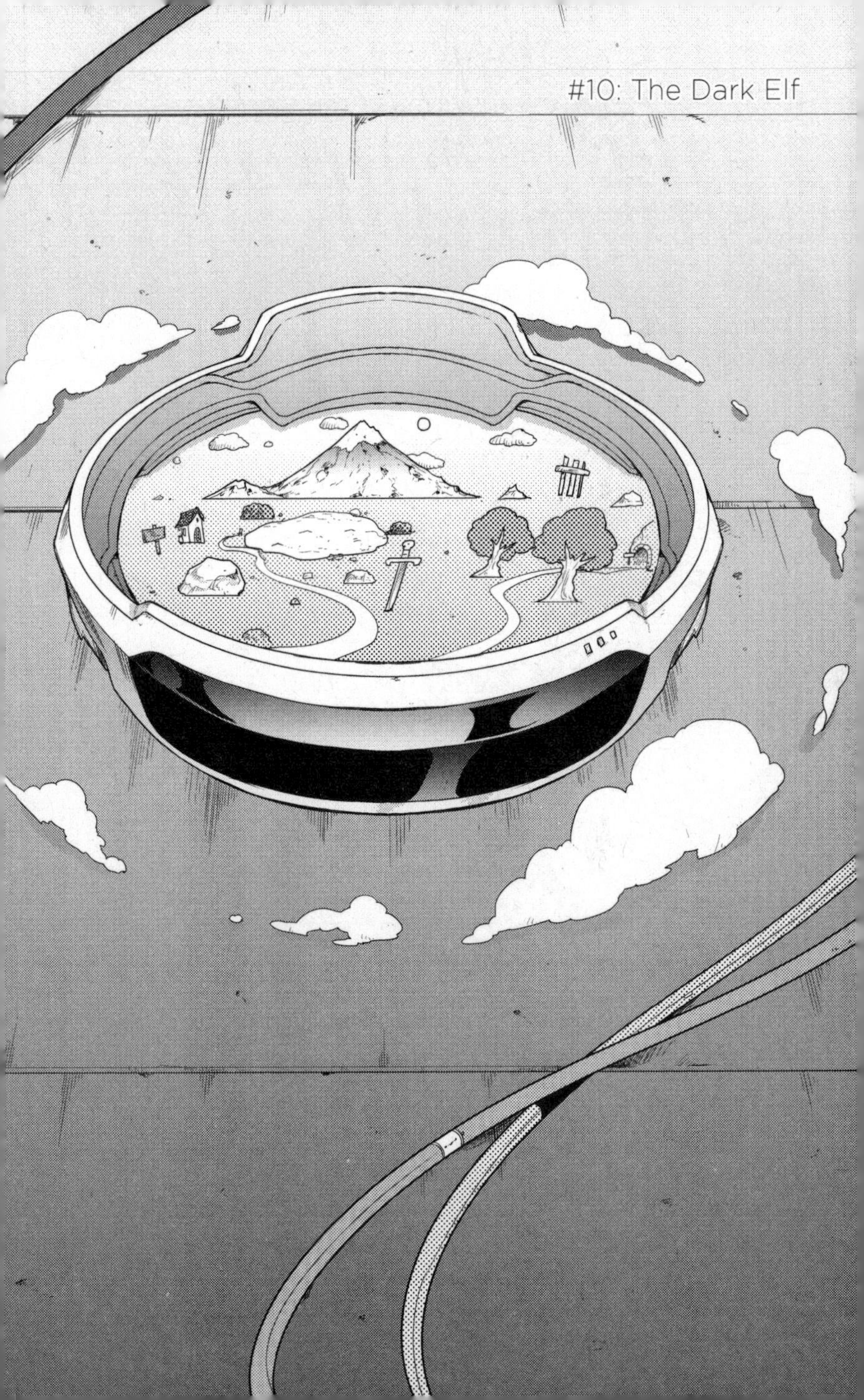

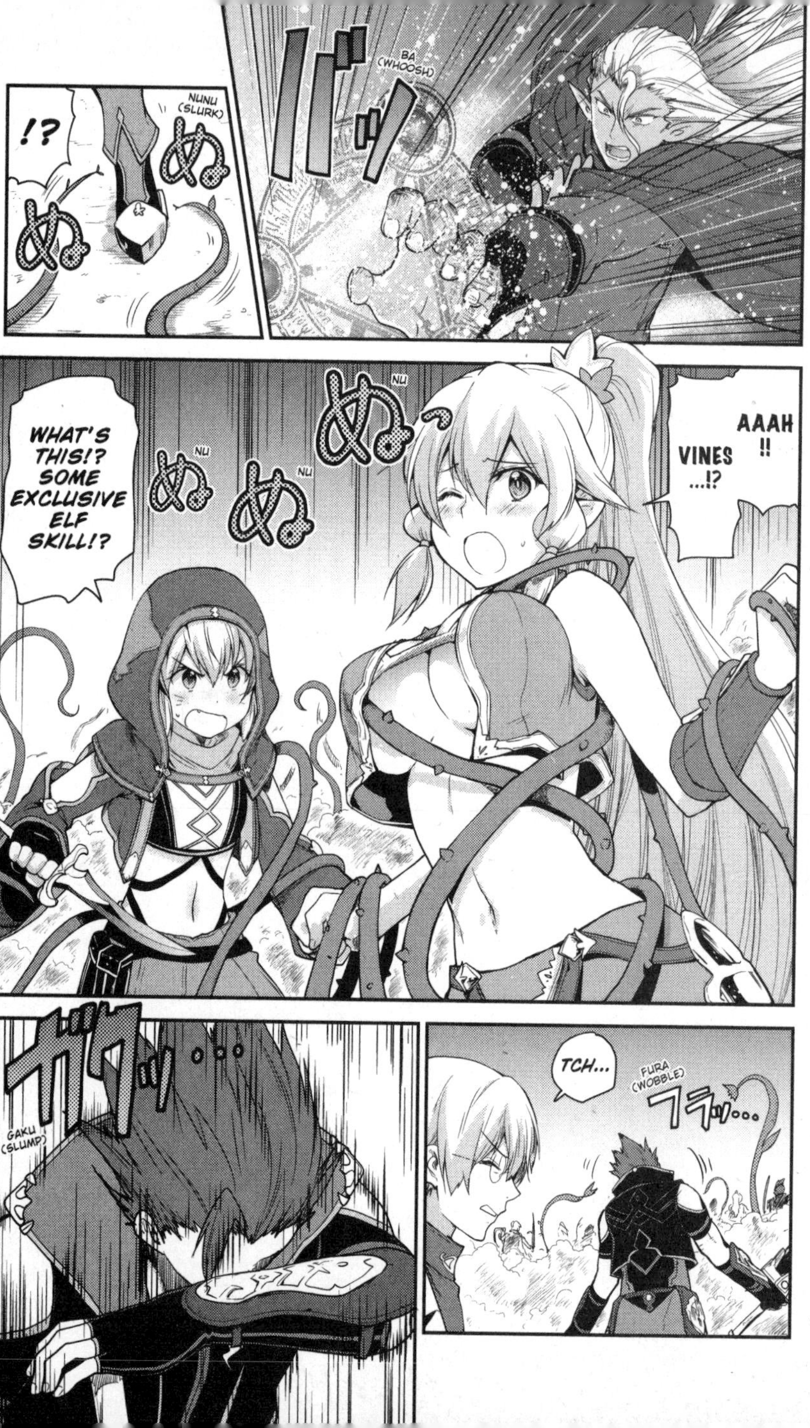

BA (WHOOSH)
NUNU (SLURK)
!?
AAAH!!
VINES ...!?
NU
NU
NU
WHAT'S THIS!? SOME EXCLUSIVE ELF SKILL!?
TCH...
FURA (WOBBLE)
GAKU (SLUMP)
...

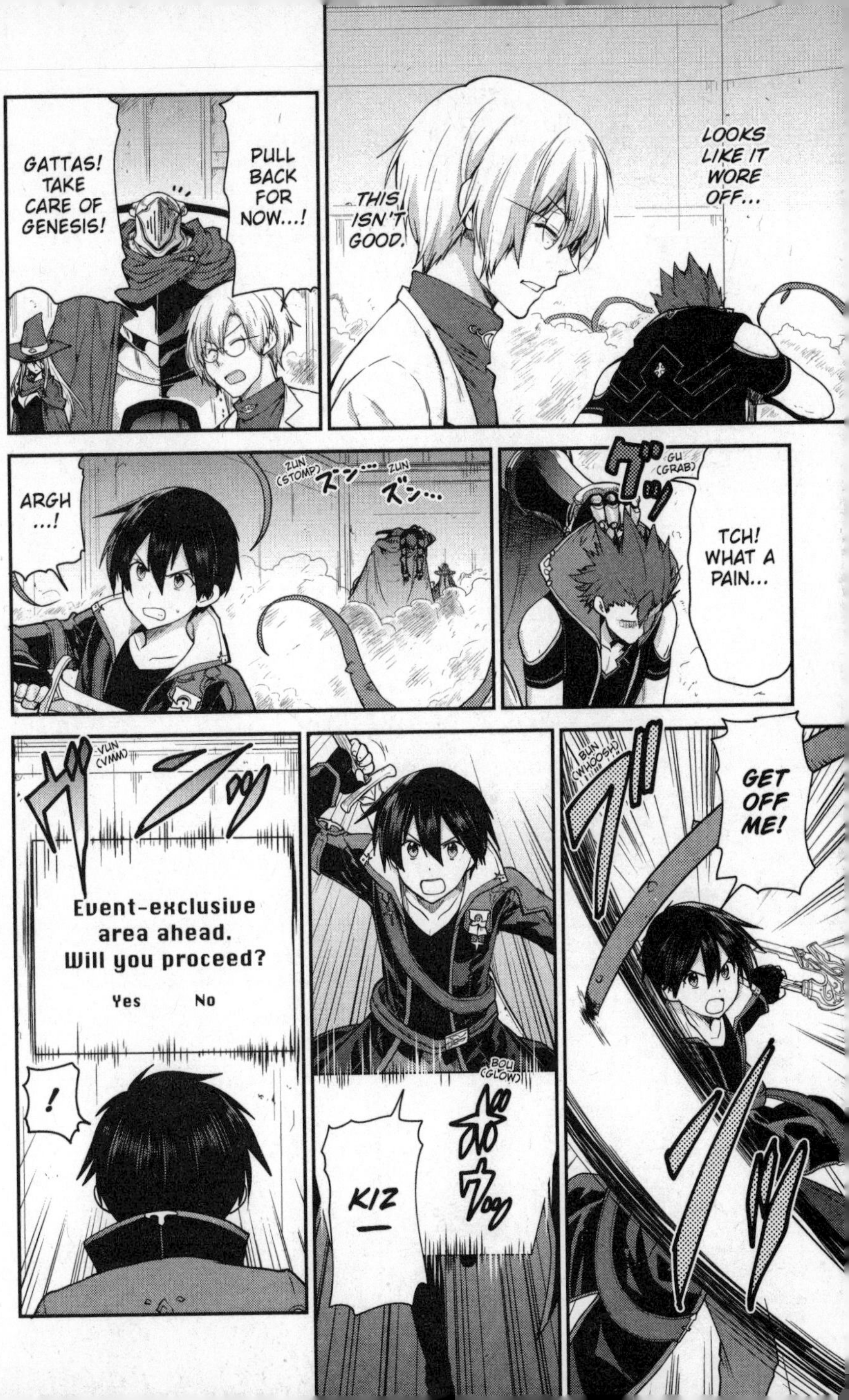

LOOKS LIKE IT WORE OFF...
THIS ISN'T GOOD.
PULL BACK FOR NOW...!
GATTAS! TAKE CARE OF GENESIS!
GU (GRAB)
TCH! WHAT A PAIN...
ZUN (STOMP)
ZUN
ARGH ...!
BUN (WHOOSH)
GET OFF ME!
BOU (GLOW)
KIZ —
VUN (VMM)
Event-exclusive area ahead. Will you proceed?
Yes No
!

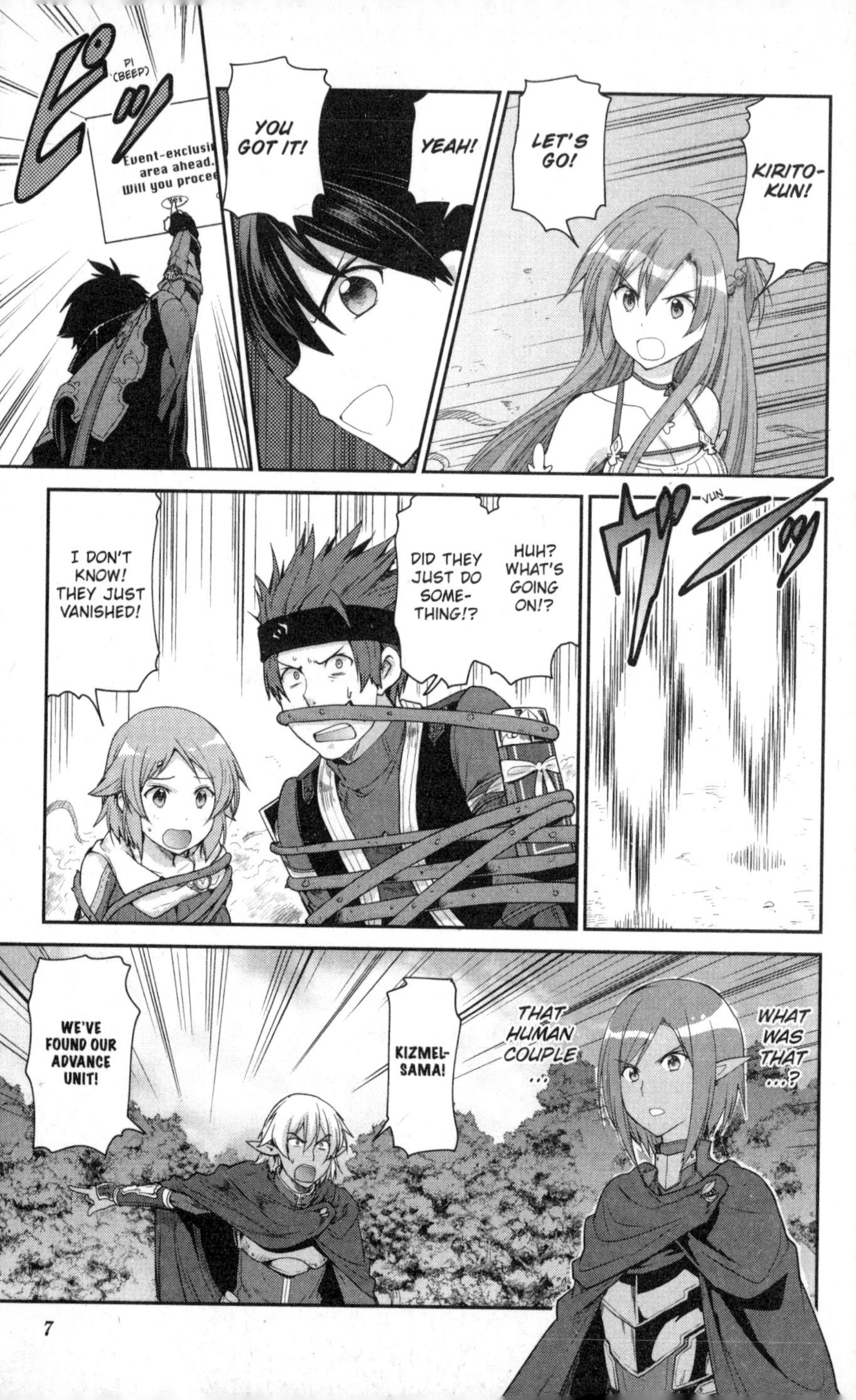
KIRITO-KUN!
LET'S GO!
YEAH!
YOU GOT IT!
PI (BEEP)
Event-exclusi
area ahead.
Will you procee
Yes
VUN
HUH? WHAT'S GOING ON!?
DID THEY JUST DO SOME-THING!?
I DON'T KNOW! THEY JUST VANISHED!
WHAT WAS THAT ...?
THAT HUMAN COUPLE ...?
KIZMEL-SAMA!
WE'VE FOUND OUR ADVANCE UNIT!

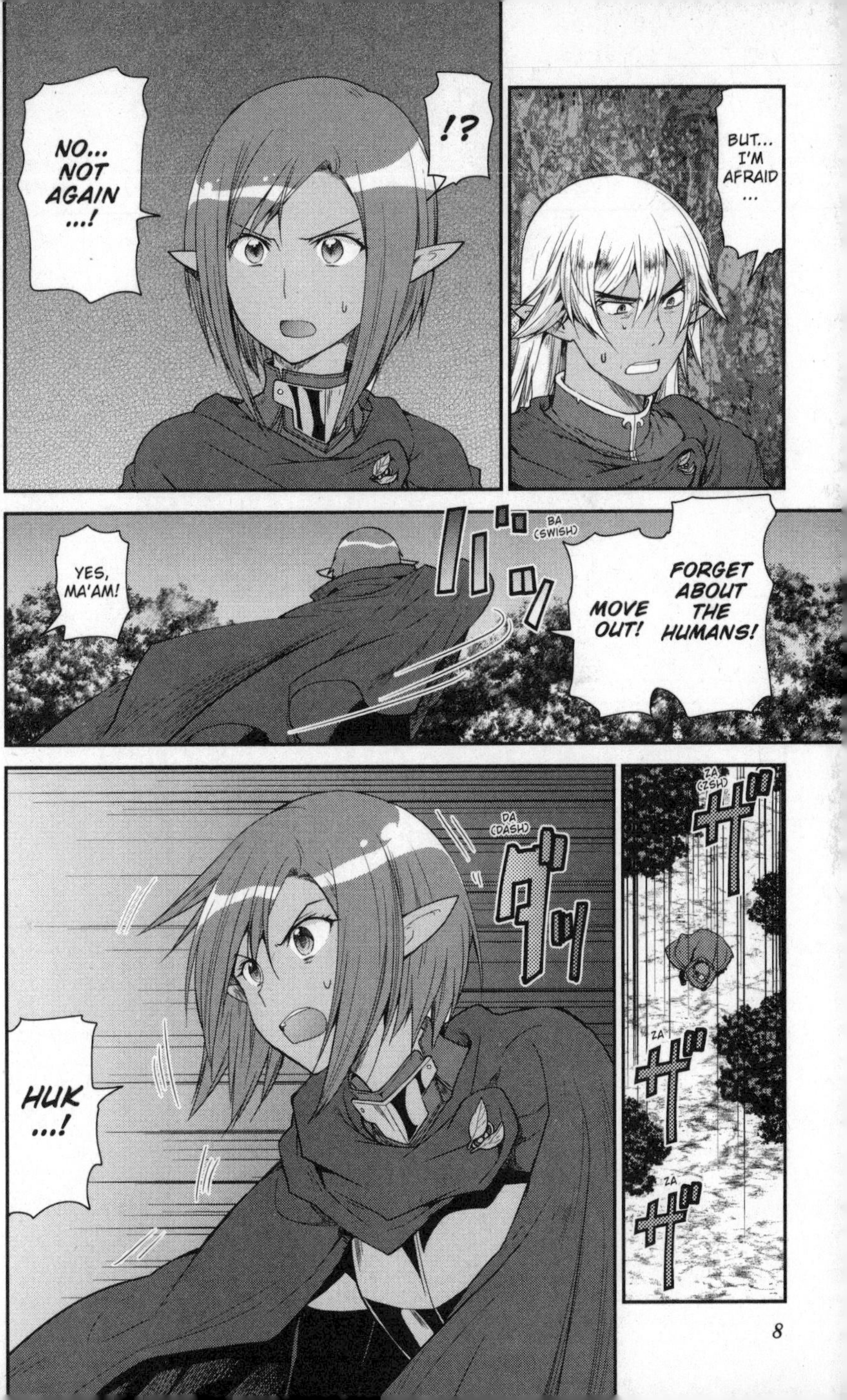
BUT... I'M AFRAID ...
!?
NO... NOT AGAIN ...!
BA (SWISH)
FORGET ABOUT THE HUMANS!
MOVE OUT!
YES, MA'AM!
ZA (ZSH)
ZA
ZA
DA (DASH)
HUK ...!

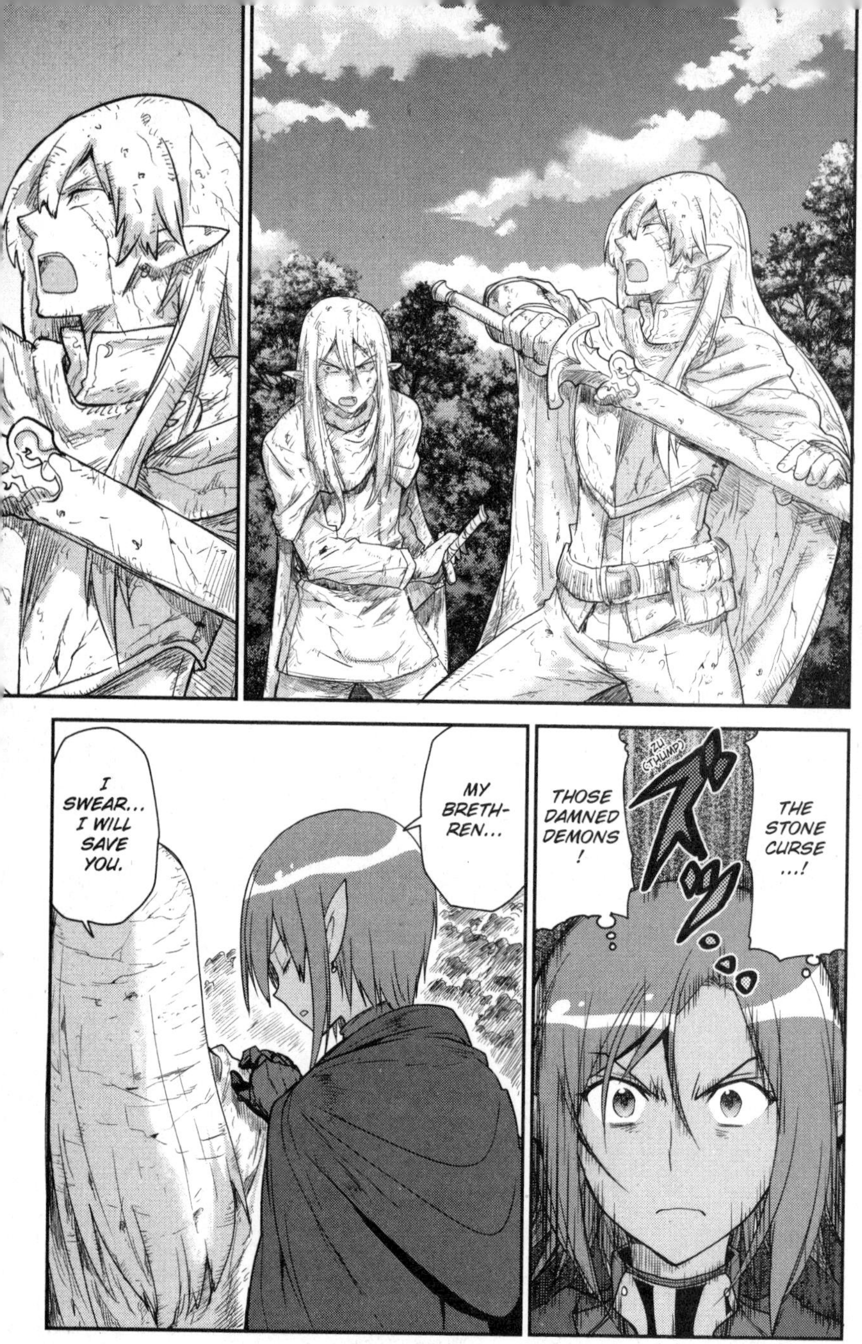
THE STONE CURSE ...!
ZU (THUMP)
THOSE DAMNED DEMONS!
MY BRETH-REN...
I SWEAR... I WILL SAVE YOU.

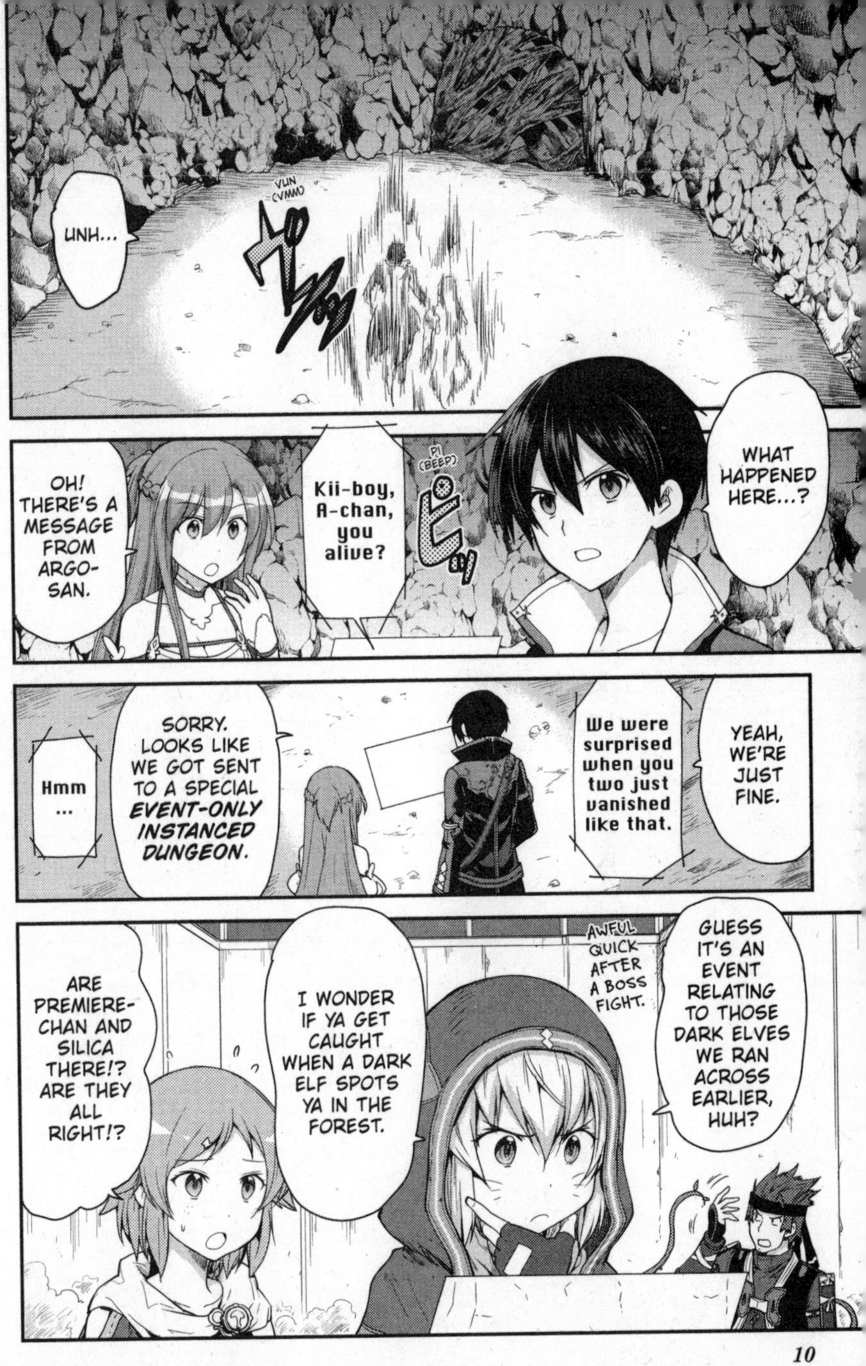
VUN (VMM)
UNH...
WHAT HAPPENED HERE...?
PI (BEEP)
Kii-boy, A-chan, you alive?
OH! THERE'S A MESSAGE FROM ARGO-SAN.
YEAH, WE'RE JUST FINE.
We were surprised when you two just vanished like that.
SORRY. LOOKS LIKE WE GOT SENT TO A SPECIAL *EVENT-ONLY INSTANCED DUNGEON*.
Hmm ...
GUESS IT'S AN EVENT RELATING TO THOSE DARK ELVES WE RAN ACROSS EARLIER, HUH?
AWFUL QUICK AFTER A BOSS FIGHT.
I WONDER IF YA GET CAUGHT WHEN A DARK ELF SPOTS YA IN THE FOREST.
ARE PREMIERE-CHAN AND SILICA THERE!? ARE THEY ALL RIGHT!?

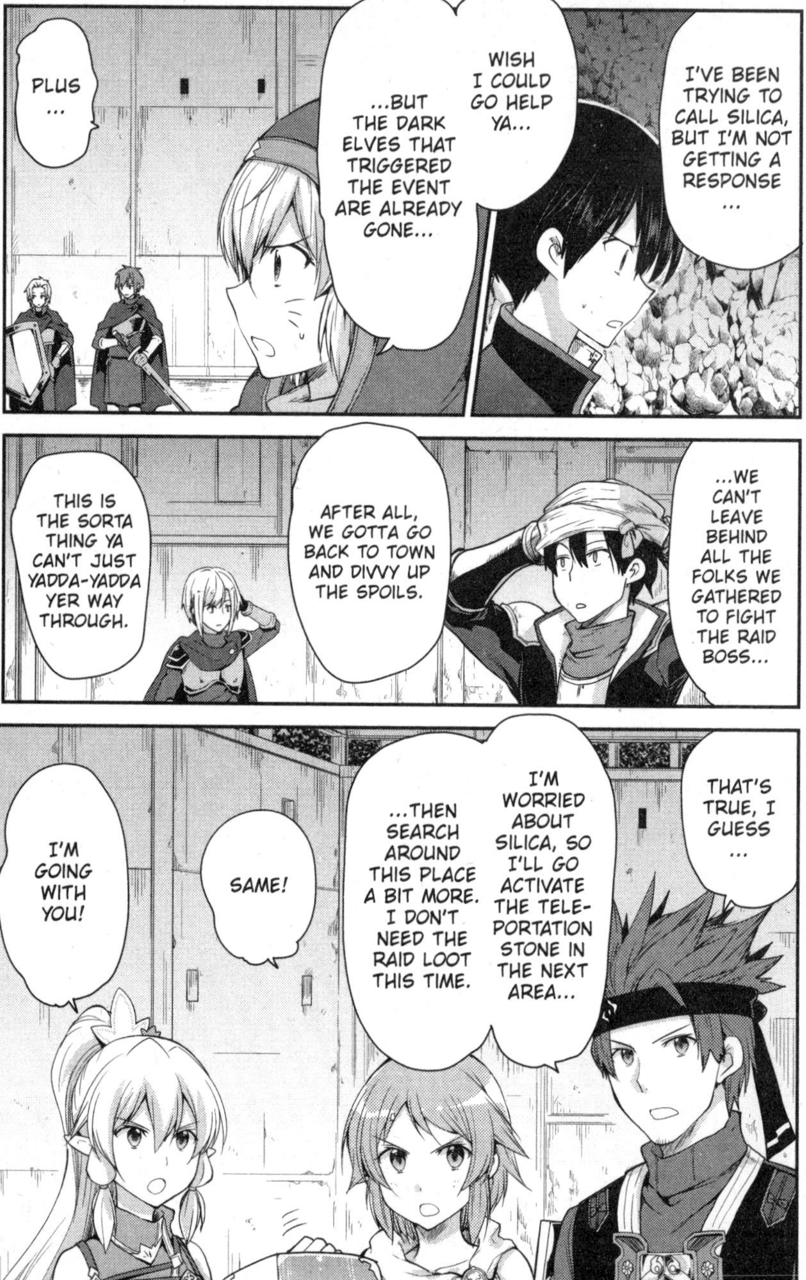
I'VE BEEN TRYING TO CALL SILICA, BUT I'M NOT GETTING A RESPONSE ...
WISH I COULD GO HELP YA...
...BUT THE DARK ELVES THAT TRIGGERED THE EVENT ARE ALREADY GONE...
PLUS ...
...WE CAN'T LEAVE BEHIND ALL THE FOLKS WE GATHERED TO FIGHT THE RAID BOSS...
AFTER ALL, WE GOTTA GO BACK TO TOWN AND DIVVY UP THE SPOILS.
THIS IS THE SORTA THING YA CAN'T JUST YADDA-YADDA YER WAY THROUGH.
THAT'S TRUE, I GUESS ...
I'M WORRIED ABOUT SILICA, SO I'LL GO ACTIVATE THE TELE-PORTATION STONE IN THE NEXT AREA...
...THEN SEARCH AROUND THIS PLACE A BIT MORE. I DON'T NEED THE RAID LOOT THIS TIME.
SAME!
I'M GOING WITH YOU!

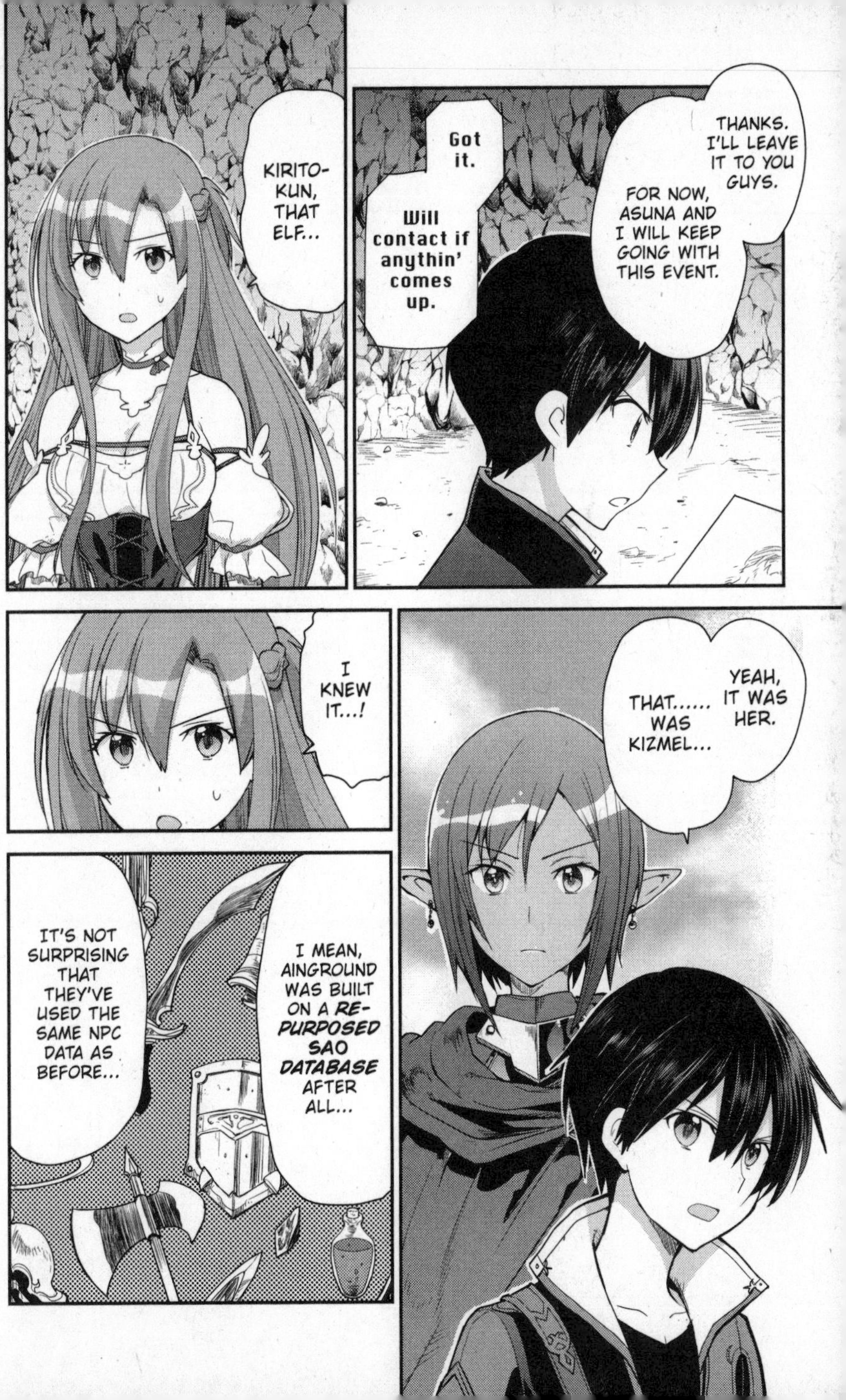
THANKS. I'LL LEAVE IT TO YOU GUYS.
FOR NOW, ASUNA AND I WILL KEEP GOING WITH THIS EVENT.
Got it.
Will contact if anythin' comes up.
KIRITO-KUN, THAT ELF...
YEAH, IT WAS HER.
THAT...... WAS KIZMEL...
I KNEW IT...!
I MEAN, AINGROUND WAS BUILT ON A ***RE-PURPOSED SAO DATABASE*** AFTER ALL...
IT'S NOT SURPRISING THAT THEY'VE USED THE SAME NPC DATA AS BEFORE...

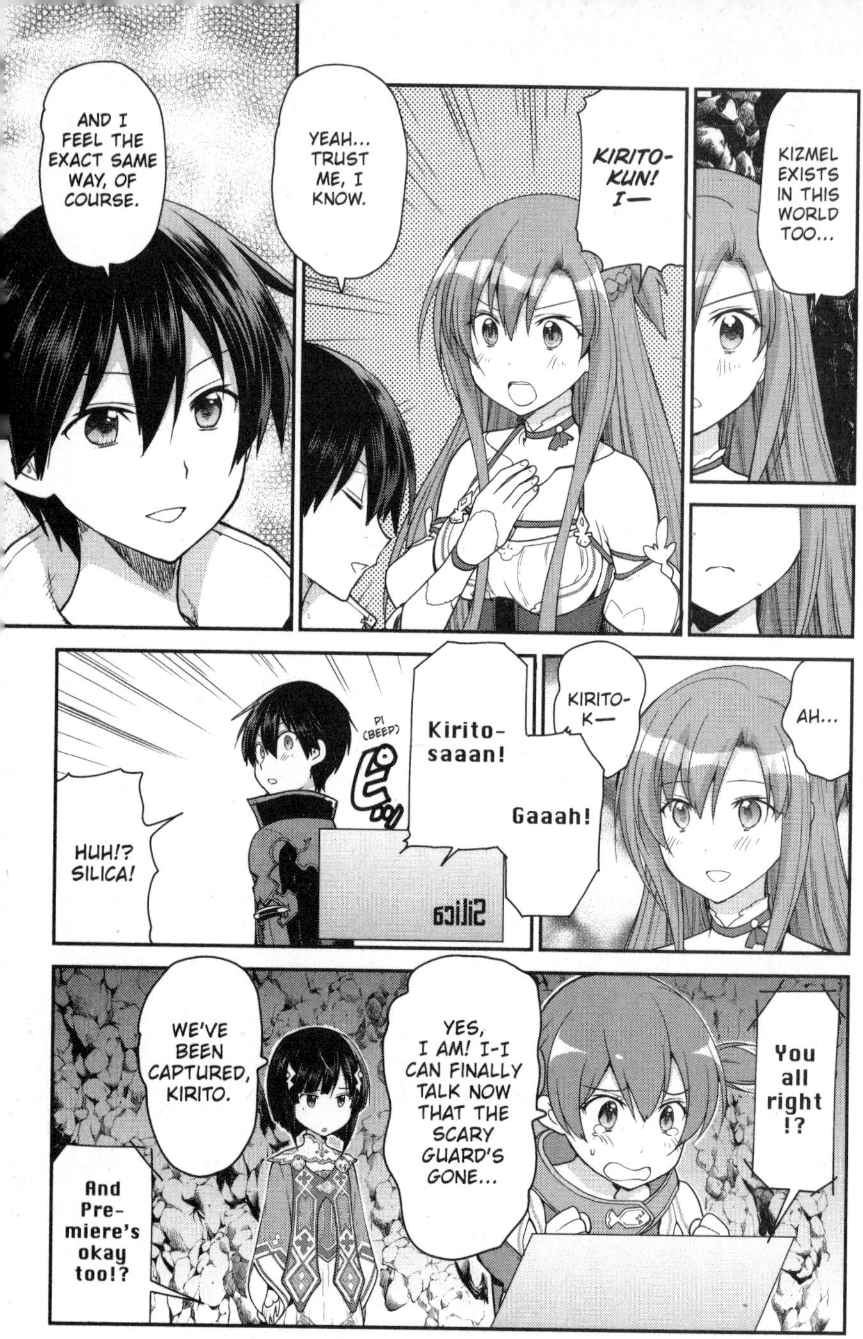
KIZMEL EXISTS IN THIS WORLD TOO...
KIRITO-KUN! I—
YEAH... TRUST ME, I KNOW.
AND I FEEL THE EXACT SAME WAY, OF COURSE.
AH...
KIRITO-K—
Kirito-saaan!
Gaaah!
PI (BEEP)
HUH!? SILICA!
Silica
You all right!?
YES, I AM! I-I CAN FINALLY TALK NOW THAT THE SCARY GUARD'S GONE...
WE'VE BEEN CAPTURED, KIRITO.
And Premiere's okay too!?

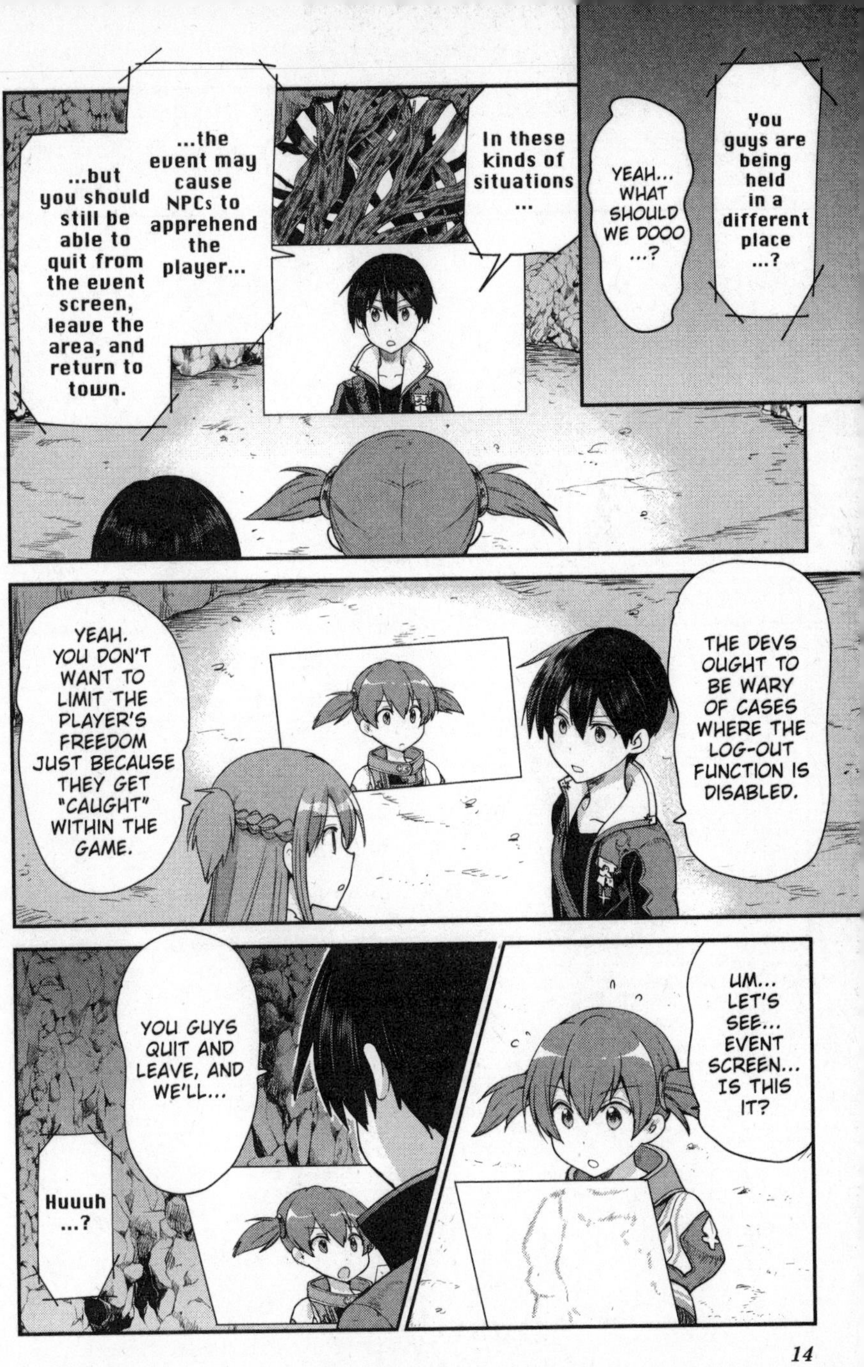
You guys are being held in a different place ...?
YEAH... WHAT SHOULD WE DOOO ...?
In these kinds of situations ...
...the event may cause NPCs to apprehend the player...
...but you should still be able to quit from the event screen, leave the area, and return to town.
THE DEVS OUGHT TO BE WARY OF CASES WHERE THE LOG-OUT FUNCTION IS DISABLED.
YEAH. YOU DON'T WANT TO LIMIT THE PLAYER'S FREEDOM JUST BECAUSE THEY GET "CAUGHT" WITHIN THE GAME.
UM... LET'S SEE... EVENT SCREEN... IS THIS IT?
YOU GUYS QUIT AND LEAVE, AND WE'LL...
Huuuh ...?

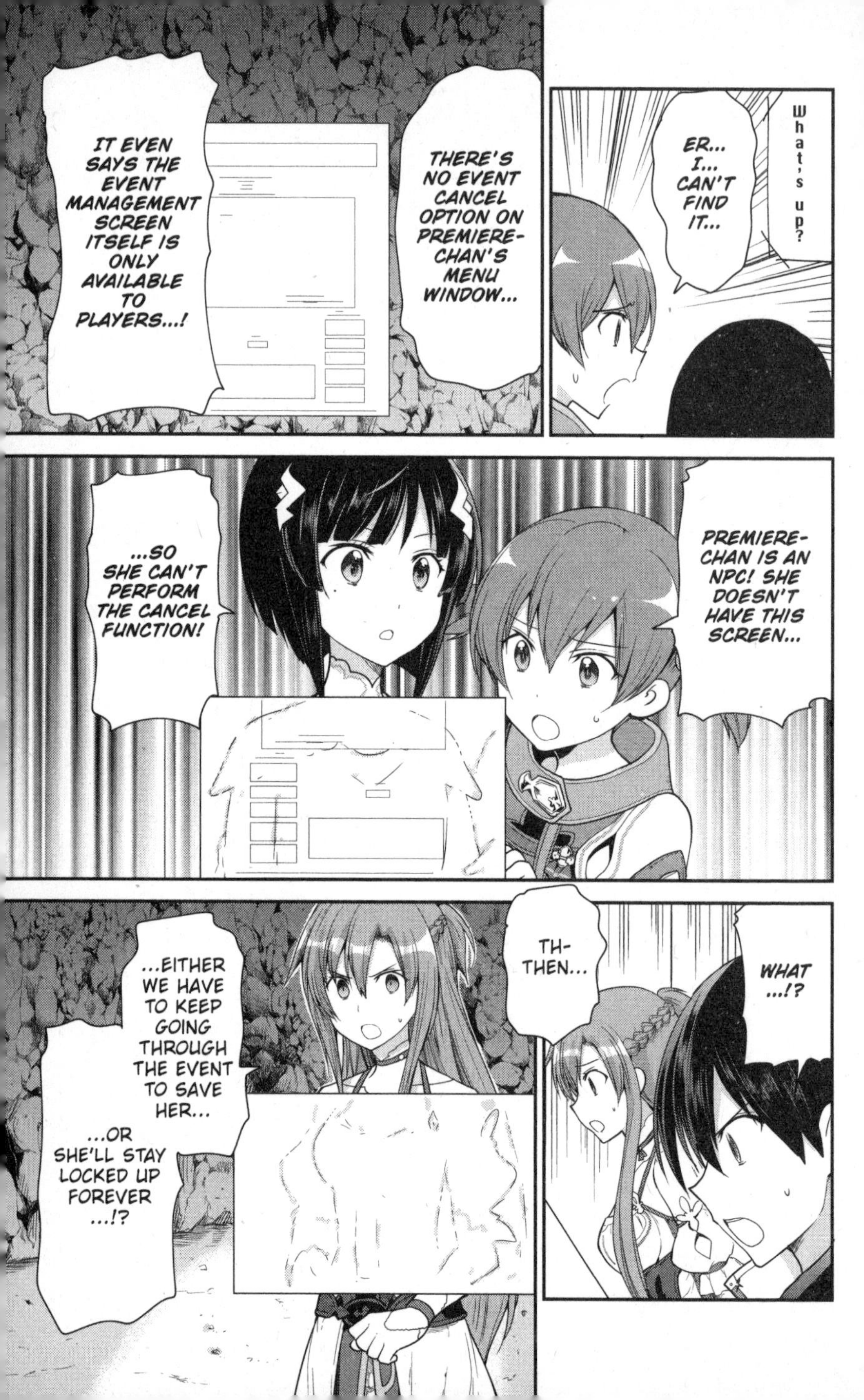
What's up?
ER... I... CAN'T FIND IT...
THERE'S NO EVENT CANCEL OPTION ON PREMIERE-CHAN'S MENU WINDOW...
IT EVEN SAYS THE EVENT MANAGEMENT SCREEN ITSELF IS ONLY AVAILABLE TO PLAYERS...!
PREMIERE-CHAN IS AN NPC! SHE DOESN'T HAVE THIS SCREEN...
...SO SHE CAN'T PERFORM THE CANCEL FUNCTION!
WHAT ...!?
TH-THEN...
...EITHER WE HAVE TO KEEP GOING THROUGH THE EVENT TO SAVE HER...
...OR SHE'LL STAY LOCKED UP FOREVER ...!?

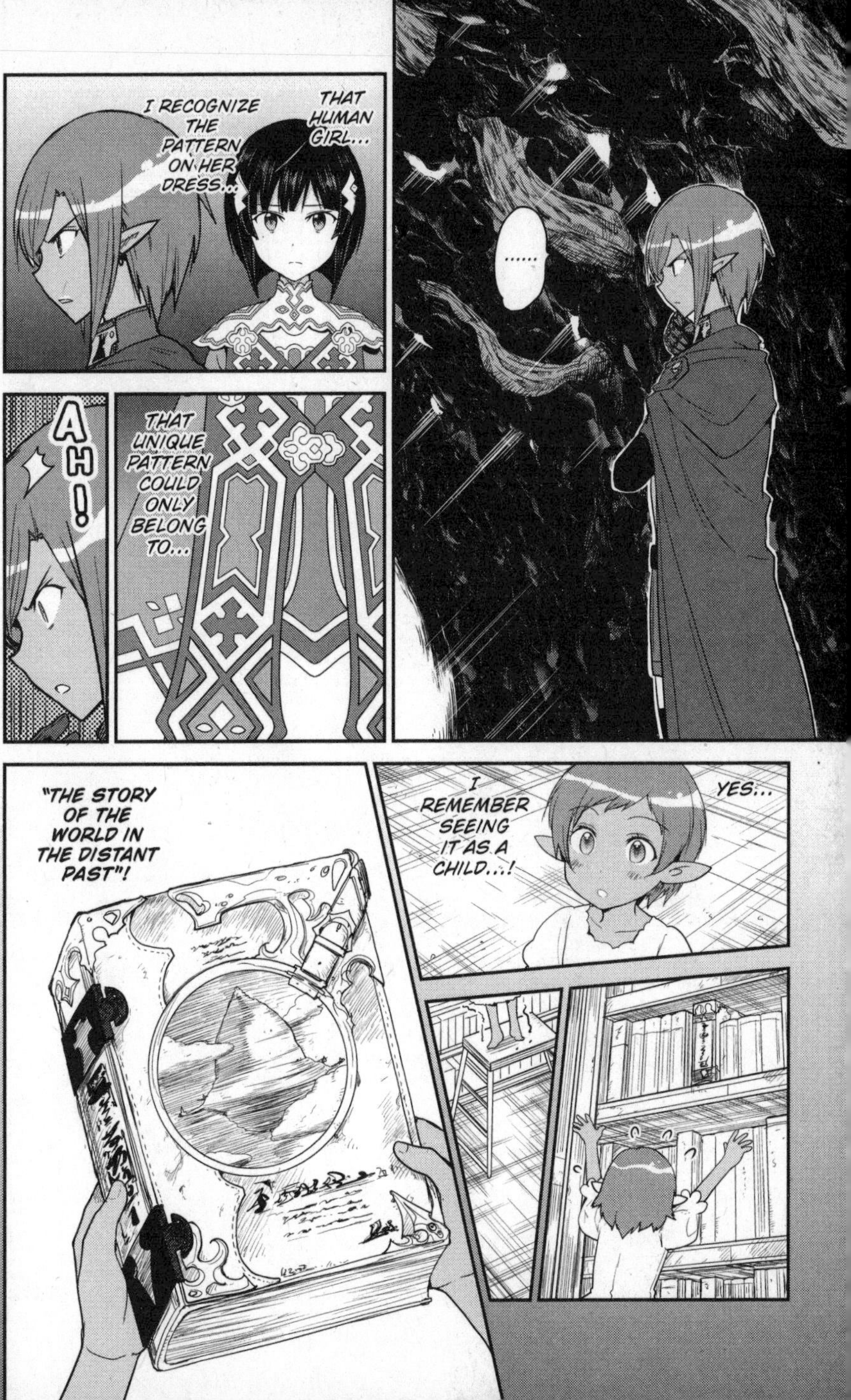
......
THAT HUMAN GIRL...
I RECOGNIZE THE PATTERN ON HER DRESS...
THAT UNIQUE PATTERN COULD ONLY BELONG TO...
AH!
YES...
I REMEMBER SEEING IT AS A CHILD...!
"THE STORY OF THE WORLD IN THE DISTANT PAST"!

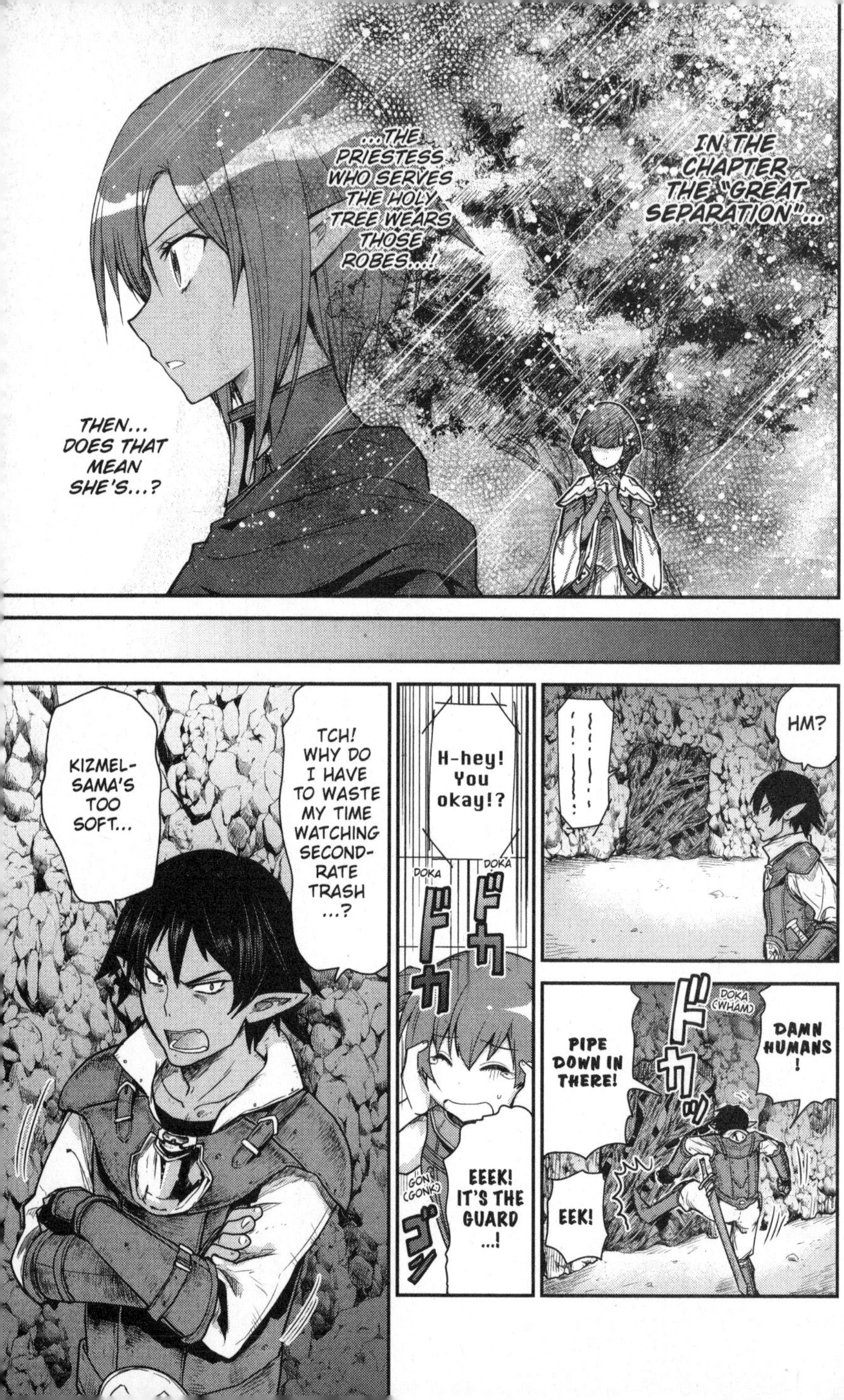
IN THE CHAPTER THE "GREAT SEPARATION"...
...THE PRIESTESS WHO SERVES THE HOLY TREE WEARS THOSE ROBES...!
THEN... DOES THAT MEAN SHE'S...?
HM?
DOKA (WHAM)
DAMN HUMANS!
PIPE DOWN IN THERE!
EEK!
H-hey! You okay!?
DOKA
DOKA
EEEK! IT'S THE GUARD...!
GON (GONK)
TCH! WHY DO I HAVE TO WASTE MY TIME WATCHING SECOND-RATE TRASH...?
KIZMEL-SAMA'S TOO SOFT...

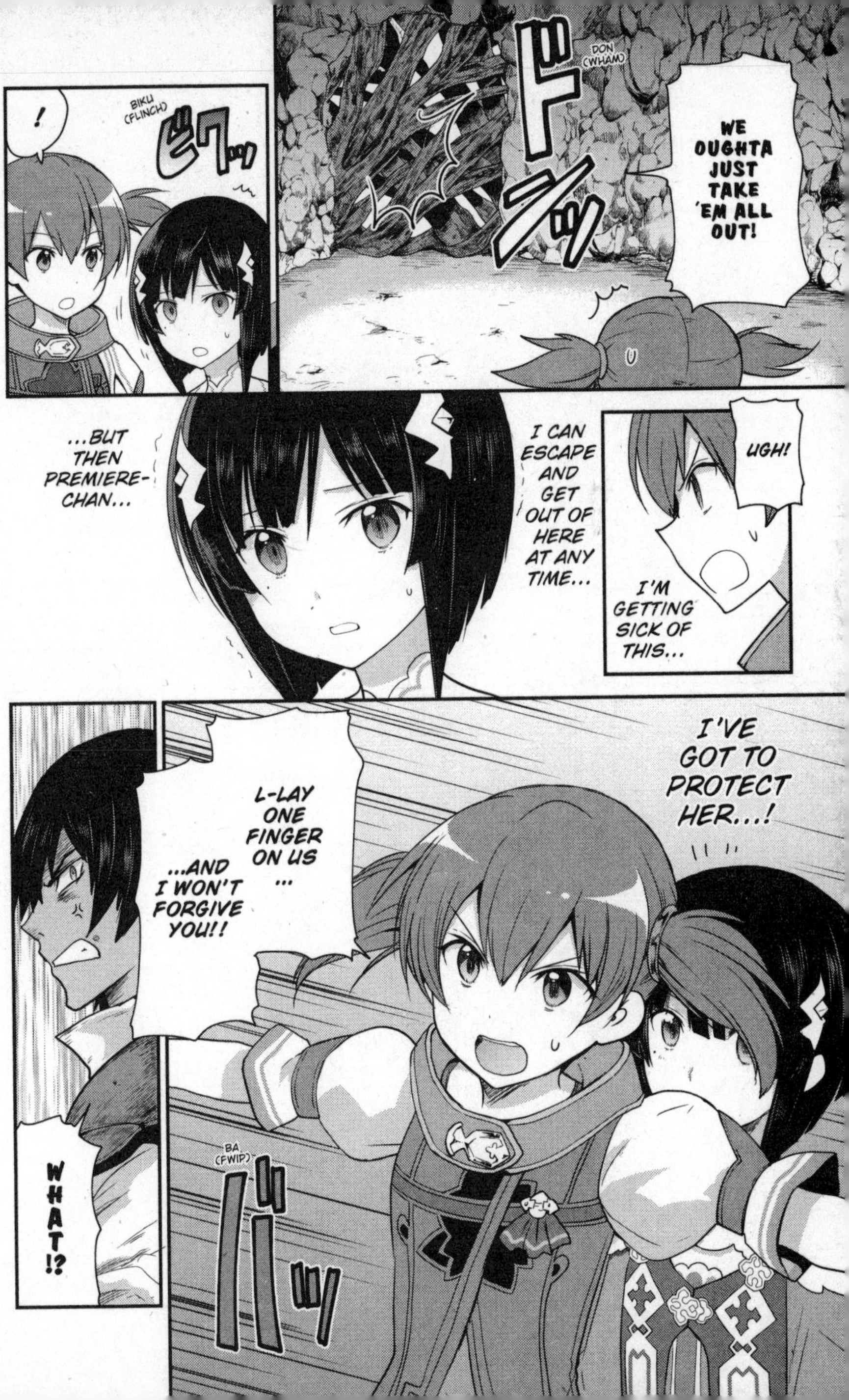
DON (WHAM)
WE OUGHTA JUST TAKE 'EM ALL OUT!
!
BIKU (FLINCH)
UGH!
I'M GETTING SICK OF THIS...
I CAN ESCAPE AND GET OUT OF HERE AT ANY TIME...
...BUT THEN PREMIERE-CHAN...
I'VE GOT TO PROTECT HER...!
L-LAY ONE FINGER ON US...
...AND I WON'T FORGIVE YOU!!
BA (FWIP)
WHAT!?

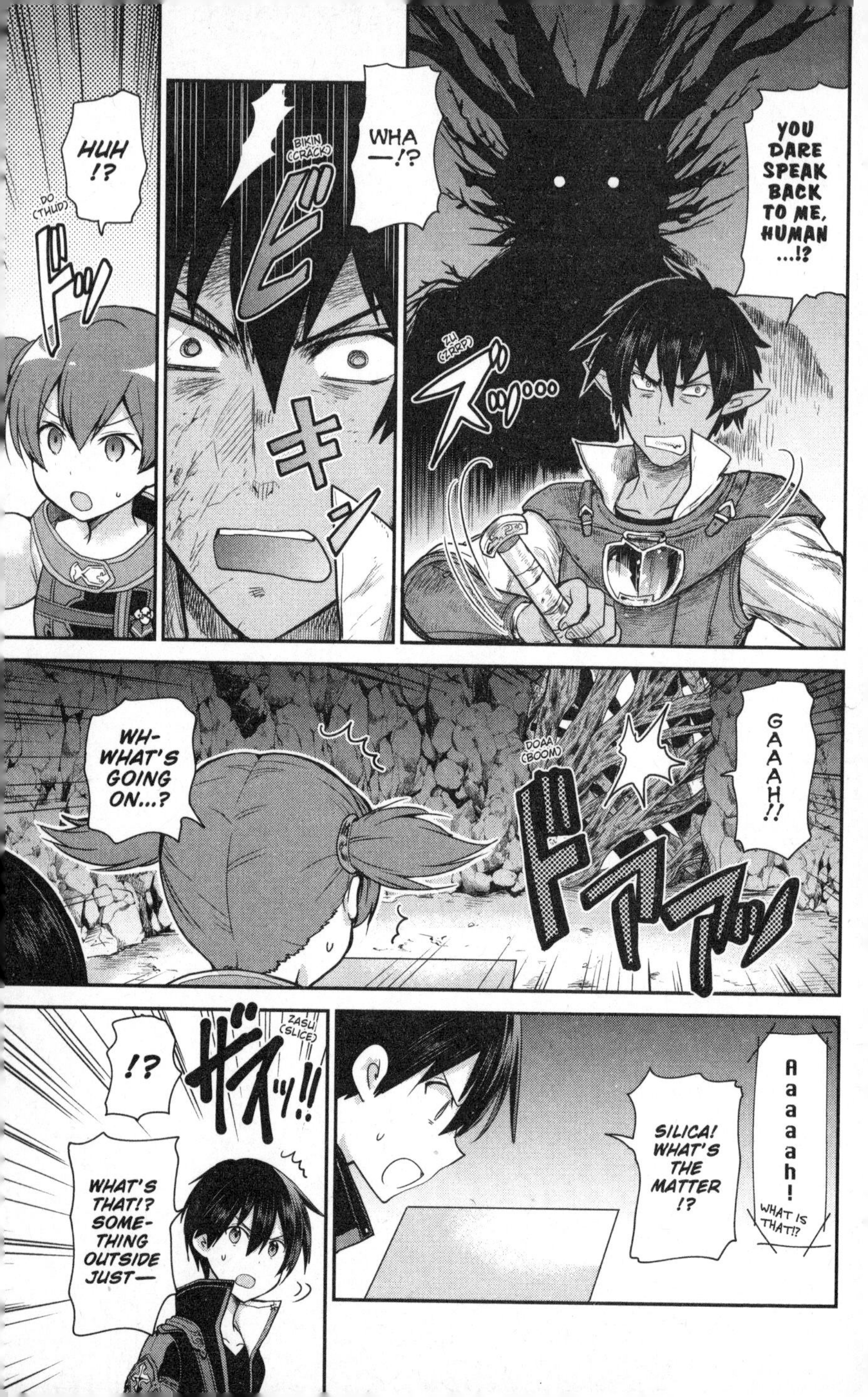
YOU DARE SPEAK BACK TO ME, HUMAN ...!?
ZU (ZRRP)
WHA—!?
BIKIN (CRACK)
HUH !?
DO (THUD)
GAAAAH!!
DOAA (BOOM)
WH-WHAT'S GOING ON...?
Aaaaah!
WHAT IS THAT!?
SILICA! WHAT'S THE MATTER !?
ZASU (SLICE)
!?
WHAT'S THAT!? SOME-THING OUTSIDE JUST—

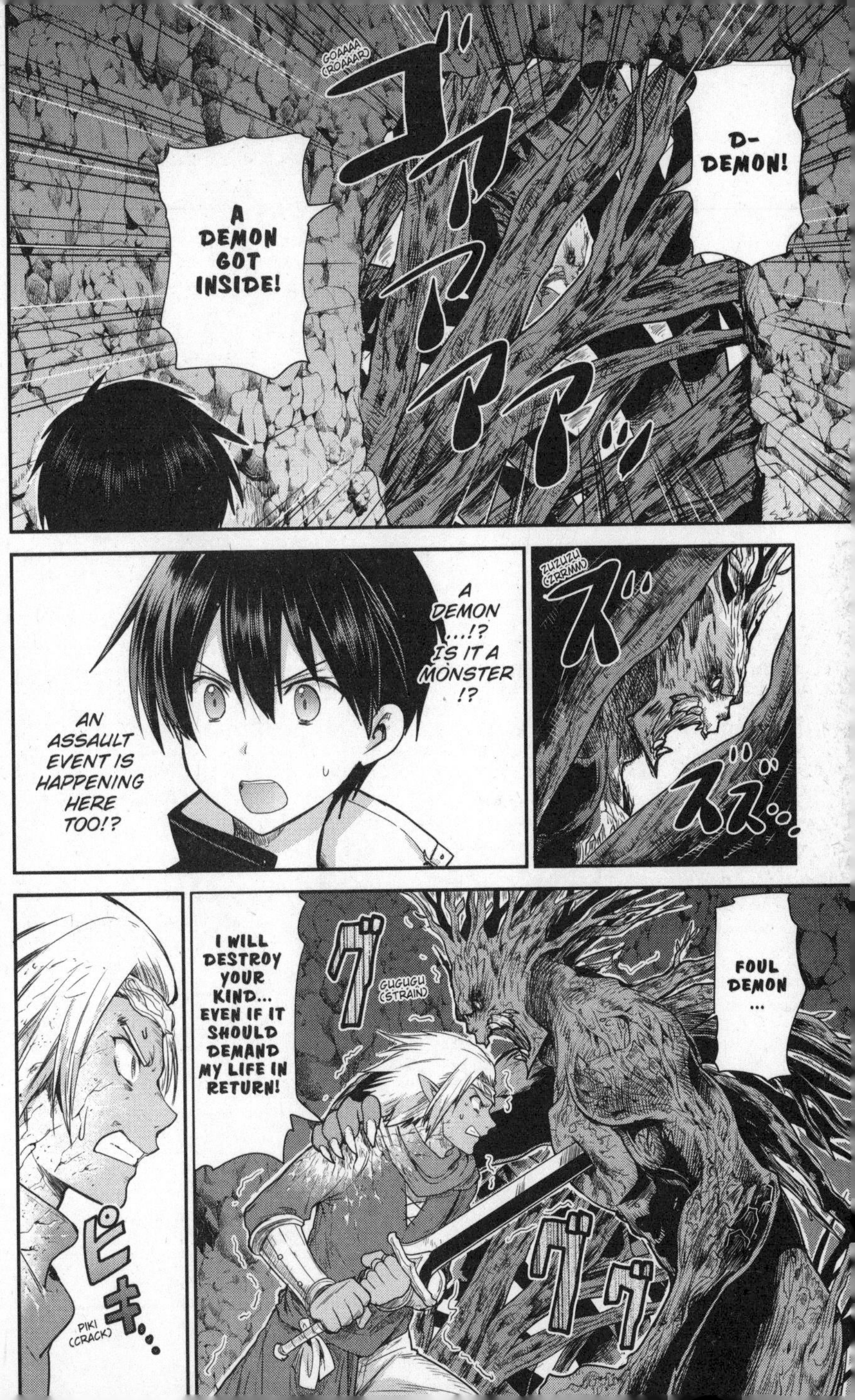
D-DEMON!
GOAAAA (ROAAAR)
A DEMON GOT INSIDE!
ZUZUZU (ZRRMM)
A DEMON...!? IS IT A MONSTER!?
AN ASSAULT EVENT IS HAPPENING HERE TOO!?
FOUL DEMON...
GUGUGU (STRAIN)
I WILL DESTROY YOUR KIND... EVEN IF IT SHOULD DEMAND MY LIFE IN RETURN!
PIKI (CRACK)

H-HE TURNED TO STONE!

IS THAT THE MONSTER'S SPECIAL ATTACK POWER!?

!!?

ピキン

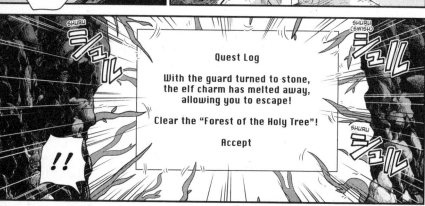

SHURU

シュル

SHURU (SWISH)

シュル

SHURU

シュル

Quest Log

With the guard turned to stone, the elf charm has melted away, allowing you to escape!

Clear the "Forest of the Holy Tree"!

Accept

!!

LET'S GO, ASUNA!

THE INTRO EVENT'S FINALLY OVER! NOW THE QUEST IS STARTING FOR REAL!

PI (BEEP)

ピッ

YEAH!

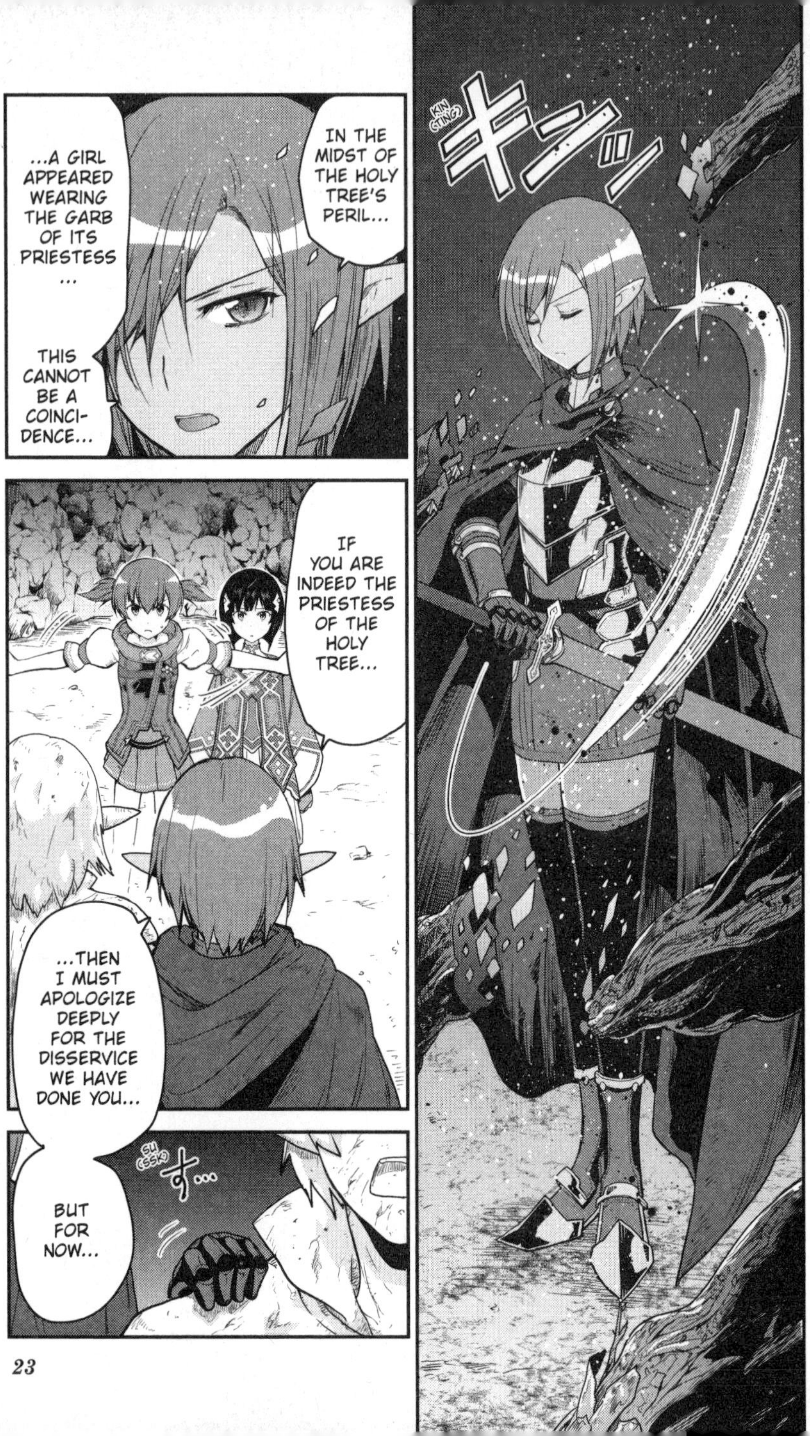
KIN (TING)
IN THE MIDST OF THE HOLY TREE'S PERIL...
...A GIRL APPEARED WEARING THE GARB OF ITS PRIESTESS...
THIS CANNOT BE A COINCIDENCE...
IF YOU ARE INDEED THE PRIESTESS OF THE HOLY TREE...
...THEN I MUST APOLOGIZE DEEPLY FOR THE DISSERVICE WE HAVE DONE YOU...
SU (SSK)
BUT FOR NOW...

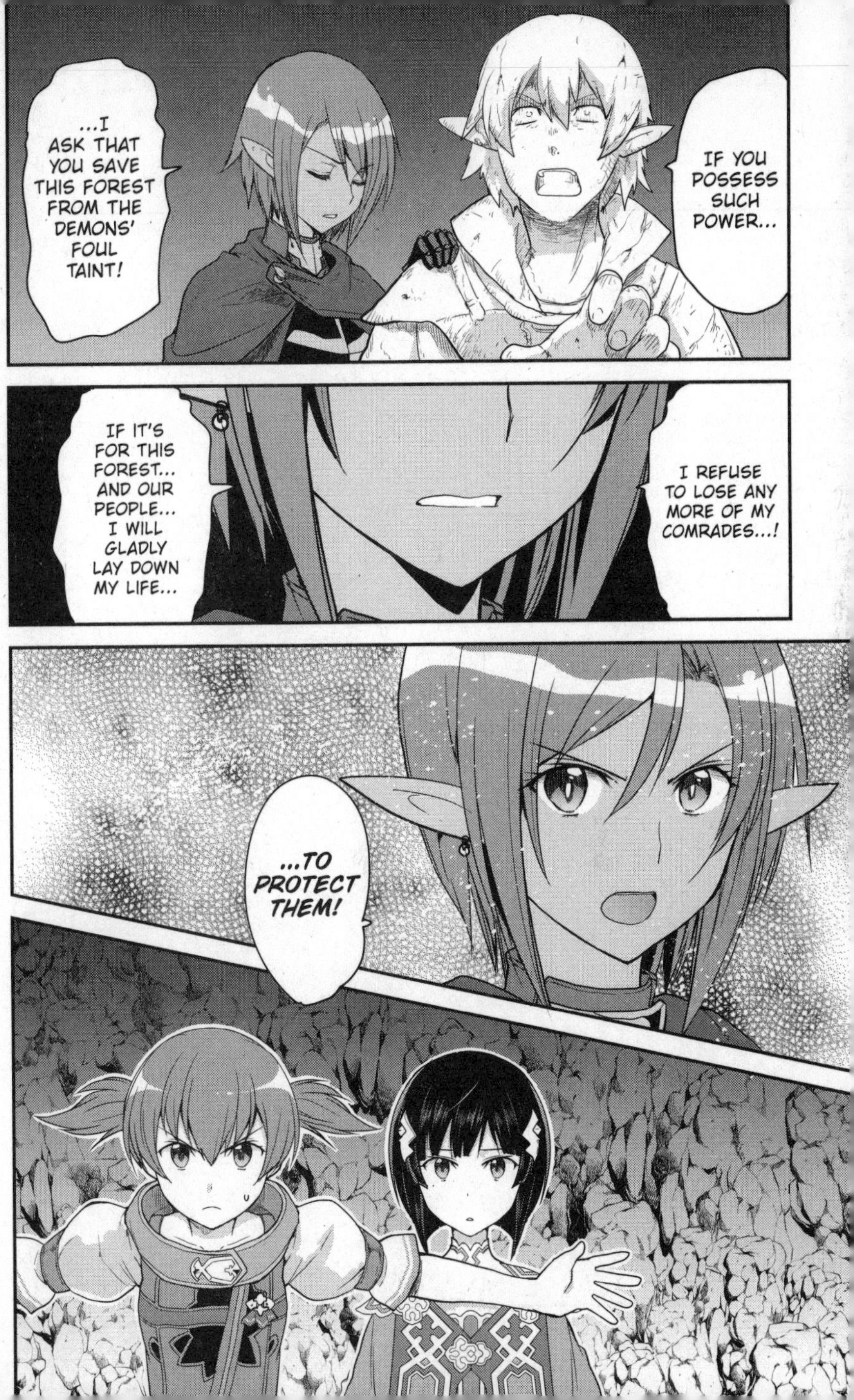
IF YOU POSSESS SUCH POWER...
...I ASK THAT YOU SAVE THIS FOREST FROM THE DEMONS' FOUL TAINT!
I REFUSE TO LOSE ANY MORE OF MY COMRADES...!
IF IT'S FOR THIS FOREST... AND OUR PEOPLE... I WILL GLADLY LAY DOWN MY LIFE...
...TO PROTECT THEM!

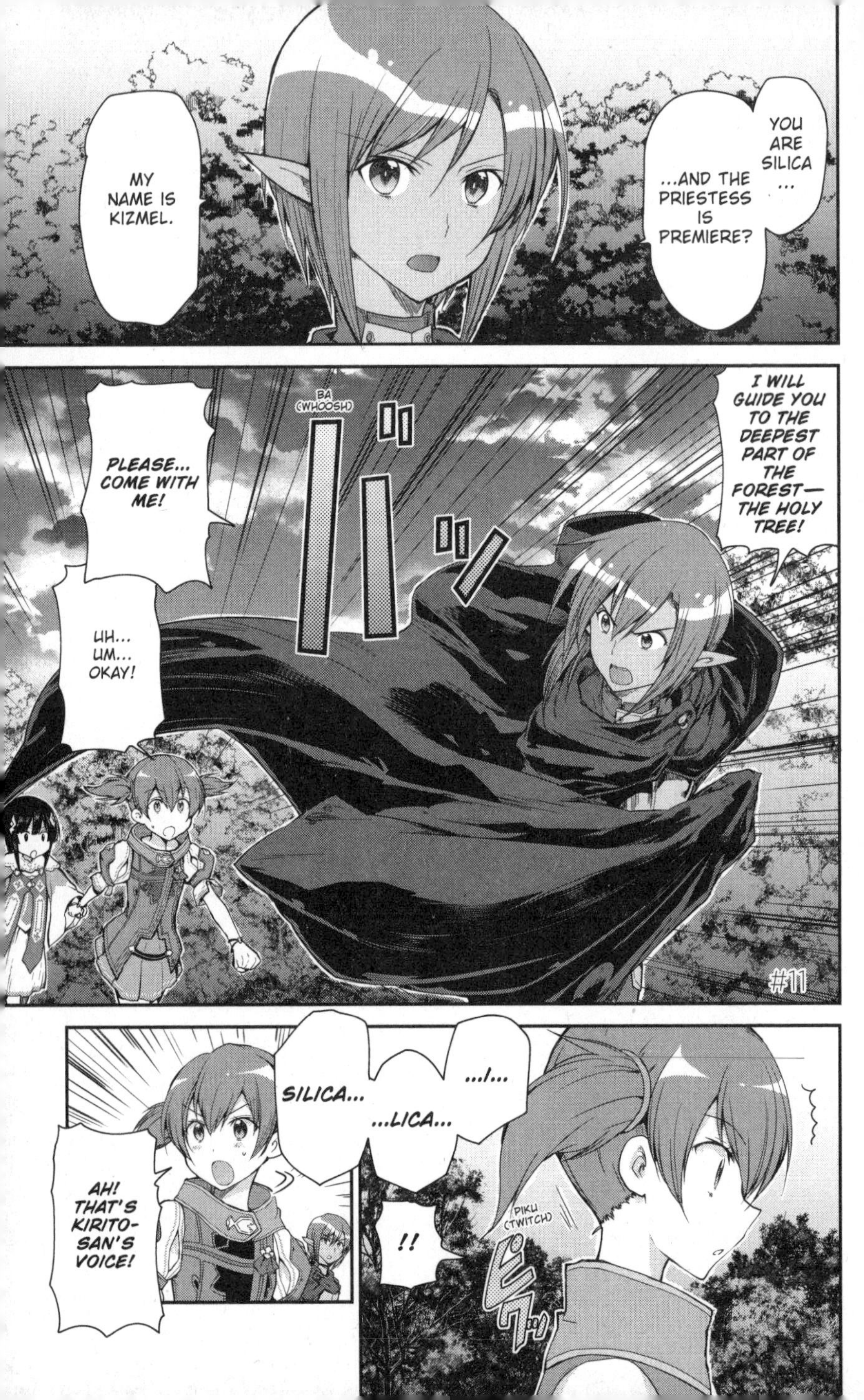
YOU ARE SILICA...
...AND THE PRIESTESS IS PREMIERE?
MY NAME IS KIZMEL.
I WILL GUIDE YOU TO THE DEEPEST PART OF THE FOREST—THE HOLY TREE!
BA (WHOOSH)
PLEASE... COME WITH ME!
UH... UM... OKAY!
#11
...I...
SILICA...
...LICA...
PIKU (TWITCH)
!!
AH! THAT'S KIRITO-SAN'S VOICE!

#11: Priestess of the Holy Tree

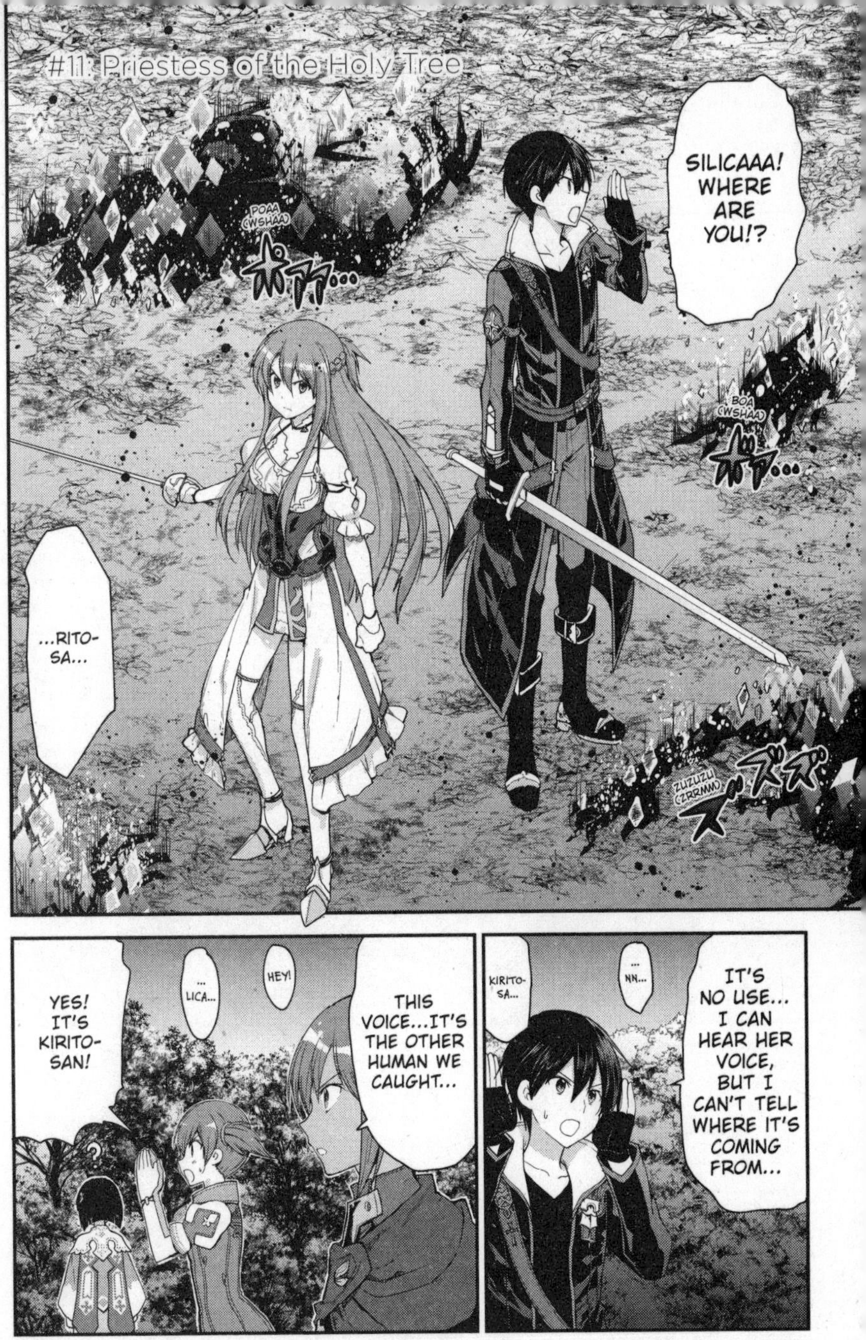
SILICAAA! WHERE ARE YOU!?
BOA (WSHAA)
POAA (WSHAA)
ZUZUZU (ZRRMM)
...RITO-SA...
IT'S NO USE... I CAN HEAR HER VOICE, BUT I CAN'T TELL WHERE IT'S COMING FROM...
... NN...
KIRITO-SA...
THIS VOICE...IT'S THE OTHER HUMAN WE CAUGHT...
HEY!
... LICA...
YES! IT'S KIRITO-SAN!

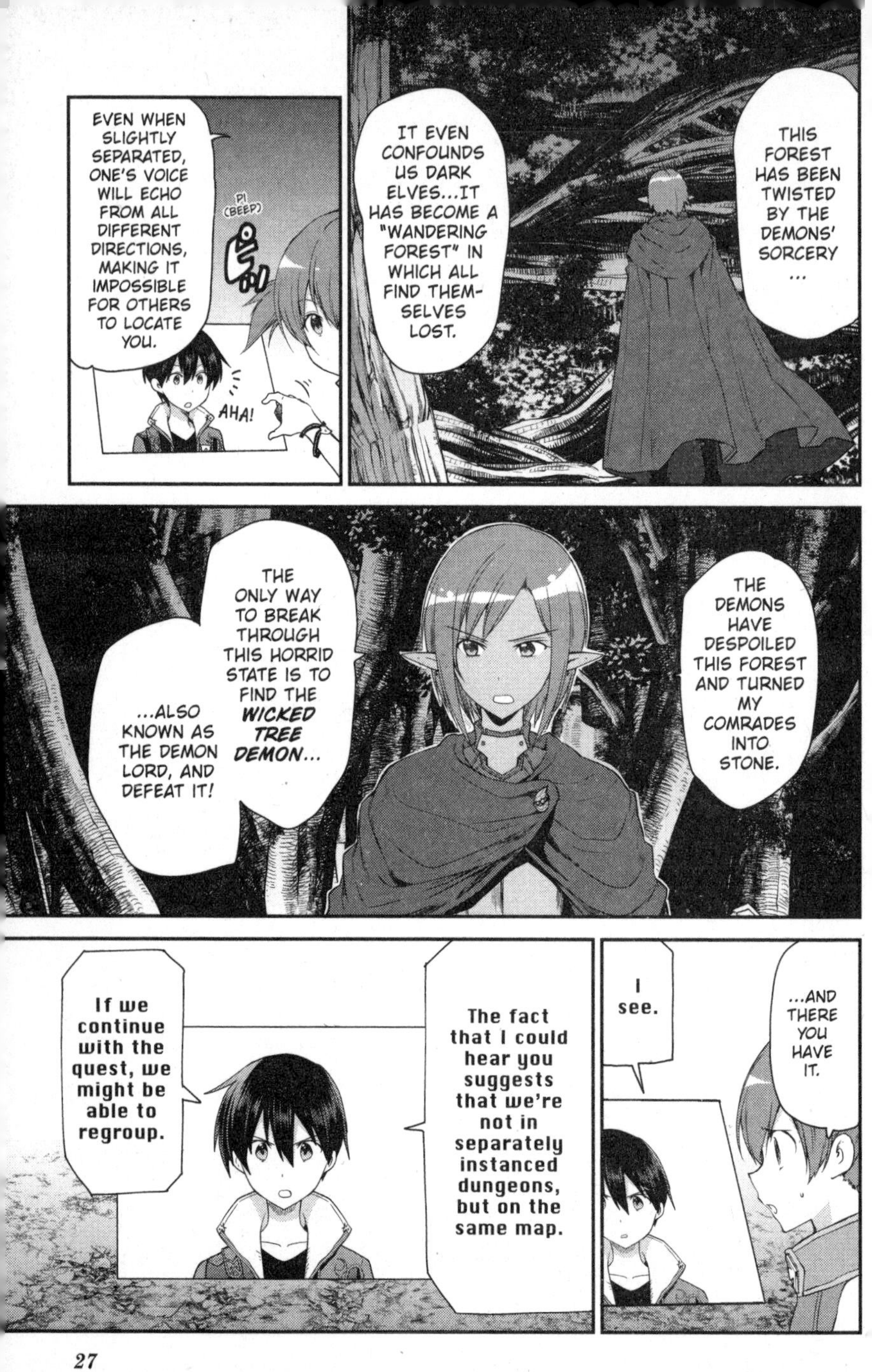
THIS FOREST HAS BEEN TWISTED BY THE DEMONS' SORCERY...
IT EVEN CONFOUNDS US DARK ELVES...IT HAS BECOME A "WANDERING FOREST" IN WHICH ALL FIND THEM-SELVES LOST.
EVEN WHEN SLIGHTLY SEPARATED, ONE'S VOICE WILL ECHO FROM ALL DIFFERENT DIRECTIONS, MAKING IT IMPOSSIBLE FOR OTHERS TO LOCATE YOU.
PI (BEEP)
AHA!
THE DEMONS HAVE DESPOILED THIS FOREST AND TURNED MY COMRADES INTO STONE.
THE ONLY WAY TO BREAK THROUGH THIS HORRID STATE IS TO FIND THE WICKED TREE DEMON...
...ALSO KNOWN AS THE DEMON LORD, AND DEFEAT IT!
...AND THERE YOU HAVE IT.
I see.
The fact that I could hear you suggests that we're not in separately instanced dungeons, but on the same map.
If we continue with the quest, we might be able to regroup.

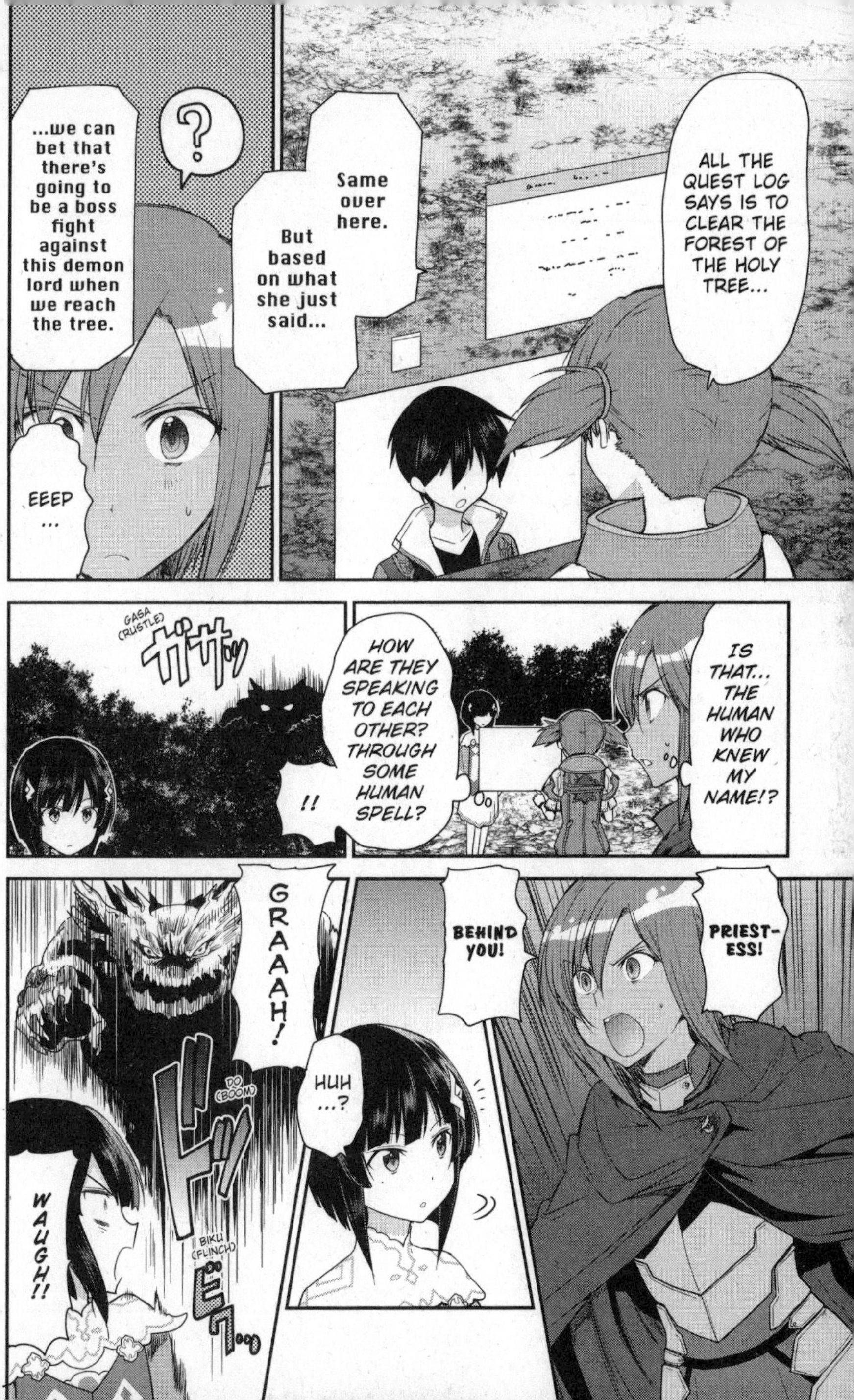
ALL THE QUEST LOG SAYS IS TO CLEAR THE FOREST OF THE HOLY TREE...
Same over here.
But based on what she just said...
?
...we can bet that there's going to be a boss fight against this demon lord when we reach the tree.
EEEP ...
IS THAT... THE HUMAN WHO KNEW MY NAME!?
HOW ARE THEY SPEAKING TO EACH OTHER? THROUGH SOME HUMAN SPELL?
!!
GASA (RUSTLE)
PRIEST-ESS!
BEHIND YOU!
HUH ...?
GRAAAAH!
DO (BOOM)
WAUGH!!
BIKU (FLINCH)

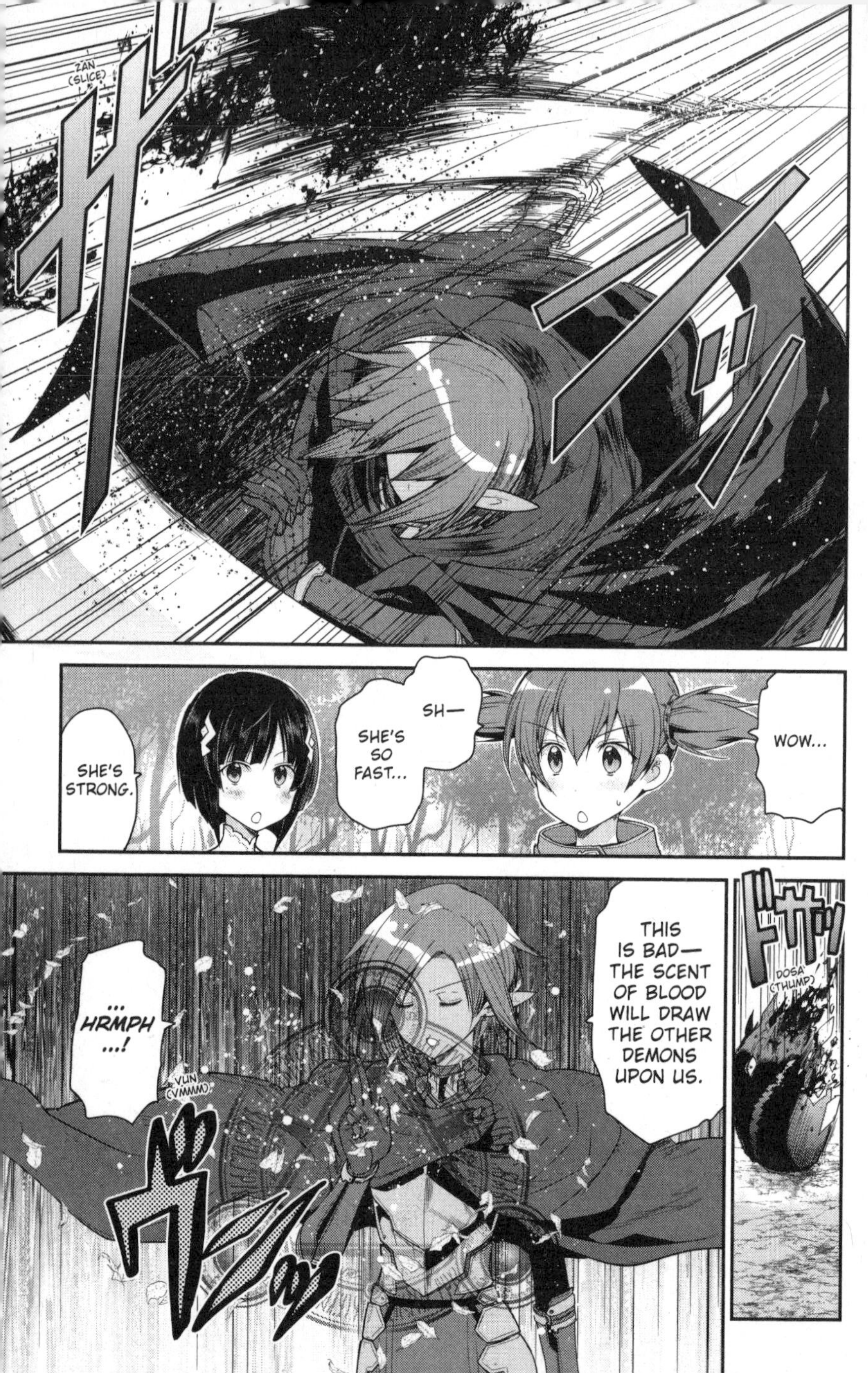
ZAN (SLICE)
WOW...
SH— SHE'S SO FAST...
SHE'S STRONG.
DOSA (THUMP)
THIS IS BAD— THE SCENT OF BLOOD WILL DRAW THE OTHER DEMONS UPON US.
...HRMPH ...!
VUN (VMMM)

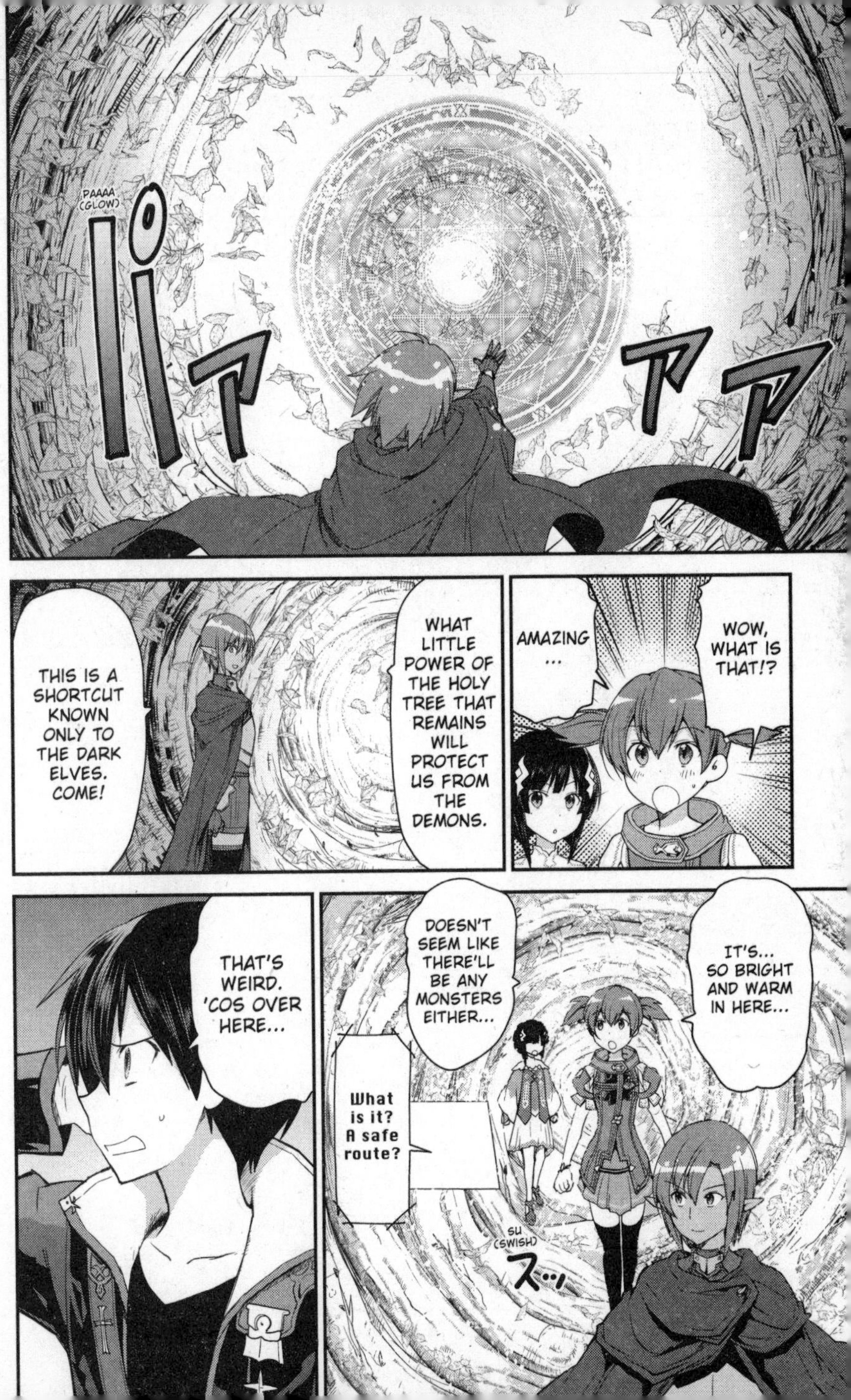
PAAAA (GLOW)
パアアア
WOW, WHAT IS THAT!?
AMAZING...
WHAT LITTLE POWER OF THE HOLY TREE THAT REMAINS WILL PROTECT US FROM THE DEMONS.
THIS IS A SHORTCUT KNOWN ONLY TO THE DARK ELVES. COME!
IT'S... SO BRIGHT AND WARM IN HERE...
DOESN'T SEEM LIKE THERE'LL BE ANY MONSTERS EITHER...
What is it? A safe route?
SU (SWISH)
スッ
THAT'S WEIRD. 'COS OVER HERE...

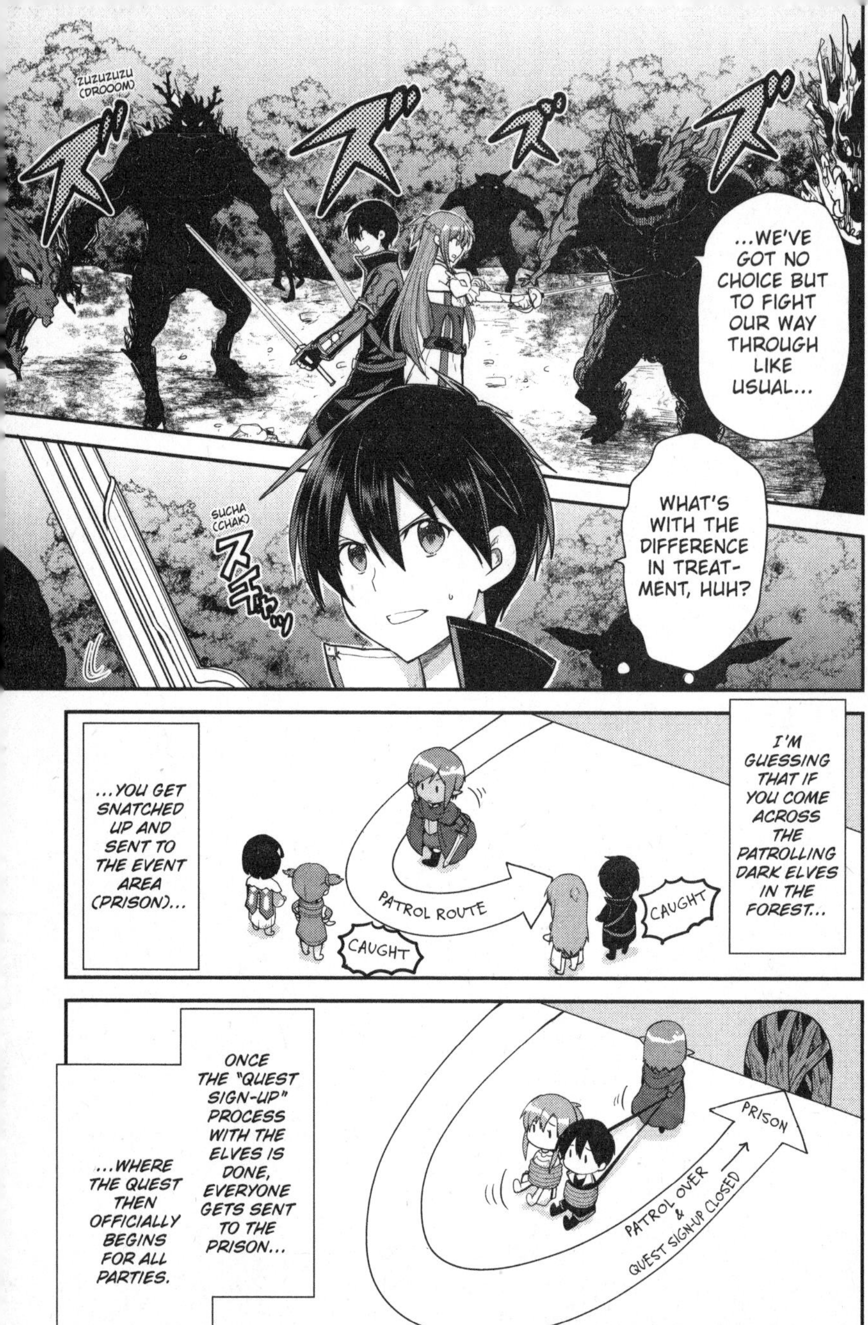
ZUZUZUZU (DROOOM)
...WE'VE GOT NO CHOICE BUT TO FIGHT OUR WAY THROUGH LIKE USUAL...
WHAT'S WITH THE DIFFERENCE IN TREAT-MENT, HUH?
SUCHA (CHAK)
I'M GUESSING THAT IF YOU COME ACROSS THE PATROLLING DARK ELVES IN THE FOREST...
CAUGHT
PATROL ROUTE
CAUGHT
...YOU GET SNATCHED UP AND SENT TO THE EVENT AREA (PRISON)...
PRISON
PATROL OVER & QUEST SIGN-UP CLOSED
ONCE THE "QUEST SIGN-UP" PROCESS WITH THE ELVES IS DONE, EVERYONE GETS SENT TO THE PRISON...
...WHERE THE QUEST THEN OFFICIALLY BEGINS FOR ALL PARTIES.

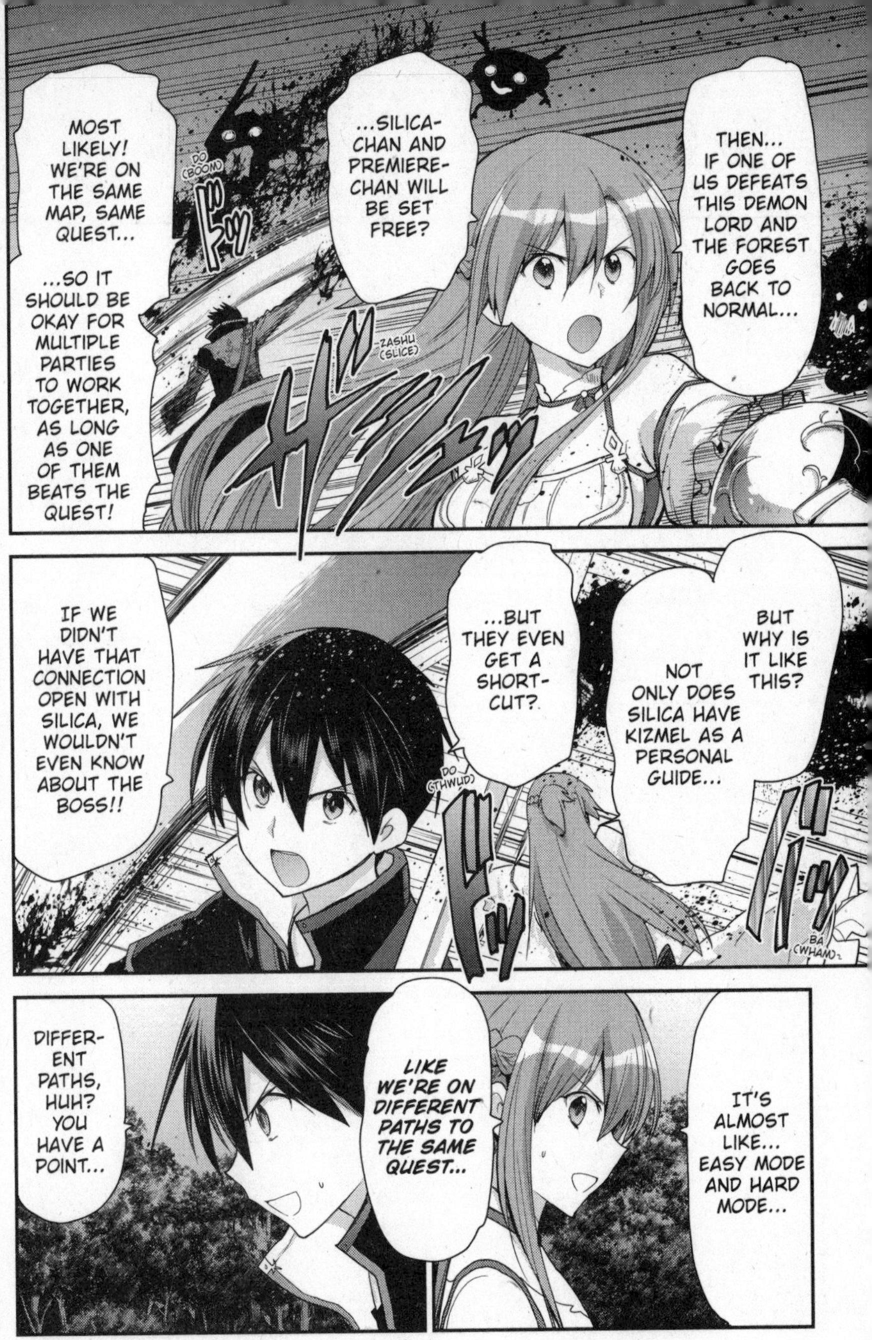
THEN... IF ONE OF US DEFEATS THIS DEMON LORD AND THE FOREST GOES BACK TO NORMAL...
...SILICA-CHAN AND PREMIERE-CHAN WILL BE SET FREE?
MOST LIKELY! WE'RE ON THE SAME MAP, SAME QUEST...
DO (BOOM)
ZASHU (SLICE)
...SO IT SHOULD BE OKAY FOR MULTIPLE PARTIES TO WORK TOGETHER, AS LONG AS ONE OF THEM BEATS THE QUEST!
BUT WHY IS IT LIKE THIS?
NOT ONLY DOES SILICA HAVE KIZMEL AS A PERSONAL GUIDE...
BA (WHAM)
...BUT THEY EVEN GET A SHORT-CUT?
DO (THWUD)
IF WE DIDN'T HAVE THAT CONNECTION OPEN WITH SILICA, WE WOULDN'T EVEN KNOW ABOUT THE BOSS!!
IT'S ALMOST LIKE... EASY MODE AND HARD MODE...
LIKE WE'RE ON DIFFERENT PATHS TO THE SAME QUEST...
DIFFERENT PATHS, HUH? YOU HAVE A POINT...

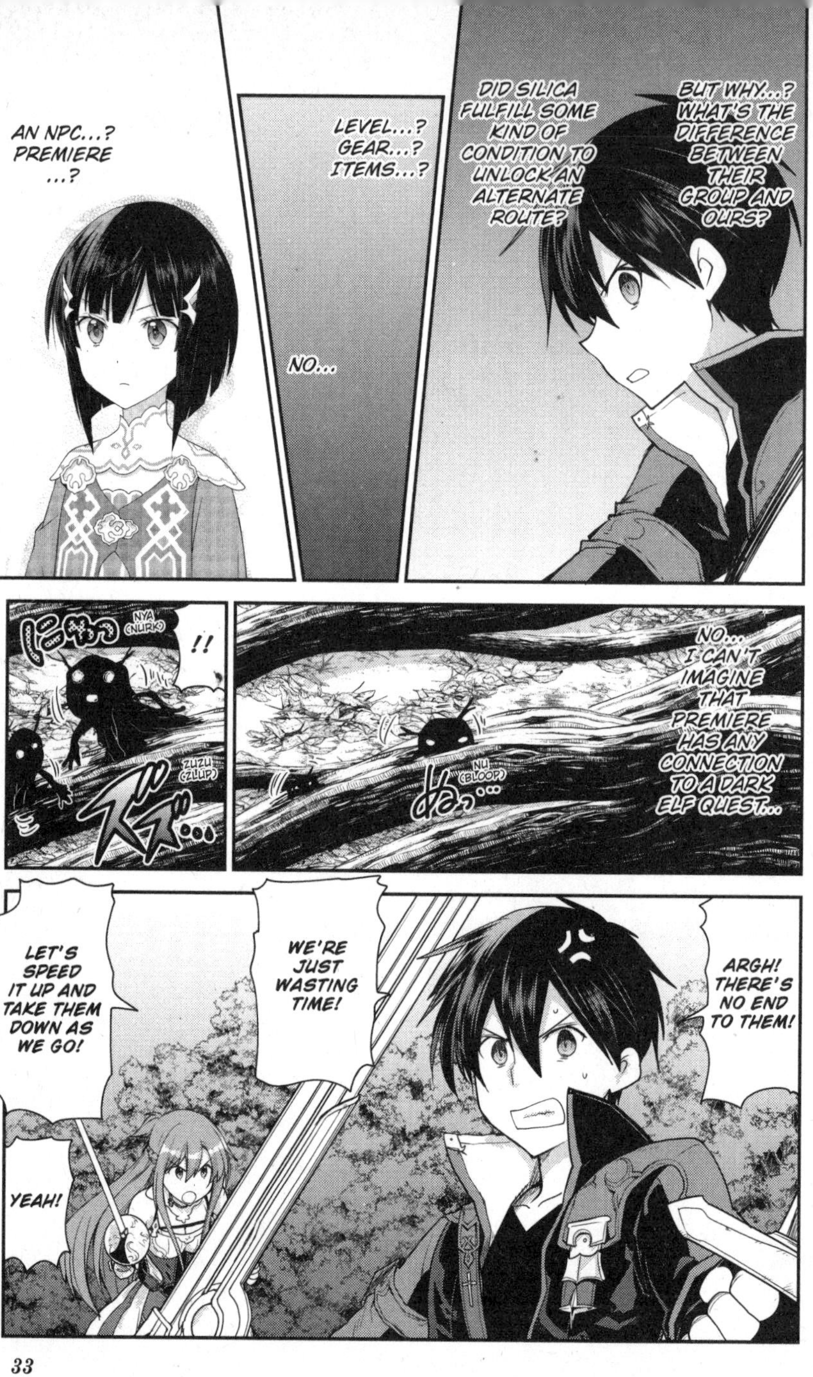
BUT WHY...? WHAT'S THE DIFFERENCE BETWEEN THEIR GROUP AND OURS?
DID SILICA FULFILL SOME KIND OF CONDITION TO UNLOCK AN ALTERNATE ROUTE?
LEVEL...? GEAR...? ITEMS...?
NO...
AN NPC...? PREMIERE ...?
NO... I CAN'T IMAGINE THAT PREMIERE HAS ANY CONNECTION TO A DARK ELF QUEST...
NU (BLOOP)
NYA (NURK)
!!
ZUZU (ZLUP)
ARGH! THERE'S NO END TO THEM!
WE'RE JUST WASTING TIME!
LET'S SPEED IT UP AND TAKE THEM DOWN AS WE GO!
YEAH!

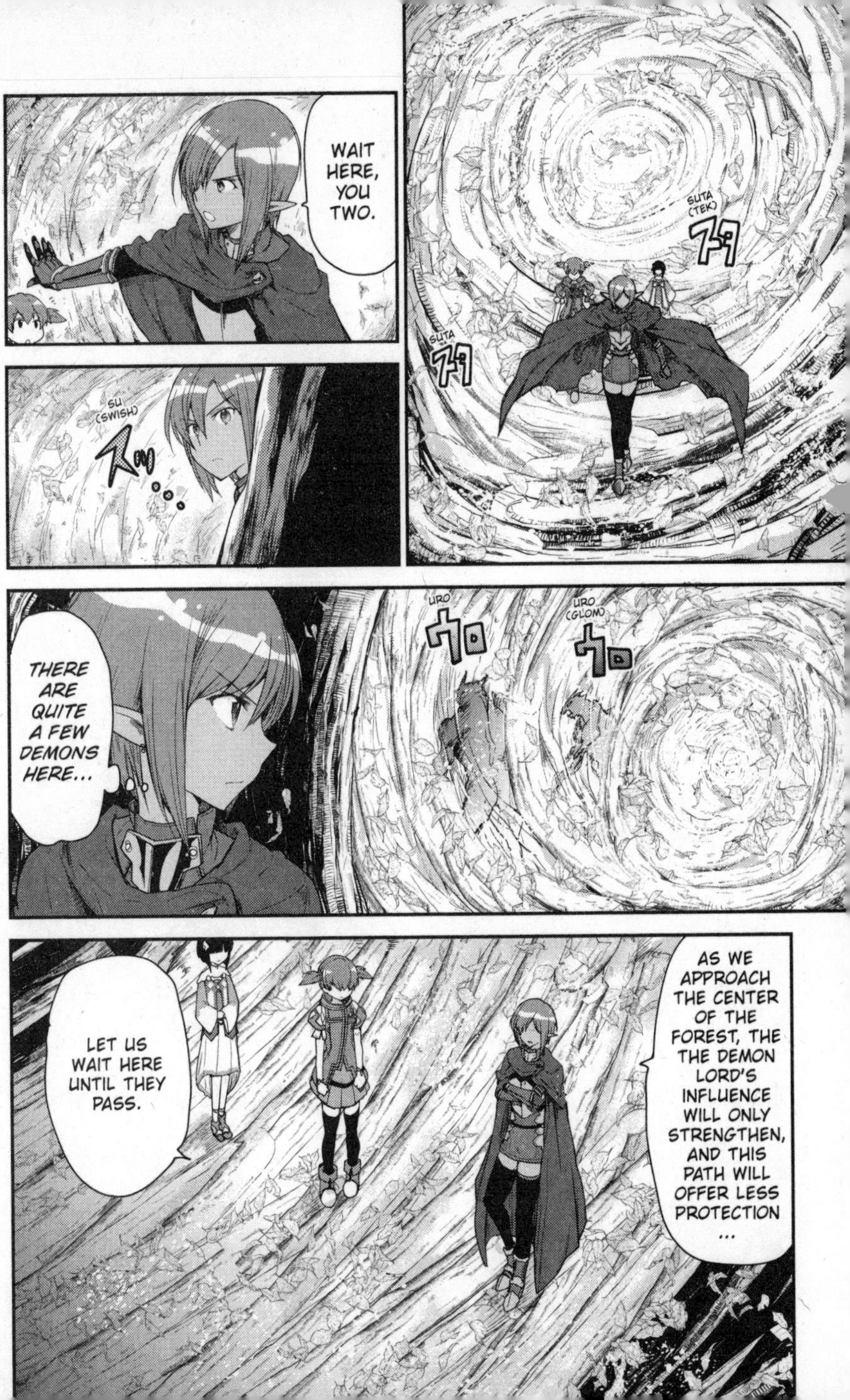
SUTA (TEK)
SUTA
WAIT HERE, YOU TWO.
SU (SWISH)
...
URO
URO (GLOM)
THERE ARE QUITE A FEW DEMONS HERE...
AS WE APPROACH THE CENTER OF THE FOREST, THE THE DEMON LORD'S INFLUENCE WILL ONLY STRENGTHEN, AND THIS PATH WILL OFFER LESS PROTECTION ...
LET US WAIT HERE UNTIL THEY PASS.

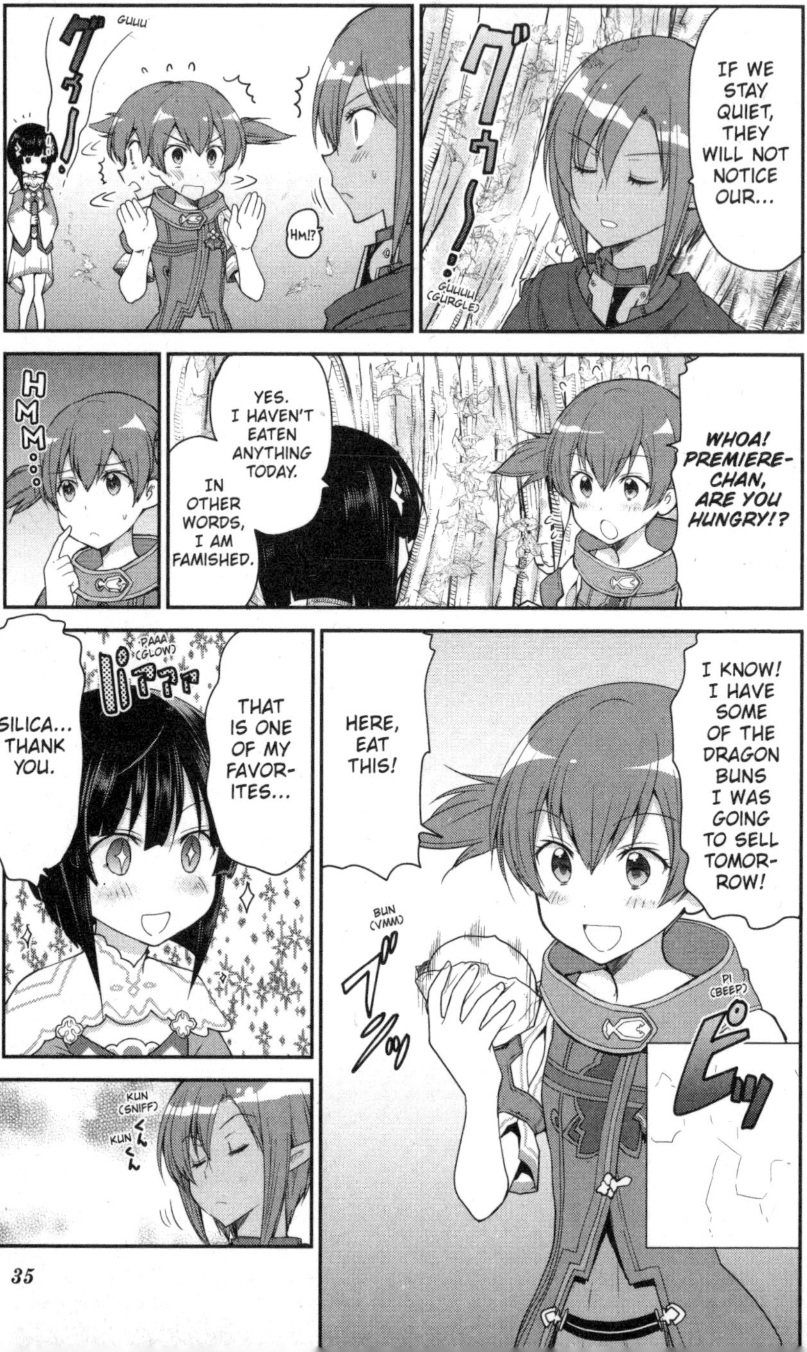
IF WE STAY QUIET, THEY WILL NOT NOTICE OUR...
GUUUU (GURGLE)
GUUU
HM!?
WHOA! PREMIERE-CHAN, ARE YOU HUNGRY!?
YES. I HAVEN'T EATEN ANYTHING TODAY.
IN OTHER WORDS, I AM FAMISHED.
HMM...
I KNOW! I HAVE SOME OF THE DRAGON BUNS I WAS GOING TO SELL TOMORROW!
PI (BEEP)
BUN (VMM)
HERE, EAT THIS!
THAT IS ONE OF MY FAVOR-ITES...
PAAA (GLOW)
SILICA... THANK YOU.
KUN (SNIFF)
KUN

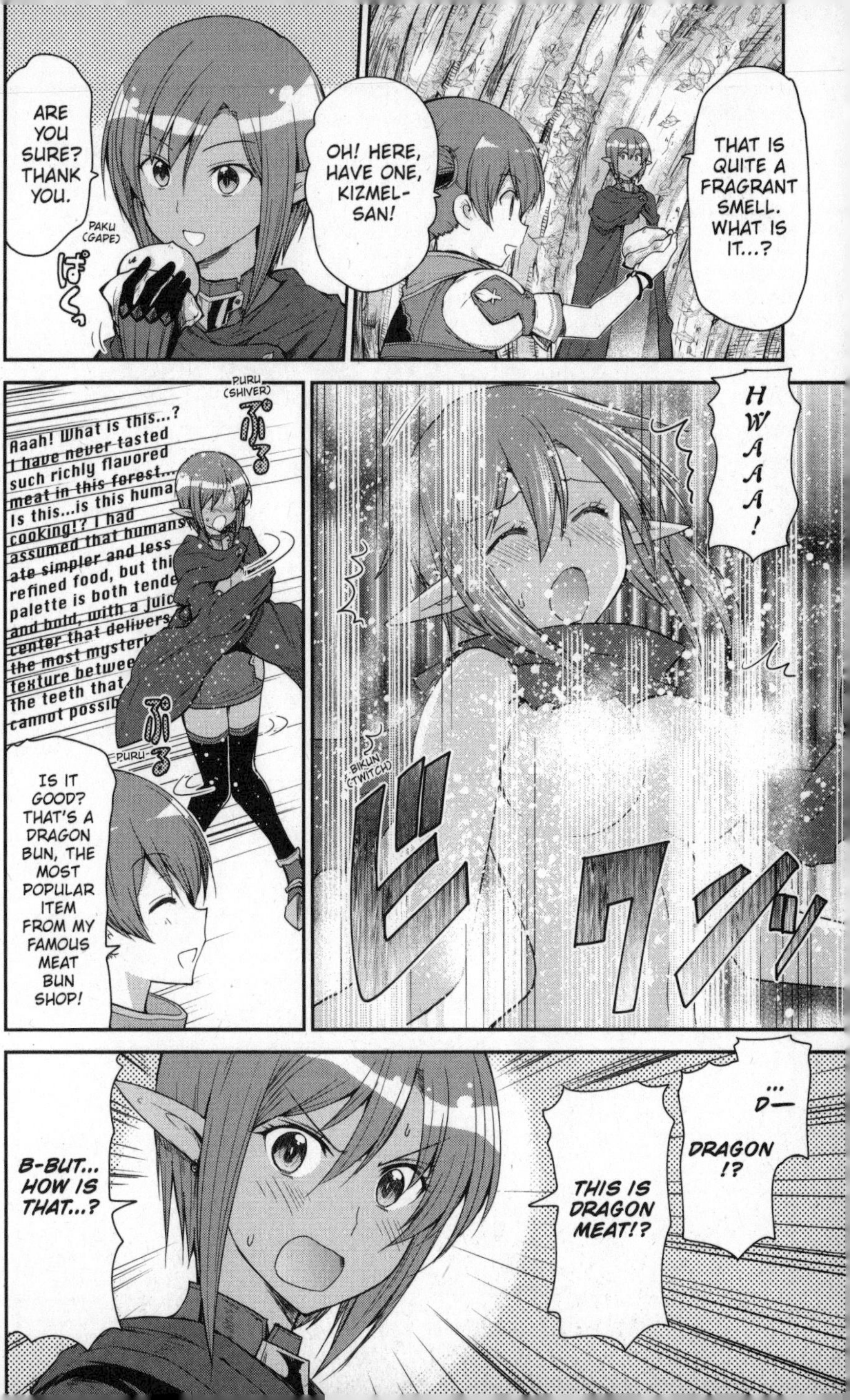
THAT IS QUITE A FRAGRANT SMELL. WHAT IS IT...?
OH! HERE, HAVE ONE, KIZMEL-SAN!
ARE YOU SURE? THANK YOU.
PAKU (GAPE)
HWAAAA!
BIKUN (TWITCH)
PURU (SHIVER)
Aaah! What is this...? I have never tasted such richly flavored meat in this forest... Is this...is this huma cooking!? I had assumed that humans ate simpler and less refined food, but thi palette is both tende and bold, with a juic center that delivers the most mysteri texture betwee the teeth that cannot possib
PURU
IS IT GOOD? THAT'S A DRAGON BUN, THE MOST POPULAR ITEM FROM MY FAMOUS MEAT BUN SHOP!
...D— DRAGON!?
THIS IS DRAGON MEAT!?
B-BUT... HOW IS THAT...?

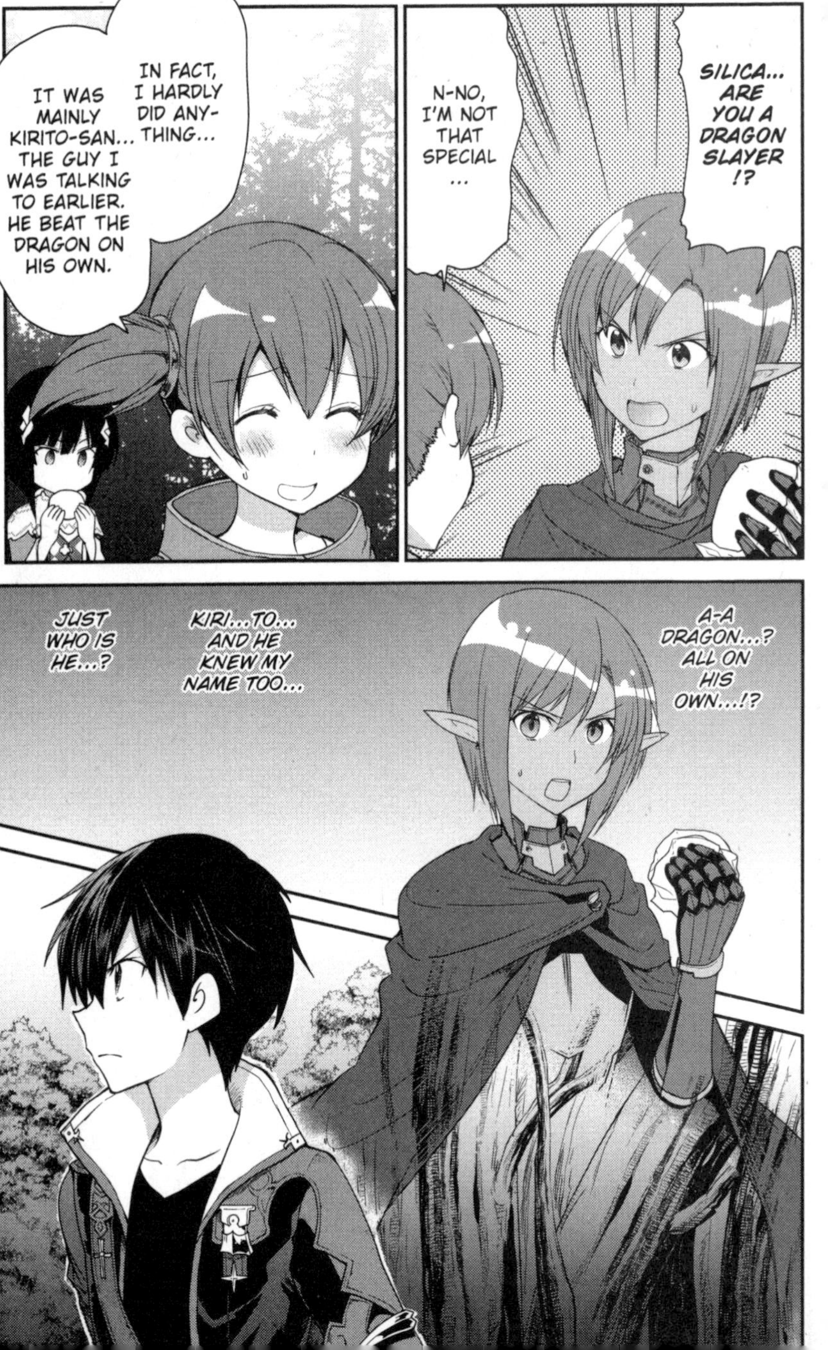
SILICA... ARE YOU A DRAGON SLAYER !?
N-NO, I'M NOT THAT SPECIAL ...
IN FACT, I HARDLY DID ANY-THING...
IT WAS MAINLY KIRITO-SAN... THE GUY I WAS TALKING TO EARLIER. HE BEAT THE DRAGON ON HIS OWN.
A-A DRAGON...? ALL ON HIS OWN...!?
KIRI...TO... AND HE KNEW MY NAME TOO...
JUST WHO IS HE...?

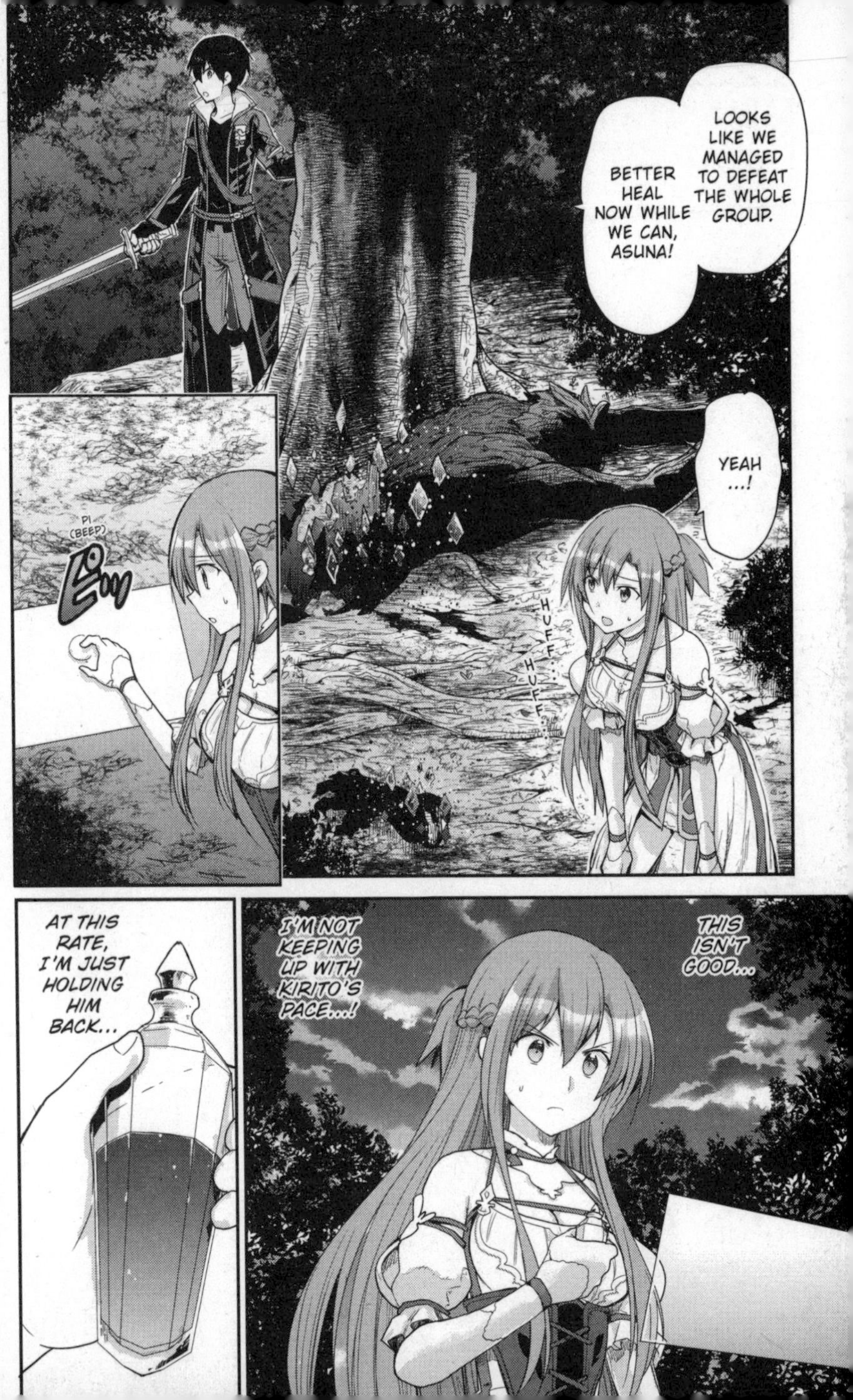
LOOKS LIKE WE MANAGED TO DEFEAT THE WHOLE GROUP.
BETTER HEAL NOW WHILE WE CAN, ASUNA!
YEAH ...!
HUFF HUFF...
PI (BEEP)
THIS ISN'T GOOD...
I'M NOT KEEPING UP WITH KIRITO'S PACE...!
AT THIS RATE, I'M JUST HOLDING HIM BACK...

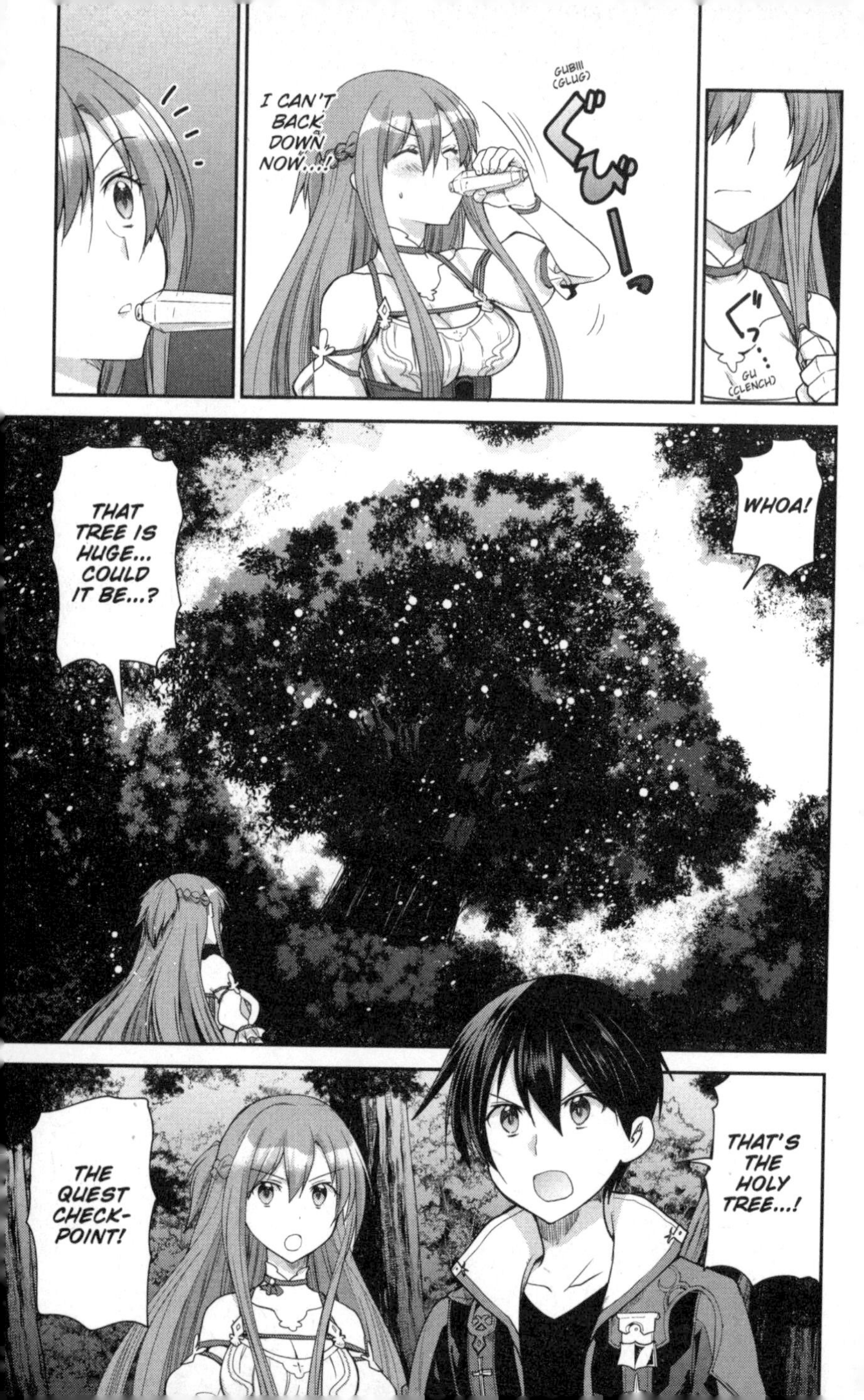
GU (CLENCH)
I CAN'T BACK DOWN NOW...!
GUBIII (GLUG)
WHOA!
THAT TREE IS HUGE... COULD IT BE...?
THAT'S THE HOLY TREE...!
THE QUEST CHECK-POINT!

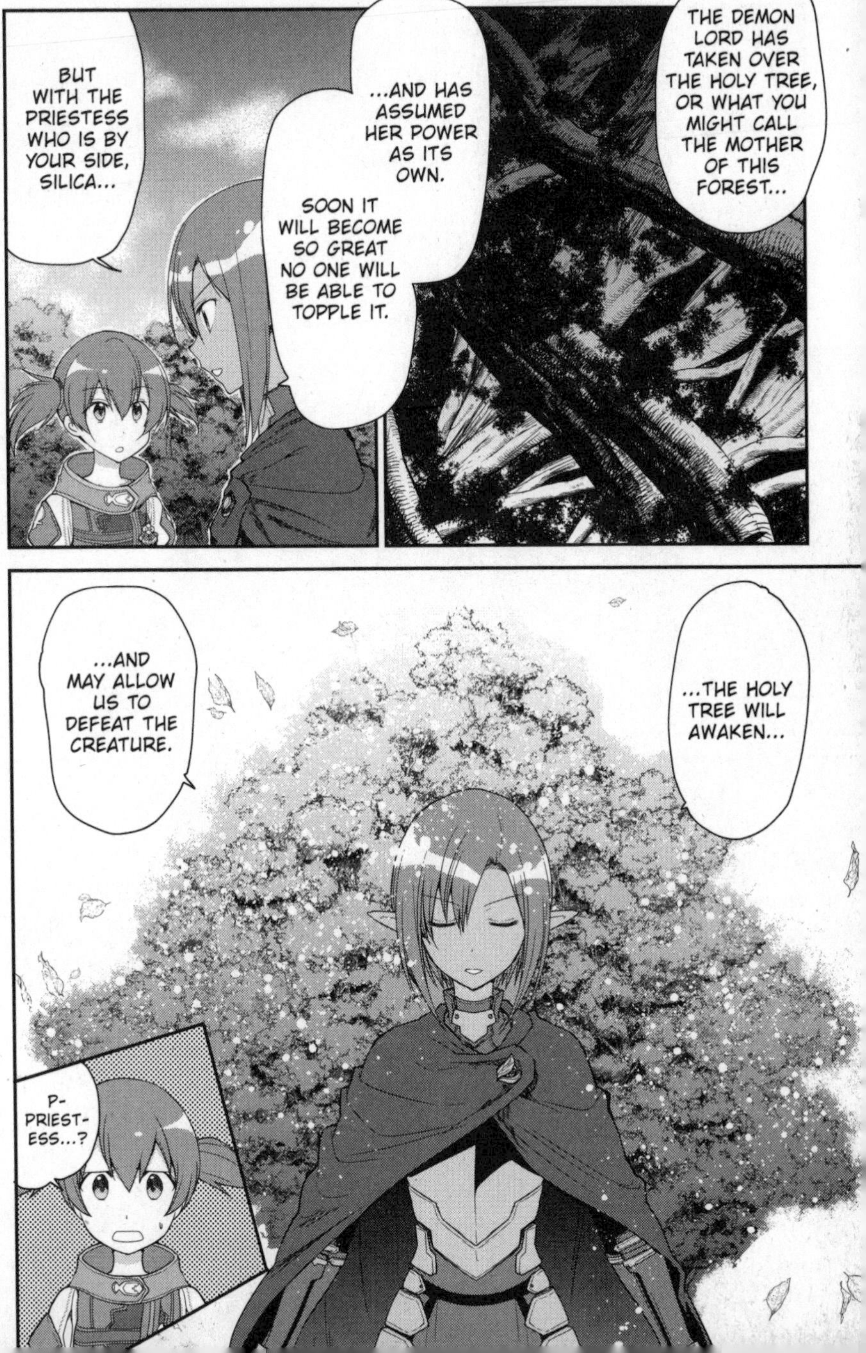
THE DEMON LORD HAS TAKEN OVER THE HOLY TREE, OR WHAT YOU MIGHT CALL THE MOTHER OF THIS FOREST...
...AND HAS ASSUMED HER POWER AS ITS OWN.
SOON IT WILL BECOME SO GREAT NO ONE WILL BE ABLE TO TOPPLE IT.
BUT WITH THE PRIESTESS WHO IS BY YOUR SIDE, SILICA...
...THE HOLY TREE WILL AWAKEN...
...AND MAY ALLOW US TO DEFEAT THE CREATURE.
P-PRIEST-ESS...?

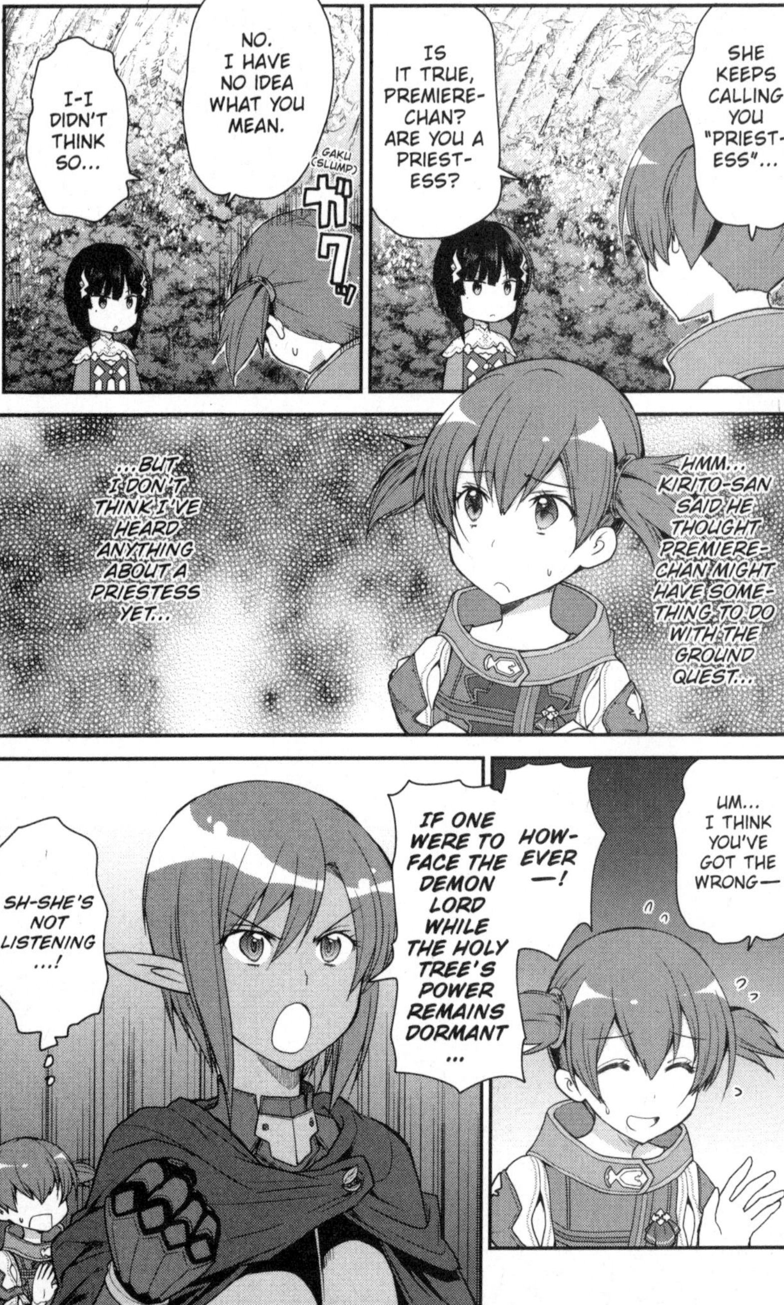
SHE KEEPS CALLING YOU "PRIEST-ESS"...
IS IT TRUE, PREMIERE-CHAN? ARE YOU A PRIEST-ESS?
NO. I HAVE NO IDEA WHAT YOU MEAN.
ガクッ
GAKU (SLUMP)
I-I DIDN'T THINK SO...
HMM... KIRITO-SAN SAID HE THOUGHT PREMIERE-CHAN MIGHT HAVE SOME-THING TO DO WITH THE GROUND QUEST...
...BUT I DON'T THINK I'VE HEARD ANYTHING ABOUT A PRIESTESS YET...
UM... I THINK YOU'VE GOT THE WRONG—
HOW-EVER—!
IF ONE WERE TO FACE THE DEMON LORD WHILE THE HOLY TREE'S POWER REMAINS DORMANT...
SH-SHE'S NOT LISTENING...!

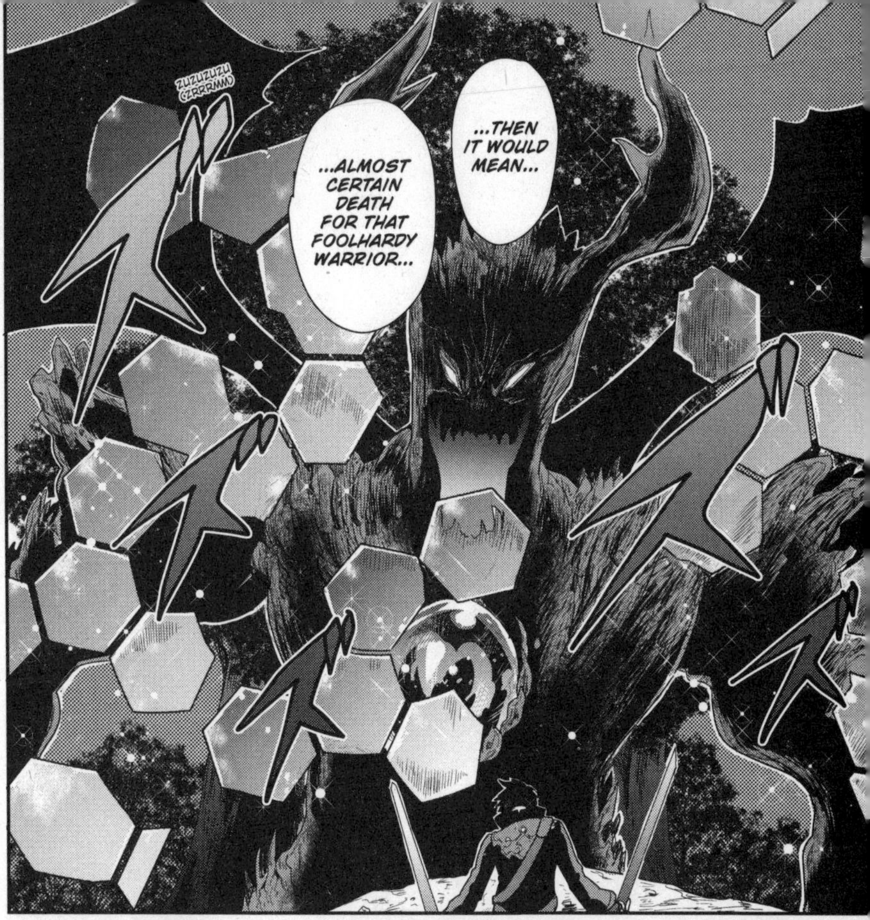
ZUZUZUZU (ZRRRMM)
...THEN IT WOULD MEAN...
...ALMOST CERTAIN DEATH FOR THAT FOOLHARDY WARRIOR...
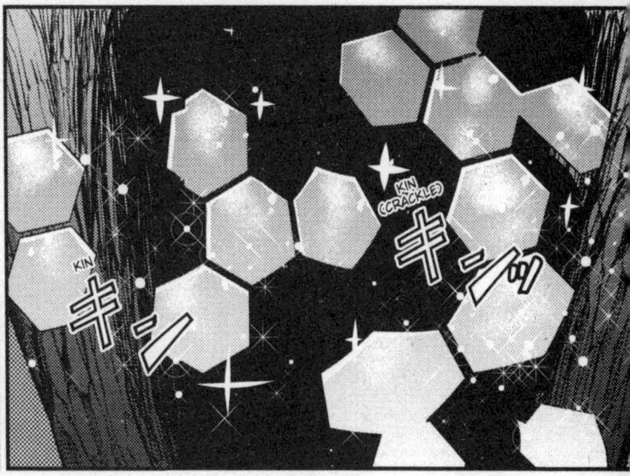
KIN (CRACKLE)
KIN
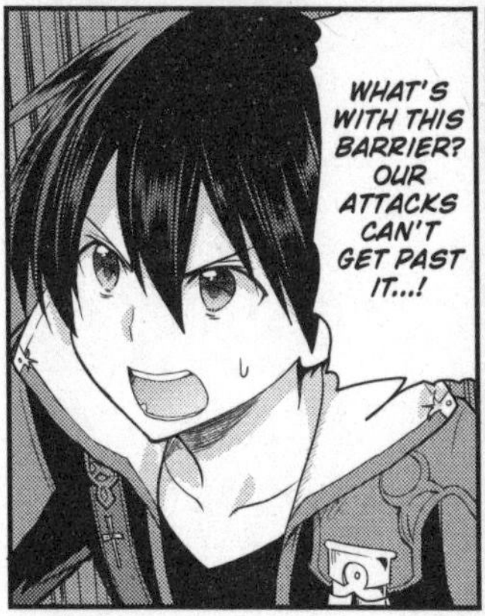
WHAT'S WITH THIS BARRIER? OUR ATTACKS CAN'T GET PAST IT...!

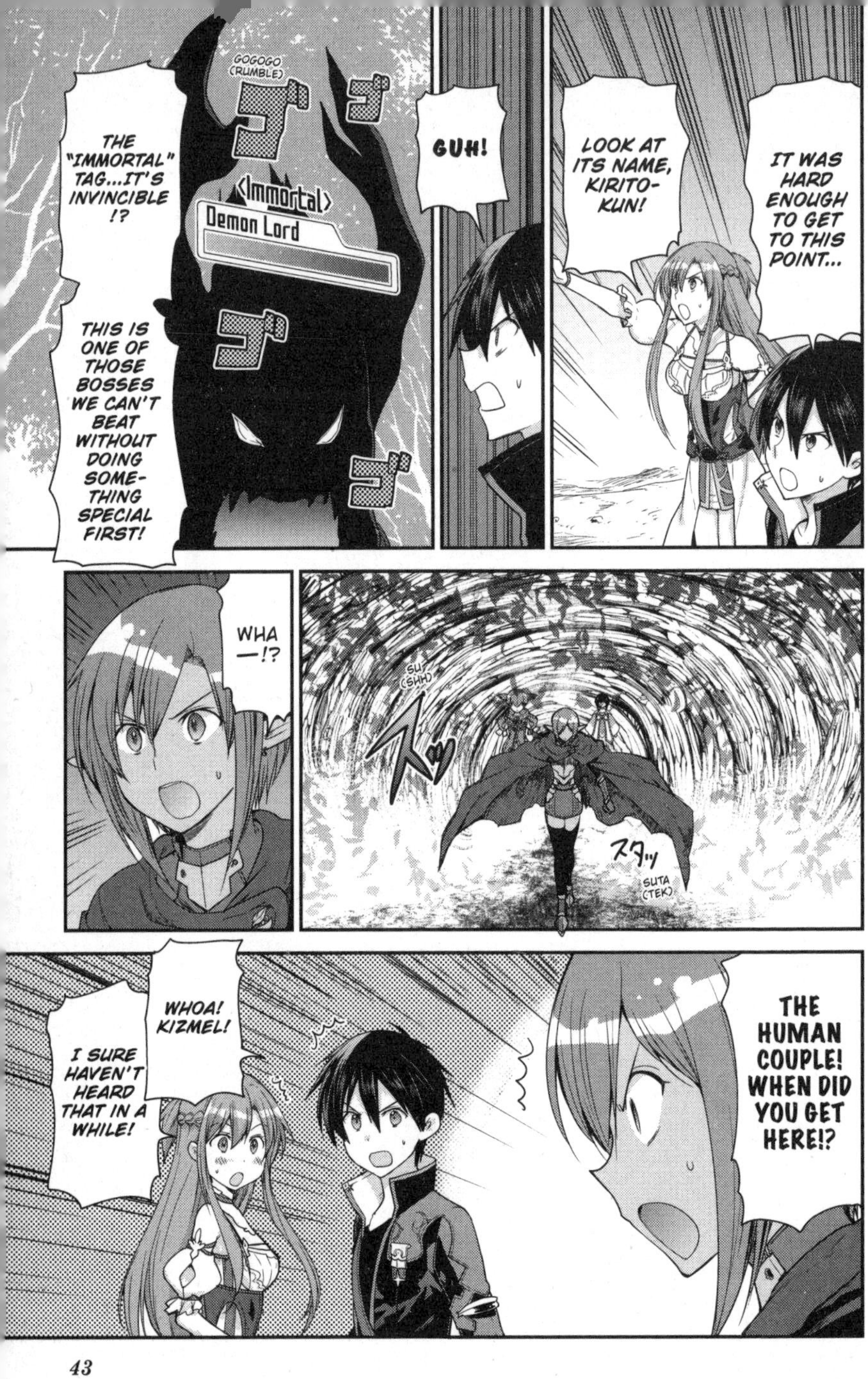
IT WAS HARD ENOUGH TO GET TO THIS POINT...
LOOK AT ITS NAME, KIRITO-KUN!
GUH!
GOGOGO (RUMBLE)
<Immortal>
Demon Lord
THE "IMMORTAL" TAG...IT'S INVINCIBLE!?
THIS IS ONE OF THOSE BOSSES WE CAN'T BEAT WITHOUT DOING SOMETHING SPECIAL FIRST!
SU (SHH)
SUTA (TEK)
WHA—!?
THE HUMAN COUPLE! WHEN DID YOU GET HERE!?
WHOA! KIZMEL!
I SURE HAVEN'T HEARD THAT IN A WHILE!

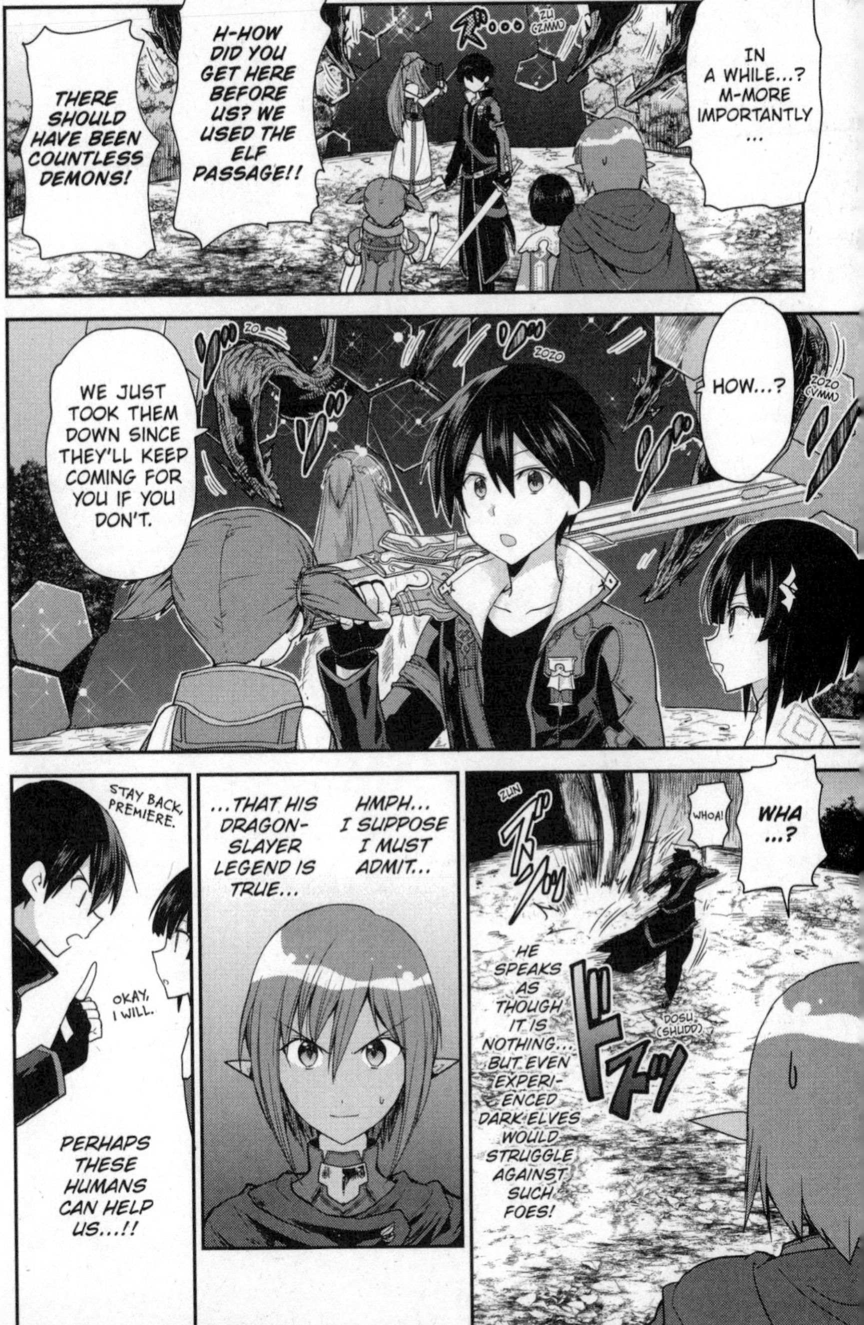
IN A WHILE...? M-MORE IMPORTANTLY ...
ZU (ZMMM)
H-HOW DID YOU GET HERE BEFORE US? WE USED THE ELF PASSAGE!!
THERE SHOULD HAVE BEEN COUNTLESS DEMONS!
HOW...?
ZOZO (VMMM)
ZOZO
ZO
WE JUST TOOK THEM DOWN SINCE THEY'LL KEEP COMING FOR YOU IF YOU DON'T.
WHA ...?
WHOA!
ZUN
DOSU (SHUDD)
HE SPEAKS AS THOUGH IT IS NOTHING... BUT EVEN EXPERI-ENCED DARK ELVES WOULD STRUGGLE AGAINST SUCH FOES!
HMPH... I SUPPOSE I MUST ADMIT...
...THAT HIS DRAGON-SLAYER LEGEND IS TRUE...
STAY BACK, PREMIERE.
OKAY, I WILL.
PERHAPS THESE HUMANS CAN HELP US...!!

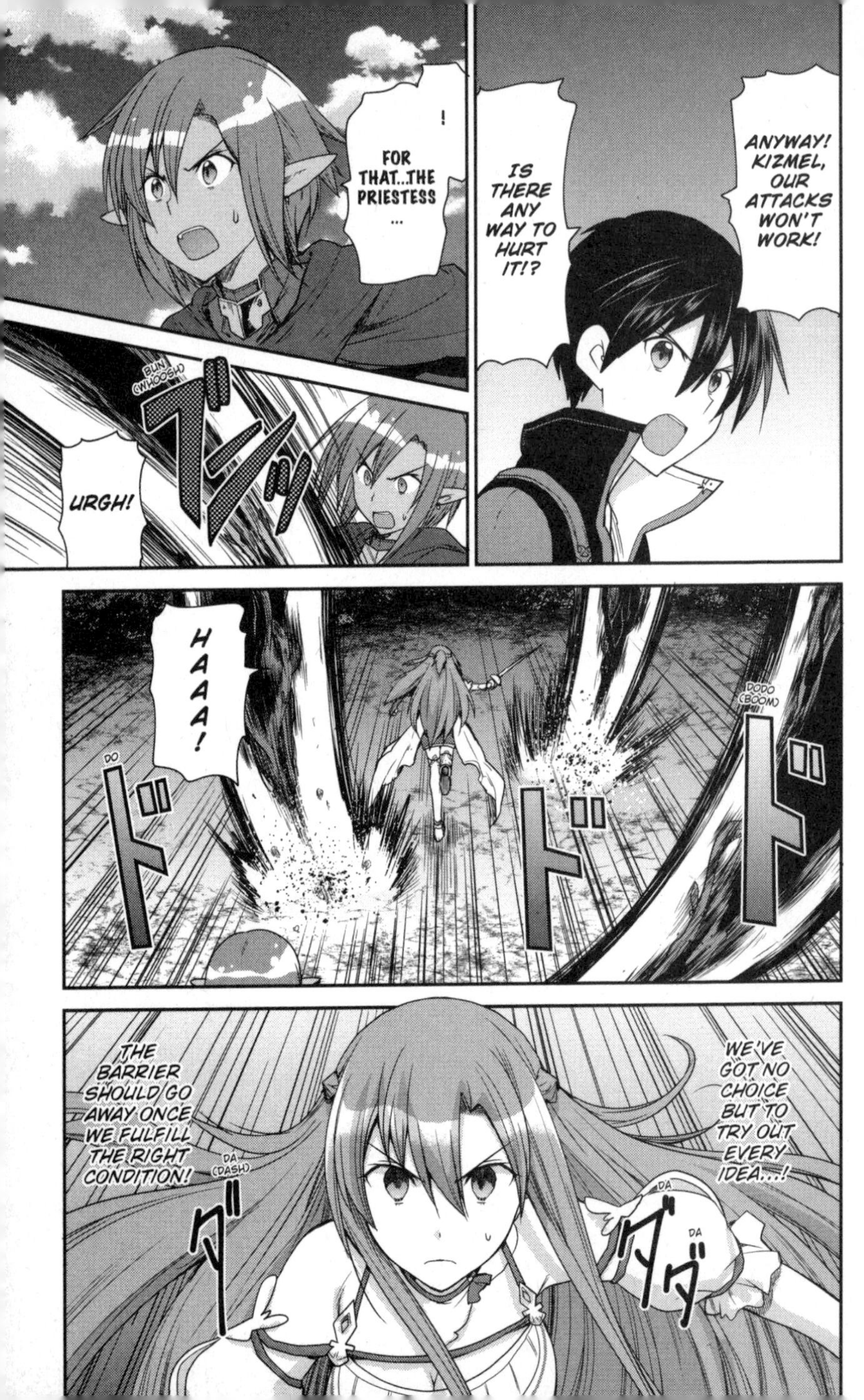
ANYWAY! KIZMEL, OUR ATTACKS WON'T WORK!
IS THERE ANY WAY TO HURT IT!?
!
FOR THAT...THE PRIESTESS ...
BUN (WHOOSH)
URGH!
HAAAA!
DODO (BOOM)
DO
WE'VE GOT NO CHOICE BUT TO TRY OUT EVERY IDEA...!
DA
DA
THE BARRIER SHOULD GO AWAY ONCE WE FULFILL THE RIGHT CONDITION!
DA (DASH)

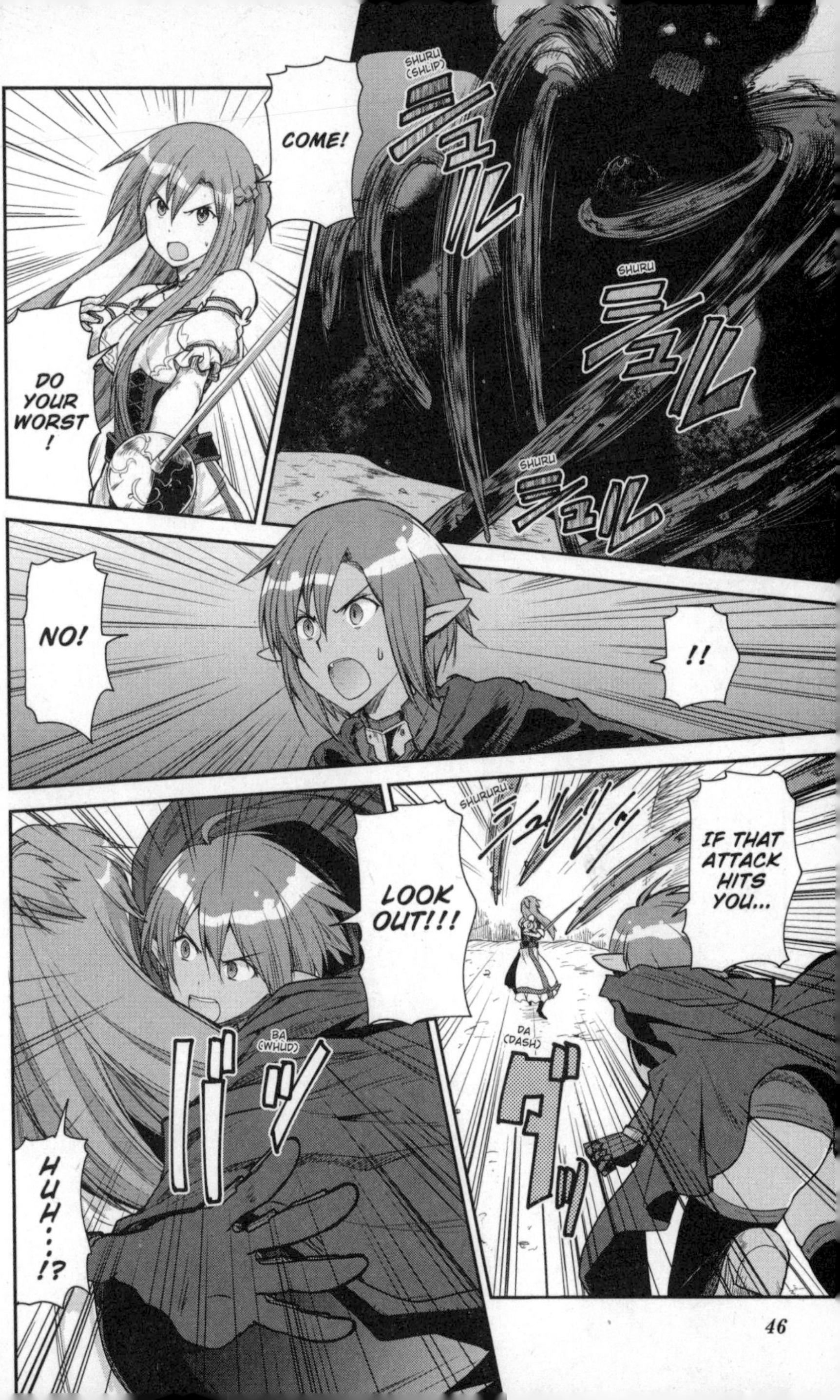
SHURU (SHLIP)
SHURU
SHURU
COME!
DO YOUR WORST!
!!
NO!
IF THAT ATTACK HITS YOU...
SHURURU
DA (DASH)
LOOK OUT!!!
BA (WHUD)
HUH...!?

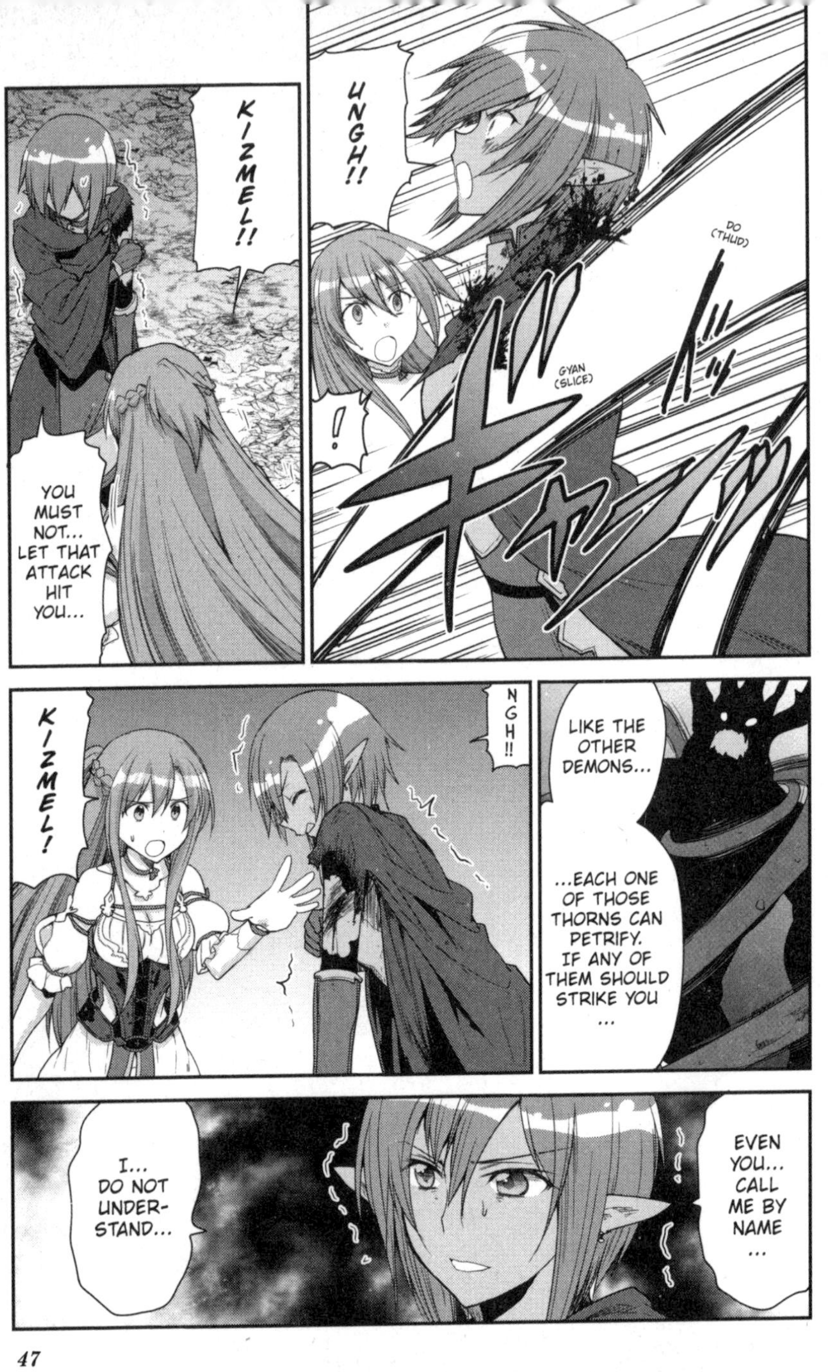
UNGH!!
DO (THUD)
GYAN (SLICE)
!
KIZMEL!!
YOU MUST NOT... LET THAT ATTACK HIT YOU...
LIKE THE OTHER DEMONS...
...EACH ONE OF THOSE THORNS CAN PETRIFY. IF ANY OF THEM SHOULD STRIKE YOU ...
NGH!!
KIZMEL!
EVEN YOU... CALL ME BY NAME ...
I... DO NOT UNDER-STAND...

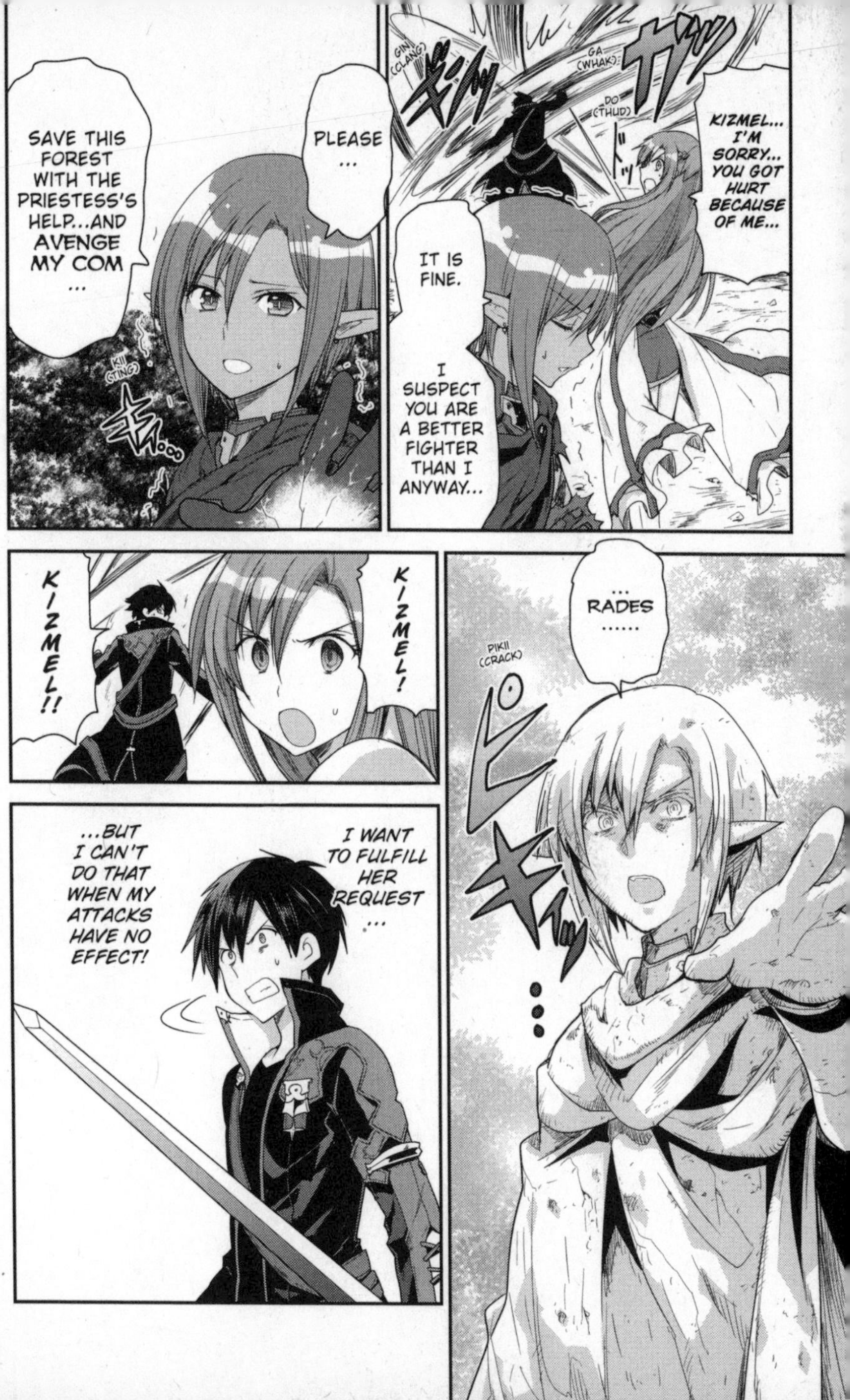
GIN (CLANG)
GA (WHAK)
DO (THUD)
KIZMEL... I'M SORRY... YOU GOT HURT BECAUSE OF ME...
IT IS FINE.
I SUSPECT YOU ARE A BETTER FIGHTER THAN I ANYWAY...
PLEASE...
SAVE THIS FOREST WITH THE PRIESTESS'S HELP...AND AVENGE MY COM...
KII (TING)
...RADES......
PIKII (CRACK)
KIZMEL!
KIZMEL!!
I WANT TO FULFILL HER REQUEST...
...BUT I CAN'T DO THAT WHEN MY ATTACKS HAVE NO EFFECT!

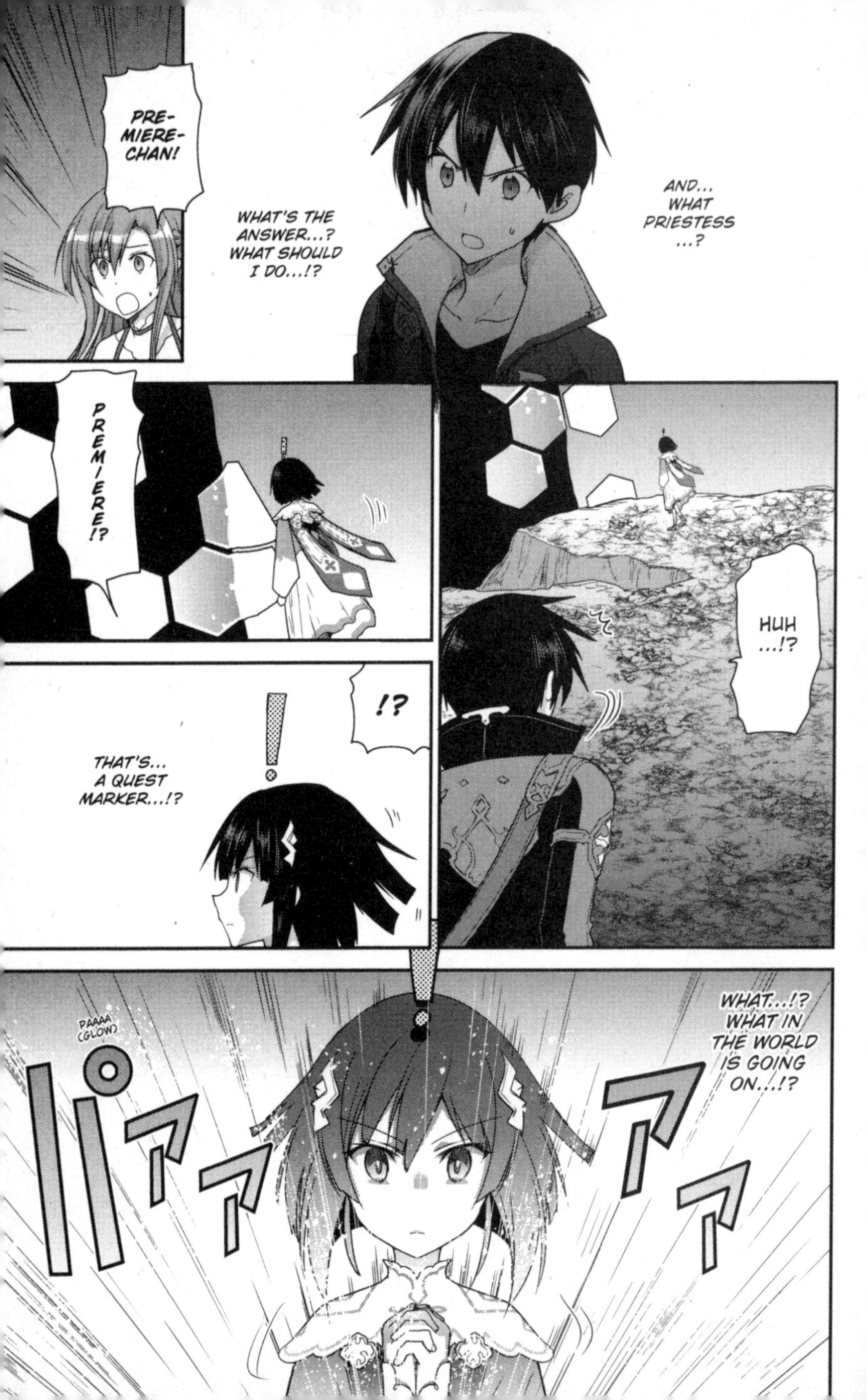
AND... WHAT PRIESTESS ...?
WHAT'S THE ANSWER...? WHAT SHOULD I DO...!?
PRE-MIERE-CHAN!
HUH ...!?
PREMIERE!?
!?
THAT'S... A QUEST MARKER...!?
WHAT...!? WHAT IN THE WORLD IS GOING ON...!?
PAAAA (GLOW)
パァァァァ

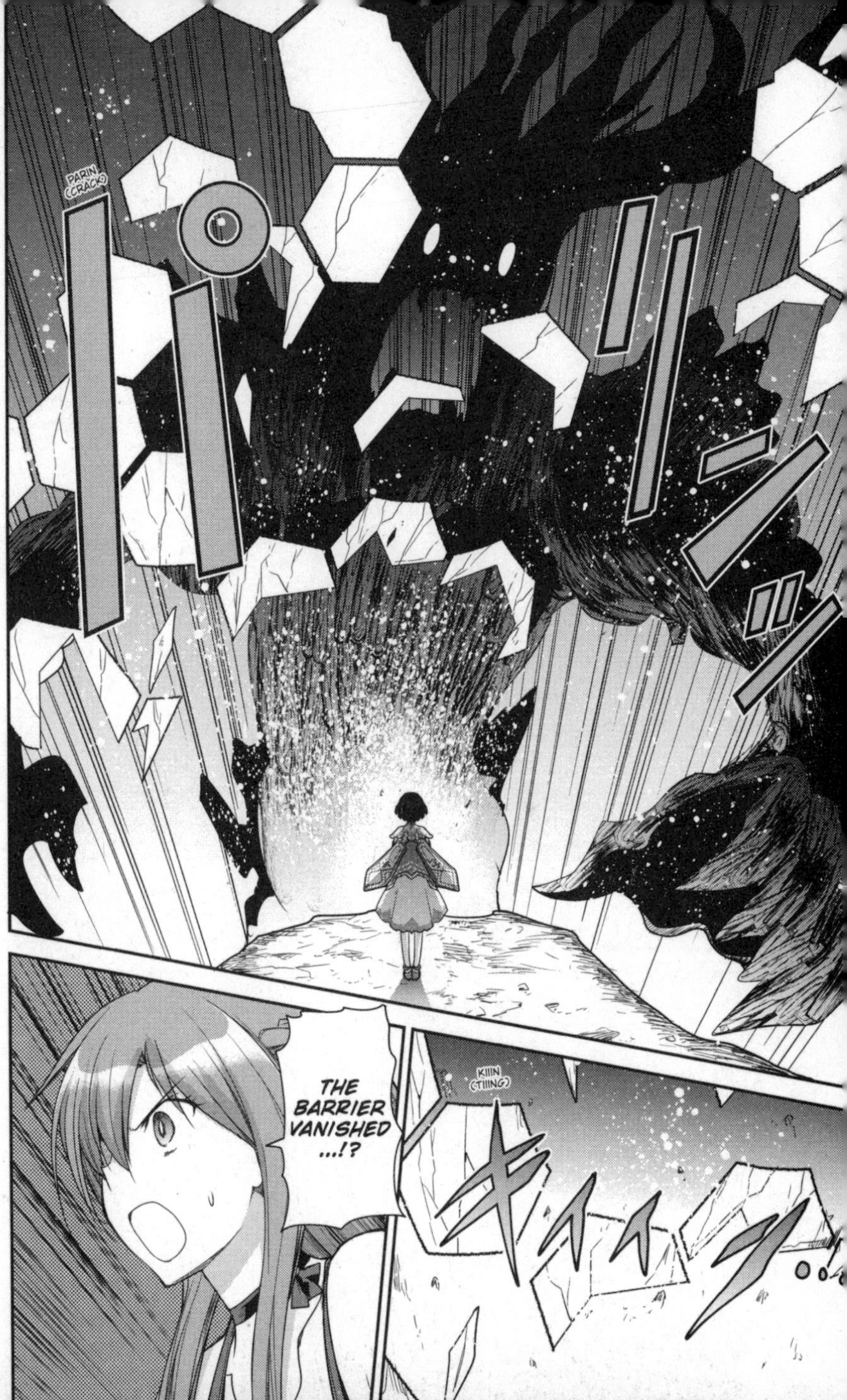
PARIN (CRACK)
KIIIN (TIIING)
THE BARRIER VANISHED ...!?

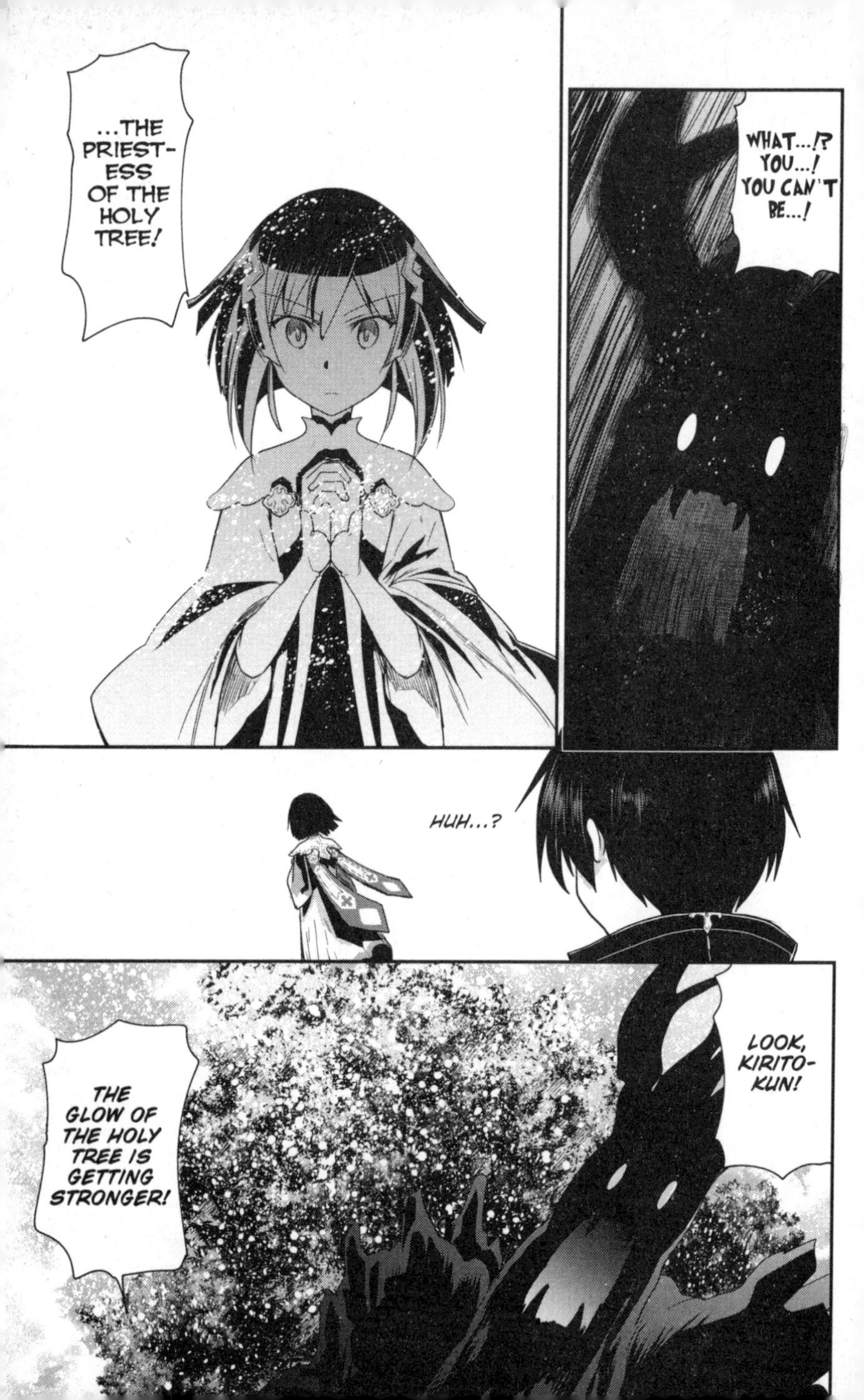
WHAT...!? YOU...! YOU CAN'T BE...!
...THE PRIEST-ESS OF THE HOLY TREE!
HUH...?
LOOK, KIRITO-KUN!
THE GLOW OF THE HOLY TREE IS GETTING STRONGER!

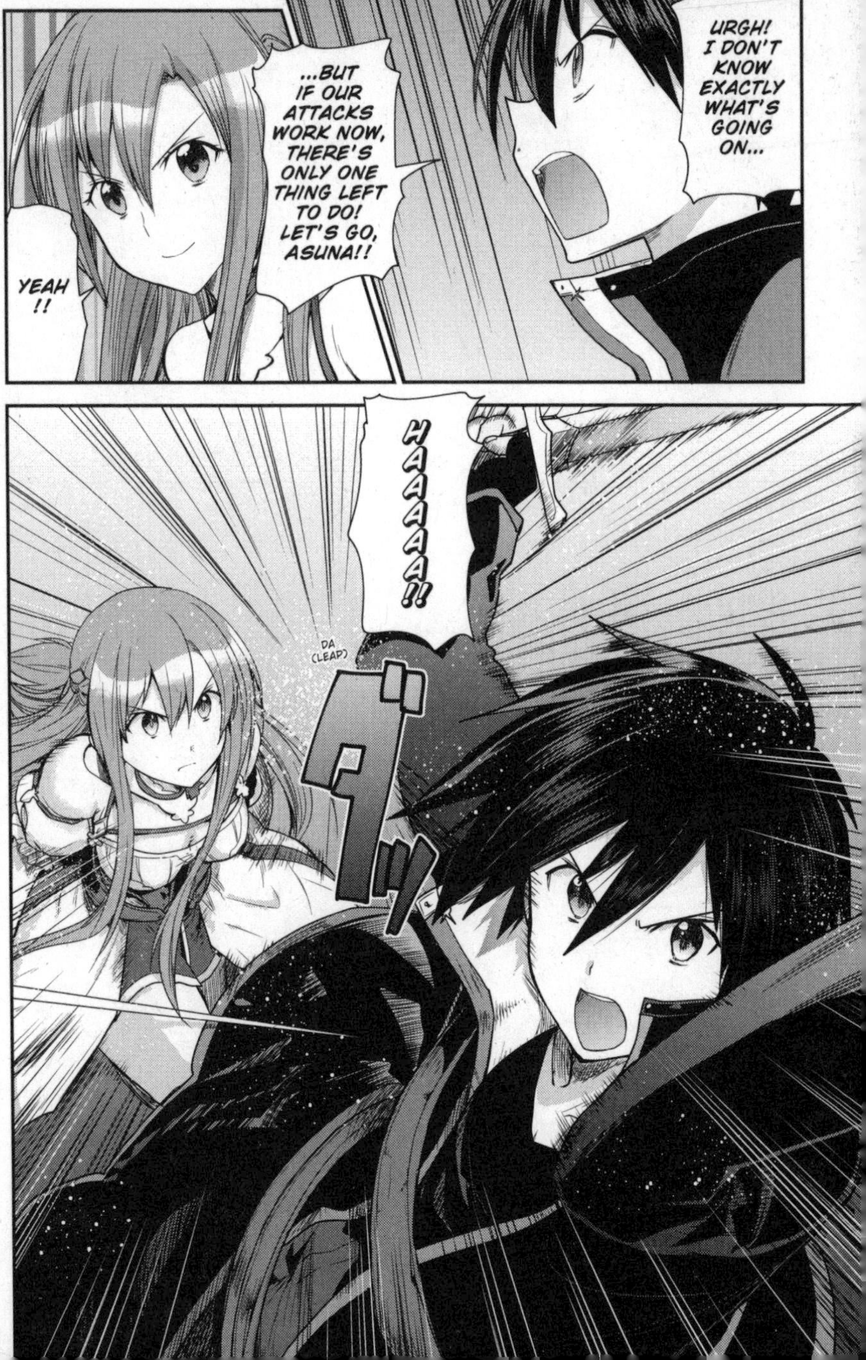
URGH! I DON'T KNOW EXACTLY WHAT'S GOING ON...
...BUT IF OUR ATTACKS WORK NOW, THERE'S ONLY ONE THING LEFT TO DO! LET'S GO, ASUNA!!
YEAH!!
HAAAAAA!!
DA (LEAP)

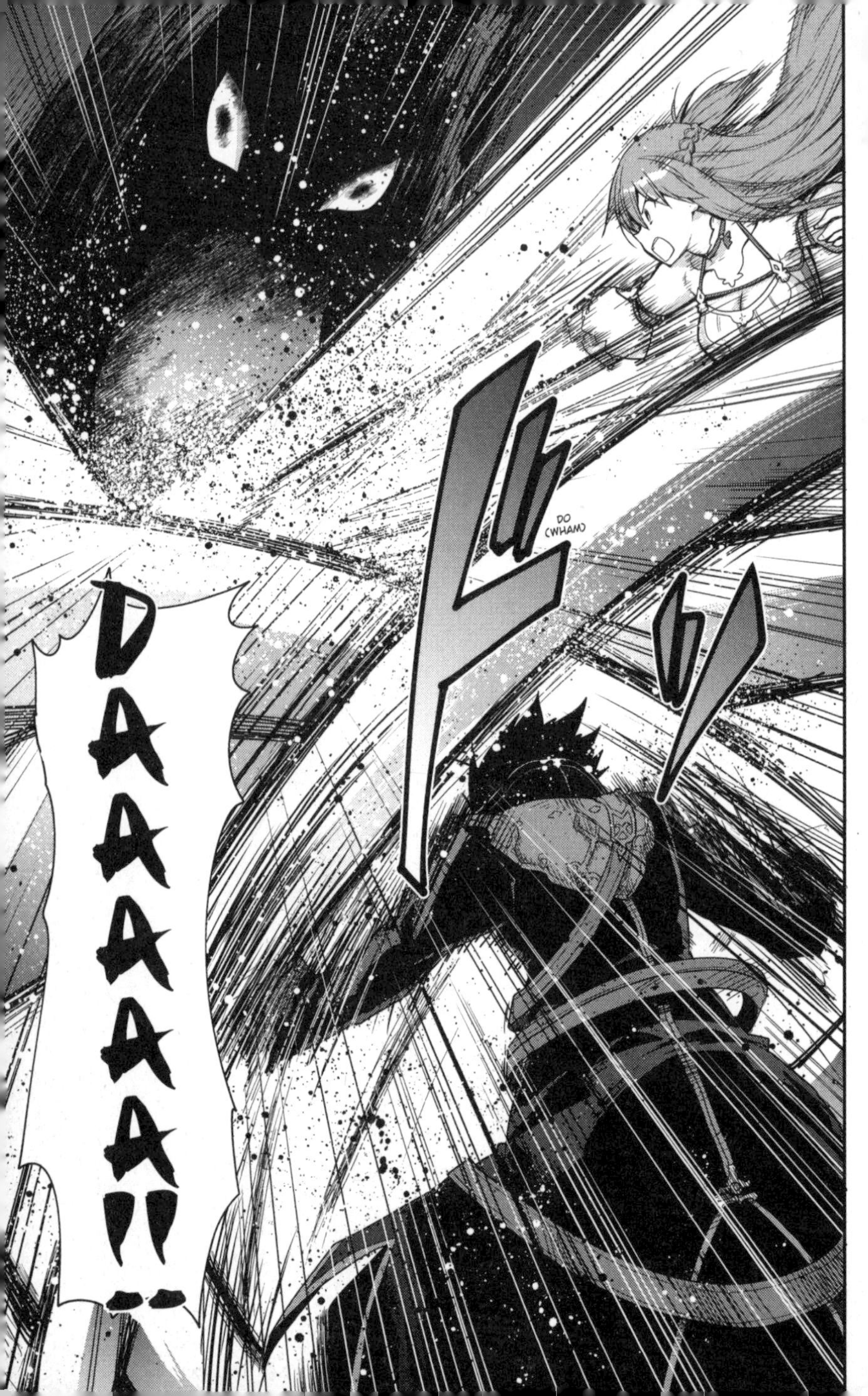
ドン
DO (WHAM)
DAAAAA!!

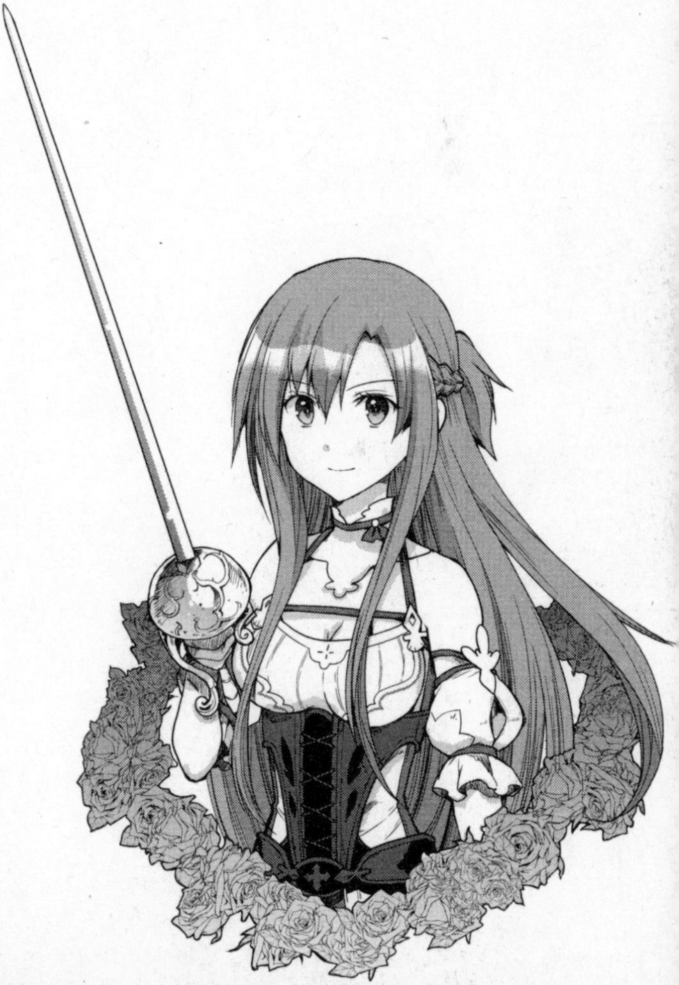

#12: A New Land, a New Room

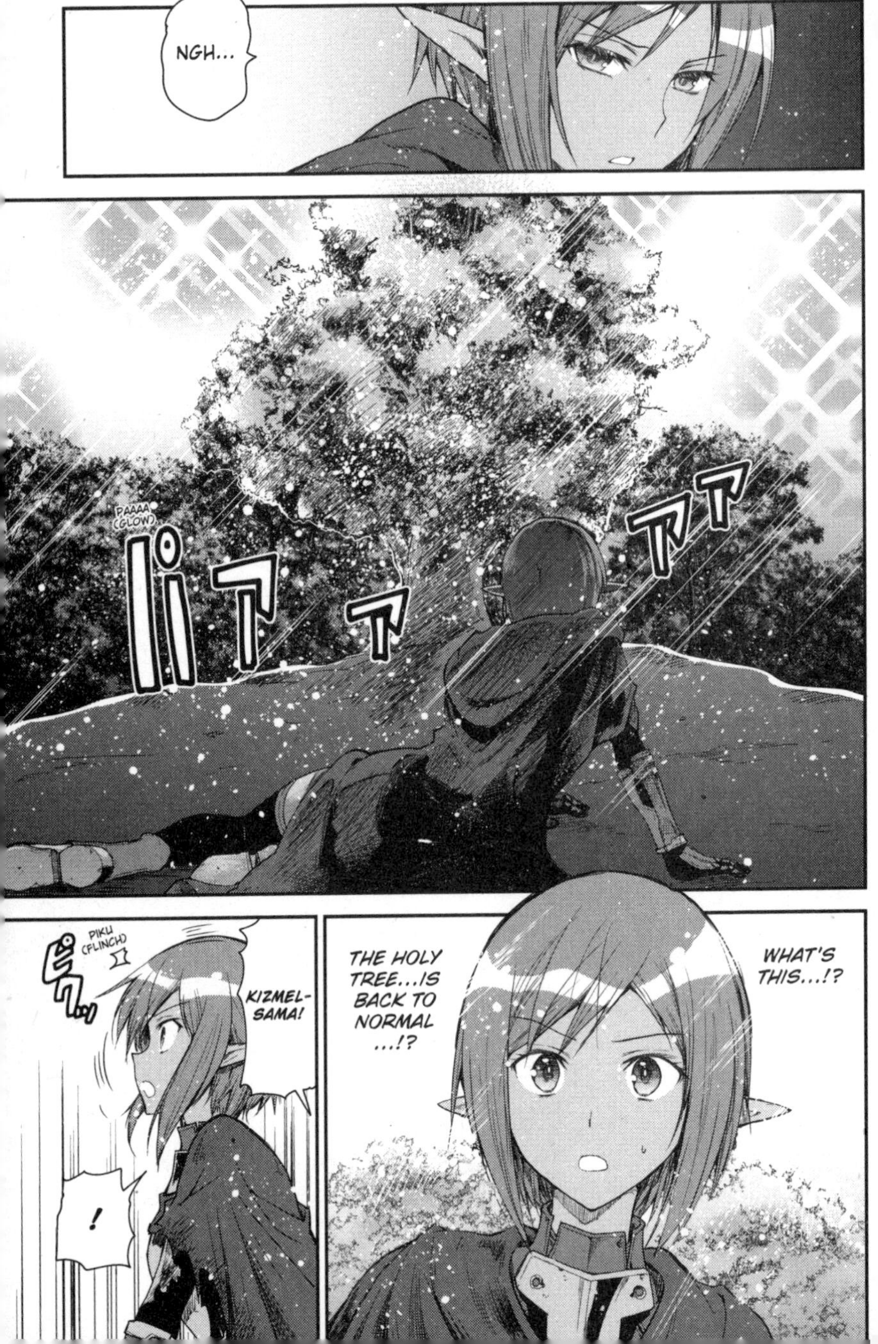
NGH...
PAAAA (GLOW)
パァァァァ
WHAT'S THIS...!?
THE HOLY TREE...IS BACK TO NORMAL...!?
PIKU (FLINCH)
KIZMEL-SAMA!
!

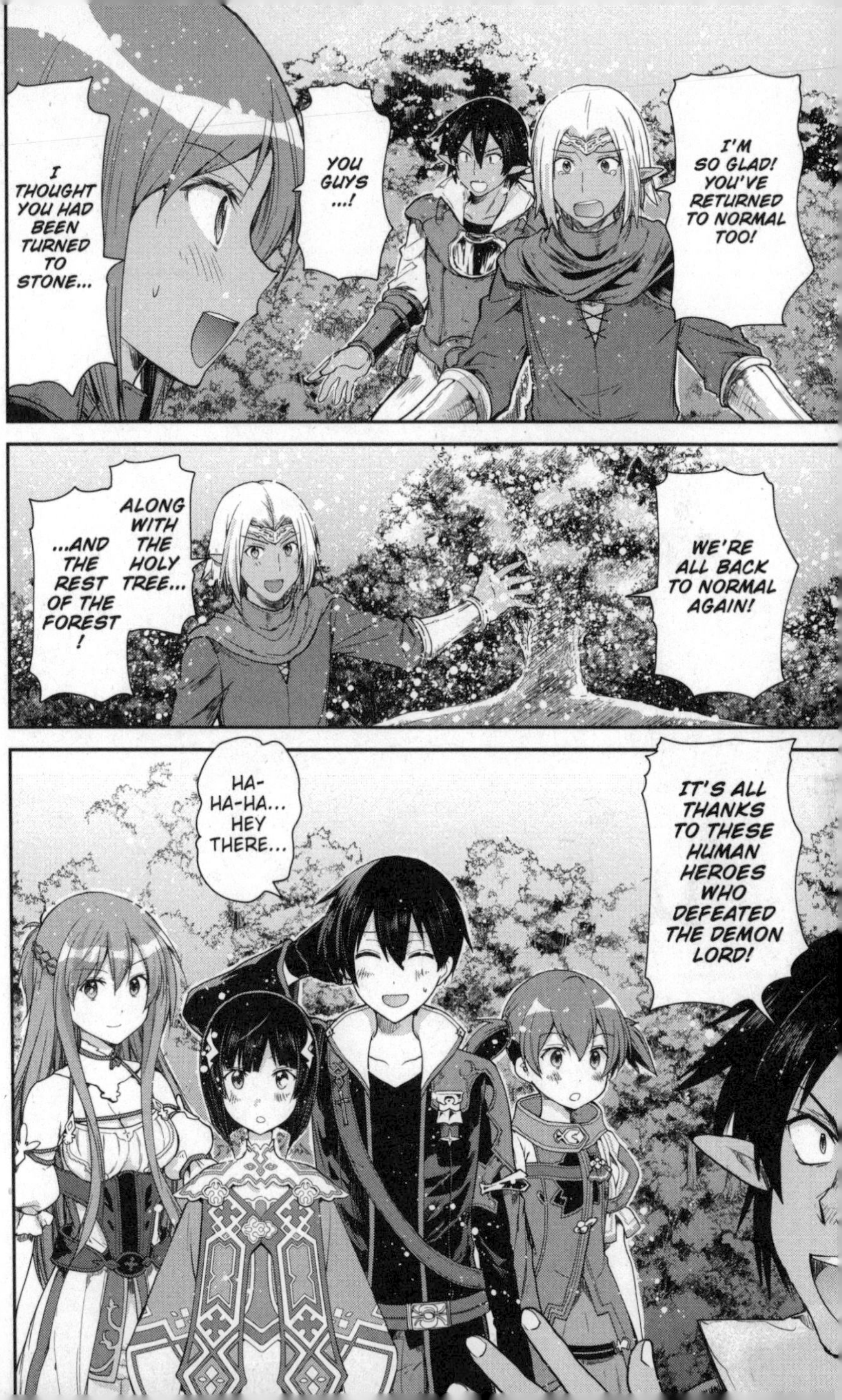
I'M SO GLAD! YOU'VE RETURNED TO NORMAL TOO!
YOU GUYS ...!
I THOUGHT YOU HAD BEEN TURNED TO STONE...
WE'RE ALL BACK TO NORMAL AGAIN!
ALONG WITH THE HOLY TREE...
...AND THE REST OF THE FOREST!
IT'S ALL THANKS TO THESE HUMAN HEROES WHO DEFEATED THE DEMON LORD!
HA-HA-HA... HEY THERE...

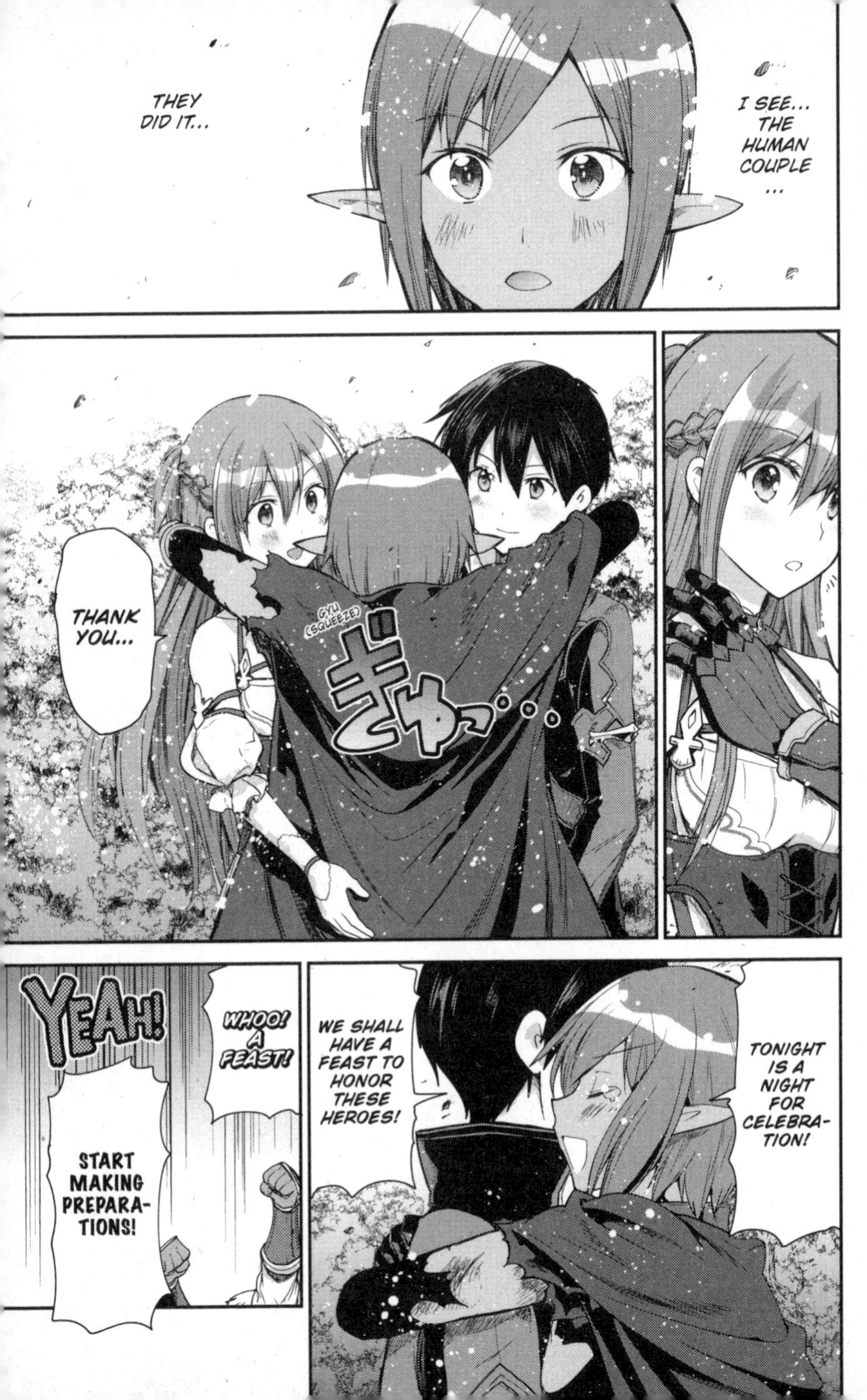
I SEE... THE HUMAN COUPLE ...
THEY DID IT...
GYU (SQUEEZE)
ぎゅっ...
THANK YOU...
TONIGHT IS A NIGHT FOR CELEBRATION!
WE SHALL HAVE A FEAST TO HONOR THESE HEROES!
WHOO! A FEAST!
YEAH!
START MAKING PREPARATIONS!

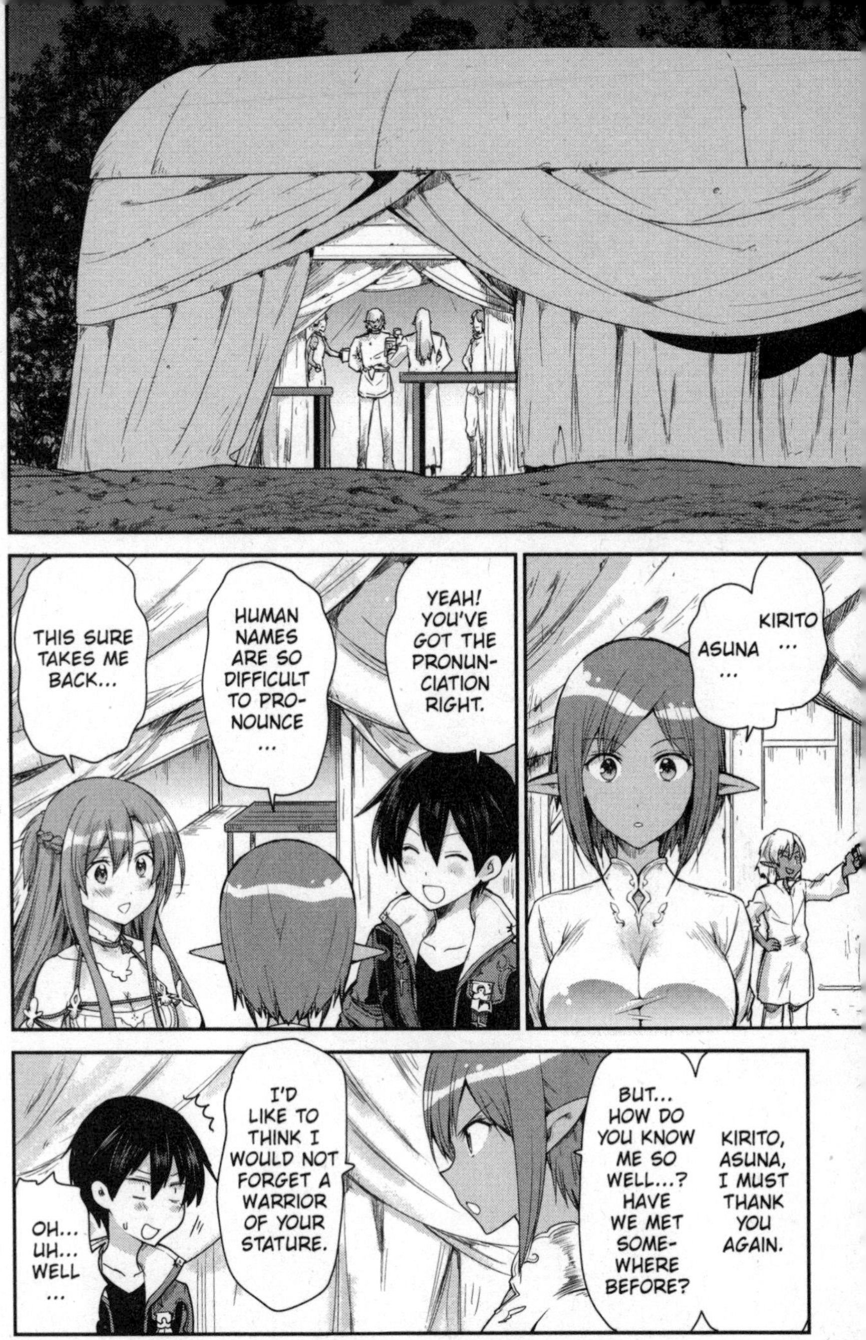
KIRITO... ASUNA...
YEAH! YOU'VE GOT THE PRONUNCIATION RIGHT.
HUMAN NAMES ARE SO DIFFICULT TO PRONOUNCE...
THIS SURE TAKES ME BACK...
KIRITO, ASUNA, I MUST THANK YOU AGAIN.
BUT... HOW DO YOU KNOW ME SO WELL...? HAVE WE MET SOMEWHERE BEFORE?
I'D LIKE TO THINK I WOULD NOT FORGET A WARRIOR OF YOUR STATURE.
OH... UH... WELL...

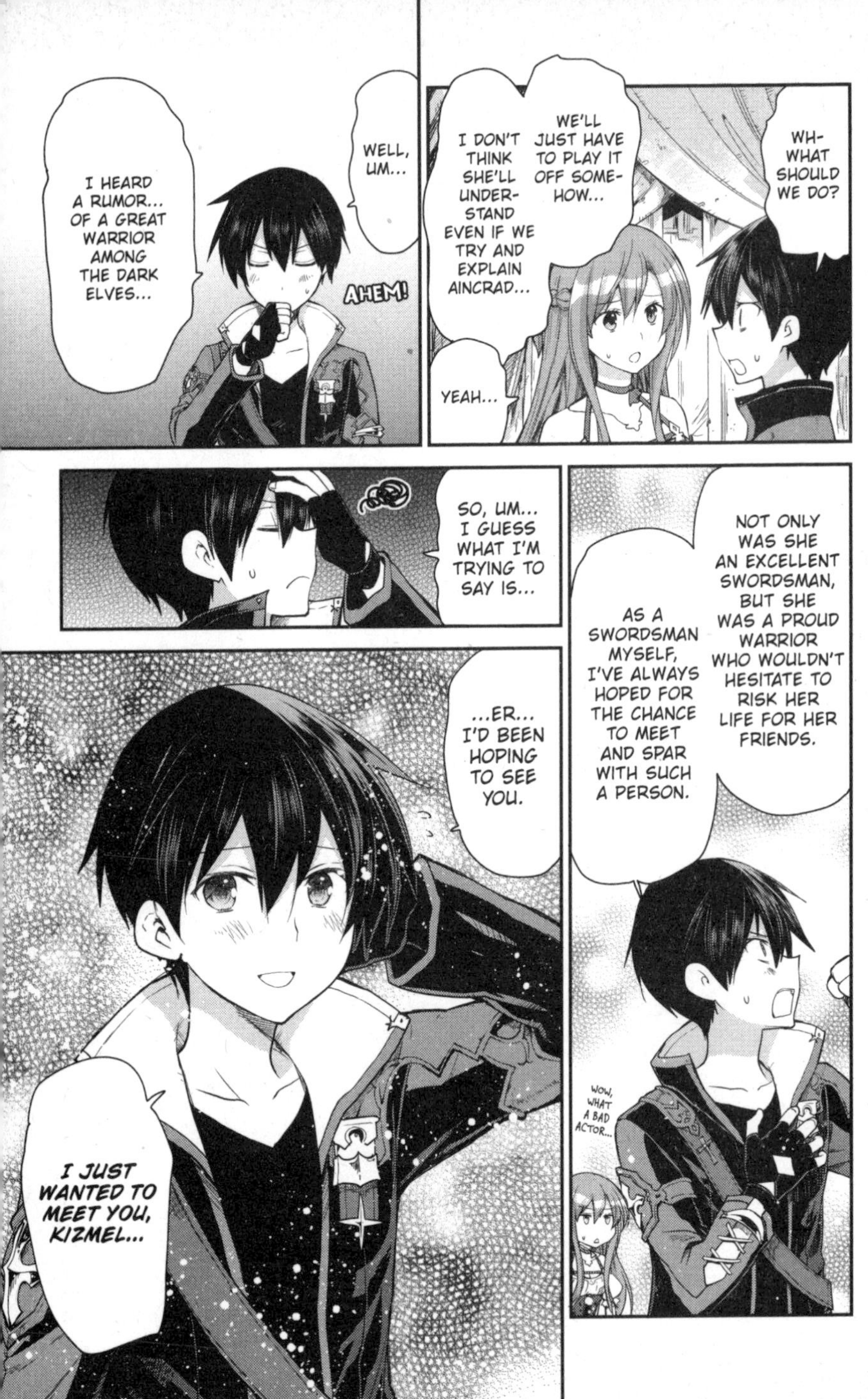
WH- WHAT SHOULD WE DO?
WE'LL JUST HAVE TO PLAY IT OFF SOME-HOW...
I DON'T THINK SHE'LL UNDER-STAND EVEN IF WE TRY AND EXPLAIN AINCRAD...
YEAH...
WELL, UM...
AHEM!
I HEARD A RUMOR... OF A GREAT WARRIOR AMONG THE DARK ELVES...
NOT ONLY WAS SHE AN EXCELLENT SWORDSMAN, BUT SHE WAS A PROUD WARRIOR WHO WOULDN'T HESITATE TO RISK HER LIFE FOR HER FRIENDS.
AS A SWORDSMAN MYSELF, I'VE ALWAYS HOPED FOR THE CHANCE TO MEET AND SPAR WITH SUCH A PERSON.
WOW, WHAT A BAD ACTOR...
SO, UM... I GUESS WHAT I'M TRYING TO SAY IS...
...ER... I'D BEEN HOPING TO SEE YOU.
I JUST WANTED TO MEET YOU, KIZMEL...

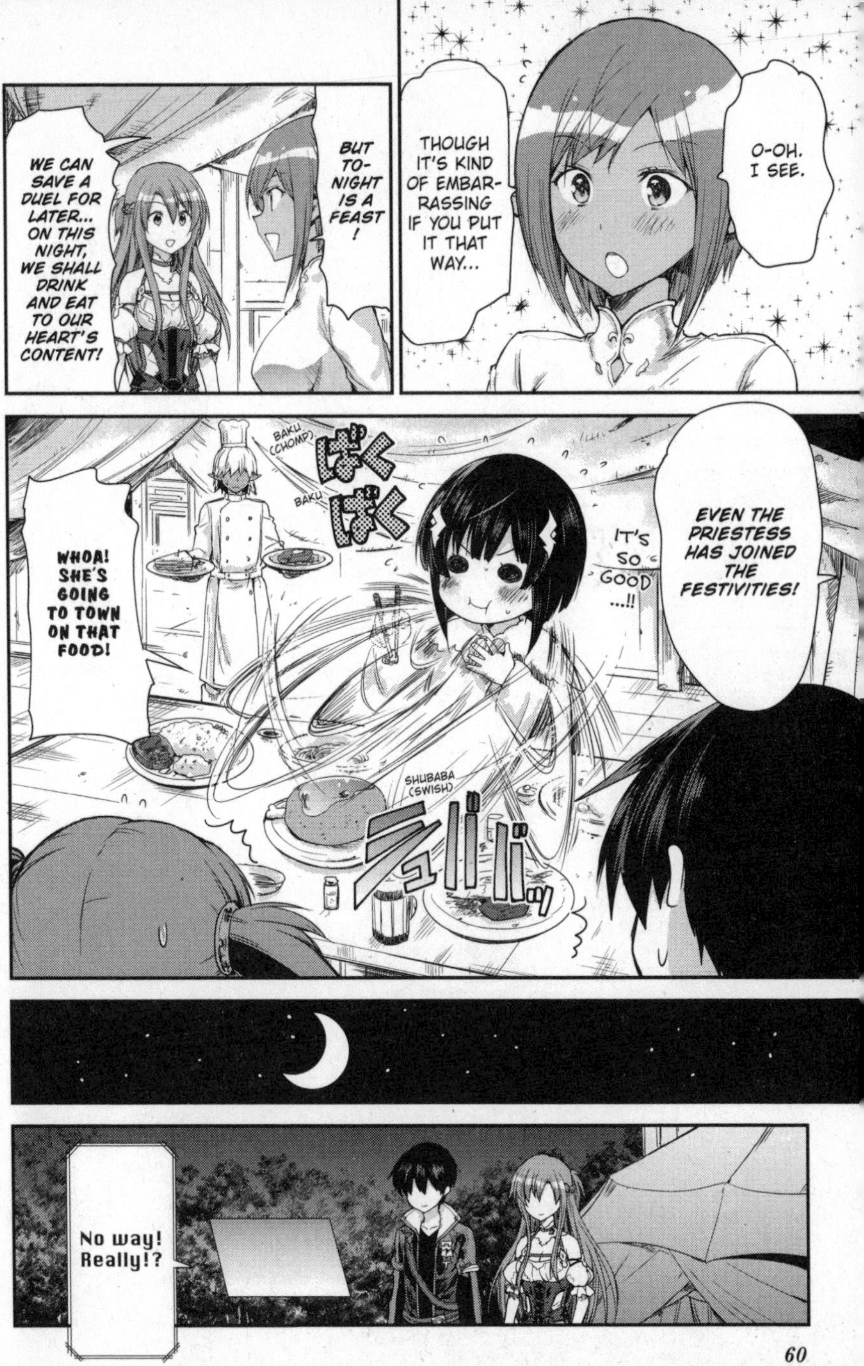
O-OH. I SEE.
THOUGH IT'S KIND OF EMBARRASSING IF YOU PUT IT THAT WAY...
BUT TONIGHT IS A FEAST!
WE CAN SAVE A DUEL FOR LATER... ON THIS NIGHT, WE SHALL DRINK AND EAT TO OUR HEART'S CONTENT!
EVEN THE PRIESTESS HAS JOINED THE FESTIVITIES!
IT'S SO GOOD ...!!
ばく
BAKU (CHOMP)
ばく
BAKU
WHOA! SHE'S GOING TO TOWN ON THAT FOOD!
シュババッ
SHUBABA (SWISH)
No way! Really!?

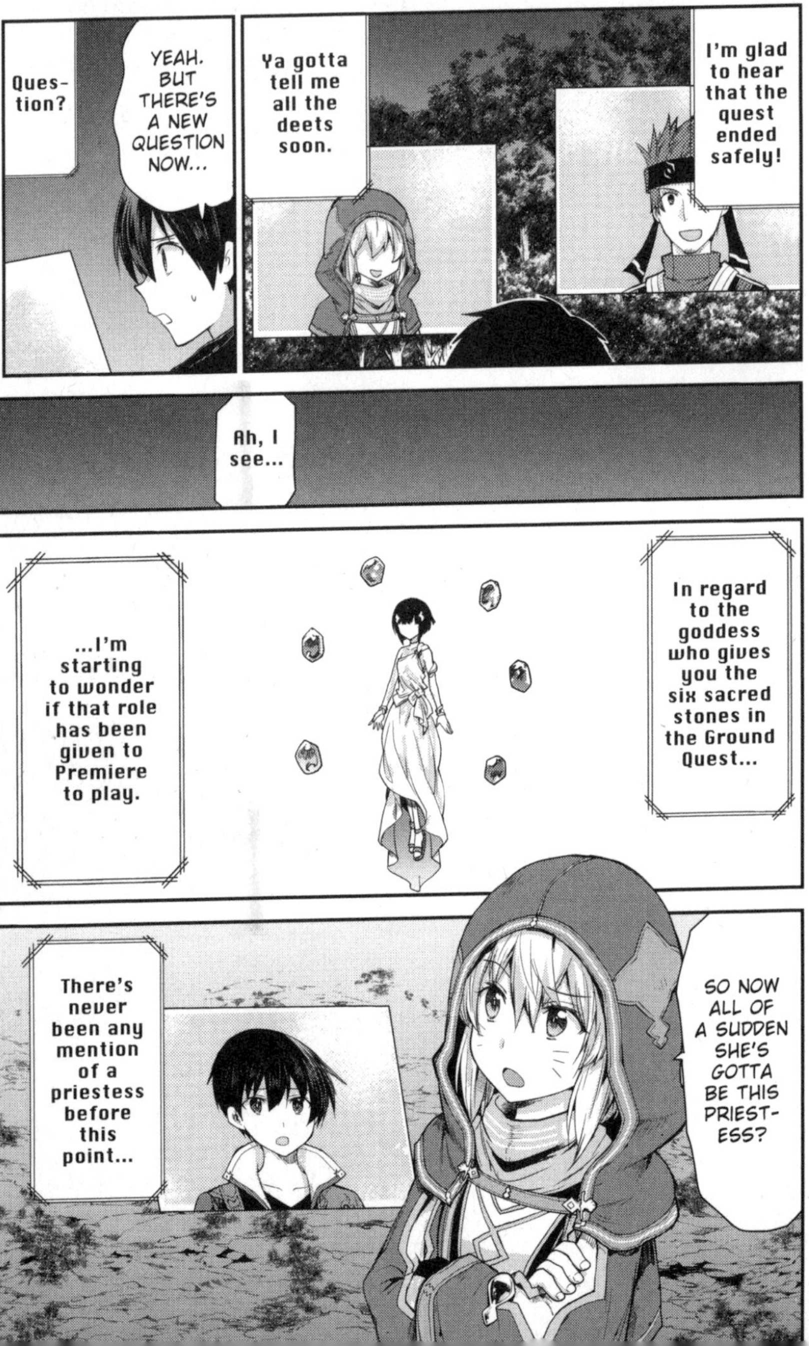
I'm glad to hear that the quest ended safely!
Ya gotta tell me all the deets soon.
YEAH. BUT THERE'S A NEW QUESTION NOW...
Ques-tion?
Ah, I see...
In regard to the goddess who gives you the six sacred stones in the Ground Quest...
...I'm starting to wonder if that role has been given to Premiere to play.
SO NOW ALL OF A SUDDEN SHE'S GOTTA BE THIS PRIEST-ESS?
There's never been any mention of a priestess before this point...

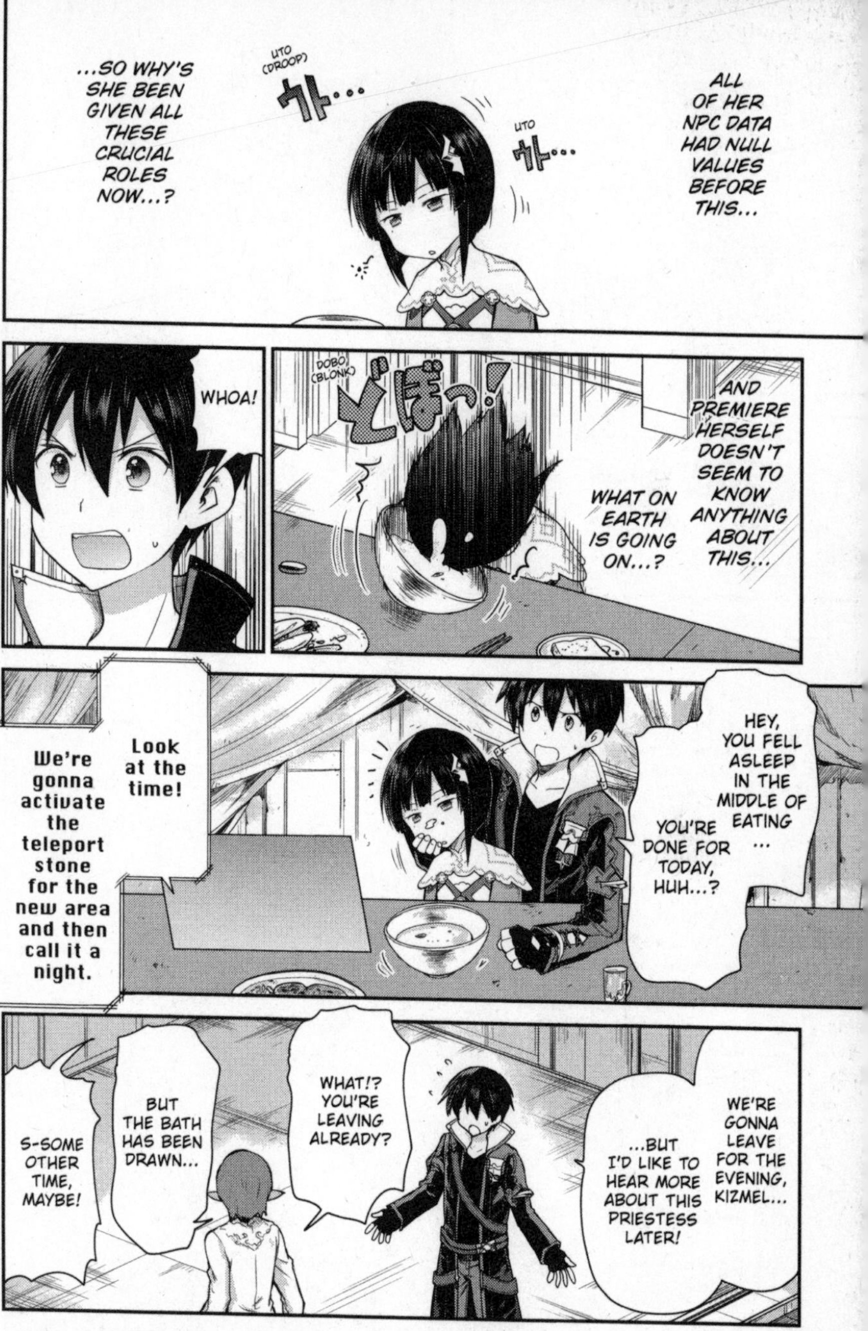
ALL OF HER NPC DATA HAD NULL VALUES BEFORE THIS...
UTO (DROOP)
ウト…
UTO
ウト…
...SO WHY'S SHE BEEN GIVEN ALL THESE CRUCIAL ROLES NOW...?
AND PREMIERE HERSELF DOESN'T SEEM TO KNOW ANYTHING ABOUT THIS...
WHAT ON EARTH IS GOING ON...?
DOBO (BLONK)
どぼっ!
WHOA!
HEY, YOU FELL ASLEEP IN THE MIDDLE OF EATING...
YOU'RE DONE FOR TODAY, HUH...?
Look at the time!
We're gonna activate the teleport stone for the new area and then call it a night.
WE'RE GONNA LEAVE FOR THE EVENING, KIZMEL...
...BUT I'D LIKE TO HEAR MORE ABOUT THIS PRIESTESS LATER!
WHAT!? YOU'RE LEAVING ALREADY?
BUT THE BATH HAS BEEN DRAWN...
S-SOME OTHER TIME, MAYBE!

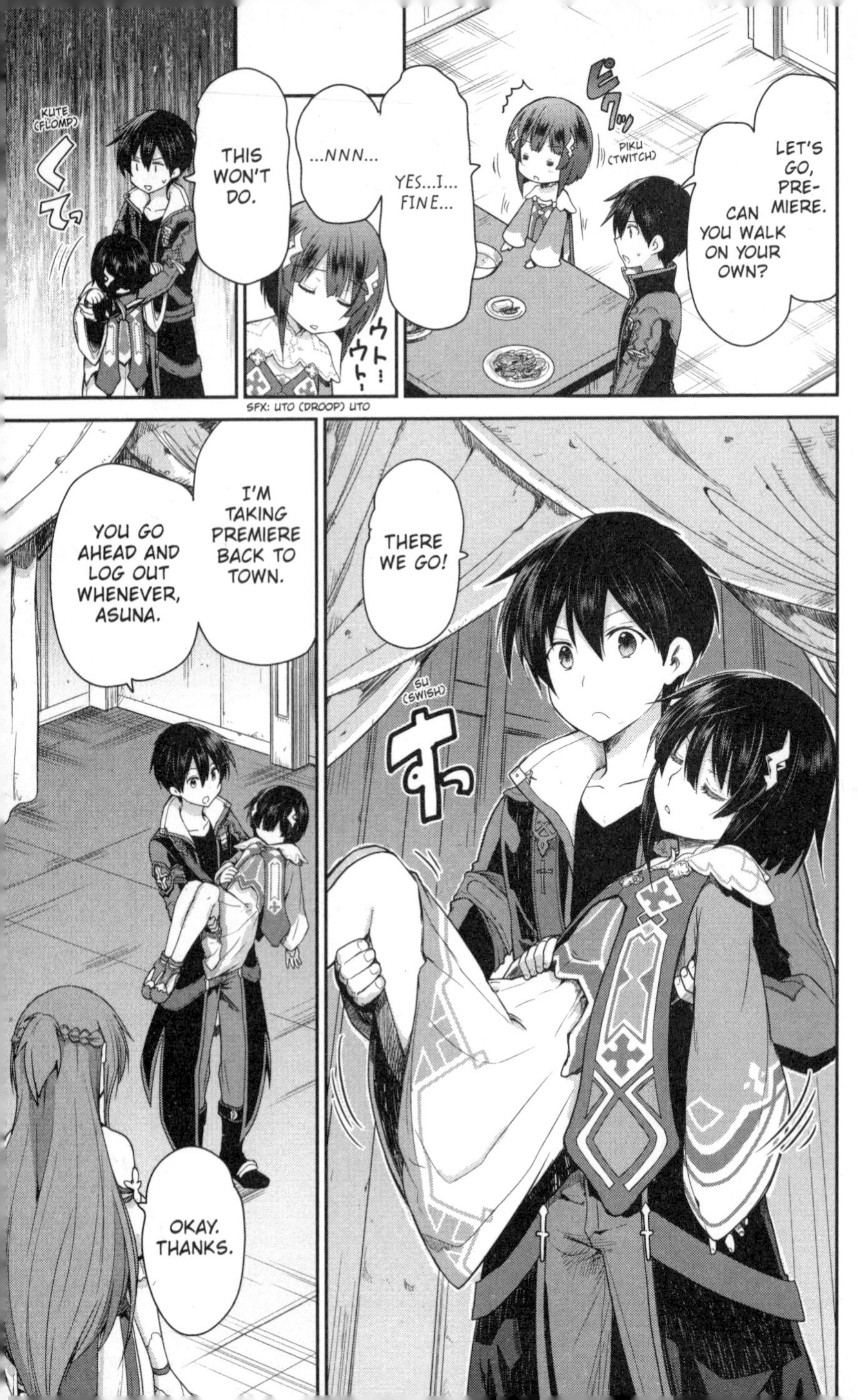
LET'S GO, PREMIERE.
CAN YOU WALK ON YOUR OWN?
ピクッ
PIKU (TWITCH)
...NNN...
YES...I... FINE...
ウトウト
THIS WON'T DO.
くてっ
KUTE (FLOMP)
SFX: UTO (DROOP) UTO
THERE WE GO!
すっ
SU (SWISH)
I'M TAKING PREMIERE BACK TO TOWN.
YOU GO AHEAD AND LOG OUT WHENEVER, ASUNA.
OKAY. THANKS.

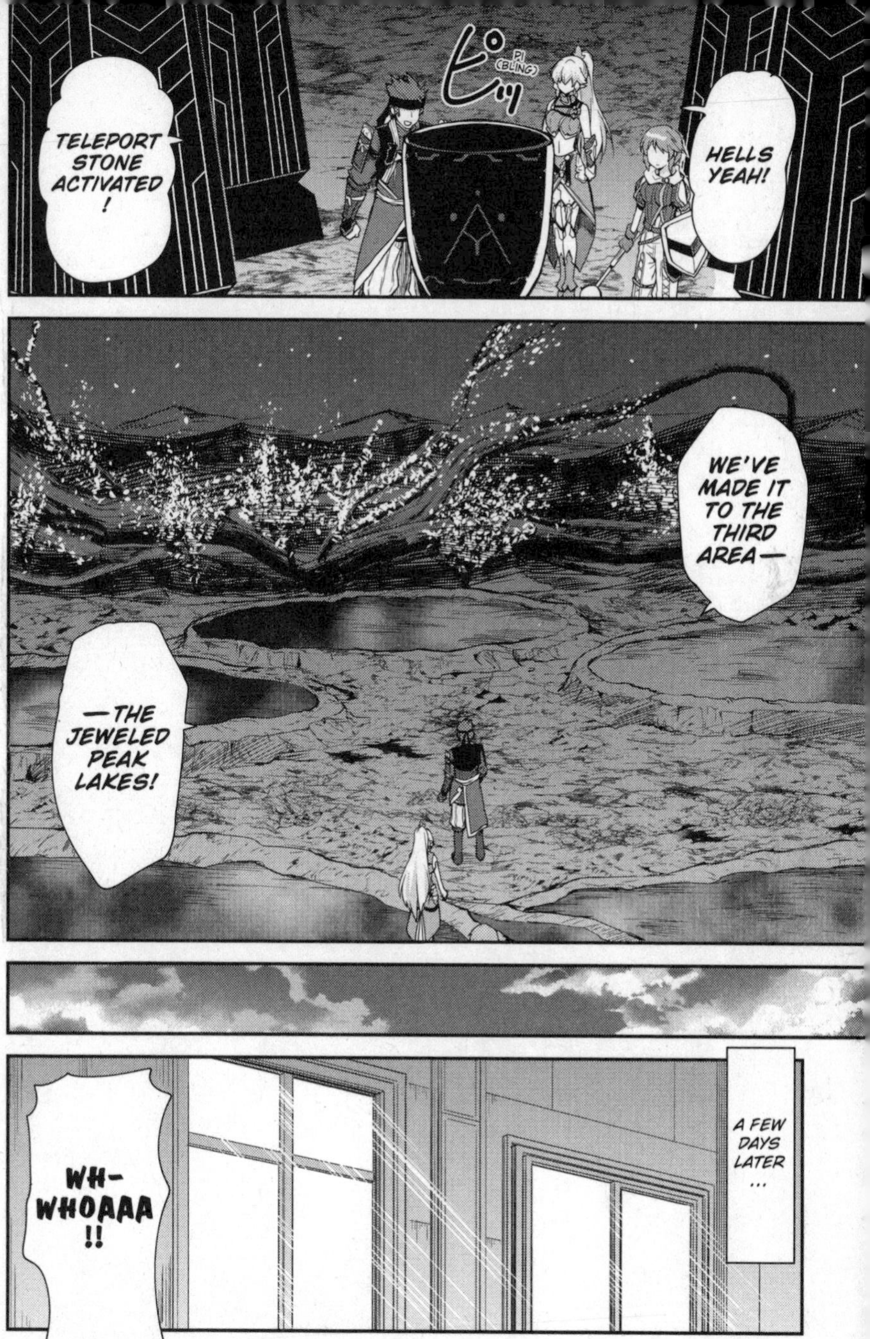
HELLS YEAH!
ピッ
PI (BLING)
TELEPORT STONE ACTIVATED!
WE'VE MADE IT TO THE THIRD AREA—
—THE JEWELED PEAK LAKES!
A FEW DAYS LATER...
WH-WHOAAA!!

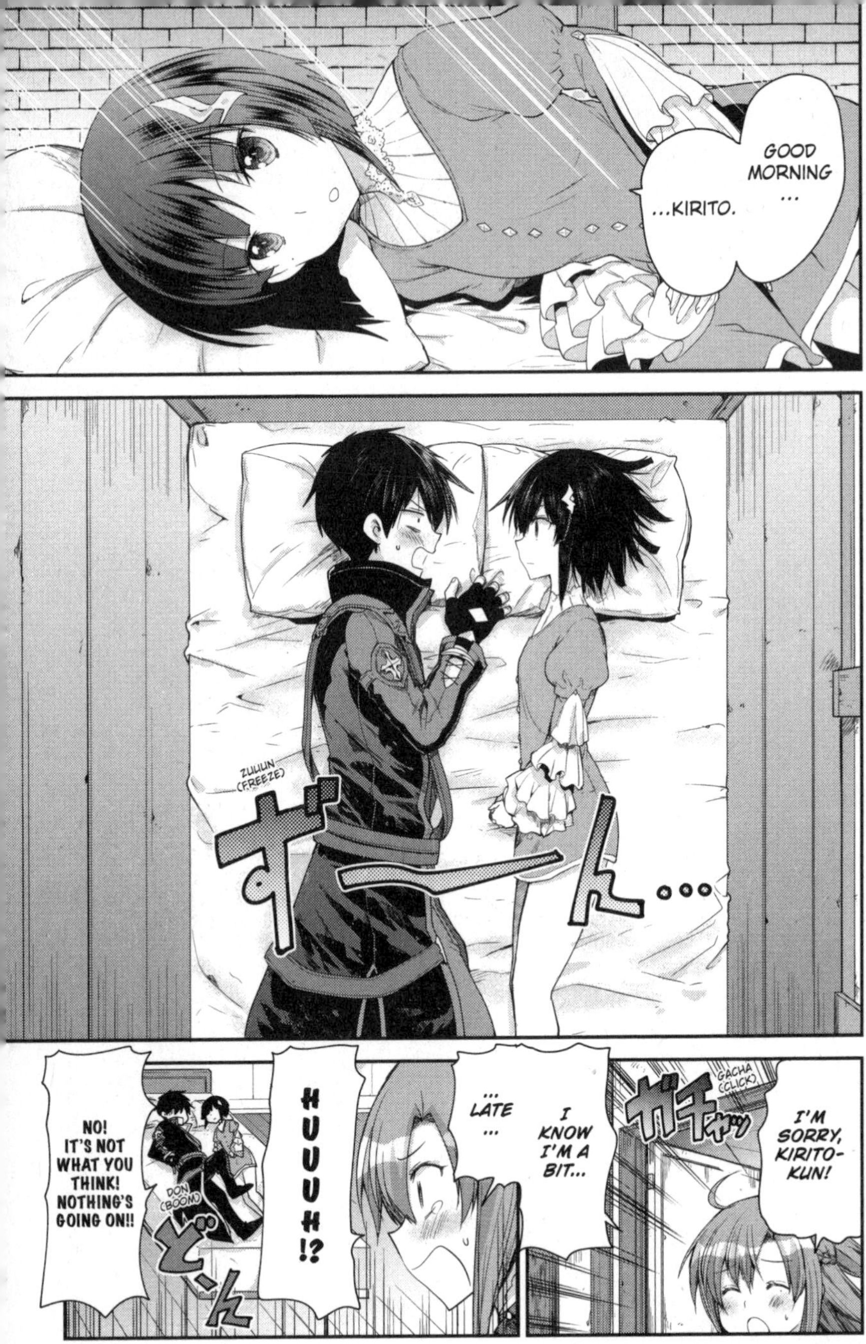
GOOD MORNING ...
...KIRITO.
ZUUUN (FREEZE)
ずーん...
GACHA (CLICK)
ガチャッ
I'M SORRY, KIRITO-KUN!
I KNOW I'M A BIT...
... LATE ...
HUUUUH!?
NO! IT'S NOT WHAT YOU THINK! NOTHING'S GOING ON!!
DON (BOOM)
どーん

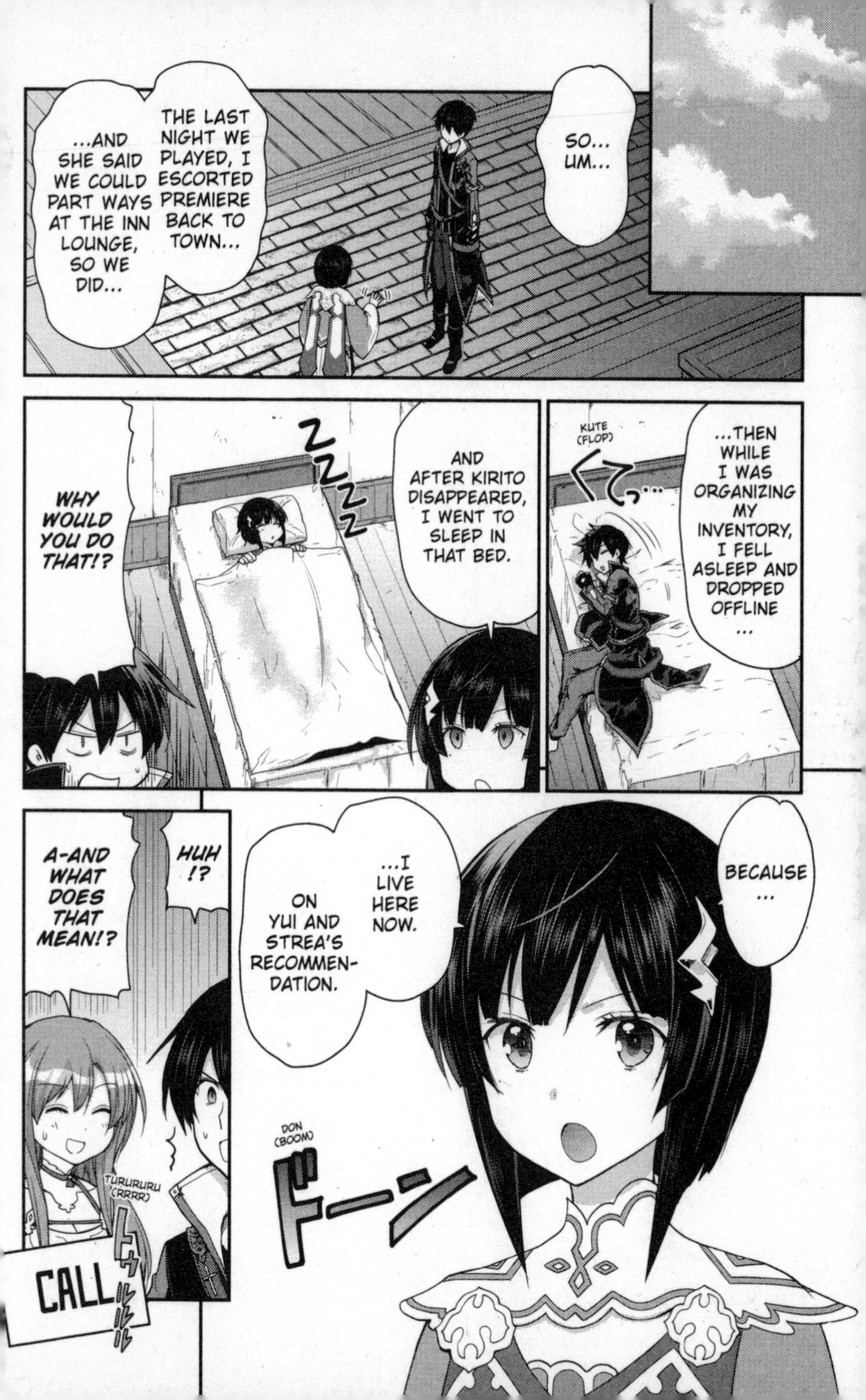
SO... UM...
THE LAST NIGHT WE PLAYED, I ESCORTED PREMIERE BACK TO TOWN...
...AND SHE SAID WE COULD PART WAYS AT THE INN LOUNGE, SO WE DID...
KUTE (FLOP)
...THEN WHILE I WAS ORGANIZING MY INVENTORY, I FELL ASLEEP AND DROPPED OFFLINE ...
AND AFTER KIRITO DISAPPEARED, I WENT TO SLEEP IN THAT BED.
WHY WOULD YOU DO THAT!?
BECAUSE ...
...I LIVE HERE NOW.
ON YUI AND STREA'S RECOMMENDATION.
DON (BOOM)
HUH !?
A-AND WHAT DOES THAT MEAN!?
TURURURU (RRRR)
CALL

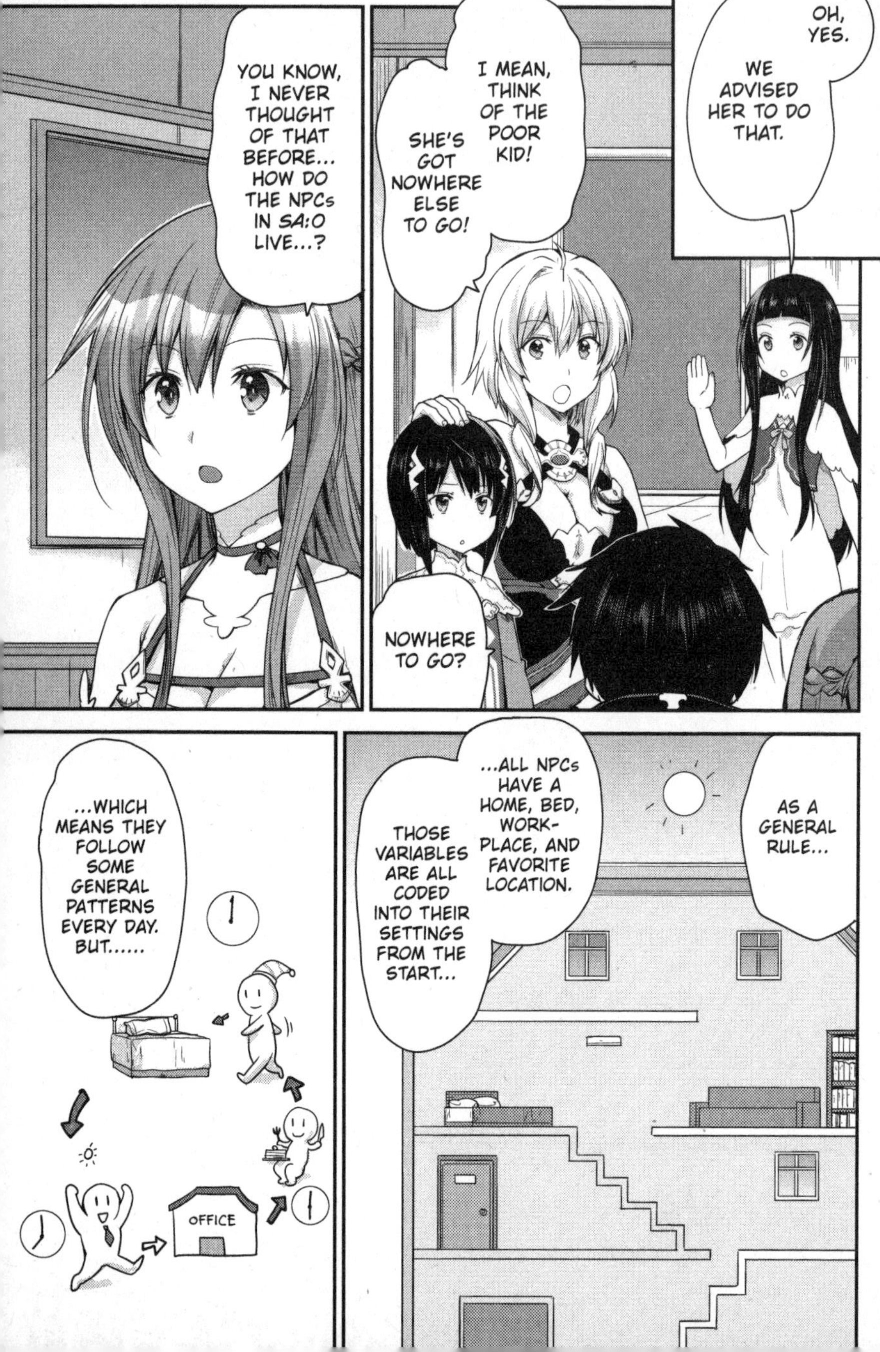
OH, YES.
WE ADVISED HER TO DO THAT.
I MEAN, THINK OF THE POOR KID!
SHE'S GOT NOWHERE ELSE TO GO!
NOWHERE TO GO?
YOU KNOW, I NEVER THOUGHT OF THAT BEFORE... HOW DO THE NPCs IN SA:O LIVE...?
AS A GENERAL RULE...
...ALL NPCs HAVE A HOME, BED, WORK-PLACE, AND FAVORITE LOCATION.
THOSE VARIABLES ARE ALL CODED INTO THEIR SETTINGS FROM THE START...
...WHICH MEANS THEY FOLLOW SOME GENERAL PATTERNS EVERY DAY. BUT......
OFFICE

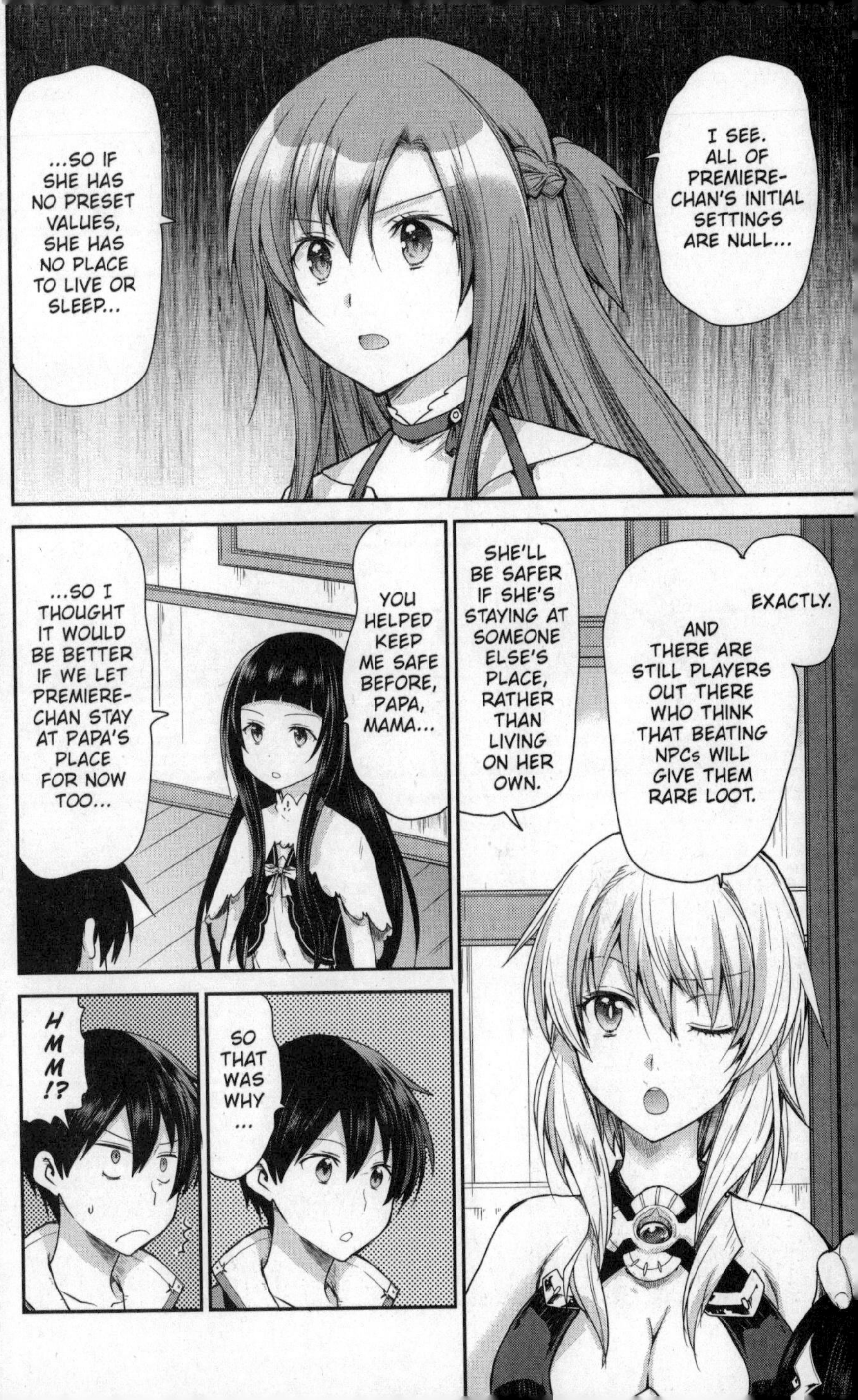
I SEE. ALL OF PREMIERE-CHAN'S INITIAL SETTINGS ARE NULL...
...SO IF SHE HAS NO PRESET VALUES, SHE HAS NO PLACE TO LIVE OR SLEEP...
EXACTLY.
AND THERE ARE STILL PLAYERS OUT THERE WHO THINK THAT BEATING NPCs WILL GIVE THEM RARE LOOT.
SHE'LL BE SAFER IF SHE'S STAYING AT SOMEONE ELSE'S PLACE, RATHER THAN LIVING ON HER OWN.
YOU HELPED KEEP ME SAFE BEFORE, PAPA, MAMA...
...SO I THOUGHT IT WOULD BE BETTER IF WE LET PREMIERE-CHAN STAY AT PAPA'S PLACE FOR NOW TOO...
SO THAT WAS WHY...
HMM!?

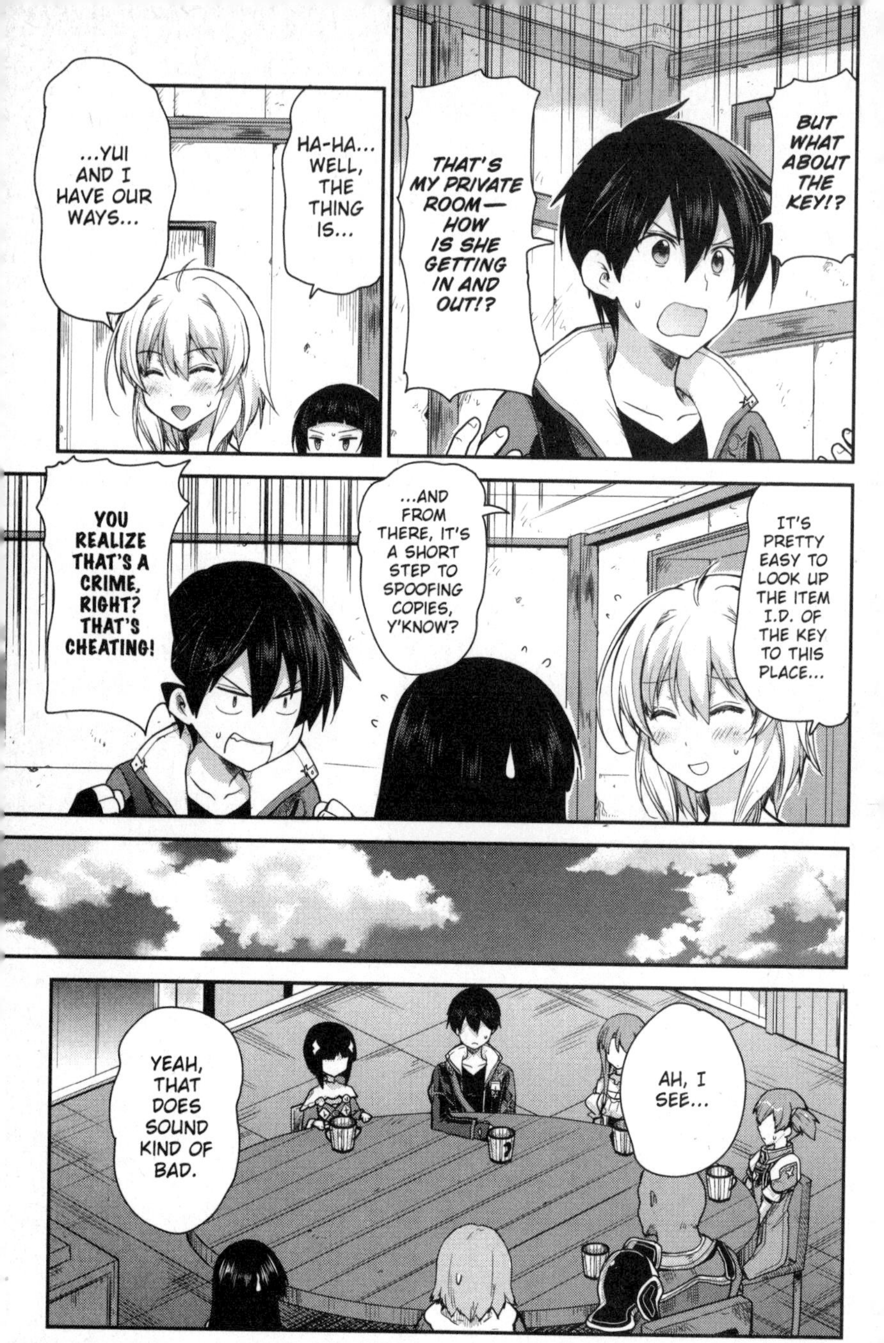
BUT WHAT ABOUT THE KEY!?
THAT'S MY PRIVATE ROOM—HOW IS SHE GETTING IN AND OUT!?
HA-HA... WELL, THE THING IS...
...YUI AND I HAVE OUR WAYS...
IT'S PRETTY EASY TO LOOK UP THE ITEM I.D. OF THE KEY TO THIS PLACE...
...AND FROM THERE, IT'S A SHORT STEP TO SPOOFING COPIES, Y'KNOW?
YOU REALIZE THAT'S A CRIME, RIGHT? THAT'S CHEATING!
AH, I SEE...
YEAH, THAT DOES SOUND KIND OF BAD.

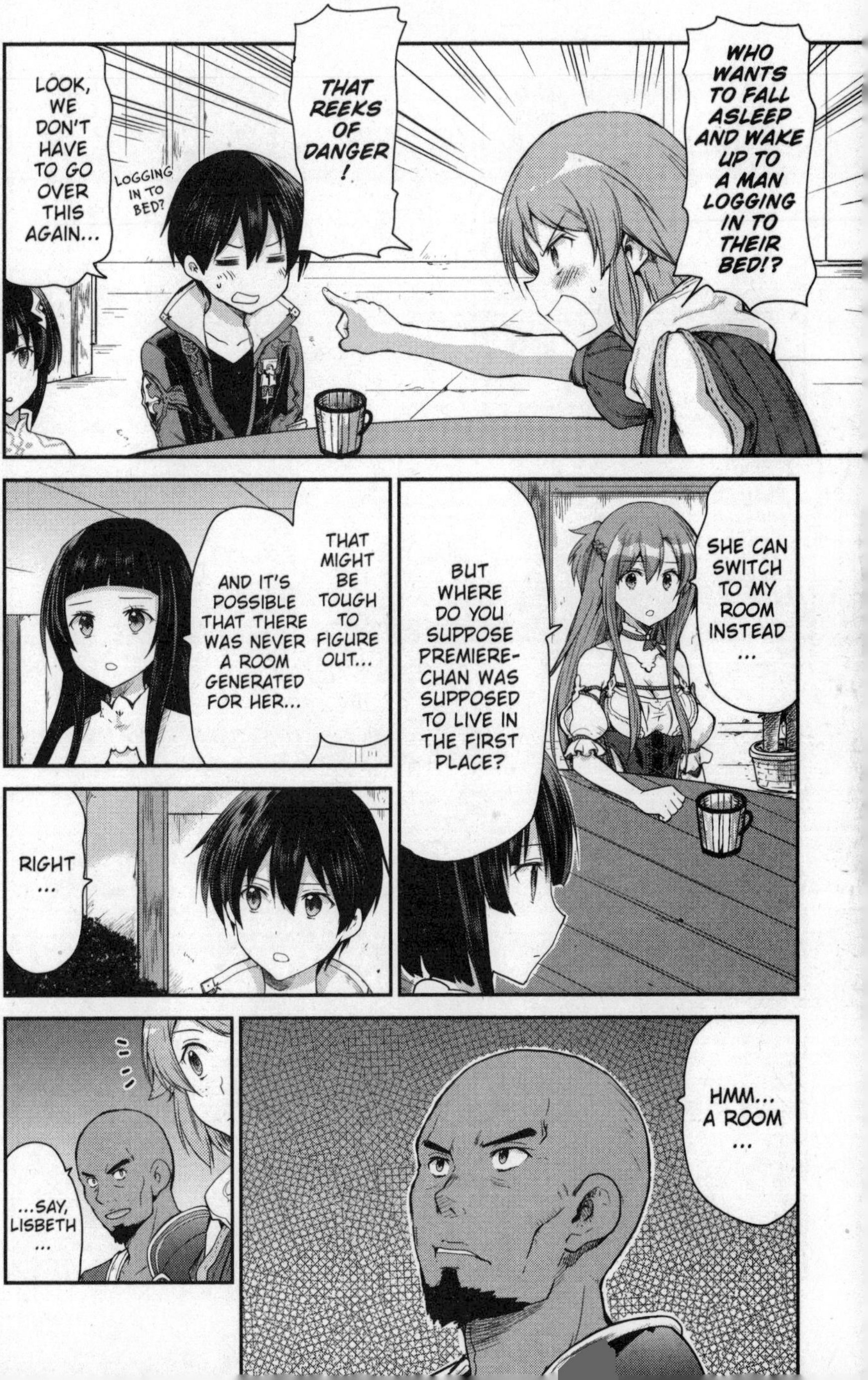
WHO WANTS TO FALL ASLEEP AND WAKE UP TO A MAN LOGGING IN TO THEIR BED!?
THAT REEKS OF DANGER!
LOGGING IN TO BED?
LOOK, WE DON'T HAVE TO GO OVER THIS AGAIN...
SHE CAN SWITCH TO MY ROOM INSTEAD...
BUT WHERE DO YOU SUPPOSE PREMIERE-CHAN WAS SUPPOSED TO LIVE IN THE FIRST PLACE?
THAT MIGHT BE TOUGH TO FIGURE OUT...
AND IT'S POSSIBLE THAT THERE WAS NEVER A ROOM GENERATED FOR HER...
RIGHT...
HMM... A ROOM...
...
...SAY, LISBETH...

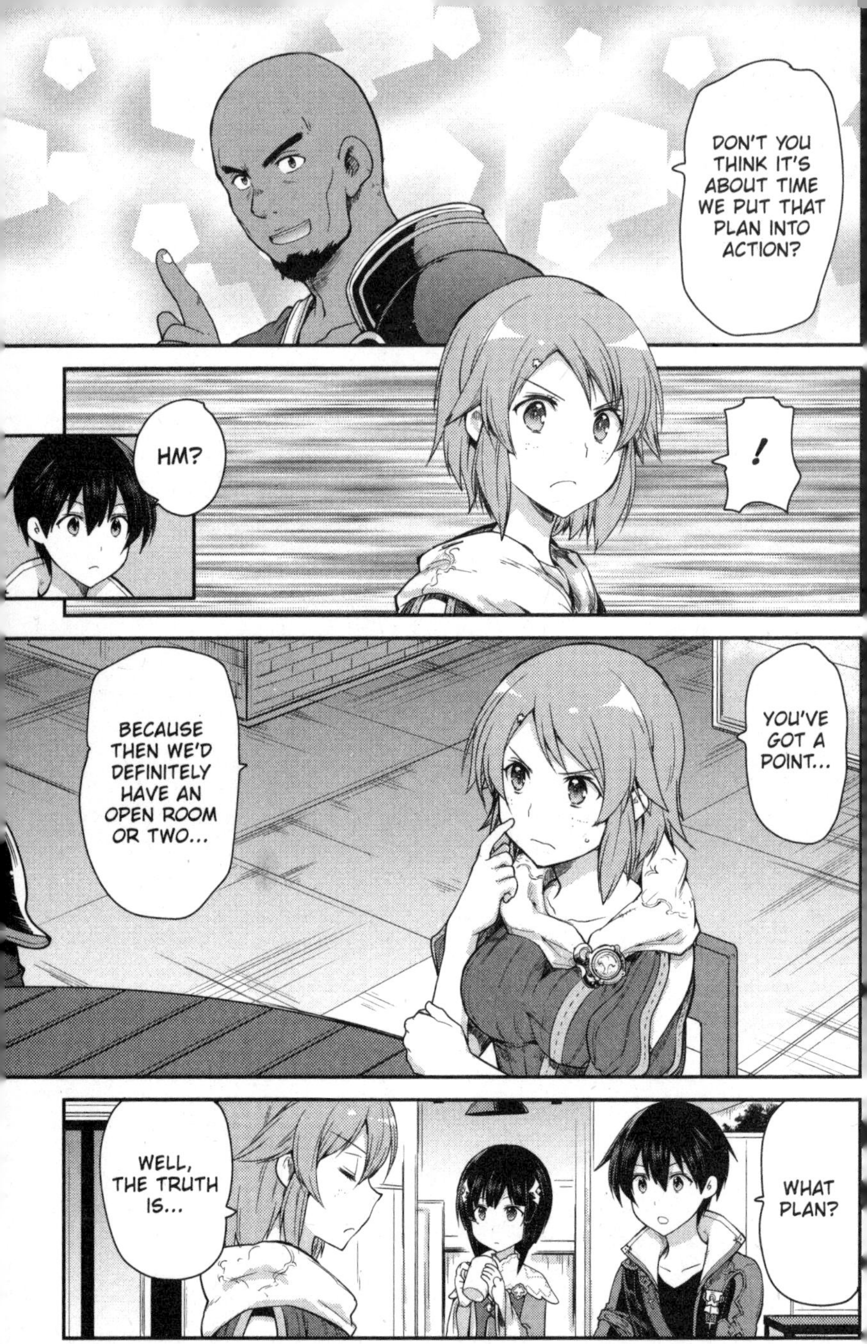
DON'T YOU THINK IT'S ABOUT TIME WE PUT THAT PLAN INTO ACTION?
!
HM?
YOU'VE GOT A POINT...
BECAUSE THEN WE'D DEFINITELY HAVE AN OPEN ROOM OR TWO...
WHAT PLAN?
WELL, THE TRUTH IS...

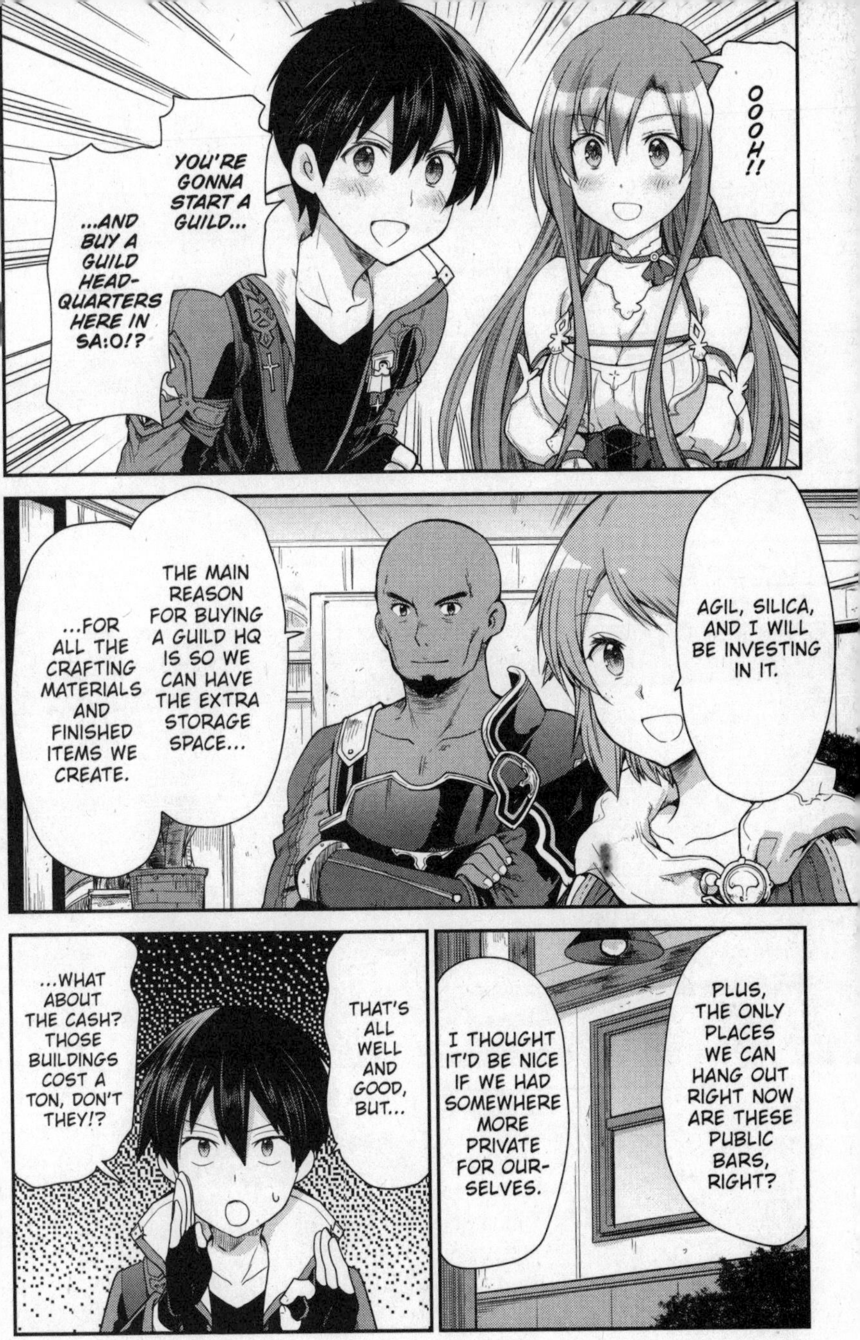
OOOH!!
YOU'RE GONNA START A GUILD...
...AND BUY A GUILD HEAD-QUARTERS HERE IN SA:O!?
AGIL, SILICA, AND I WILL BE INVESTING IN IT.
THE MAIN REASON FOR BUYING A GUILD HQ IS SO WE CAN HAVE THE EXTRA STORAGE SPACE...
...FOR ALL THE CRAFTING MATERIALS AND FINISHED ITEMS WE CREATE.
PLUS, THE ONLY PLACES WE CAN HANG OUT RIGHT NOW ARE THESE PUBLIC BARS, RIGHT?
I THOUGHT IT'D BE NICE IF WE HAD SOMEWHERE MORE PRIVATE FOR OUR-SELVES.
THAT'S ALL WELL AND GOOD, BUT...
...WHAT ABOUT THE CASH? THOSE BUILDINGS COST A TON, DON'T THEY!?

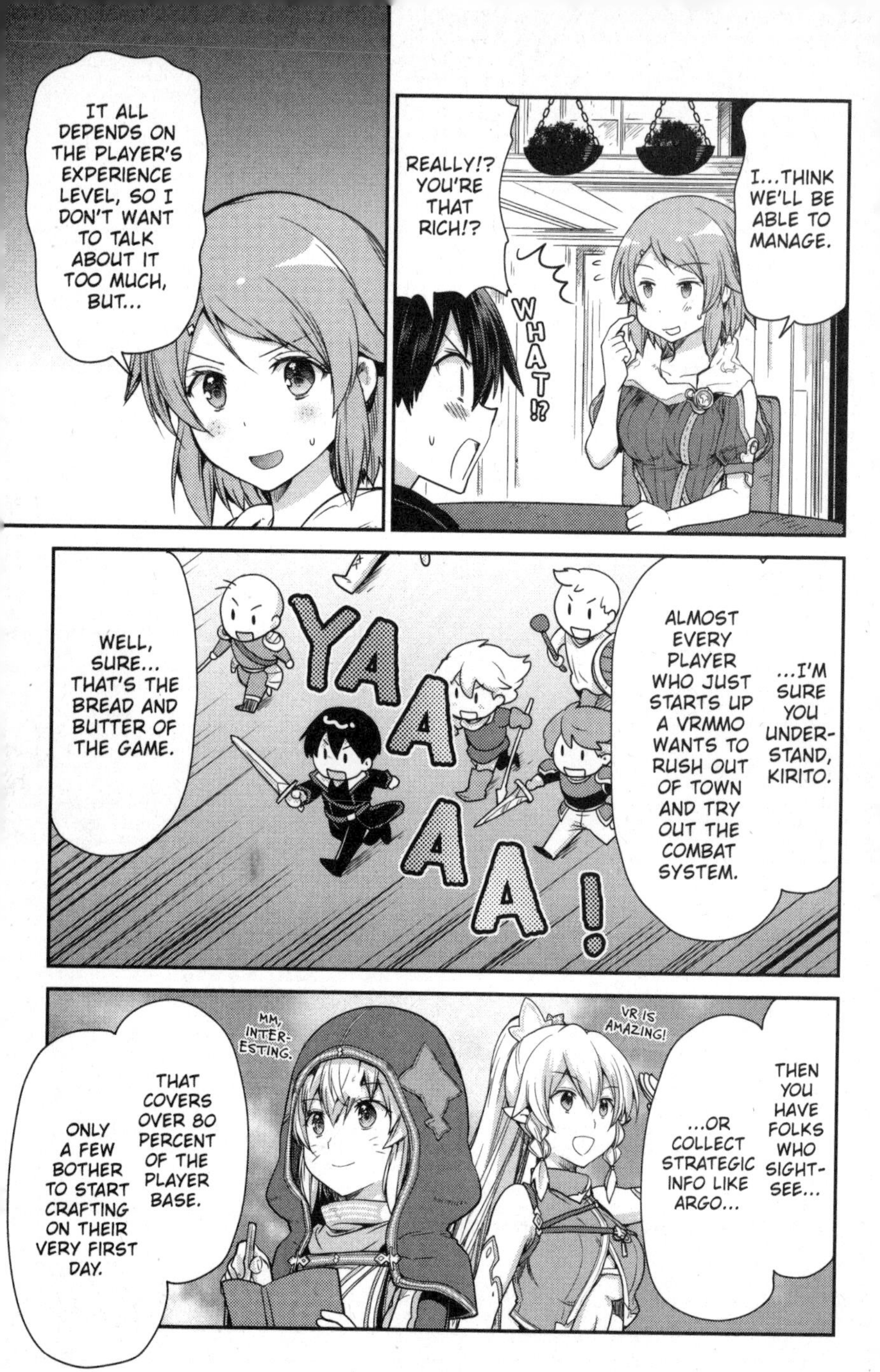
I...THINK WE'LL BE ABLE TO MANAGE.
REALLY!? YOU'RE THAT RICH!?
WHAT!?
IT ALL DEPENDS ON THE PLAYER'S EXPERIENCE LEVEL, SO I DON'T WANT TO TALK ABOUT IT TOO MUCH, BUT...
...I'M SURE YOU UNDERSTAND, KIRITO.
ALMOST EVERY PLAYER WHO JUST STARTS UP A VRMMO WANTS TO RUSH OUT OF TOWN AND TRY OUT THE COMBAT SYSTEM.
YAAAA!
WELL, SURE... THAT'S THE BREAD AND BUTTER OF THE GAME.
THEN YOU HAVE FOLKS WHO SIGHT-SEE...
VR IS AMAZING!
...OR COLLECT STRATEGIC INFO LIKE ARGO...
MM, INTER-ESTING.
THAT COVERS OVER 80 PERCENT OF THE PLAYER BASE.
ONLY A FEW BOTHER TO START CRAFTING ON THEIR VERY FIRST DAY.

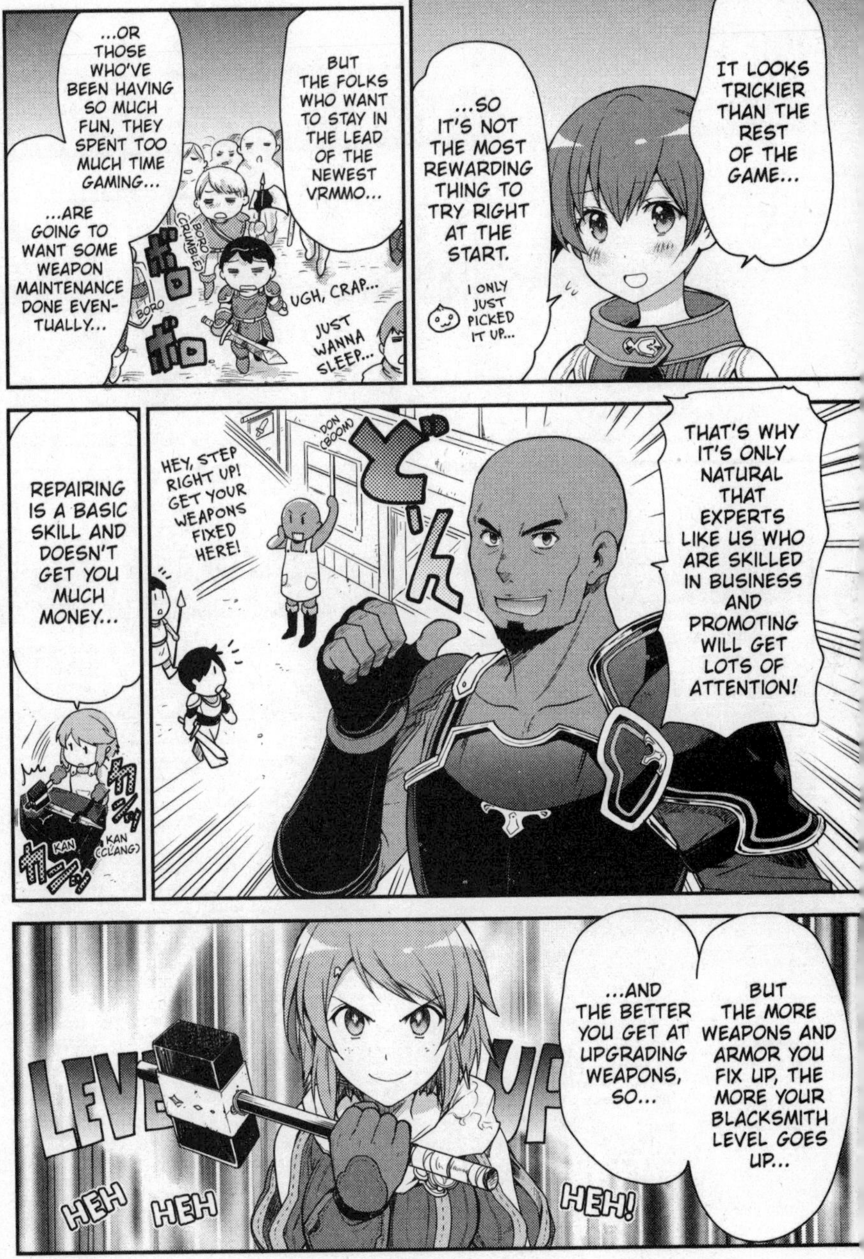

IT LOOKS TRICKIER THAN THE REST OF THE GAME...
...SO IT'S NOT THE MOST REWARDING THING TO TRY RIGHT AT THE START.
I ONLY JUST PICKED IT UP...
BUT THE FOLKS WHO WANT TO STAY IN THE LEAD OF THE NEWEST VRMMO...
...OR THOSE WHO'VE BEEN HAVING SO MUCH FUN, THEY SPENT TOO MUCH TIME GAMING...
...ARE GOING TO WANT SOME WEAPON MAINTENANCE DONE EVENTUALLY...
BORO (CRUMBLE)
BORO
UGH, CRAP...
JUST WANNA SLEEP...
THAT'S WHY IT'S ONLY NATURAL THAT EXPERTS LIKE US WHO ARE SKILLED IN BUSINESS AND PROMOTING WILL GET LOTS OF ATTENTION!
DON (BOOM)
HEY, STEP RIGHT UP! GET YOUR WEAPONS FIXED HERE!
REPAIRING IS A BASIC SKILL AND DOESN'T GET YOU MUCH MONEY...
KAN
KAN (CLANG)
BUT THE MORE WEAPONS AND ARMOR YOU FIX UP, THE MORE YOUR BLACKSMITH LEVEL GOES UP...
...AND THE BETTER YOU GET AT UPGRADING WEAPONS, SO...
HEH HEH HEH!

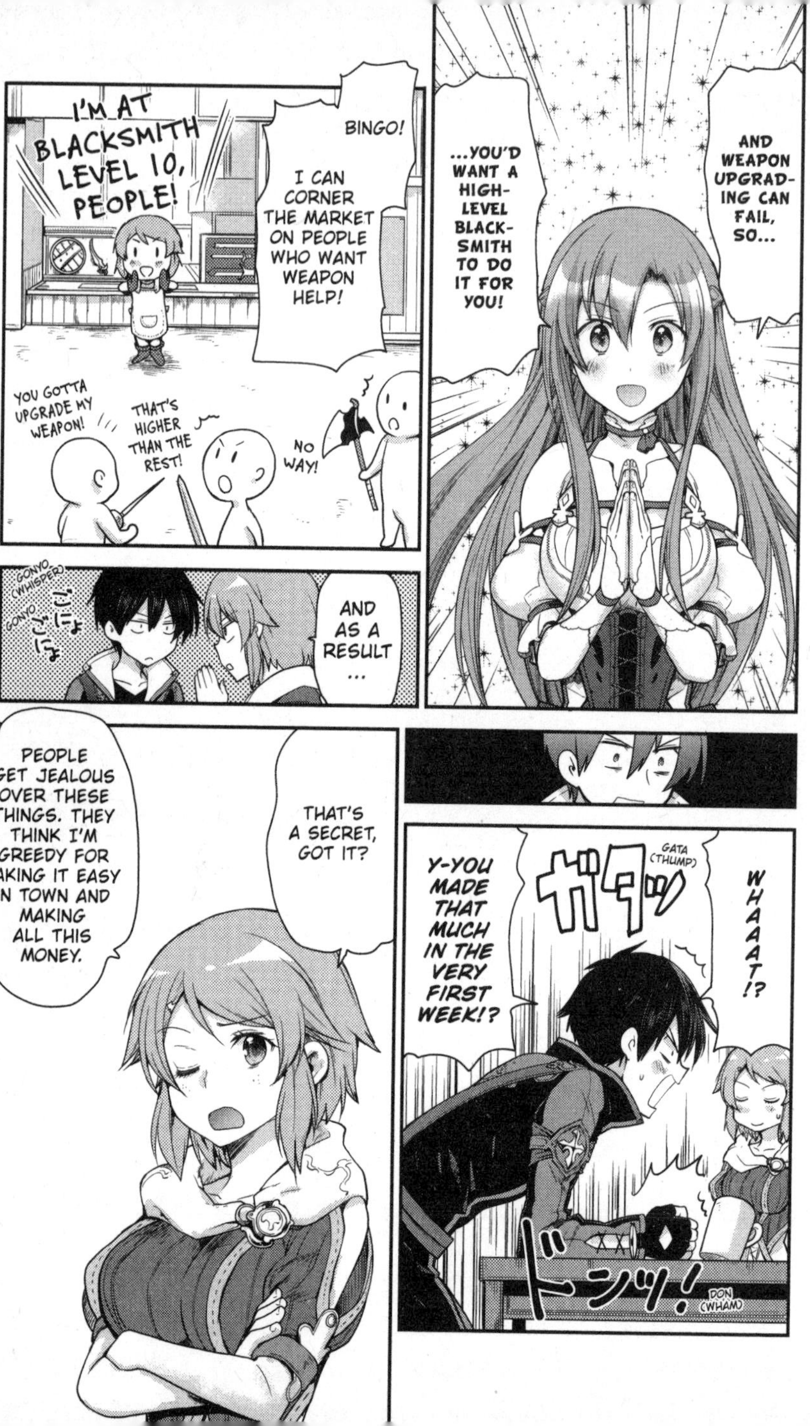
AND WEAPON UPGRADING CAN FAIL, SO...
...YOU'D WANT A HIGH-LEVEL BLACKSMITH TO DO IT FOR YOU!
BINGO!
I CAN CORNER THE MARKET ON PEOPLE WHO WANT WEAPON HELP!
I'M AT BLACKSMITH LEVEL 10, PEOPLE!
NO WAY!
THAT'S HIGHER THAN THE REST!
YOU GOTTA UPGRADE MY WEAPON!
AND AS A RESULT ...
ごにょごにょ
GONYO GONYO (WHISPER)
W H A A A A T!?
ガタッ
GATA (THUMP)
Y-YOU MADE THAT MUCH IN THE VERY FIRST WEEK!?
ドンッ!
DON (WHAM)
THAT'S A SECRET, GOT IT?
PEOPLE GET JEALOUS OVER THESE THINGS. THEY THINK I'M GREEDY FOR TAKING IT EASY IN TOWN AND MAKING ALL THIS MONEY.

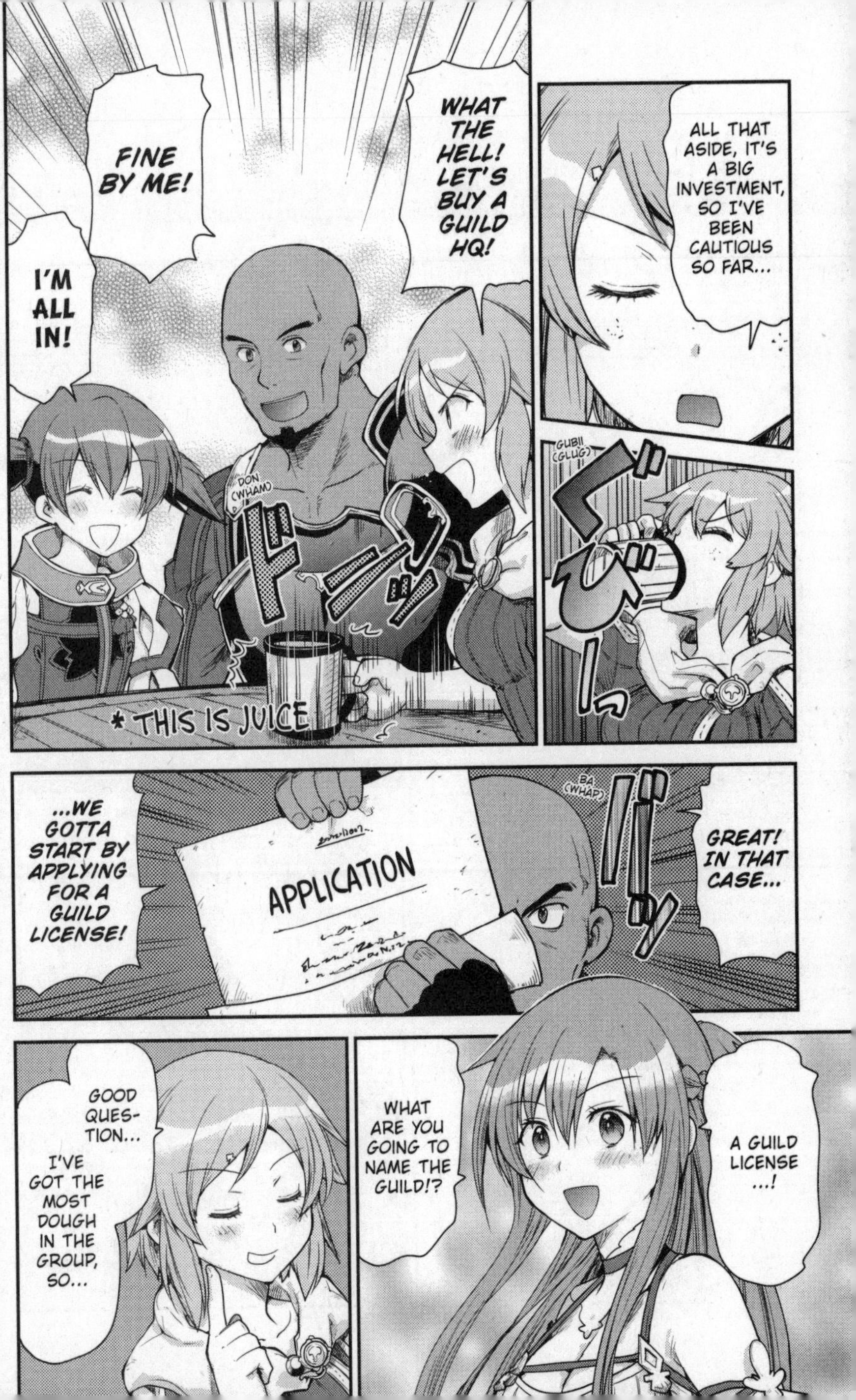
ALL THAT ASIDE, IT'S A BIG INVESTMENT, SO I'VE BEEN CAUTIOUS SO FAR...
GUBI (GLUG)
WHAT THE HELL! LET'S BUY A GUILD HQ!
FINE BY ME!
I'M ALL IN!
DON (WHAM)
* THIS IS JUICE
GREAT! IN THAT CASE...
BA (WHAP)
...WE GOTTA START BY APPLYING FOR A GUILD LICENSE!
APPLICATION
A GUILD LICENSE ...!
WHAT ARE YOU GOING TO NAME THE GUILD!?
GOOD QUES-TION...
I'VE GOT THE MOST DOUGH IN THE GROUP, SO...

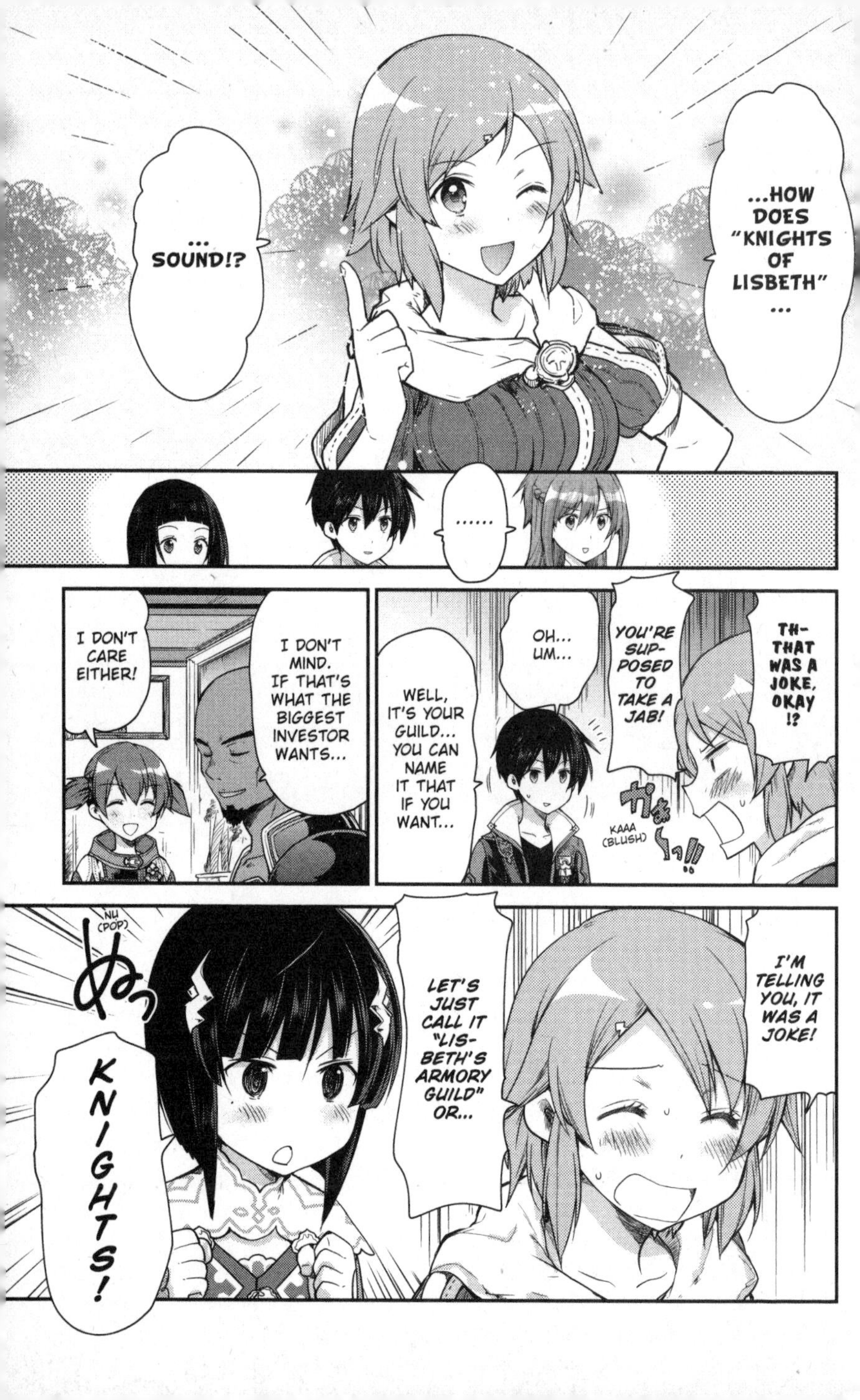
...HOW DOES "KNIGHTS OF LISBETH" ...
... SOUND!?
......
TH-THAT WAS A JOKE, OKAY!?
YOU'RE SUP-POSED TO TAKE A JAB!
KAAA (BLUSH)
OH... UM...
WELL, IT'S YOUR GUILD... YOU CAN NAME IT THAT IF YOU WANT...
I DON'T MIND. IF THAT'S WHAT THE BIGGEST INVESTOR WANTS...
I DON'T CARE EITHER!
I'M TELLING YOU, IT WAS A JOKE!
LET'S JUST CALL IT "LIS-BETH'S ARMORY GUILD" OR...
NU (POP)
KNIGHTS!

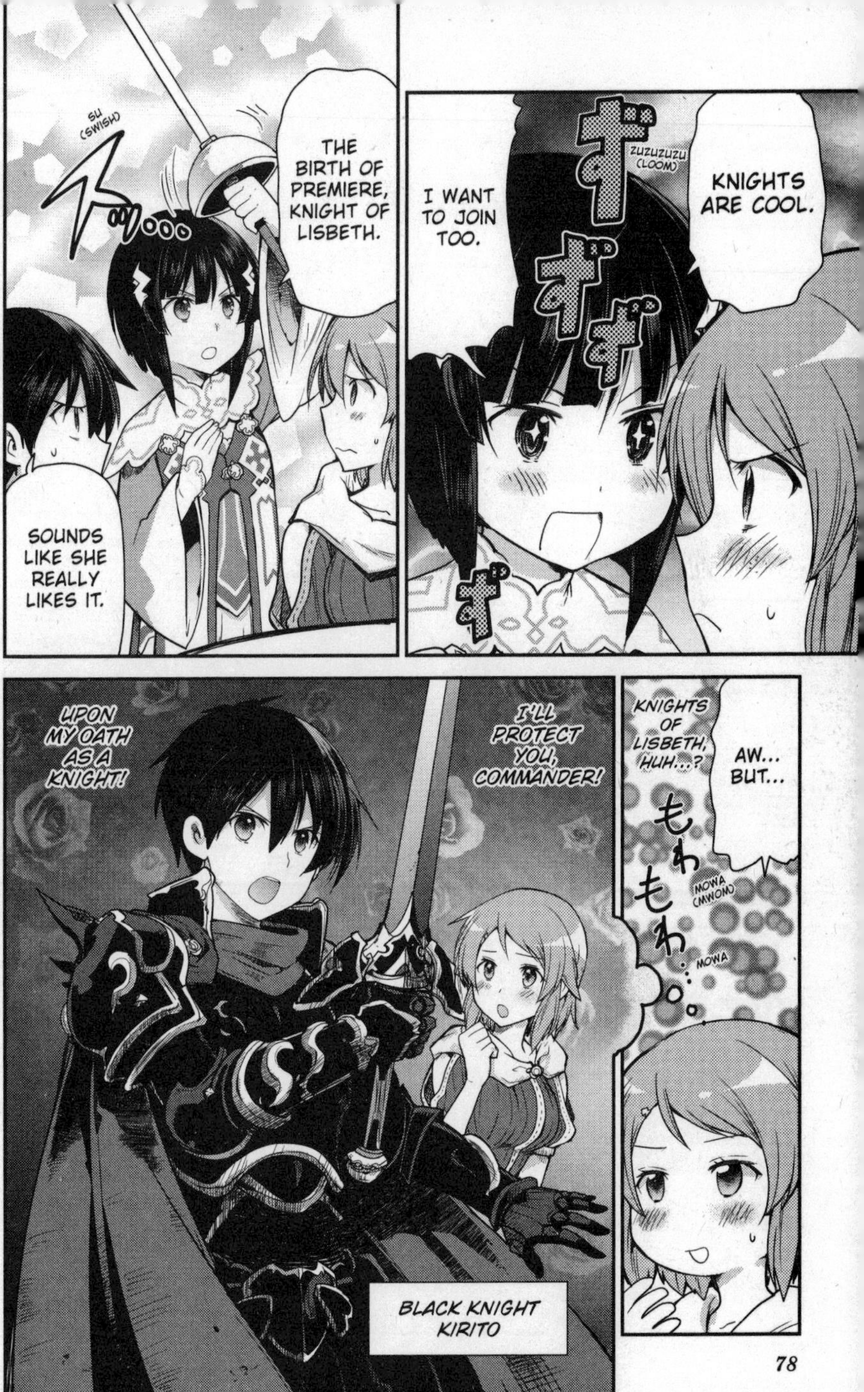

KNIGHTS ARE COOL.
ZUZUZUZU (LOOM)
I WANT TO JOIN TOO.
THE BIRTH OF PREMIERE, KNIGHT OF LISBETH.
SU (SWISH)
SOUNDS LIKE SHE REALLY LIKES IT.
AW... BUT...
KNIGHTS OF LISBETH, HUH...?
MOWA (MWOM)
MOWA
I'LL PROTECT YOU, COMMANDER!
UPON MY OATH AS A KNIGHT!
BLACK KNIGHT KIRITO

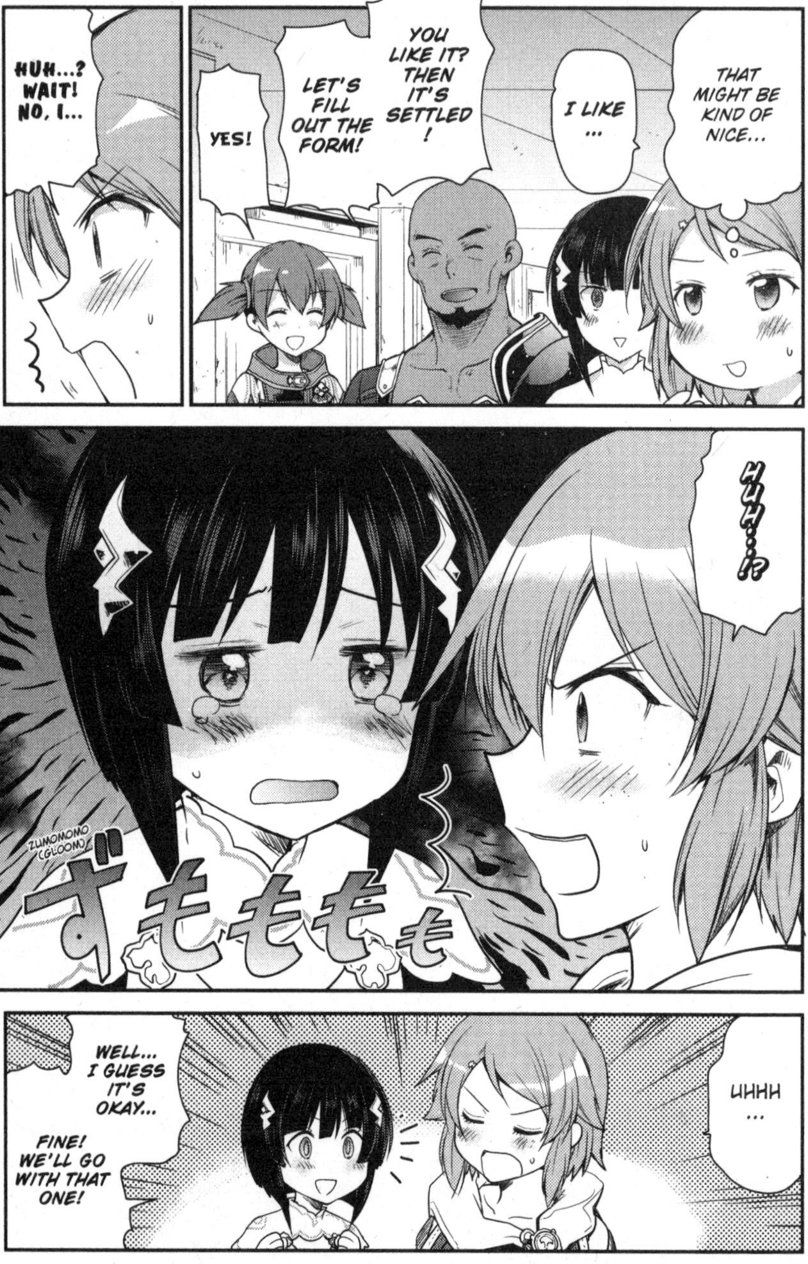
THAT MIGHT BE KIND OF NICE...
I LIKE...
YOU LIKE IT? THEN IT'S SETTLED!
LET'S FILL OUT THE FORM!
YES!
HUH...? WAIT! NO, I...
HUH...!?
ZUMOMOMO (GLOOM)
ずももももも
UHHH...
WELL... I GUESS IT'S OKAY...
FINE! WE'LL GO WITH THAT ONE!

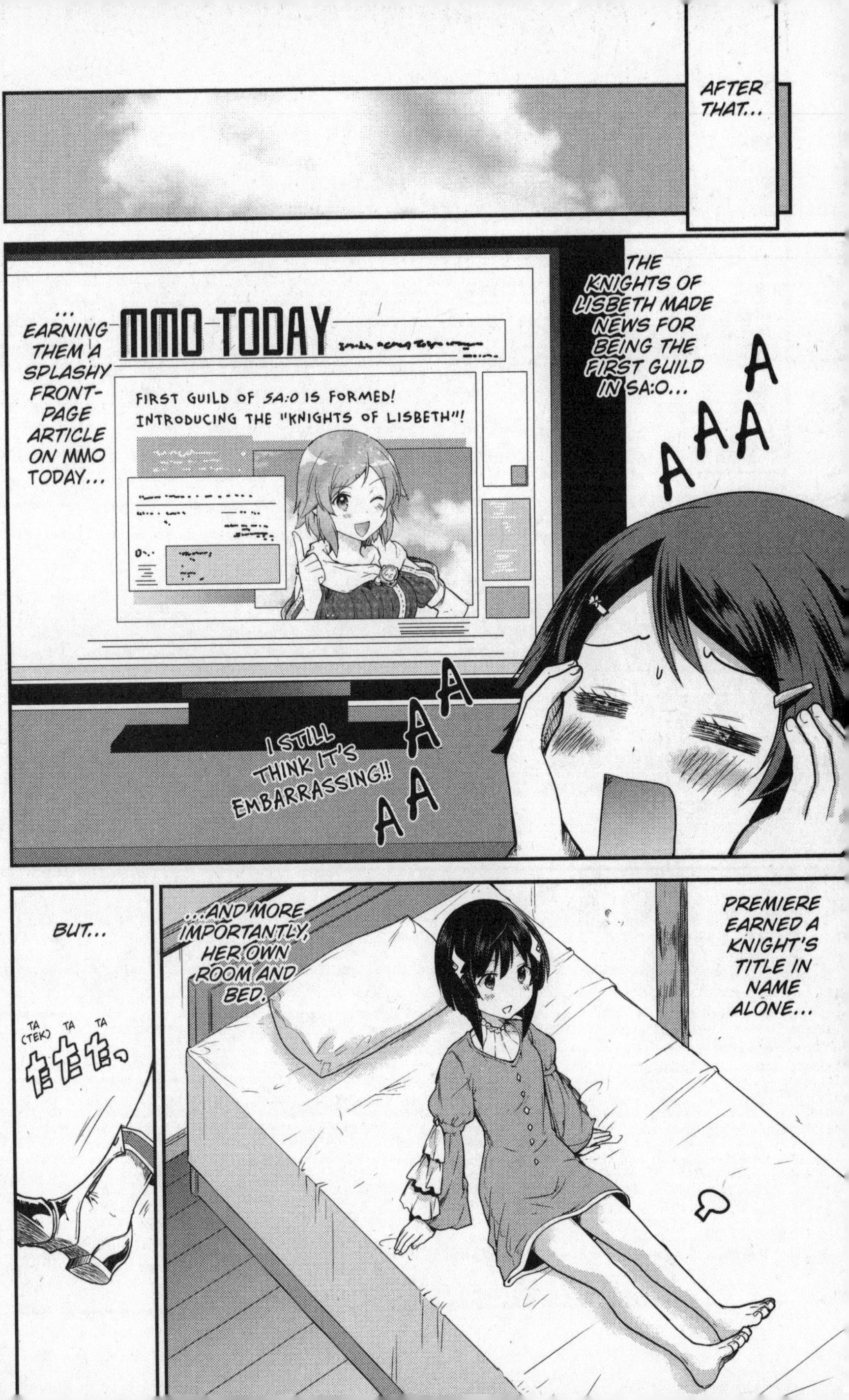
AFTER THAT...
THE KNIGHTS OF LISBETH MADE NEWS FOR BEING THE FIRST GUILD IN SA:O...
...EARNING THEM A SPLASHY FRONT-PAGE ARTICLE ON MMO TODAY...
MMO TODAY
FIRST GUILD OF SA:O IS FORMED! INTRODUCING THE "KNIGHTS OF LISBETH"!
AAAAA
I STILL THINK IT'S EMBARRASSING!!
AAAA
PREMIERE EARNED A KNIGHT'S TITLE IN NAME ALONE...
...AND MORE IMPORTANTLY, HER OWN ROOM AND BED.
BUT...
TA (TEK) TA TA

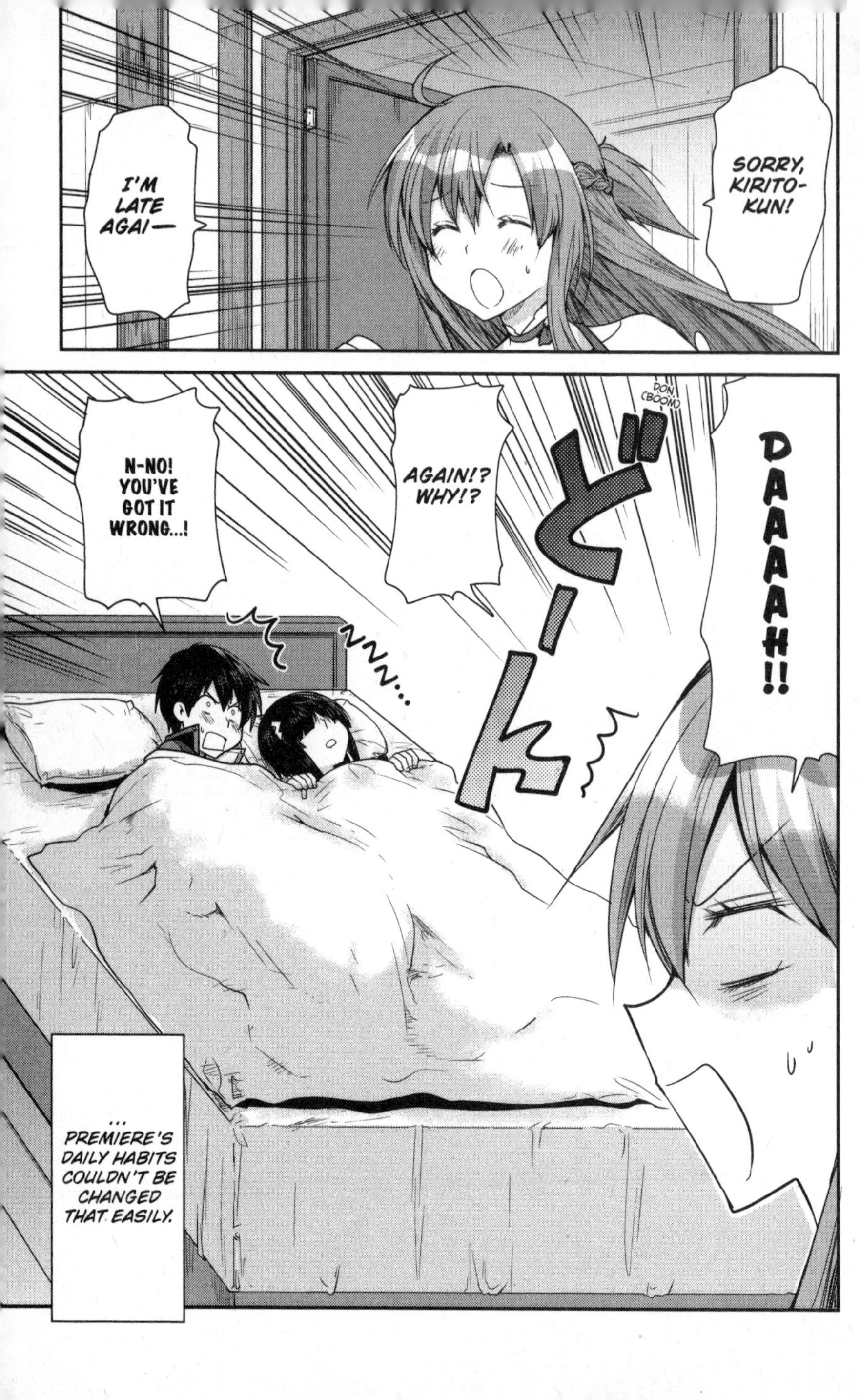
SORRY, KIRITO-KUN!
I'M LATE AGAI—
DAAAAAH!!
DON (BOOM)
AGAIN!? WHY!?
N-NO! YOU'VE GOT IT WRONG...!
NNN...
...PREMIERE'S DAILY HABITS COULDN'T BE CHANGED THAT EASILY.

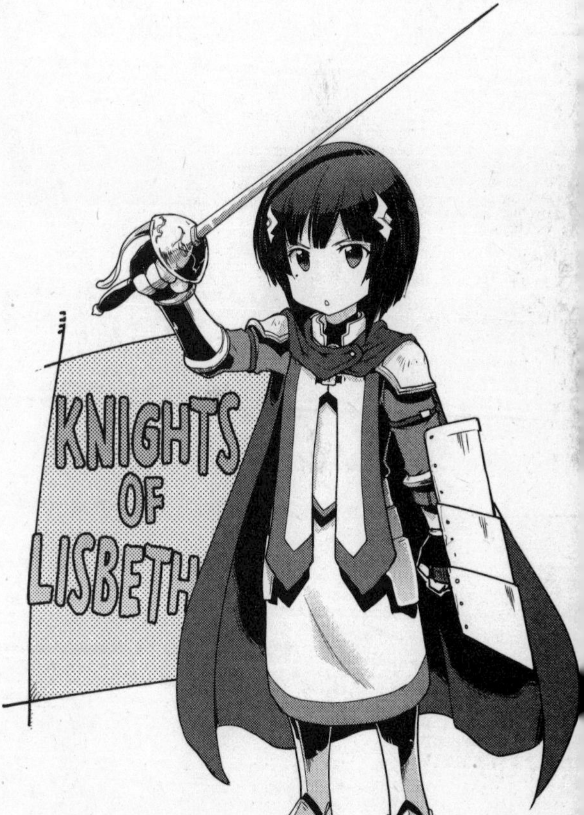
KNIGHTS
OF
LISBETH

#13

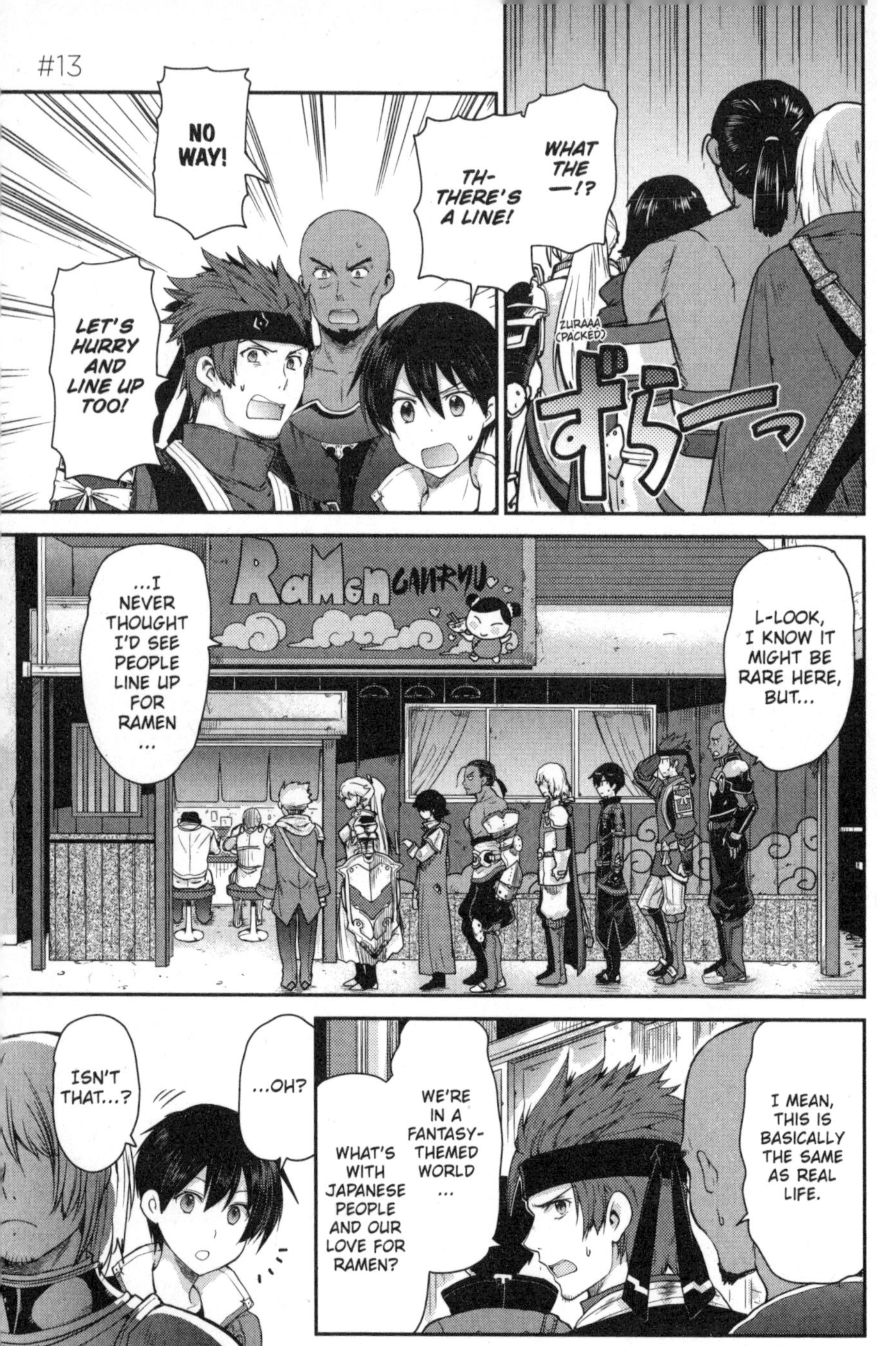
WHAT THE —!?
ZURAAA (PACKED)
TH- THERE'S A LINE!
NO WAY!
LET'S HURRY AND LINE UP TOO!
L-LOOK, I KNOW IT MIGHT BE RARE HERE, BUT...
RaMen GANRYU
...I NEVER THOUGHT I'D SEE PEOPLE LINE UP FOR RAMEN ...
I MEAN, THIS IS BASICALLY THE SAME AS REAL LIFE.
WE'RE IN A FANTASY-THEMED WORLD ...
WHAT'S WITH JAPANESE PEOPLE AND OUR LOVE FOR RAMEN?
...OH?
ISN'T THAT...?

#13: Tia

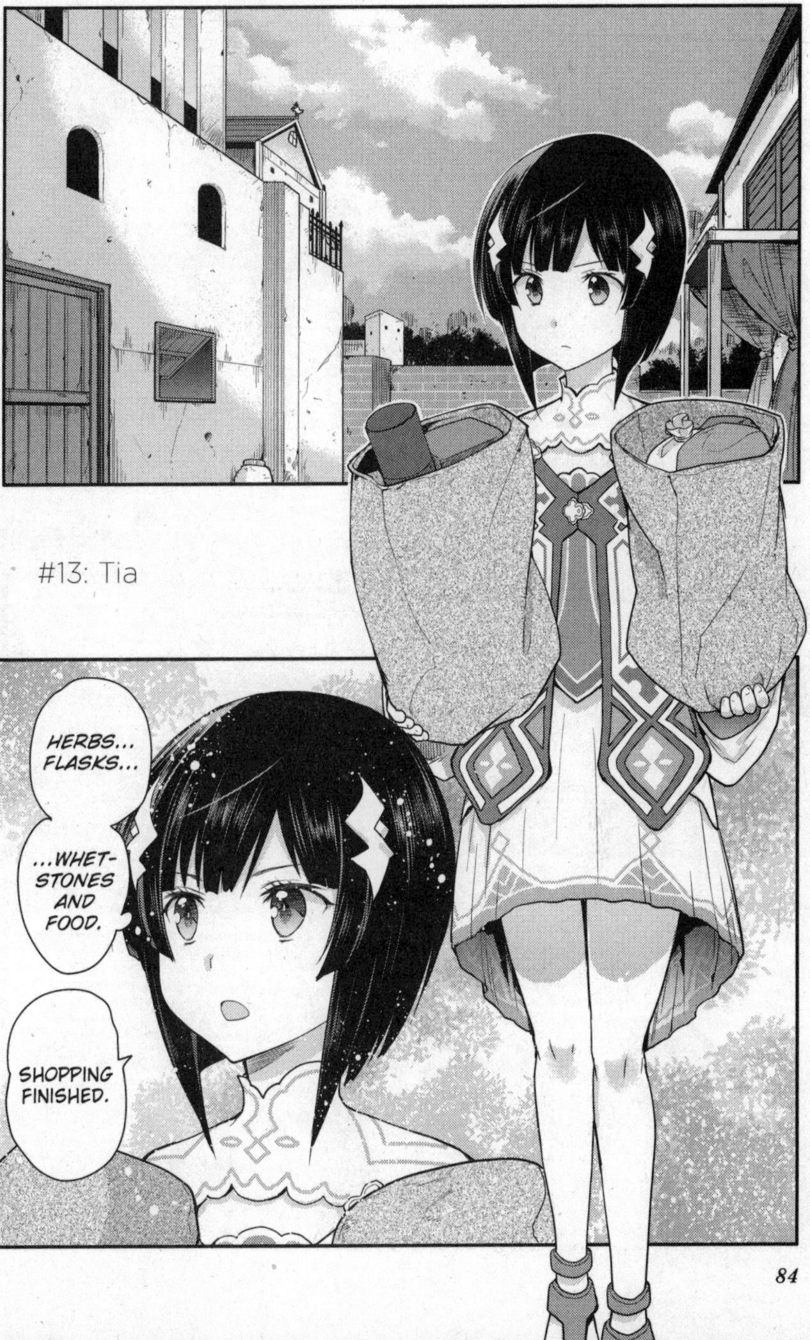
HERBS... FLASKS...
...WHET-STONES AND FOOD.
SHOPPING FINISHED.

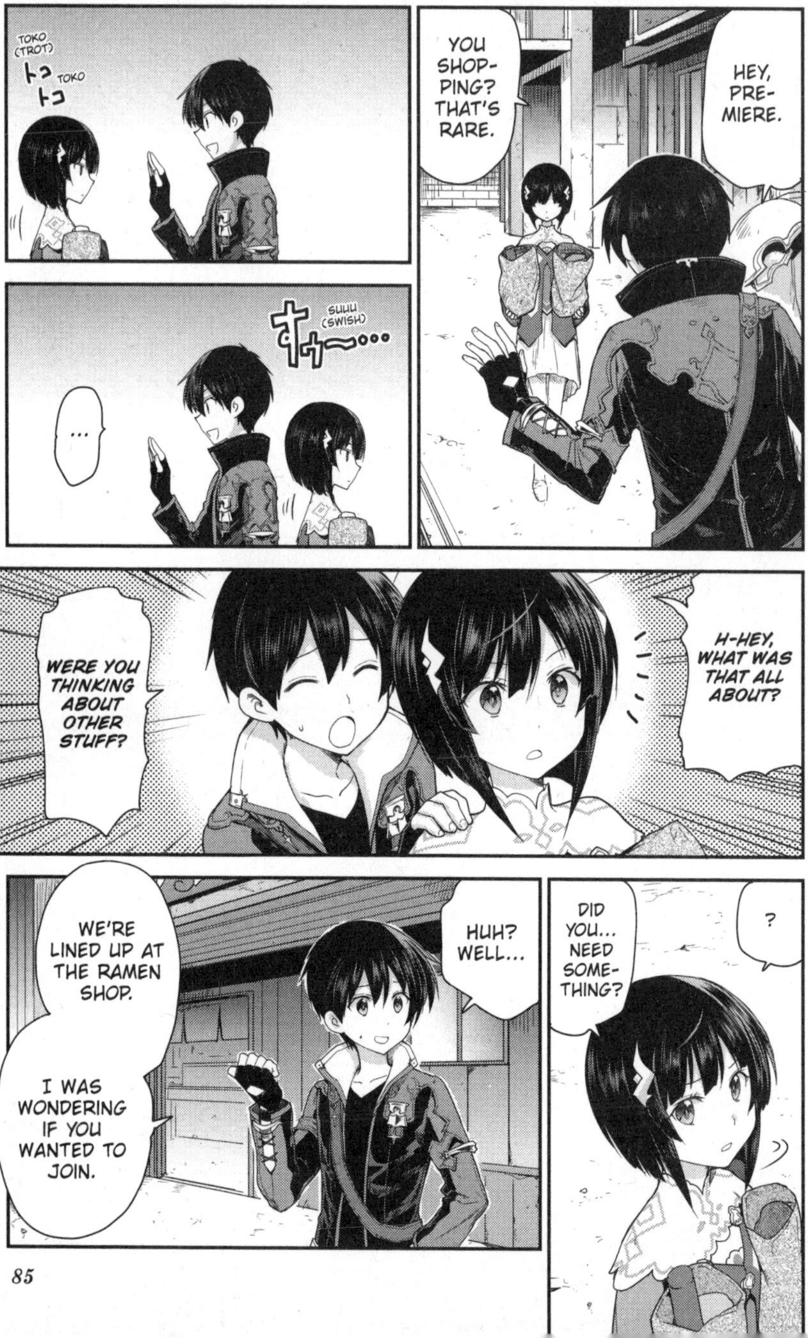
HEY, PREMIERE.
YOU SHOPPING? THAT'S RARE.
トコ トコ
TOKO (TROT) TOKO
スゥ～…
SUUU (SWISH)
...
H-HEY, WHAT WAS THAT ALL ABOUT?
WERE YOU THINKING ABOUT OTHER STUFF?
?
DID YOU... NEED SOMETHING?
HUH? WELL...
WE'RE LINED UP AT THE RAMEN SHOP.
I WAS WONDERING IF YOU WANTED TO JOIN.

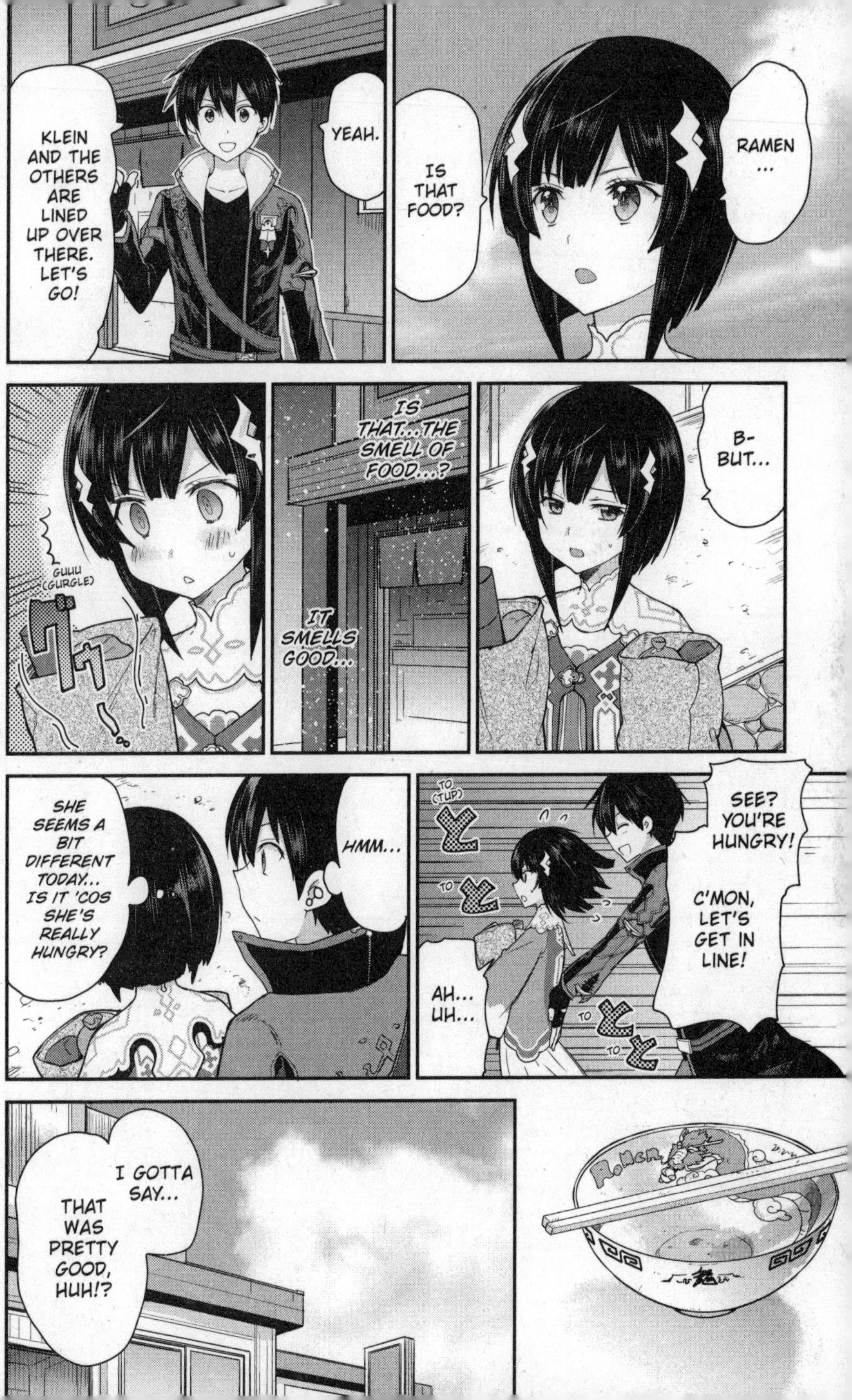
RAMEN ...
IS THAT FOOD?
YEAH.
KLEIN AND THE OTHERS ARE LINED UP OVER THERE. LET'S GO!
B-BUT...
IS THAT... THE SMELL OF FOOD...?
IT SMELLS GOOD...
GUUU (GURGLE)
SEE? YOU'RE HUNGRY!
C'MON, LET'S GET IN LINE!
TO (TUP)
TO
TO
TO
AH... UH...
HMM...
SHE SEEMS A BIT DIFFERENT TODAY... IS IT 'COS SHE'S REALLY HUNGRY?
I GOTTA SAY...
THAT WAS PRETTY GOOD, HUH!?

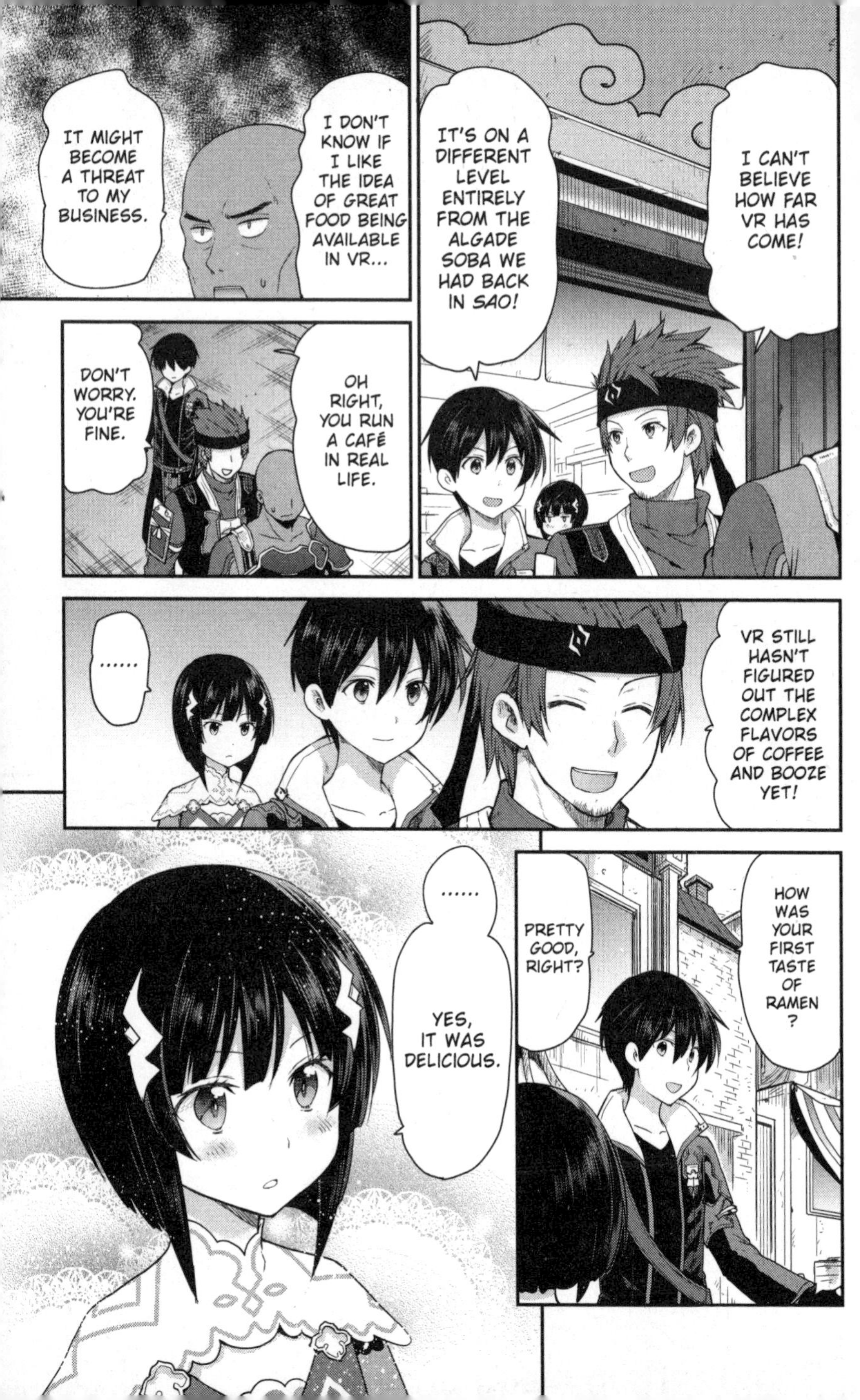
I CAN'T BELIEVE HOW FAR VR HAS COME!
IT'S ON A DIFFERENT LEVEL ENTIRELY FROM THE ALGADE SOBA WE HAD BACK IN SAO!
I DON'T KNOW IF I LIKE THE IDEA OF GREAT FOOD BEING AVAILABLE IN VR...
IT MIGHT BECOME A THREAT TO MY BUSINESS.
OH RIGHT, YOU RUN A CAFÉ IN REAL LIFE.
DON'T WORRY. YOU'RE FINE.
VR STILL HASN'T FIGURED OUT THE COMPLEX FLAVORS OF COFFEE AND BOOZE YET!
......
HOW WAS YOUR FIRST TASTE OF RAMEN?
PRETTY GOOD, RIGHT?
...... YES, IT WAS DELICIOUS.

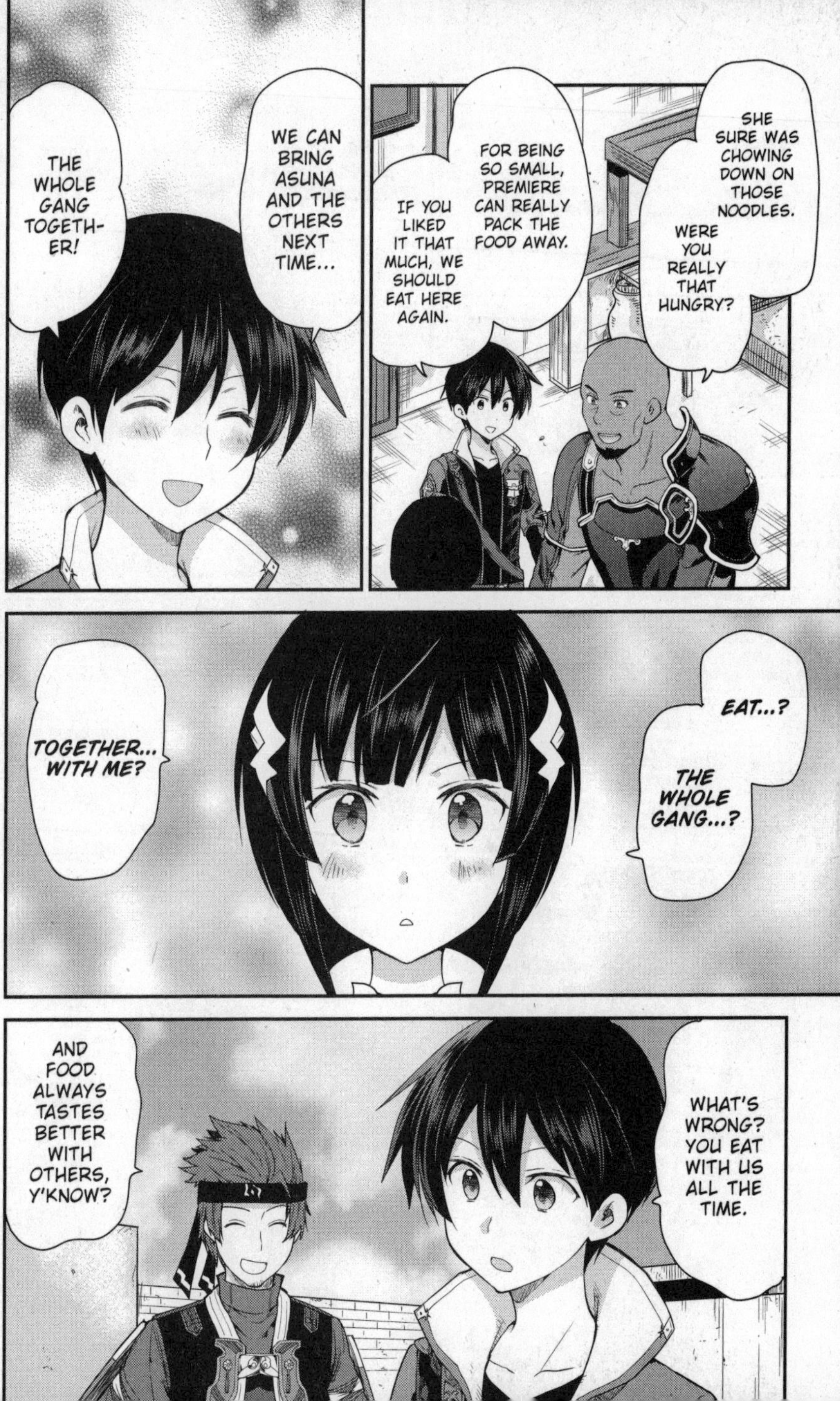
SHE SURE WAS CHOWING DOWN ON THOSE NOODLES.
WERE YOU REALLY THAT HUNGRY?
FOR BEING SO SMALL, PREMIERE CAN REALLY PACK THE FOOD AWAY.
IF YOU LIKED IT THAT MUCH, WE SHOULD EAT HERE AGAIN.
WE CAN BRING ASUNA AND THE OTHERS NEXT TIME...
THE WHOLE GANG TOGETH-ER!
EAT...?
THE WHOLE GANG...?
TOGETHER... WITH ME?
WHAT'S WRONG? YOU EAT WITH US ALL THE TIME.
AND FOOD ALWAYS TASTES BETTER WITH OTHERS, Y'KNOW?

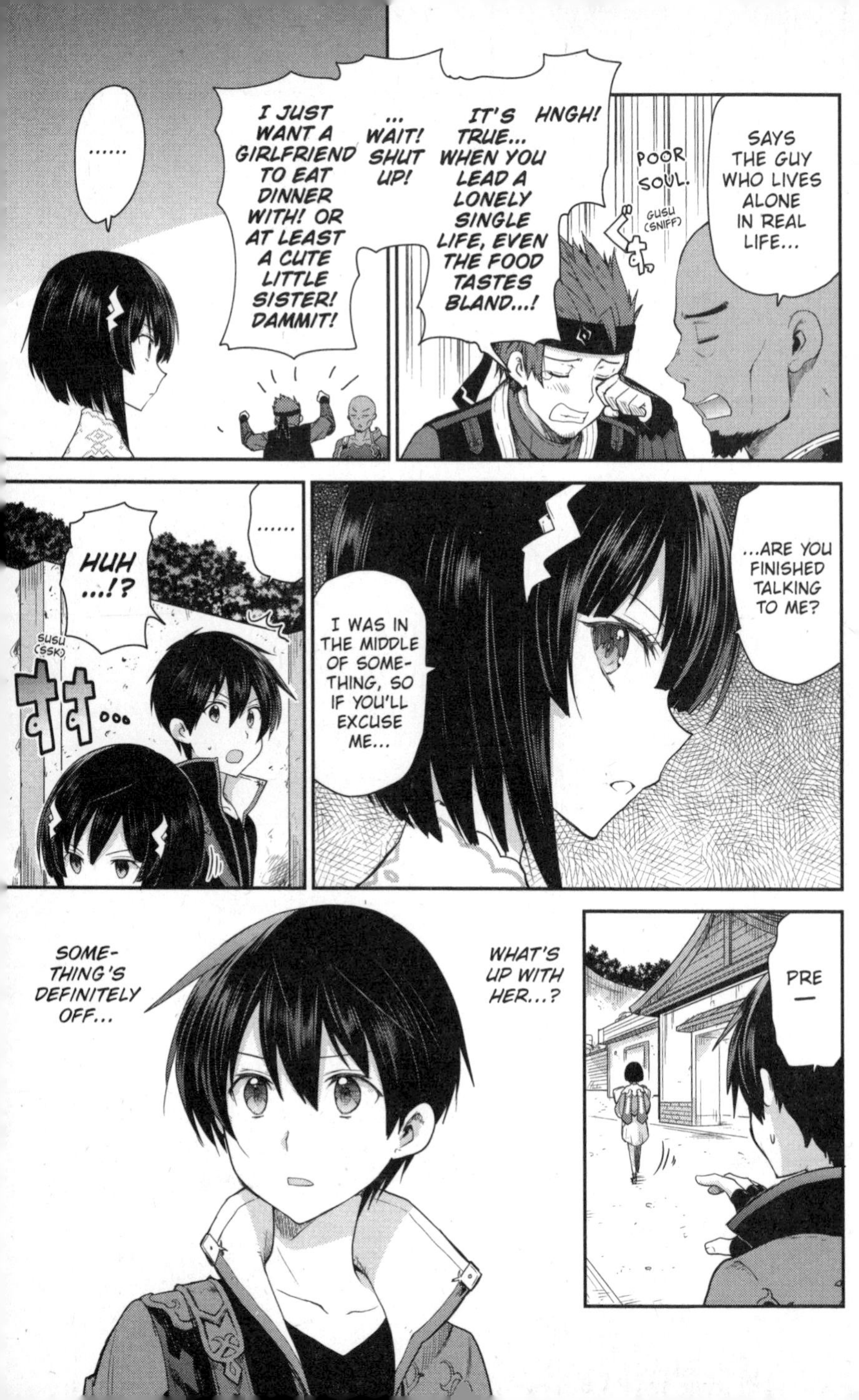
SAYS THE GUY WHO LIVES ALONE IN REAL LIFE...
POOR SOUL.
GUSU (SNIFF)
HNGH!
IT'S TRUE... WHEN YOU LEAD A LONELY SINGLE LIFE, EVEN THE FOOD TASTES BLAND...!
...WAIT! SHUT UP!
I JUST WANT A GIRLFRIEND TO EAT DINNER WITH! OR AT LEAST A CUTE LITTLE SISTER! DAMMIT!
......
...ARE YOU FINISHED TALKING TO ME?
I WAS IN THE MIDDLE OF SOME-THING, SO IF YOU'LL EXCUSE ME...
......
HUH ...!?
SUSU (SSK)
PRE—
WHAT'S UP WITH HER...?
SOME-THING'S DEFINITELY OFF...

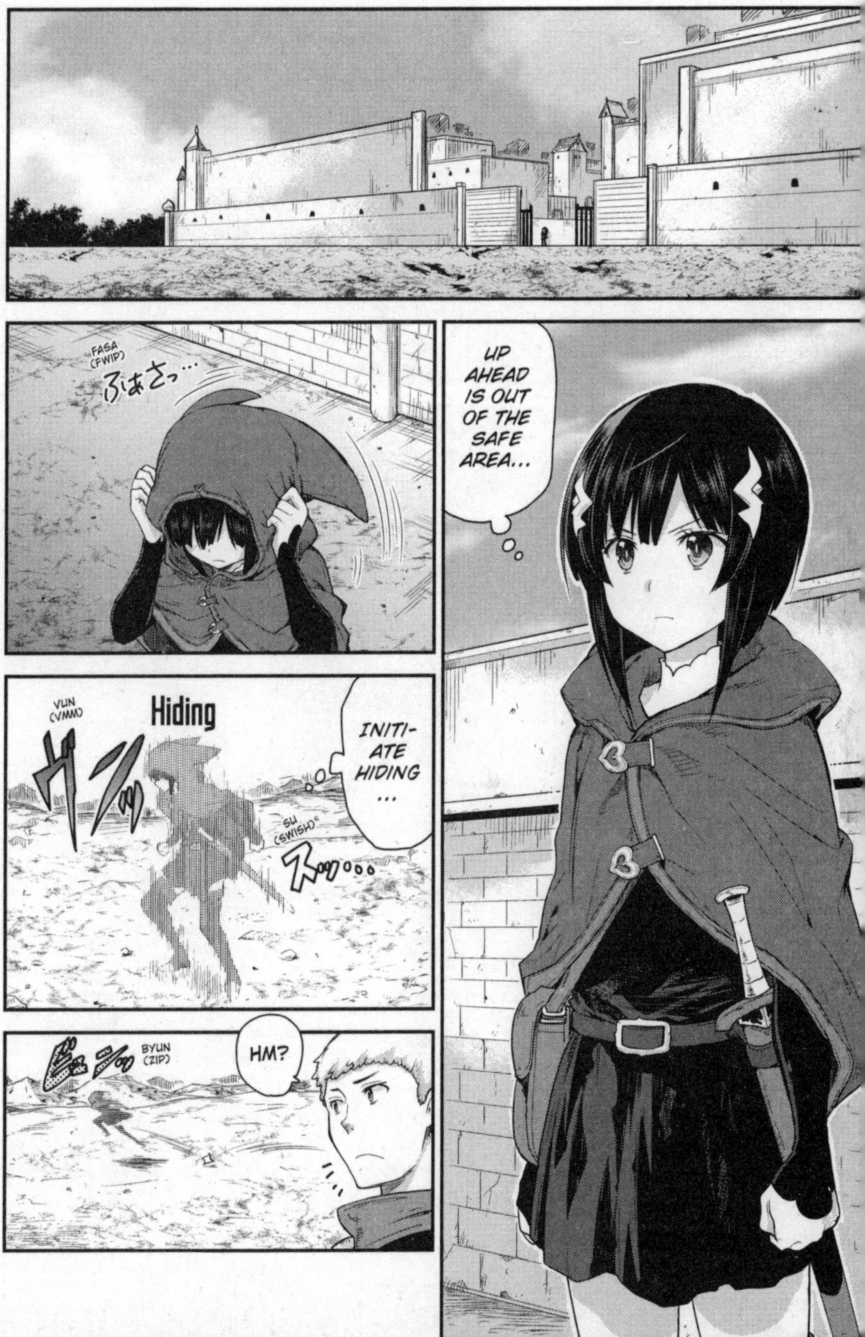
UP AHEAD IS OUT OF THE SAFE AREA...
FASA (FWIP)
ふぁさっ…
INITI-ATE HIDING ...
Hiding
VUN (VMM)
SU (SWISH)
HM?
BYUN (ZIP)

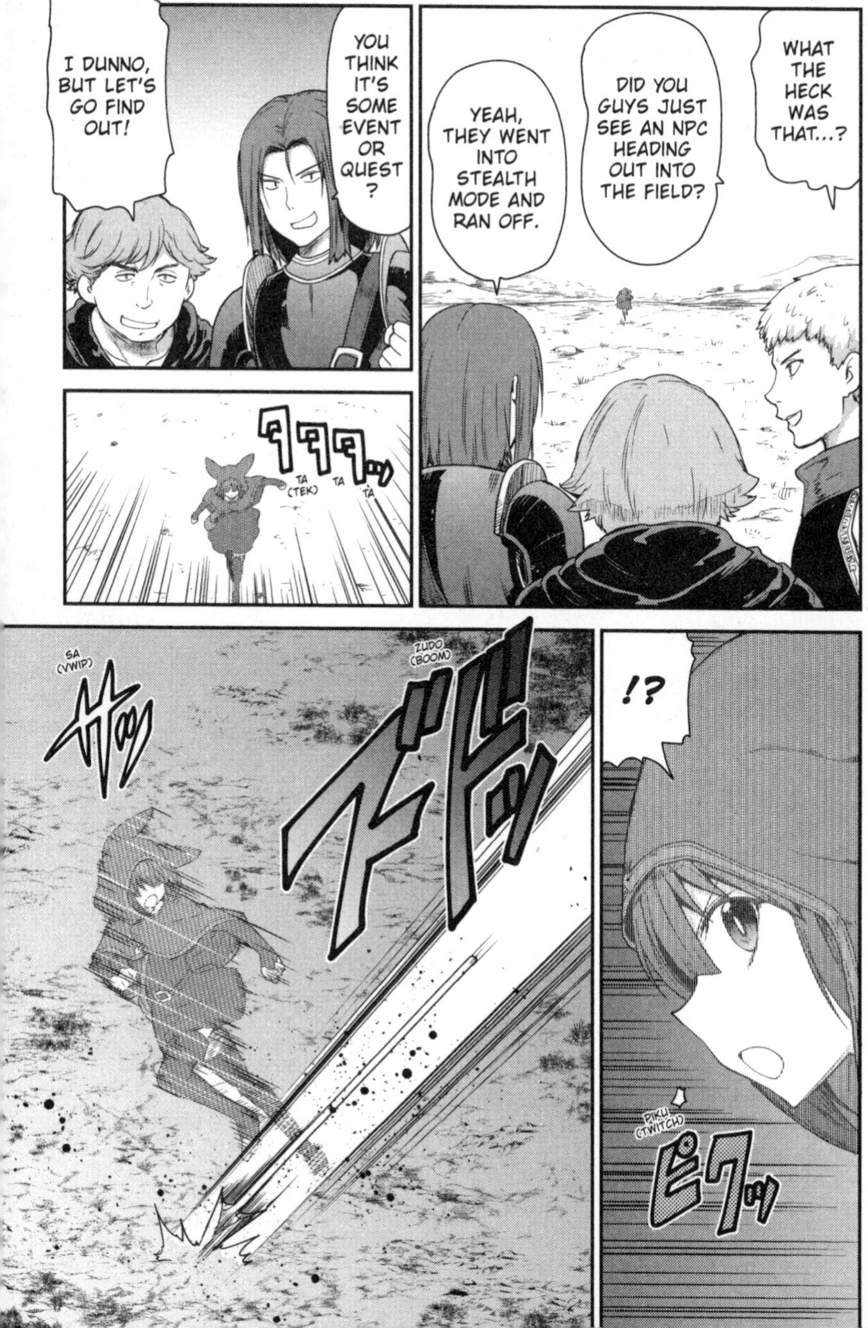
WHAT THE HECK WAS THAT...?
DID YOU GUYS JUST SEE AN NPC HEADING OUT INTO THE FIELD?
YEAH, THEY WENT INTO STEALTH MODE AND RAN OFF.
YOU THINK IT'S SOME EVENT OR QUEST?
I DUNNO, BUT LET'S GO FIND OUT!
TA (TEK) TA TA
!?
PIKU (TWITCH)
ZUDO (BOOM)
SA (VWIP)

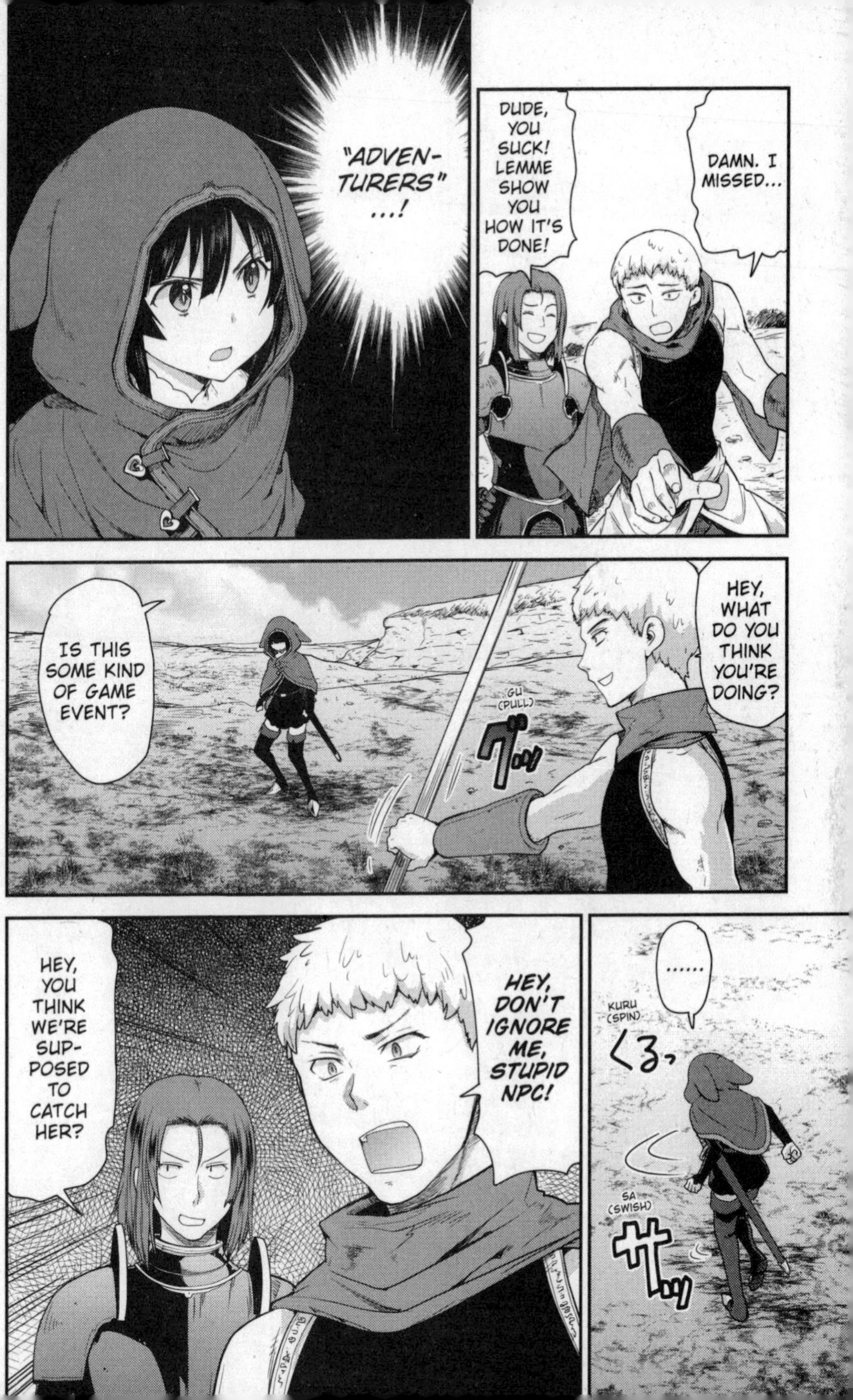
DAMN. I MISSED...
DUDE, YOU SUCK! LEMME SHOW YOU HOW IT'S DONE!
"ADVEN-TURERS" ...!
HEY, WHAT DO YOU THINK YOU'RE DOING?
GU (PULL)
ゴッ
IS THIS SOME KIND OF GAME EVENT?
......
KURU (SPIN)
くるっ
SA (SWISH)
サッ
HEY, DON'T IGNORE ME, STUPID NPC!
HEY, YOU THINK WE'RE SUP-POSED TO CATCH HER?

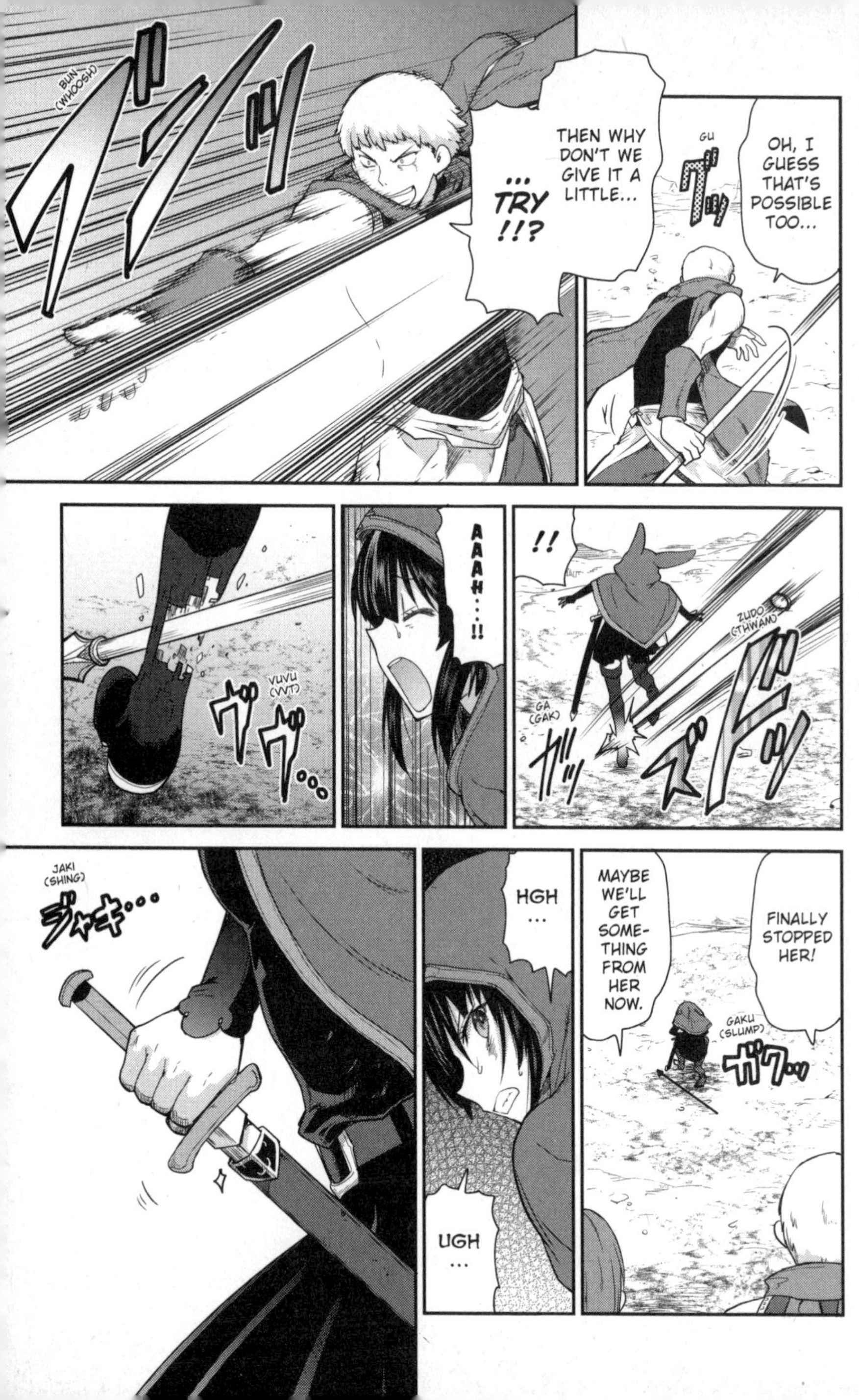
GU
OH, I GUESS THAT'S POSSIBLE TOO...
THEN WHY DON'T WE GIVE IT A LITTLE...
...TRY!!?
BUN (WHOOSH)
!!
ZUDO (THWAM)
GA (GAK)
AAAH...!!
VUVU (VVT)
FINALLY STOPPED HER!
MAYBE WE'LL GET SOME-THING FROM HER NOW.
GAKU (SLUMP)
HGH...
UGH...
JAKI (SHING)

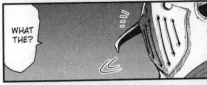

WHAT
THE?

HFE...

HFE...

UH...
WHAT'S
YOUR
NAME
AGAIN?
YOU
DIDN'T
HAVE
ONE,
RIGHT?

OH,
IT'S
YOU...

HAAH
...

HAAH
...

YORO
(WOBBLE)

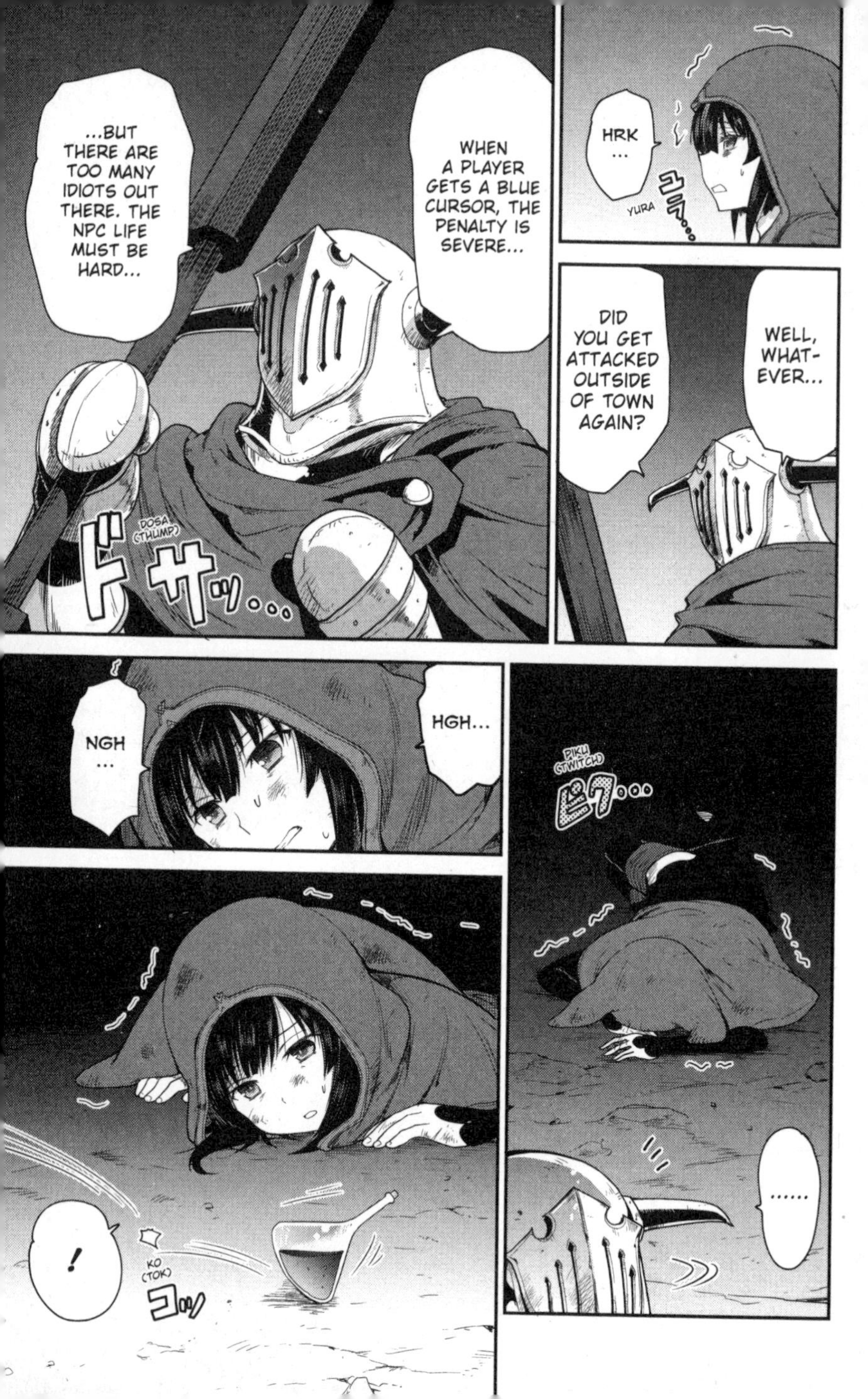
HRK...
YURA
WELL, WHATEVER...
DID YOU GET ATTACKED OUTSIDE OF TOWN AGAIN?
WHEN A PLAYER GETS A BLUE CURSOR, THE PENALTY IS SEVERE...
...BUT THERE ARE TOO MANY IDIOTS OUT THERE. THE NPC LIFE MUST BE HARD...
DOSA (THUMP)
PIKU (TWITCH)
HGH...
NGH...
......
!
KO (TOK)

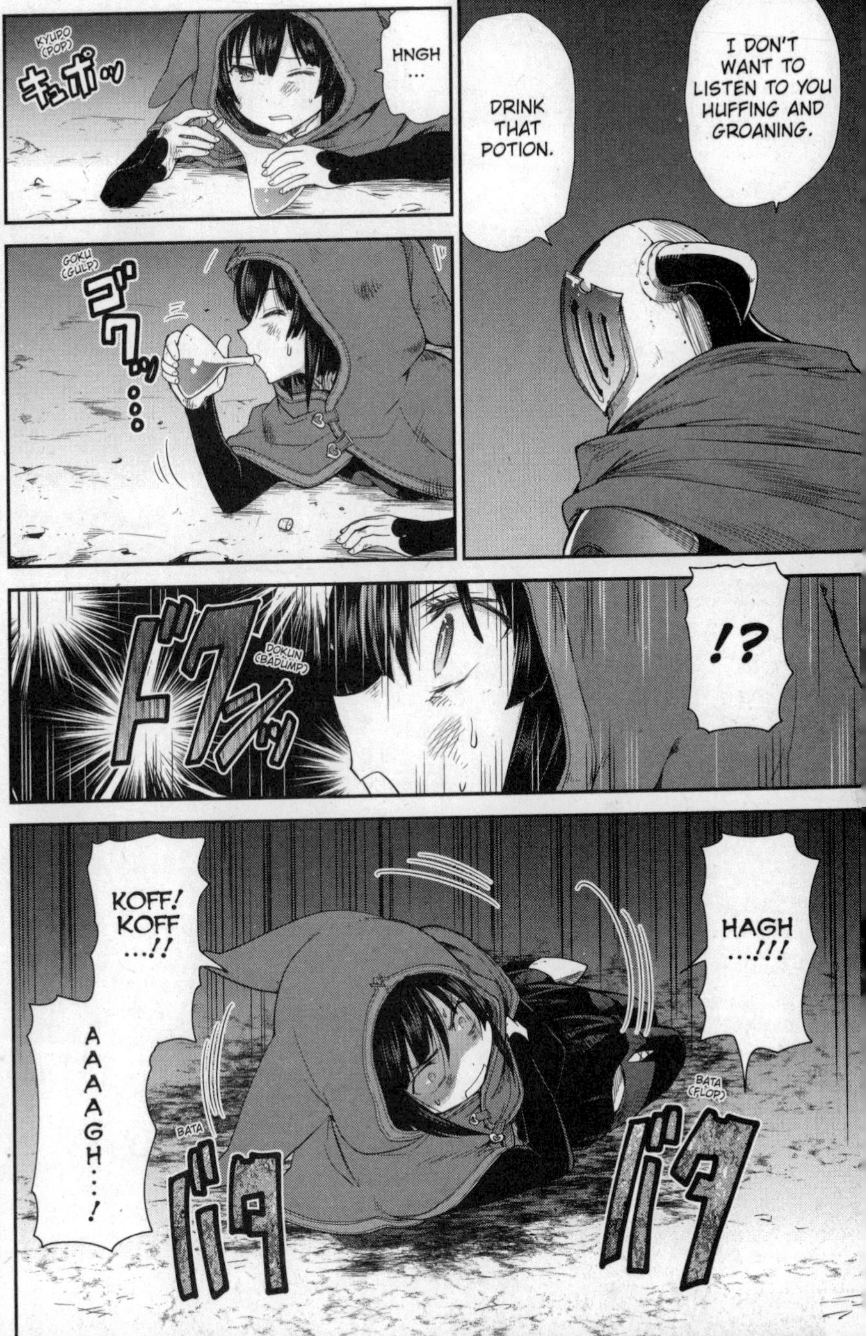
I DON'T WANT TO LISTEN TO YOU HUFFING AND GROANING.
DRINK THAT POTION.
HNGH ...
KYUPO (POP)
GOKU (GULP)
!?
DOKUN (BADUMP)
HAGH ...!!!
BATA (FLOP)
KOFF! KOFF ...!!
AAAAAGH...!
BATA

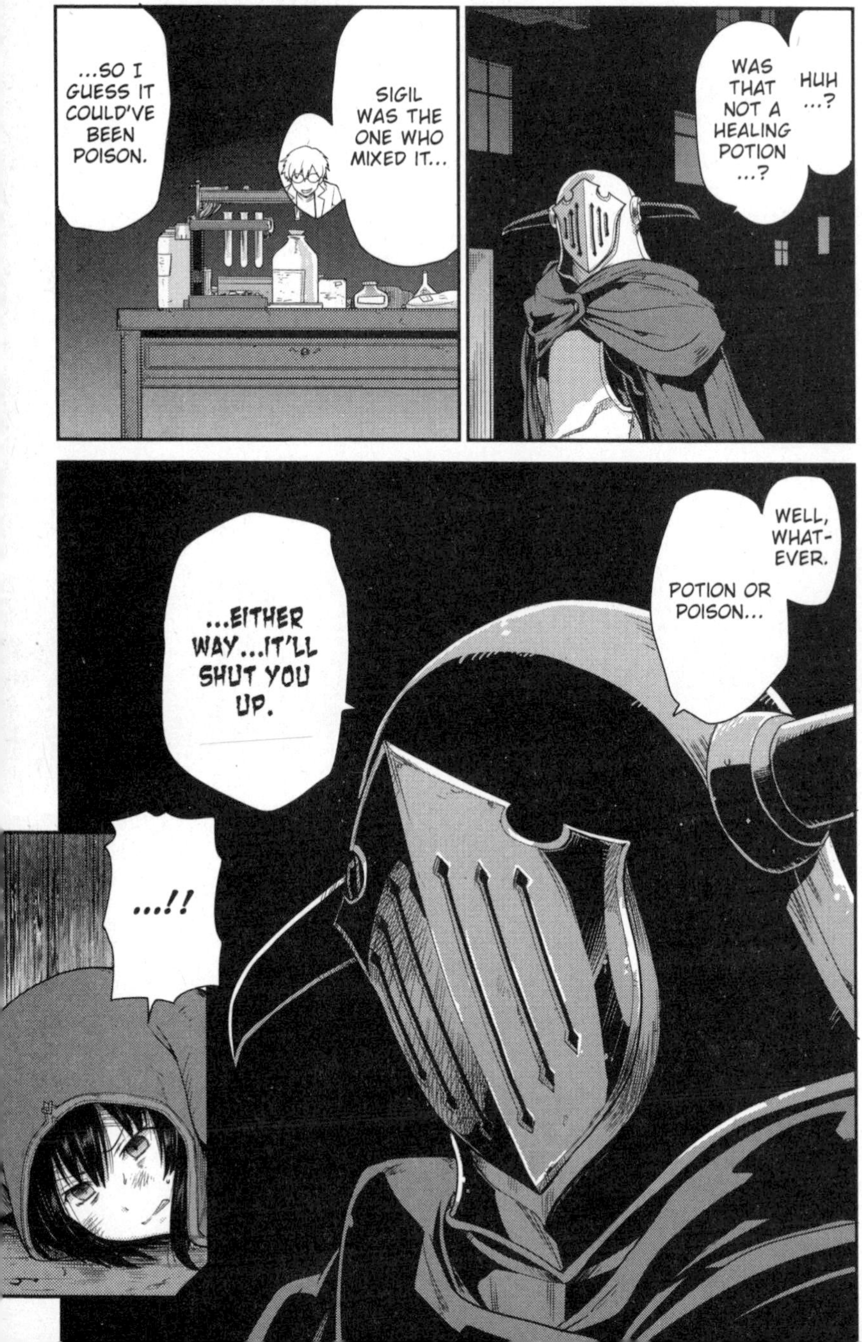
HUH...?
WAS THAT NOT A HEALING POTION...?
SIGIL WAS THE ONE WHO MIXED IT...
...SO I GUESS IT COULD'VE BEEN POISON.
WELL, WHAT-EVER.
POTION OR POISON...
...EITHER WAY...IT'LL SHUT YOU UP.
...!!

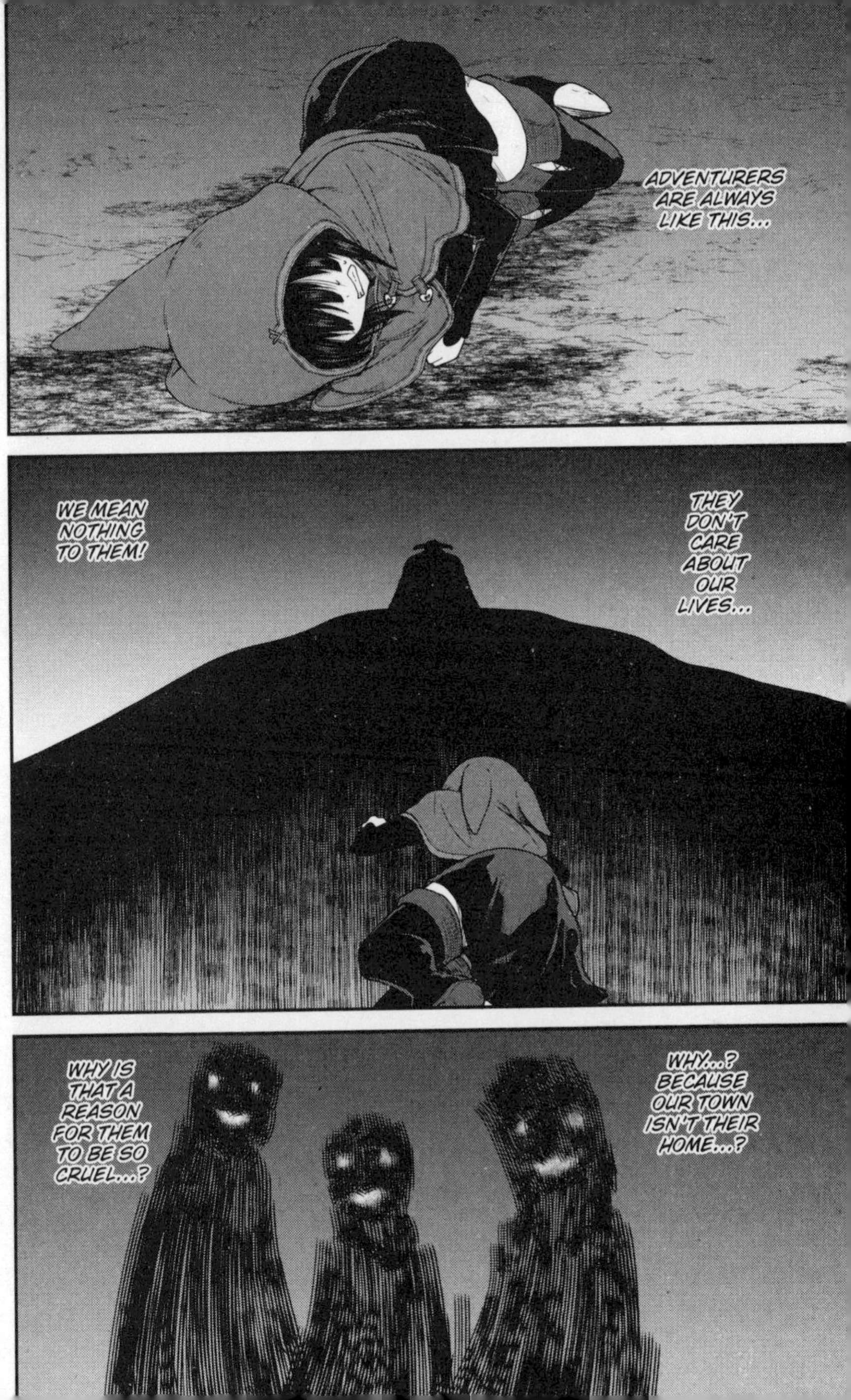
ADVENTURERS ARE ALWAYS LIKE THIS...
THEY DON'T CARE ABOUT OUR LIVES...
WE MEAN NOTHING TO THEM!
WHY...? BECAUSE OUR TOWN ISN'T THEIR HOME...?
WHY IS THAT A REASON FOR THEM TO BE SO CRUEL...?

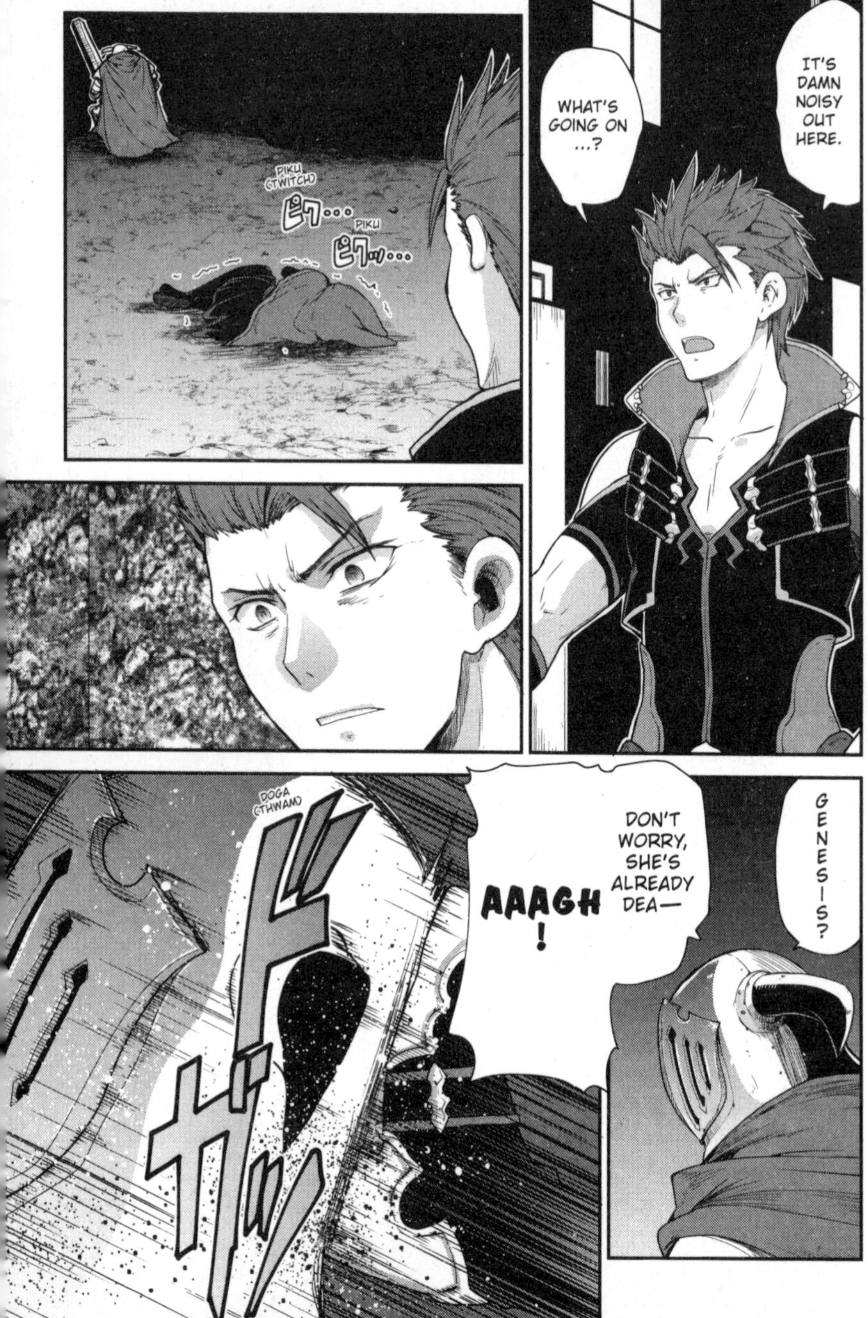
IT'S DAMN NOISY OUT HERE.
WHAT'S GOING ON ...?
PIKU (TWITCH)
ピク…
PIKU
ピクッ…
GENESIS?
DON'T WORRY, SHE'S ALREADY DEA—
AAAGH!
DOGA (THWAM)
ドガッ

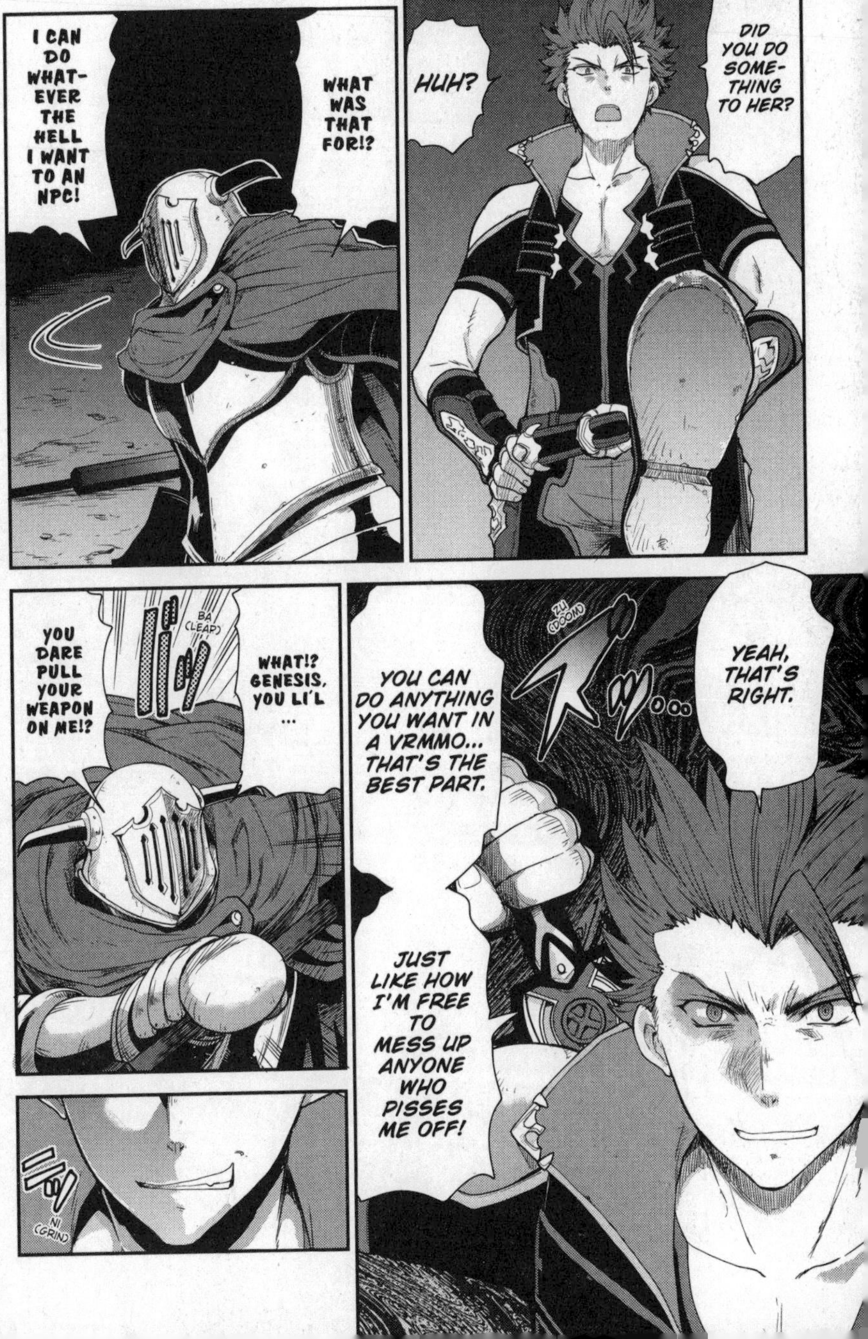
DID YOU DO SOMETHING TO HER?
HUH?
WHAT WAS THAT FOR!?
I CAN DO WHATEVER THE HELL I WANT TO AN NPC!
YEAH, THAT'S RIGHT.
ZU (DOOM)
YOU CAN DO ANYTHING YOU WANT IN A VRMMO... THAT'S THE BEST PART.
JUST LIKE HOW I'M FREE TO MESS UP ANYONE WHO PISSES ME OFF!
WHAT!? GENESIS, YOU LI'L ...
BA (LEAP)
YOU DARE PULL YOUR WEAPON ON ME!?
NI (GRIN)

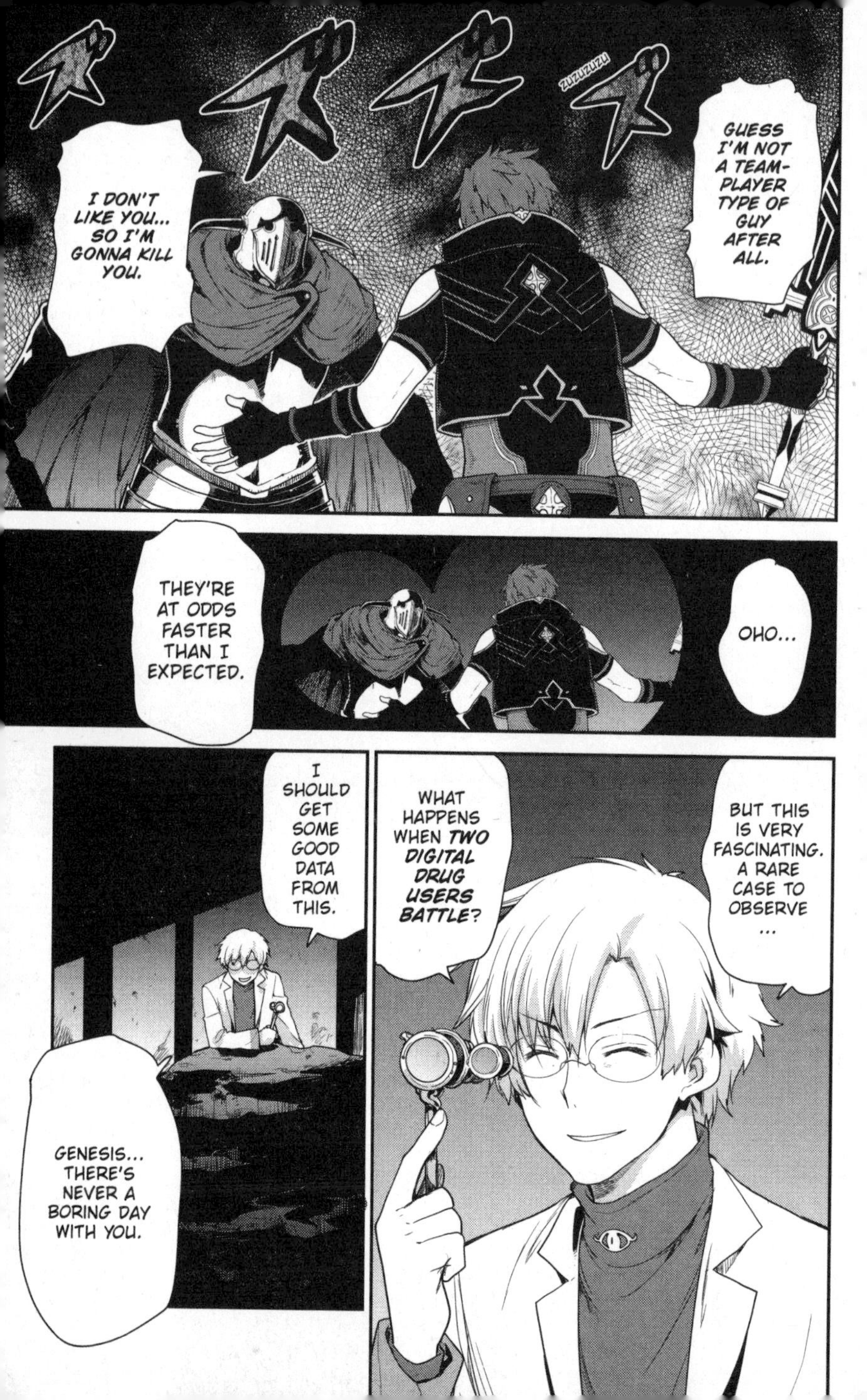
ZUZUZUZU
GUESS I'M NOT A TEAM-PLAYER TYPE OF GUY AFTER ALL.
I DON'T LIKE YOU... SO I'M GONNA KILL YOU.
OHO...
THEY'RE AT ODDS FASTER THAN I EXPECTED.
BUT THIS IS VERY FASCINATING. A RARE CASE TO OBSERVE...
WHAT HAPPENS WHEN TWO DIGITAL DRUG USERS BATTLE?
I SHOULD GET SOME GOOD DATA FROM THIS.
GENESIS... THERE'S NEVER A BORING DAY WITH YOU.

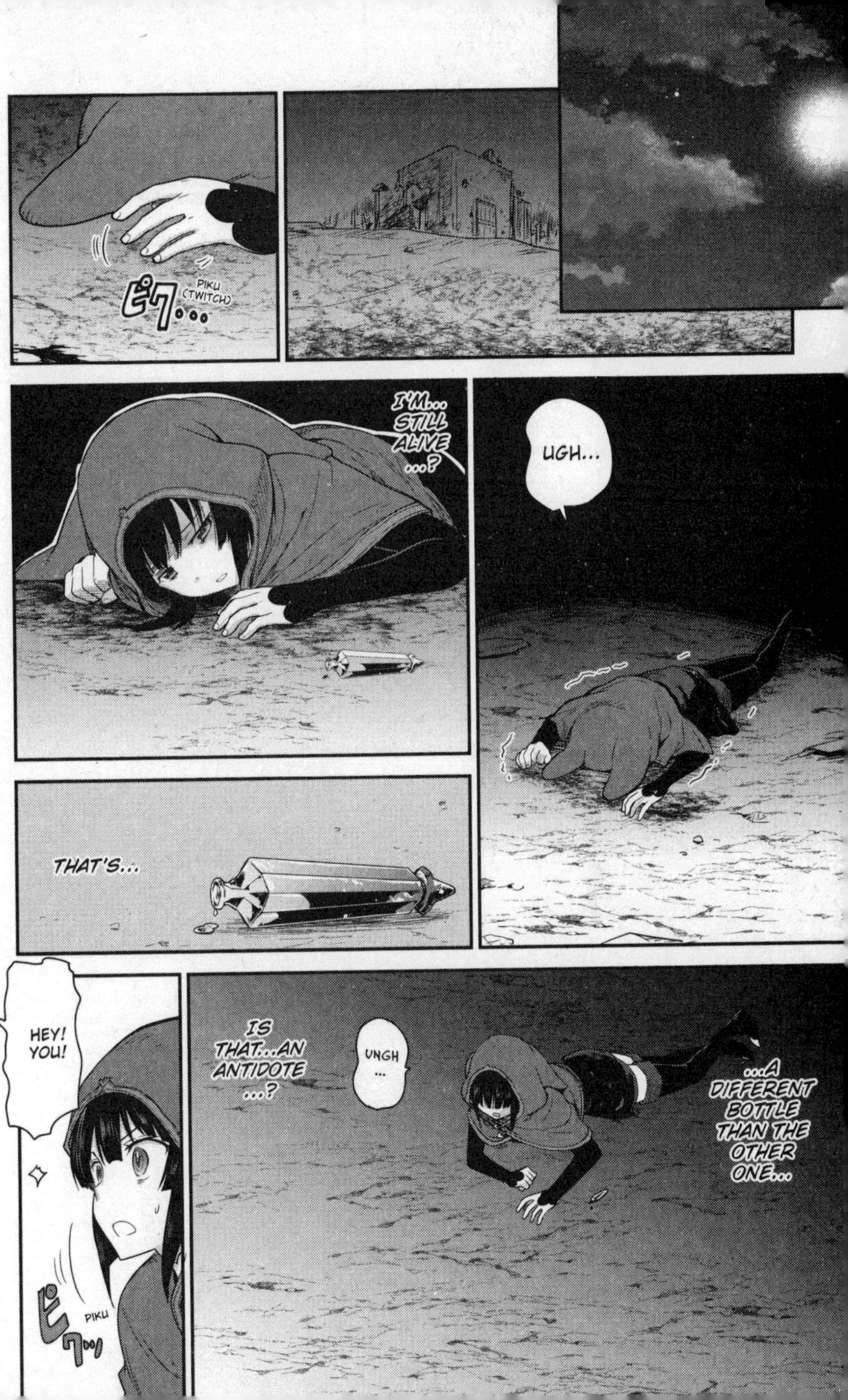
ピク...
PIKU (TWITCH)
UGH...
I'M... STILL ALIVE ...?
THAT'S...
...A DIFFERENT BOTTLE THAN THE OTHER ONE...
UNGH ...
IS THAT...AN ANTIDOTE ...?
HEY! YOU!
ピク
PIKU

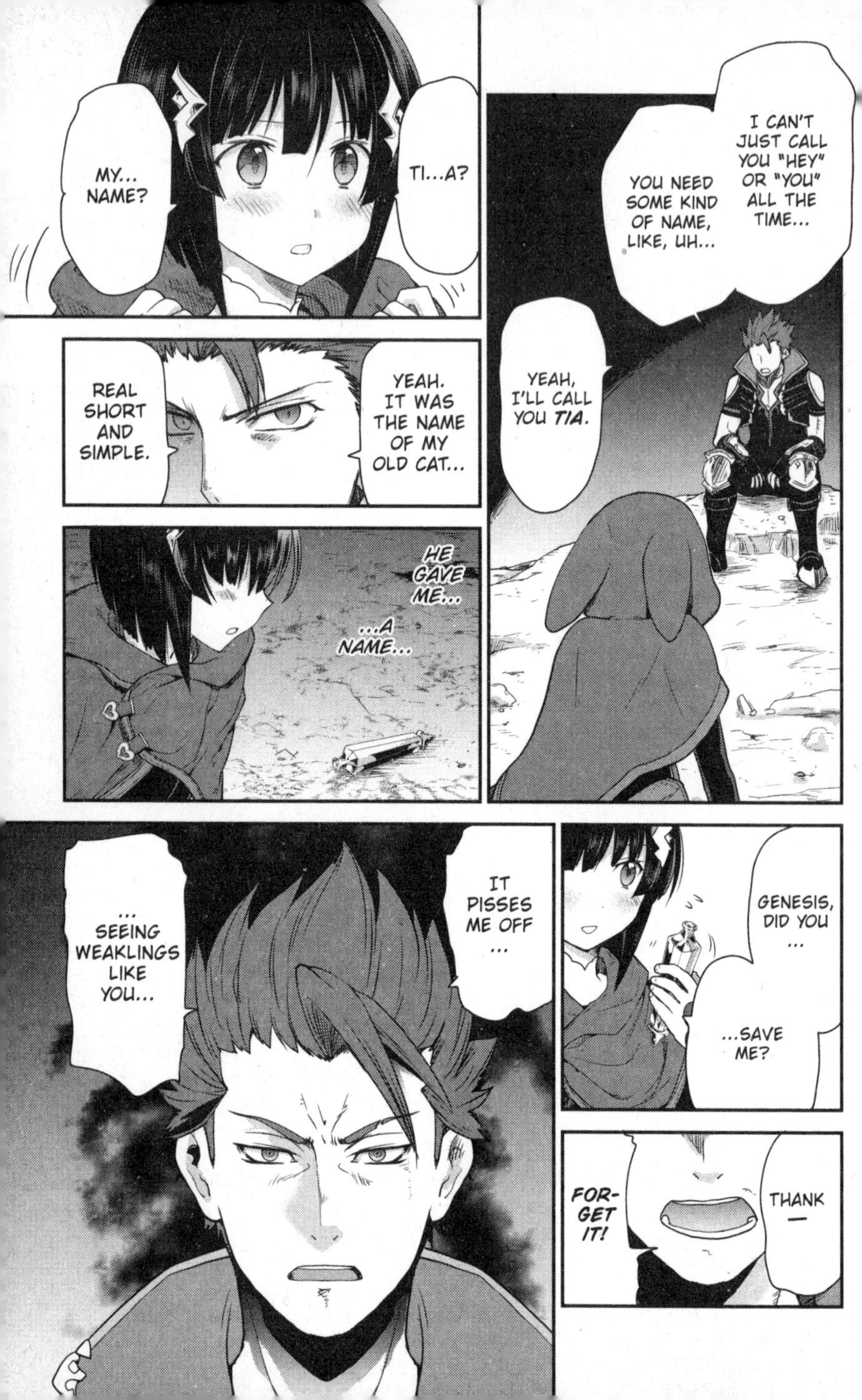

I CAN'T JUST CALL YOU "HEY" OR "YOU" ALL THE TIME...
YOU NEED SOME KIND OF NAME, LIKE, UH...
YEAH, I'LL CALL YOU *TIA*.
TI...A?
MY... NAME?
YEAH. IT WAS THE NAME OF MY OLD CAT...
REAL SHORT AND SIMPLE.
HE GAVE ME...
...A NAME...
GENESIS, DID YOU ...
...SAVE ME?
THANK—
FOR-GET IT!
IT PISSES ME OFF ...
... SEEING WEAKLINGS LIKE YOU...

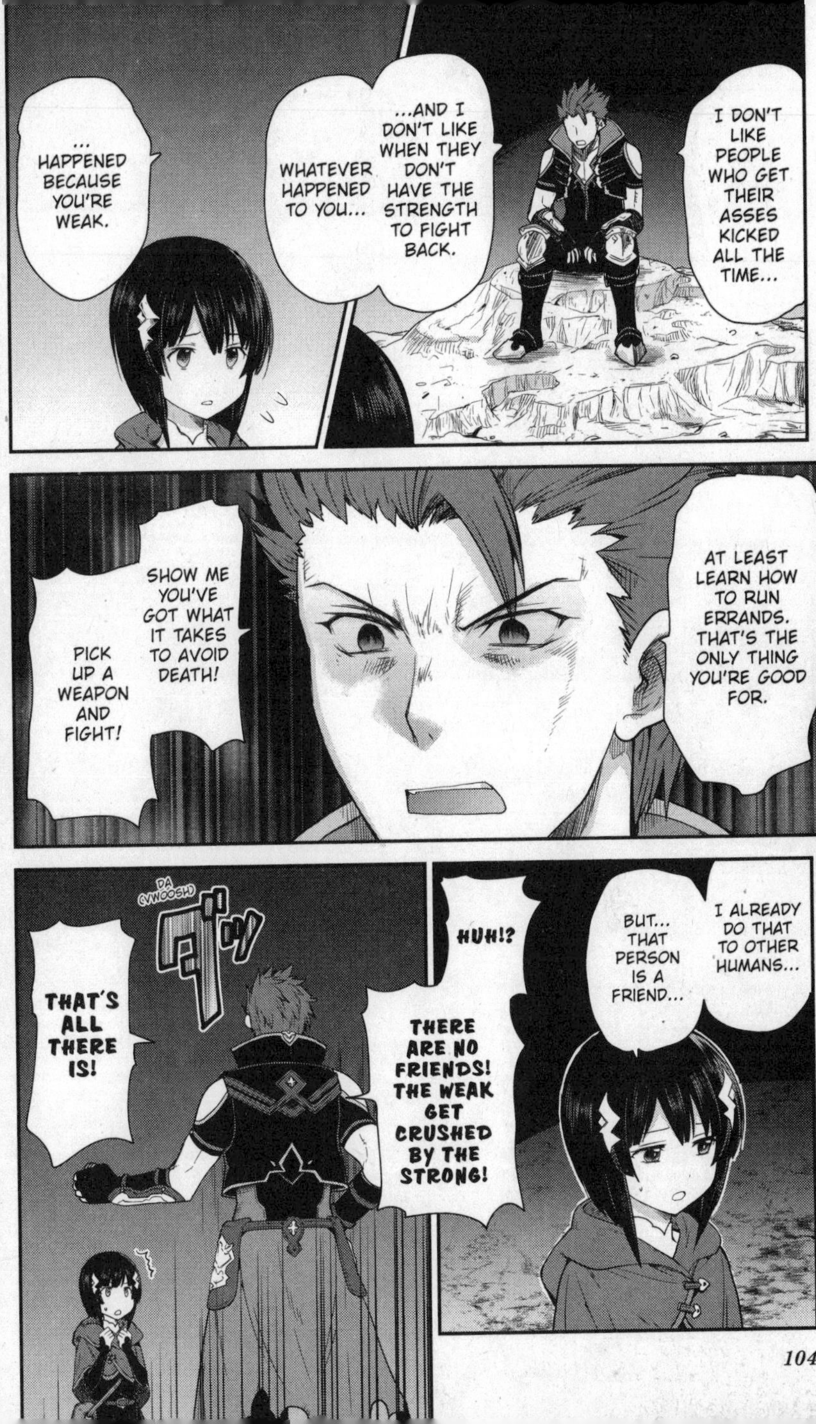
I DON'T LIKE PEOPLE WHO GET THEIR ASSES KICKED ALL THE TIME...
...AND I DON'T LIKE WHEN THEY DON'T HAVE THE STRENGTH TO FIGHT BACK.
WHATEVER HAPPENED TO YOU...
... HAPPENED BECAUSE YOU'RE WEAK.
AT LEAST LEARN HOW TO RUN ERRANDS. THAT'S THE ONLY THING YOU'RE GOOD FOR.
SHOW ME YOU'VE GOT WHAT IT TAKES TO AVOID DEATH!
PICK UP A WEAPON AND FIGHT!
I ALREADY DO THAT TO OTHER HUMANS...
BUT... THAT PERSON IS A FRIEND...
HUH!?
DA (VWOOSH)
THERE ARE NO FRIENDS! THE WEAK GET CRUSHED BY THE STRONG!
THAT'S ALL THERE IS!

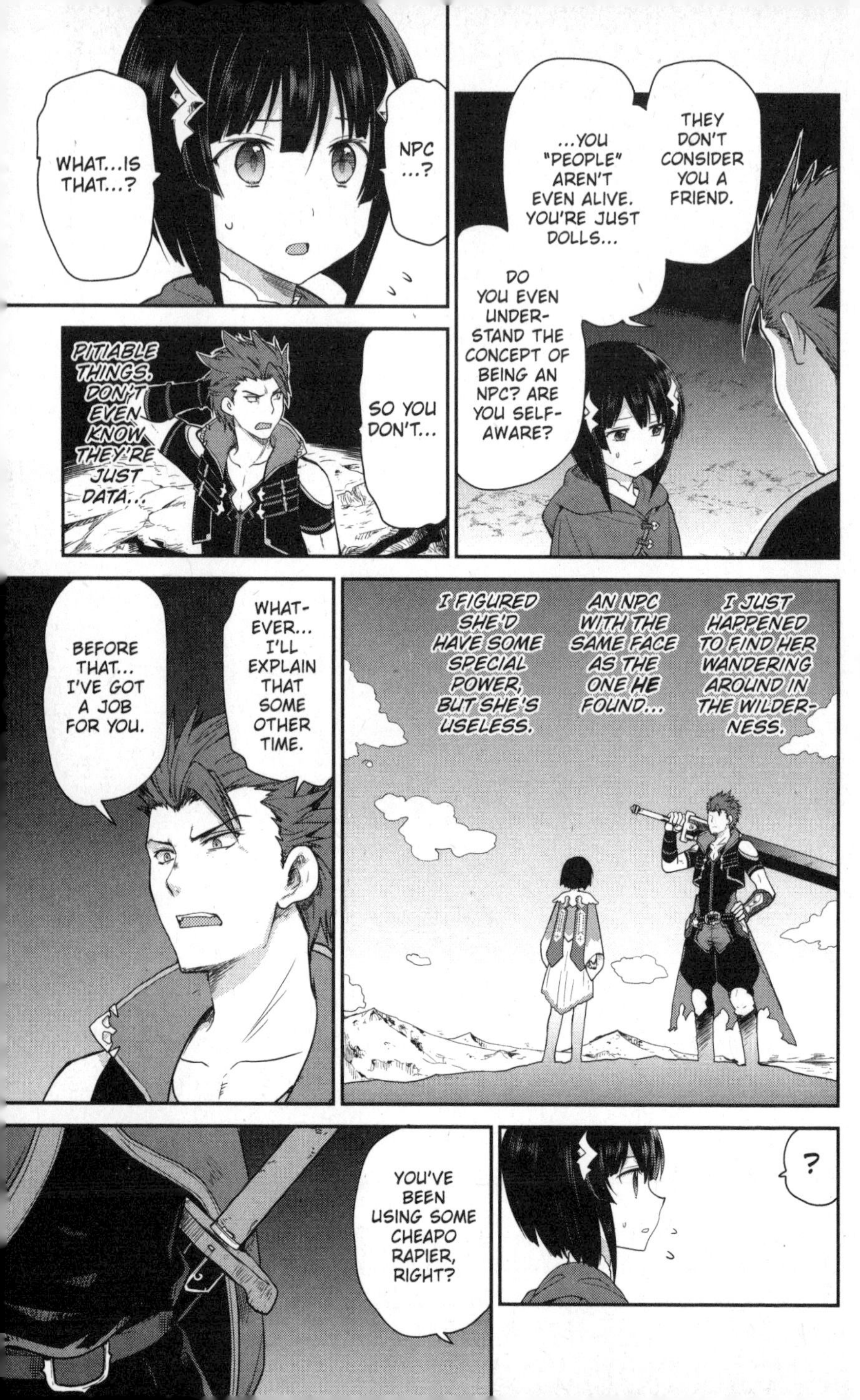
THEY DON'T CONSIDER YOU A FRIEND.
...YOU "PEOPLE" AREN'T EVEN ALIVE. YOU'RE JUST DOLLS...
DO YOU EVEN UNDER-STAND THE CONCEPT OF BEING AN NPC? ARE YOU SELF-AWARE?
NPC ...?
WHAT...IS THAT...?
SO YOU DON'T...
PITIABLE THINGS. DON'T EVEN KNOW THEY'RE JUST DATA...
I JUST HAPPENED TO FIND HER WANDERING AROUND IN THE WILDER-NESS.
AN NPC WITH THE SAME FACE AS THE ONE HE FOUND...
I FIGURED SHE'D HAVE SOME SPECIAL POWER, BUT SHE'S USELESS.
WHAT-EVER... I'LL EXPLAIN THAT SOME OTHER TIME.
BEFORE THAT... I'VE GOT A JOB FOR YOU.
?
YOU'VE BEEN USING SOME CHEAPO RAPIER, RIGHT?

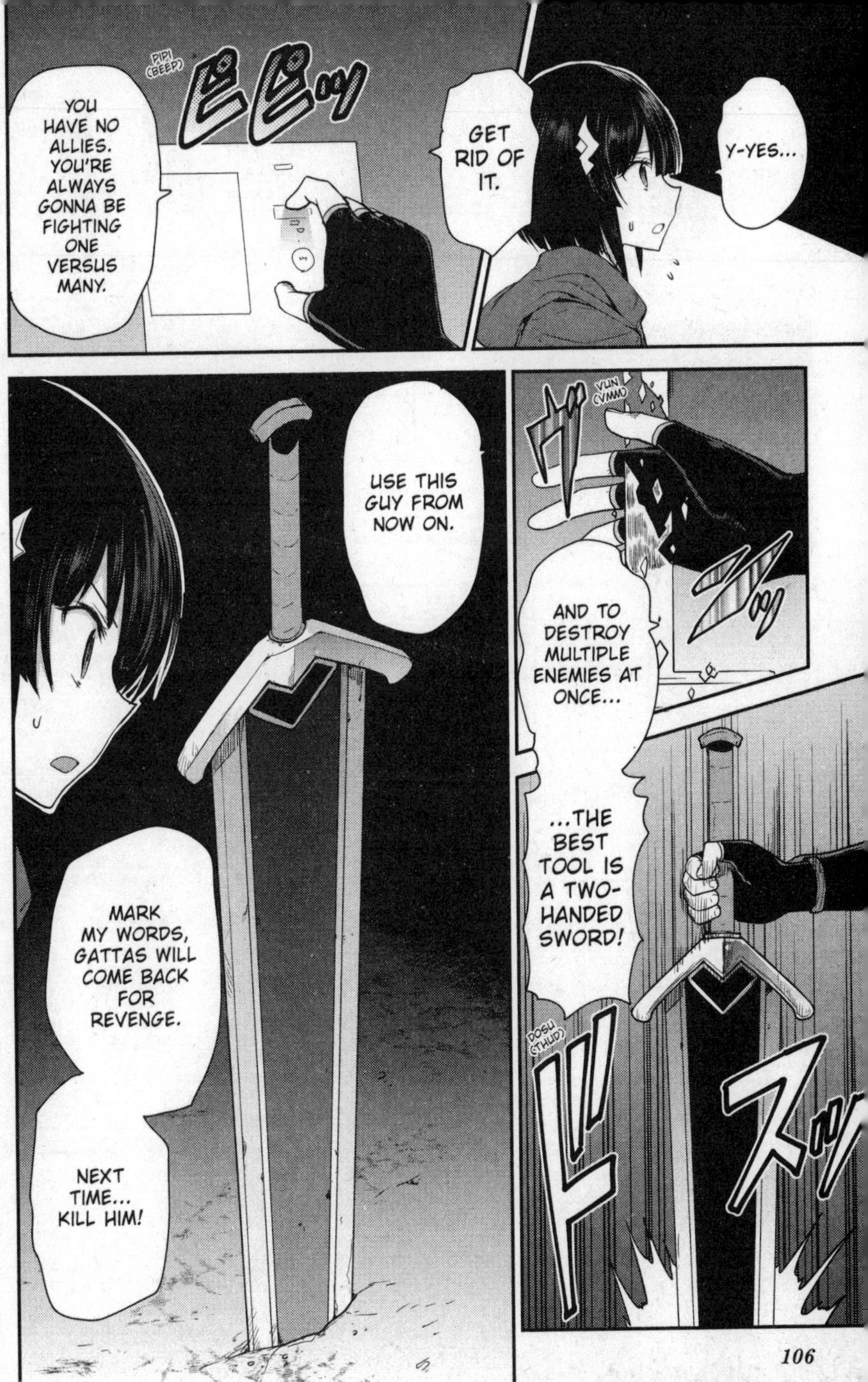
Y-YES...
GET RID OF IT.
PIPI (BEEP)
YOU HAVE NO ALLIES. YOU'RE ALWAYS GONNA BE FIGHTING ONE VERSUS MANY.
VUN (VMM)
AND TO DESTROY MULTIPLE ENEMIES AT ONCE...
...THE BEST TOOL IS A TWO-HANDED SWORD!
DOSU (THUD)
USE THIS GUY FROM NOW ON.
MARK MY WORDS, GATTAS WILL COME BACK FOR REVENGE.
NEXT TIME... KILL HIM!

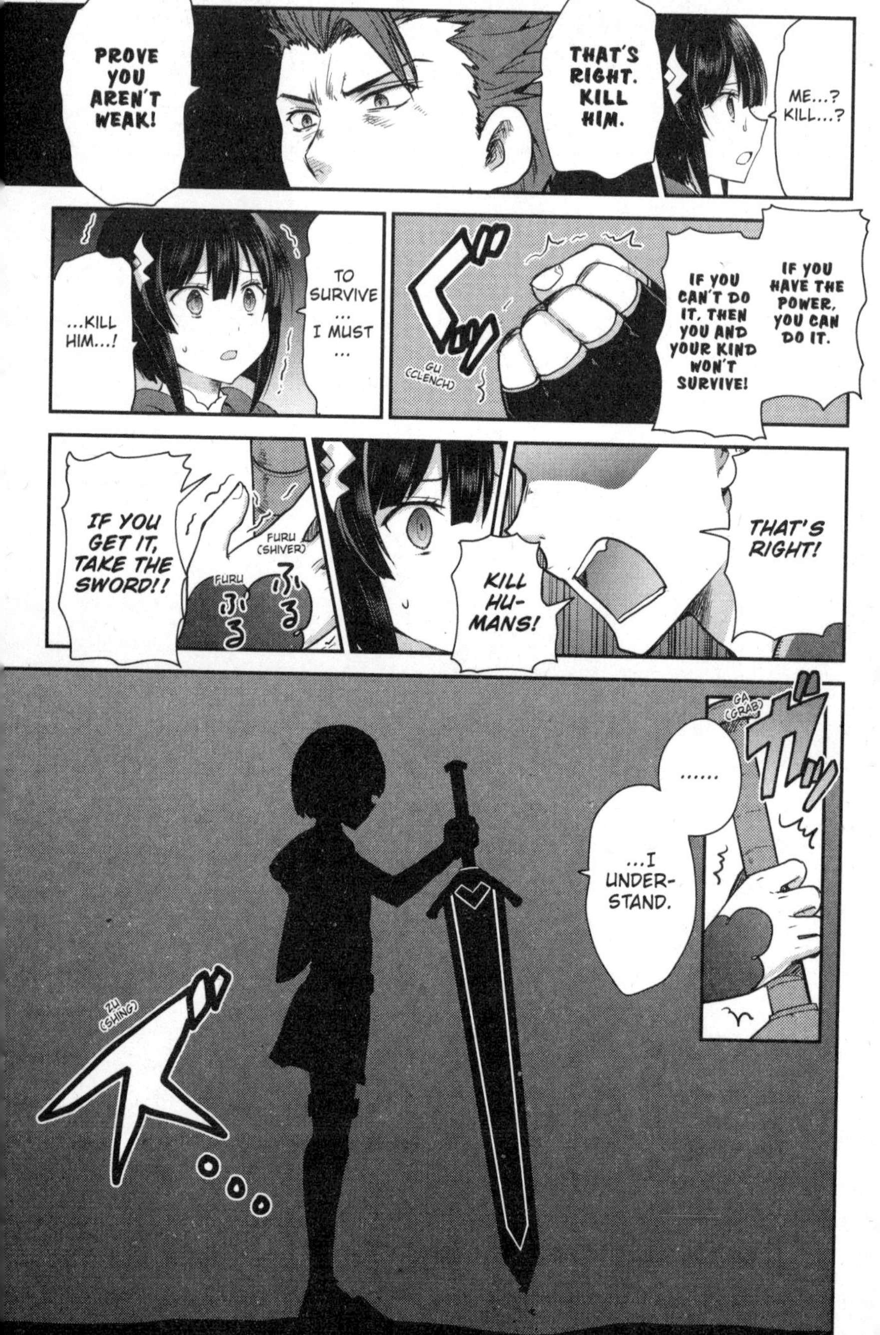
ME...? KILL...?
THAT'S RIGHT. KILL HIM.
PROVE YOU AREN'T WEAK!
IF YOU HAVE THE POWER, YOU CAN DO IT.
IF YOU CAN'T DO IT, THEN YOU AND YOUR KIND WON'T SURVIVE!
GU (CLENCH)
TO SURVIVE... I MUST...
...KILL HIM...!
THAT'S RIGHT!
KILL HUMANS!
FURU (SHIVER)
ふる
FURU
ふる
IF YOU GET IT, TAKE THE SWORD!!
GA (GRAB)
......
...I UNDERSTAND.
ZU (SHING)

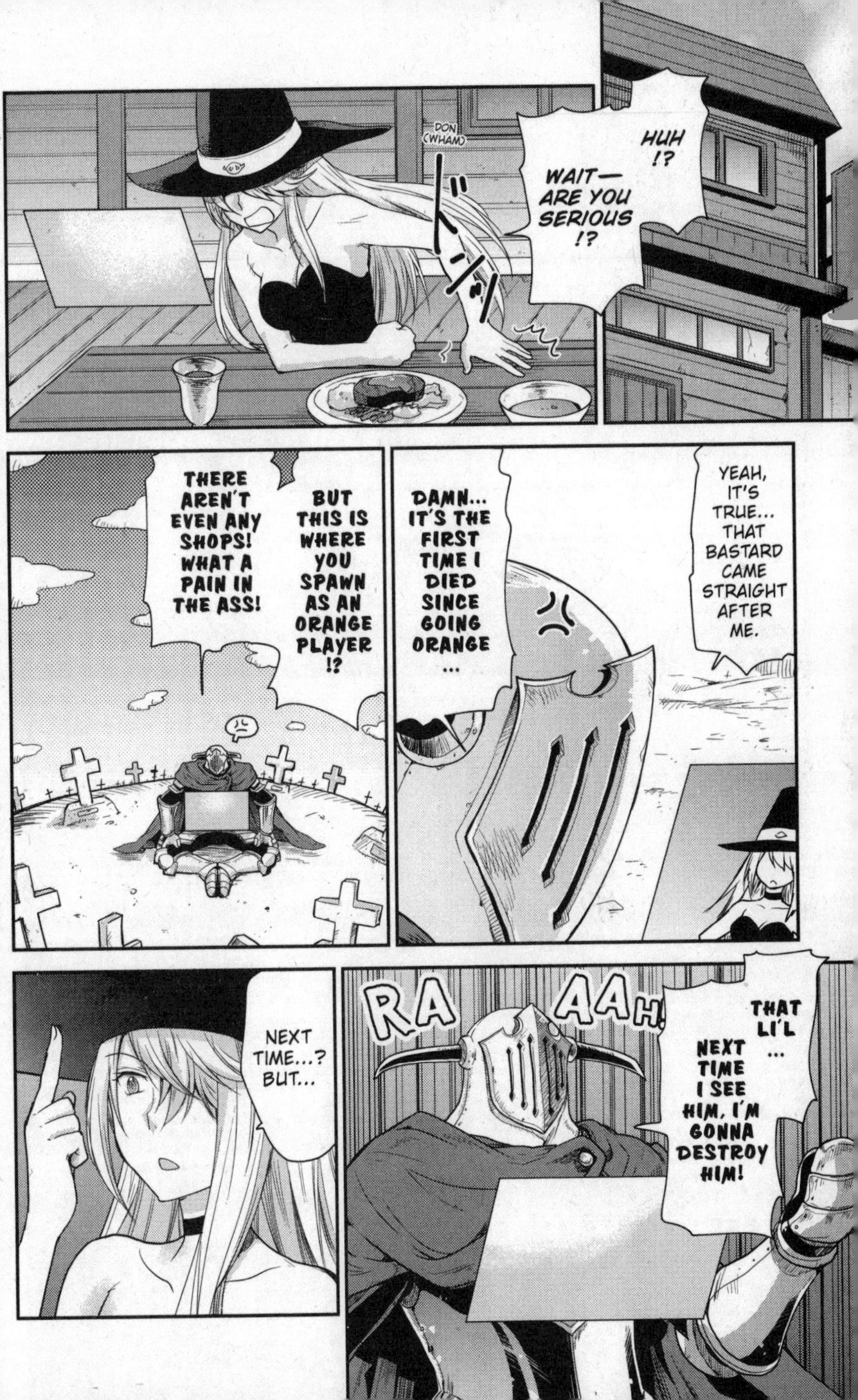
HUH!?
WAIT— ARE YOU SERIOUS!?
DON (WHAM)
YEAH, IT'S TRUE... THAT BASTARD CAME STRAIGHT AFTER ME.
DAMN... IT'S THE FIRST TIME I DIED SINCE GOING ORANGE...
BUT THIS IS WHERE YOU SPAWN AS AN ORANGE PLAYER!?
THERE AREN'T EVEN ANY SHOPS! WHAT A PAIN IN THE ASS!
THAT LI'L ...
NEXT TIME I SEE HIM, I'M GONNA DESTROY HIM!
RA AAH!
NEXT TIME...? BUT...

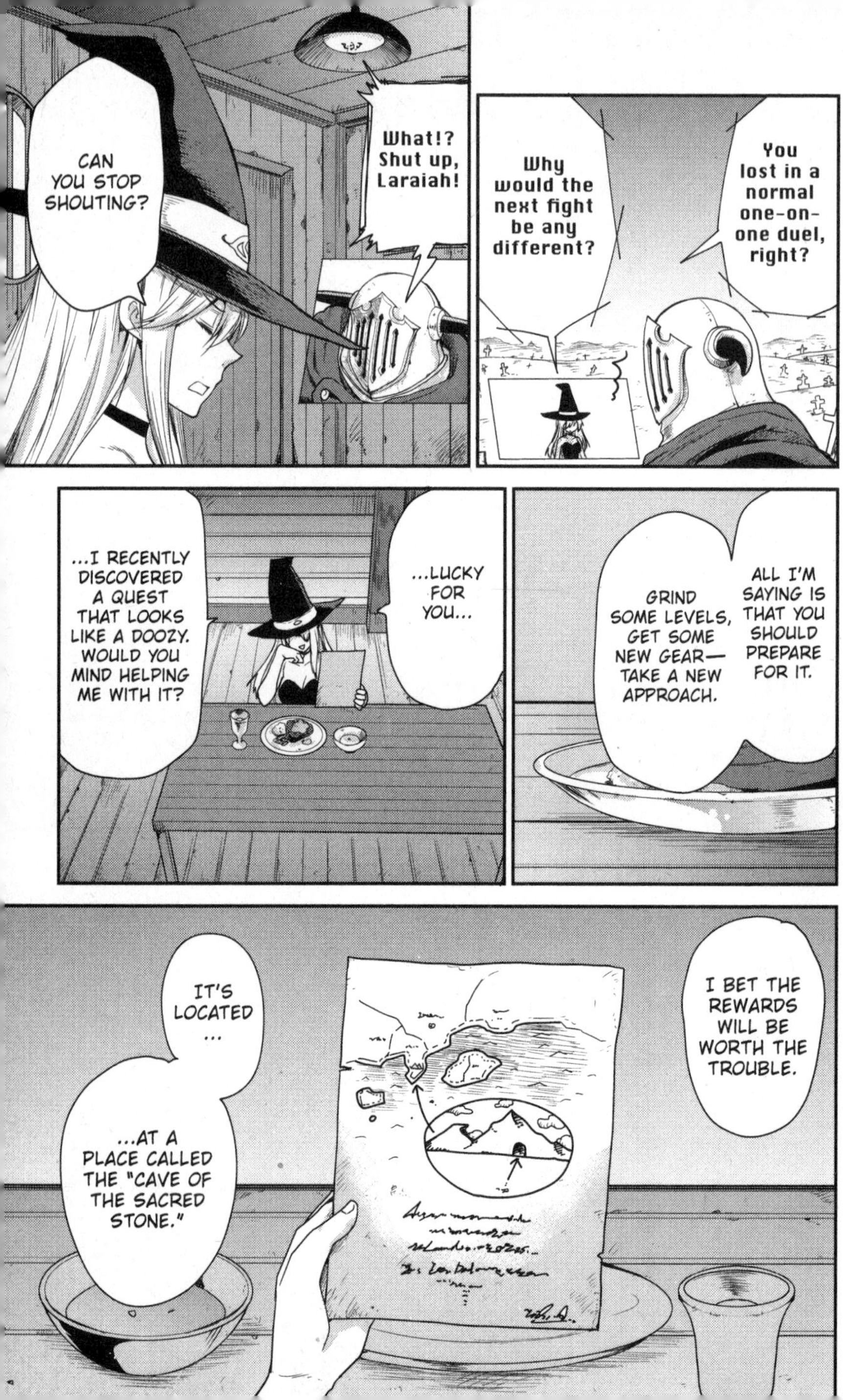
You lost in a normal one-on-one duel, right?
Why would the next fight be any different?
What!? Shut up, Laraiah!
CAN YOU STOP SHOUTING?
ALL I'M SAYING IS THAT YOU SHOULD PREPARE FOR IT.
GRIND SOME LEVELS, GET SOME NEW GEAR—TAKE A NEW APPROACH.
...LUCKY FOR YOU...
...I RECENTLY DISCOVERED A QUEST THAT LOOKS LIKE A DOOZY. WOULD YOU MIND HELPING ME WITH IT?
I BET THE REWARDS WILL BE WORTH THE TROUBLE.
IT'S LOCATED...
...AT A PLACE CALLED THE "CAVE OF THE SACRED STONE."

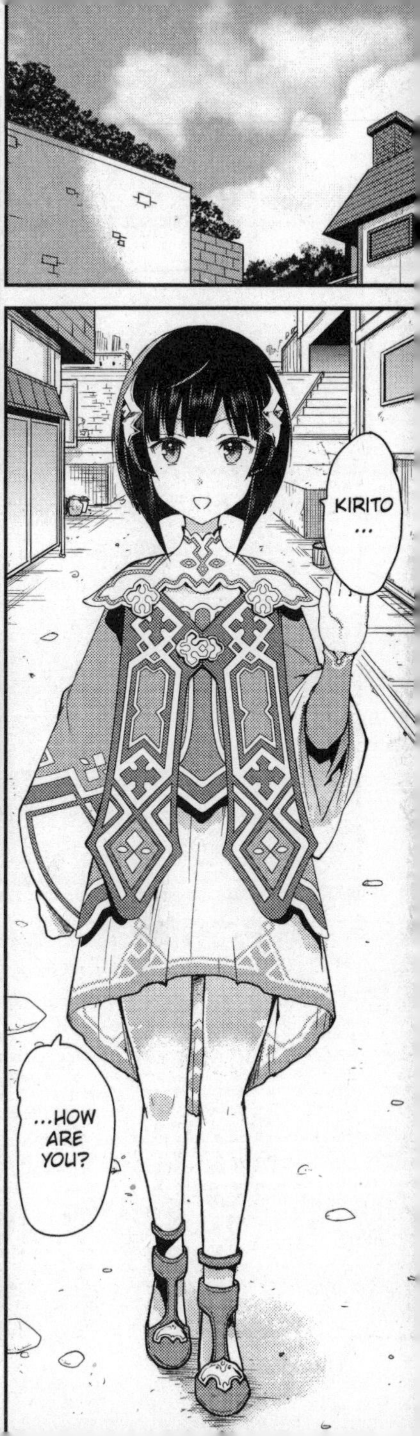
KIRITO ...
...HOW ARE YOU?

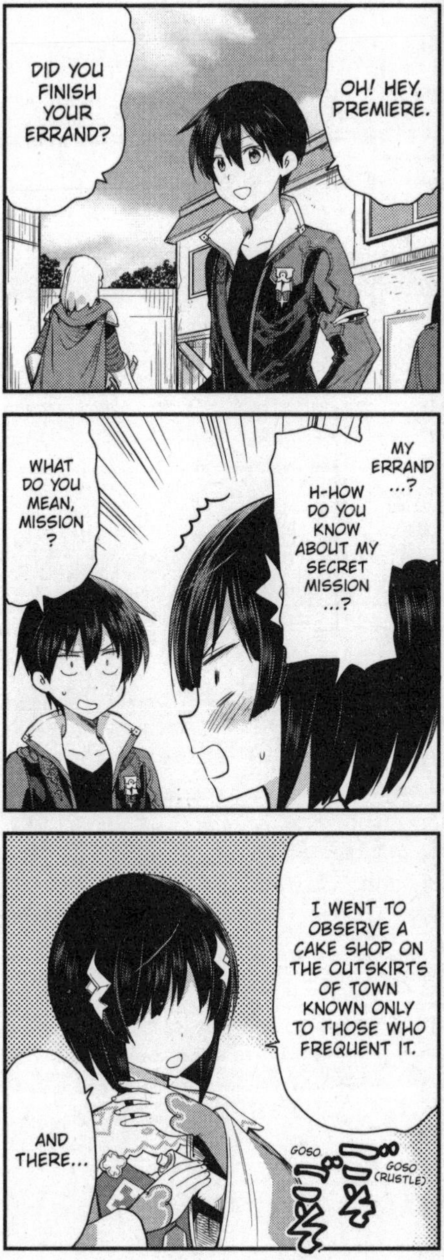
OH! HEY, PREMIERE.
DID YOU FINISH YOUR ERRAND?
MY ERRAND ...?
H-HOW DO YOU KNOW ABOUT MY SECRET MISSION ...?
WHAT DO YOU MEAN, MISSION?
I WENT TO OBSERVE A CAKE SHOP ON THE OUTSKIRTS OF TOWN KNOWN ONLY TO THOSE WHO FREQUENT IT.
AND THERE...
GOSO
GOSO (RUSTLE)

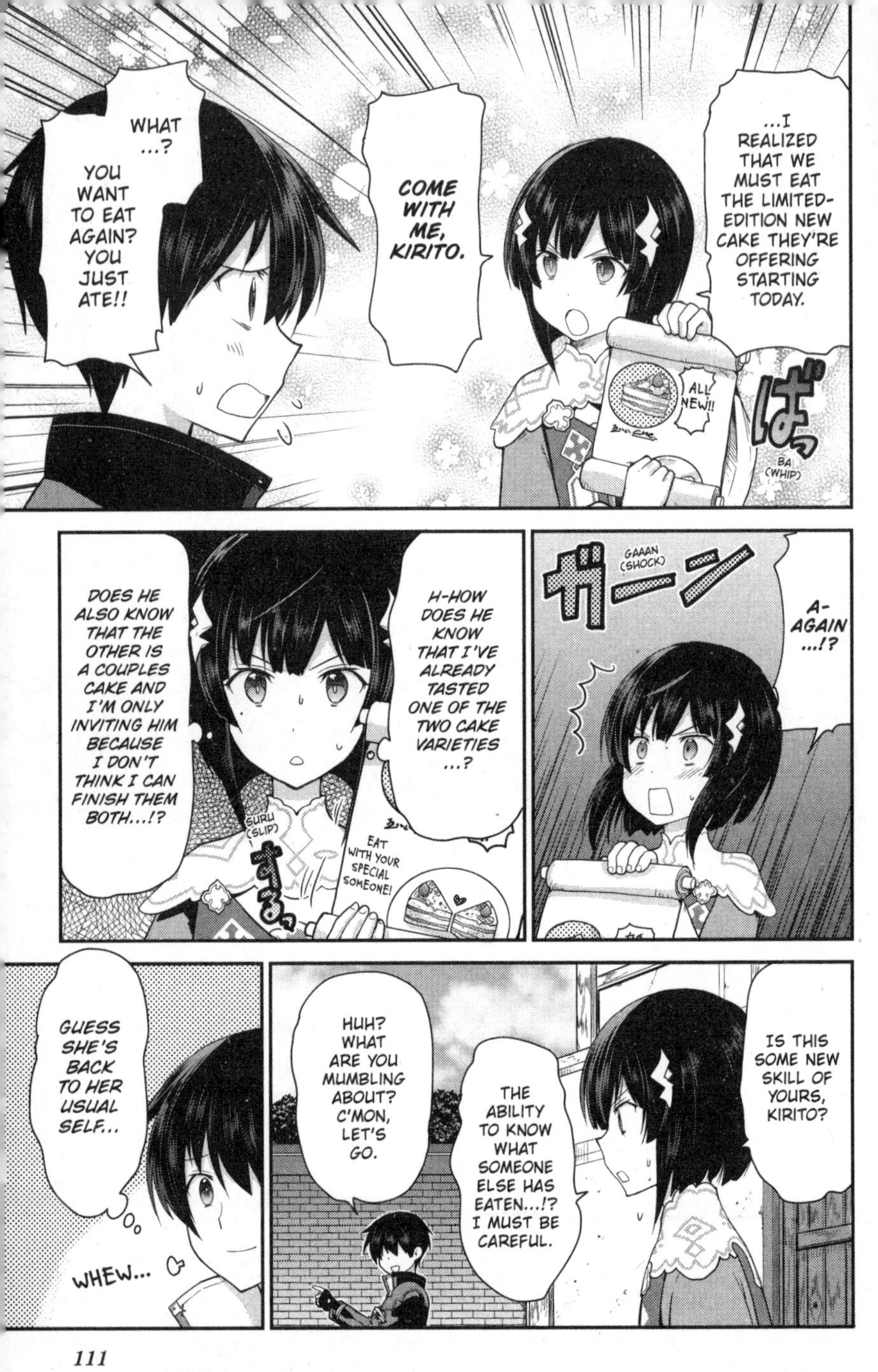
...I REALIZED THAT WE MUST EAT THE LIMITED-EDITION NEW CAKE THEY'RE OFFERING STARTING TODAY.
ALL NEW!!
ばっ
BA (WHIP)
COME WITH ME, KIRITO.
WHAT...? YOU WANT TO EAT AGAIN? YOU JUST ATE!!
ガーン
GAAAN (SHOCK)
A-AGAIN...!?
H-HOW DOES HE KNOW THAT I'VE ALREADY TASTED ONE OF THE TWO CAKE VARIETIES...?
DOES HE ALSO KNOW THAT THE OTHER IS A COUPLES CAKE AND I'M ONLY INVITING HIM BECAUSE I DON'T THINK I CAN FINISH THEM BOTH...!?
EAT WITH YOUR SPECIAL SOMEONE!
する
SURU (SLIP)
IS THIS SOME NEW SKILL OF YOURS, KIRITO?
THE ABILITY TO KNOW WHAT SOMEONE ELSE HAS EATEN...!? I MUST BE CAREFUL.
HUH? WHAT ARE YOU MUMBLING ABOUT? C'MON, LET'S GO.
GUESS SHE'S BACK TO HER USUAL SELF...
WHEW...

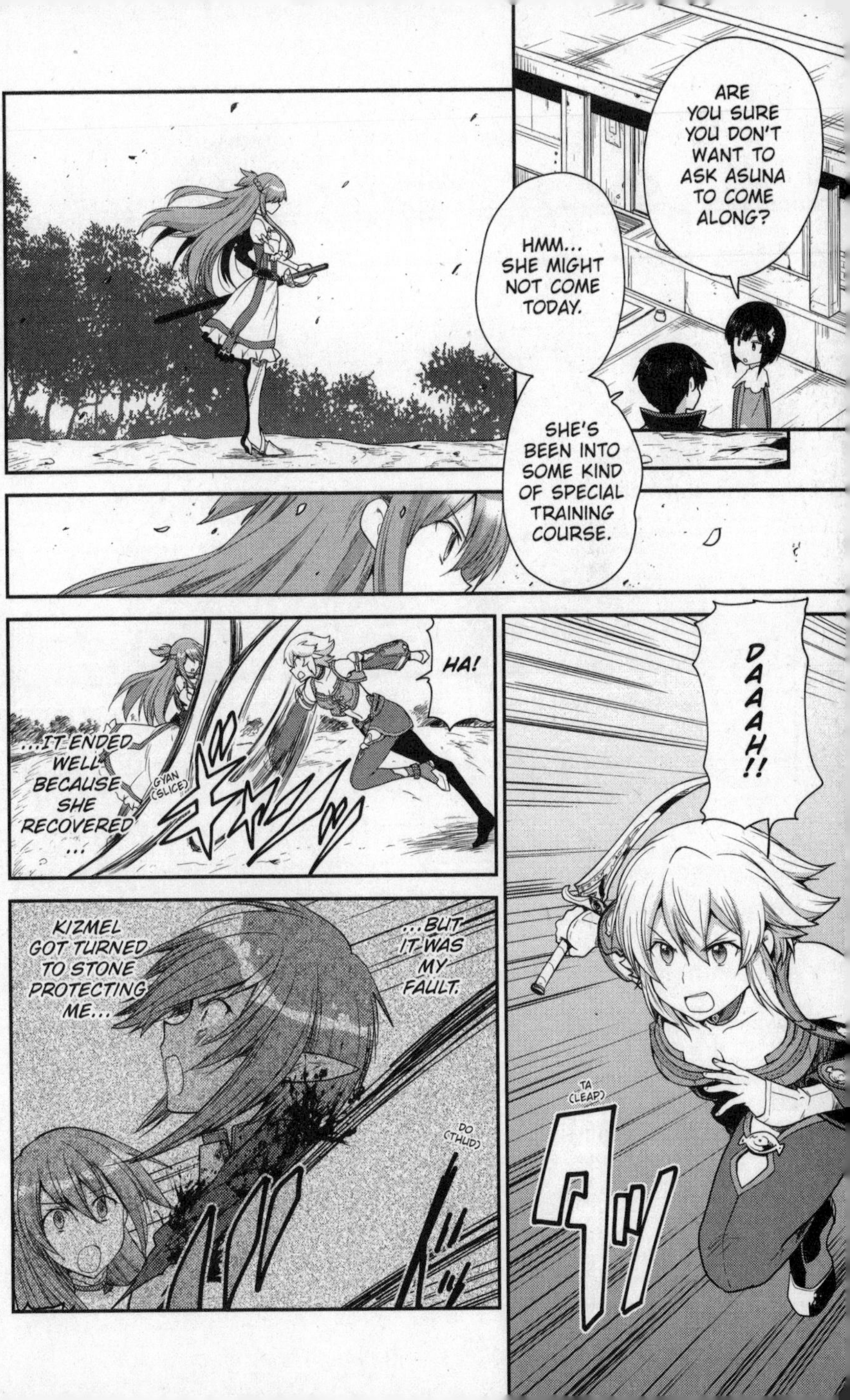
ARE YOU SURE YOU DON'T WANT TO ASK ASUNA TO COME ALONG?
HMM... SHE MIGHT NOT COME TODAY.
SHE'S BEEN INTO SOME KIND OF SPECIAL TRAINING COURSE.
DAAAAH!!
TA (LEAP)
ダッ
HA!
GYAN (SLICE)
...IT ENDED WELL BECAUSE SHE RECOVERED...
...BUT IT WAS MY FAULT.
KIZMEL GOT TURNED TO STONE PROTECTING ME...
DO (THUD)

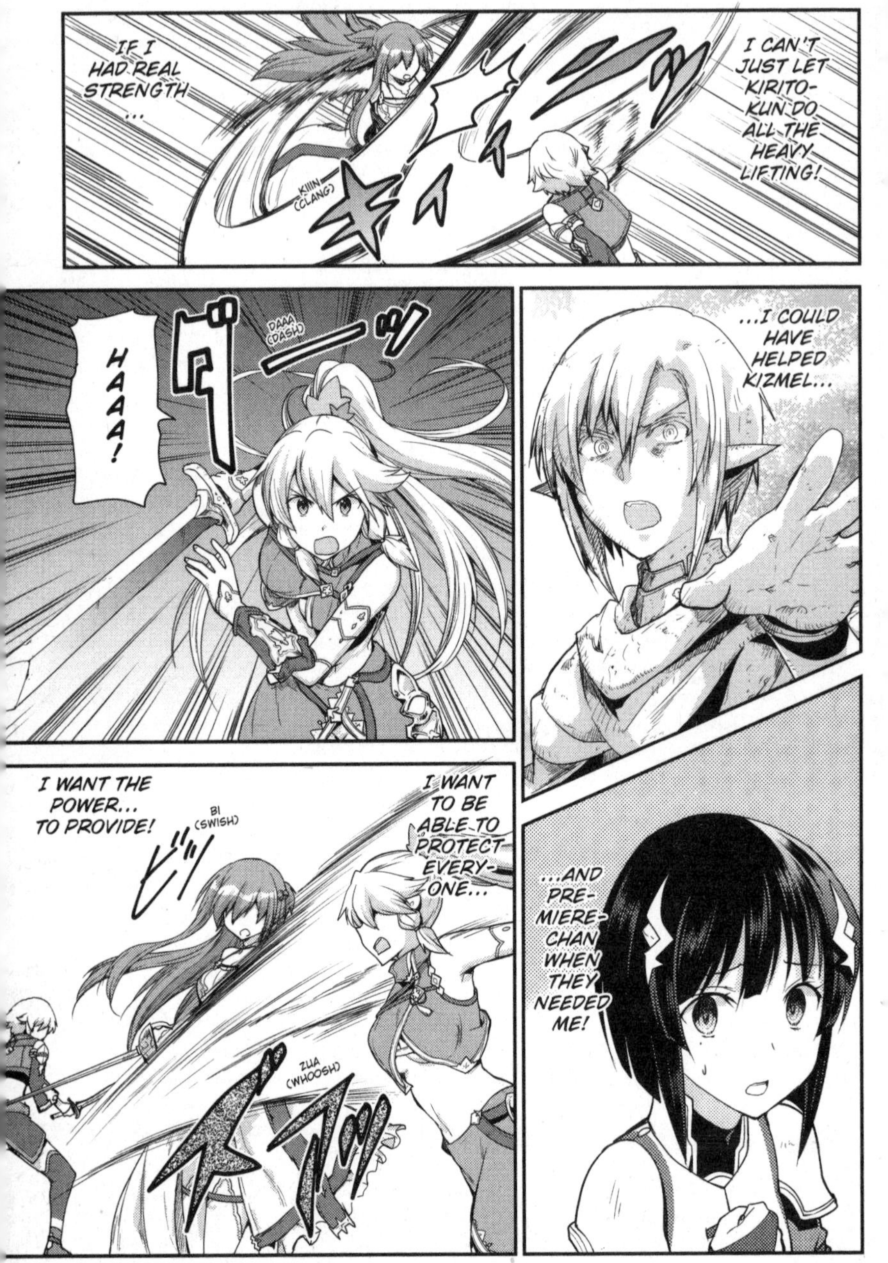
I CAN'T JUST LET KIRITO-KUN DO ALL THE HEAVY LIFTING!
IF I HAD REAL STRENGTH...
KIIIN (CLANG)
...I COULD HAVE HELPED KIZMEL...
DAAA (DASH)
HAAAA!
...AND PREMIERE-CHAN WHEN THEY NEEDED ME!
I WANT TO BE ABLE TO PROTECT EVERYONE...
I WANT THE POWER... TO PROVIDE!
BI (SWISH)
ZUA (WHOOSH)

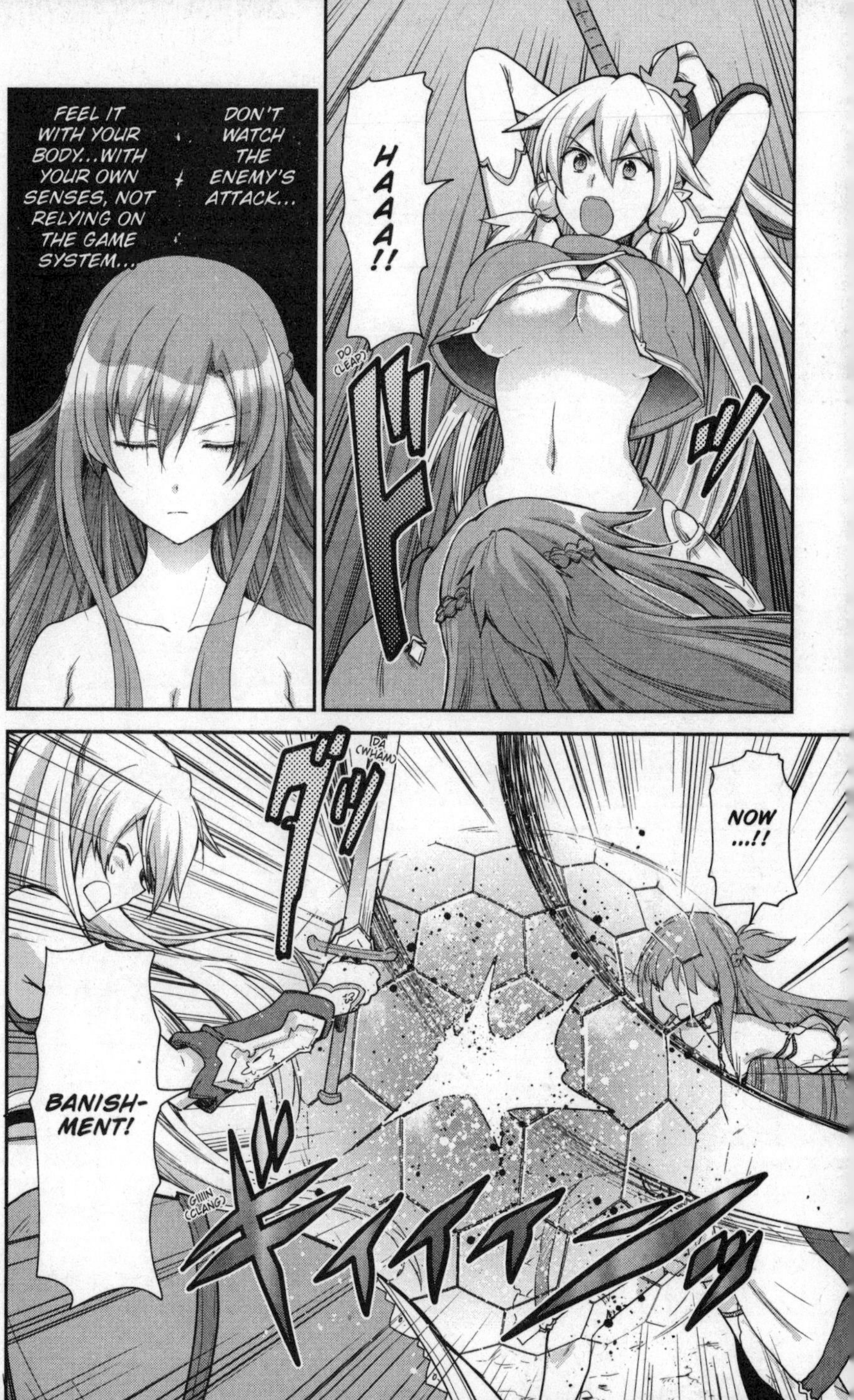
HAAAA!!
DO (LEAP)
DON'T WATCH THE ENEMY'S ATTACK...
FEEL IT WITH YOUR BODY...WITH YOUR OWN SENSES, NOT RELYING ON THE GAME SYSTEM...
NOW ...!!
DA (WHAM)
BANISH-MENT!
GIIIN (CLANG)

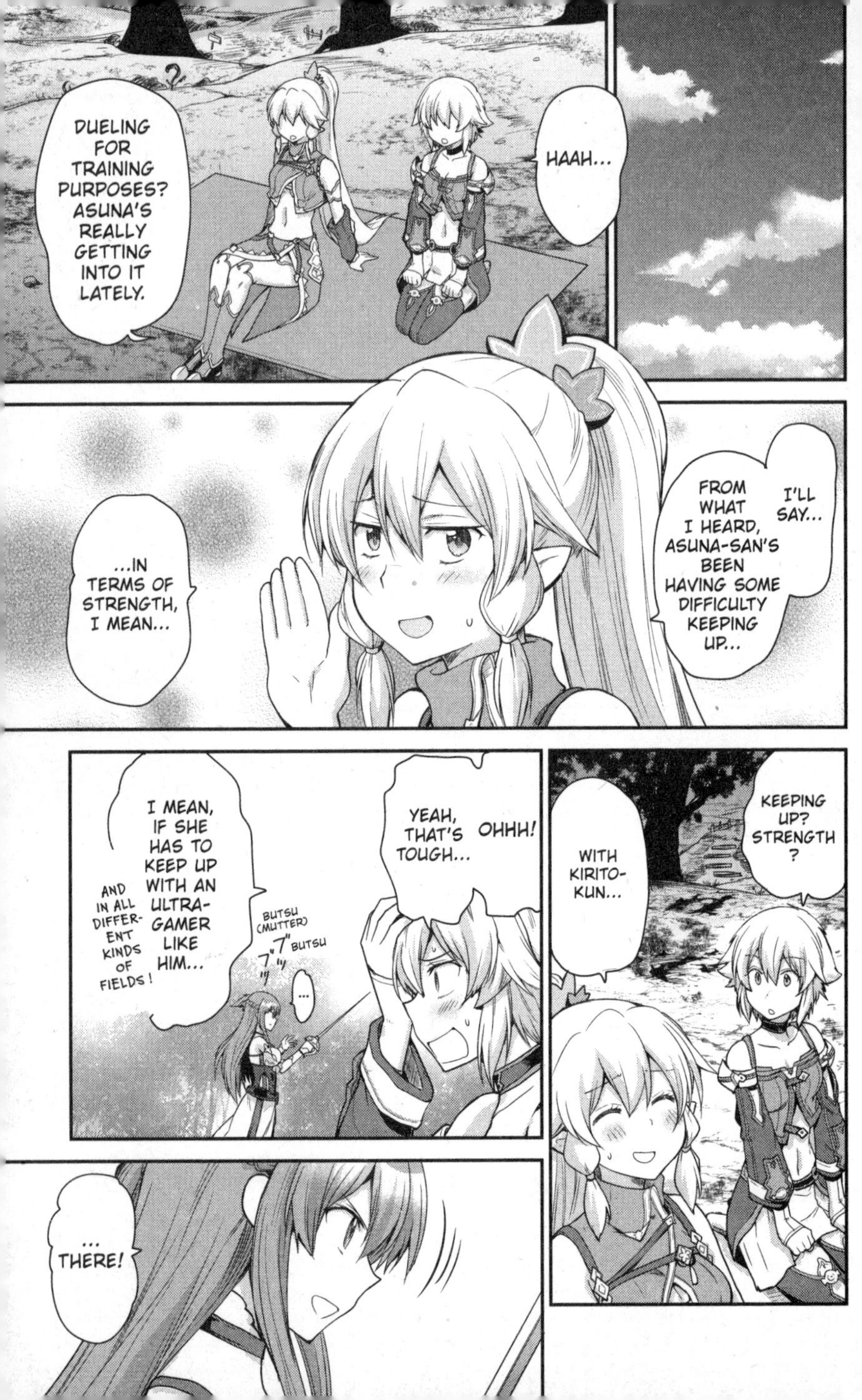
HAAH...
DUELING FOR TRAINING PURPOSES? ASUNA'S REALLY GETTING INTO IT LATELY.
I'LL SAY...
FROM WHAT I HEARD, ASUNA-SAN'S BEEN HAVING SOME DIFFICULTY KEEPING UP...
...IN TERMS OF STRENGTH, I MEAN...
KEEPING UP? STRENGTH?
WITH KIRITO-KUN...
OHHH!
YEAH, THAT'S TOUGH...
I MEAN, IF SHE HAS TO KEEP UP WITH AN ULTRA-GAMER LIKE HIM...
AND IN ALL DIFFERENT KINDS OF FIELDS!
BUTSU (MUTTER) BUTSU
...
...THERE!

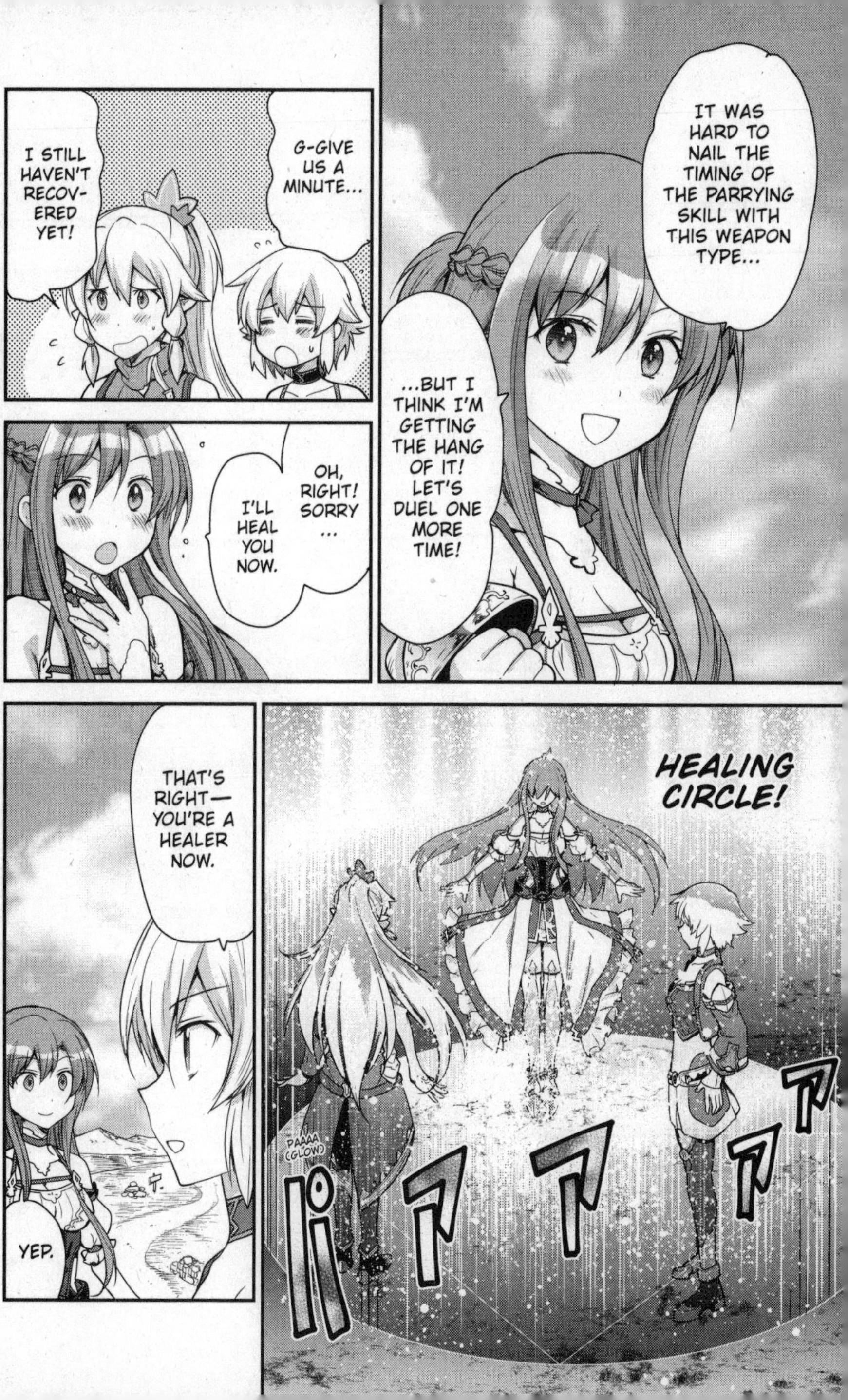
IT WAS HARD TO NAIL THE TIMING OF THE PARRYING SKILL WITH THIS WEAPON TYPE...
...BUT I THINK I'M GETTING THE HANG OF IT! LET'S DUEL ONE MORE TIME!
G-GIVE US A MINUTE...
I STILL HAVEN'T RECOV-ERED YET!
OH, RIGHT! SORRY...
I'LL HEAL YOU NOW.
HEALING CIRCLE!
パアアアア
PAAAA (GLOW)
THAT'S RIGHT—YOU'RE A HEALER NOW.
YEP.

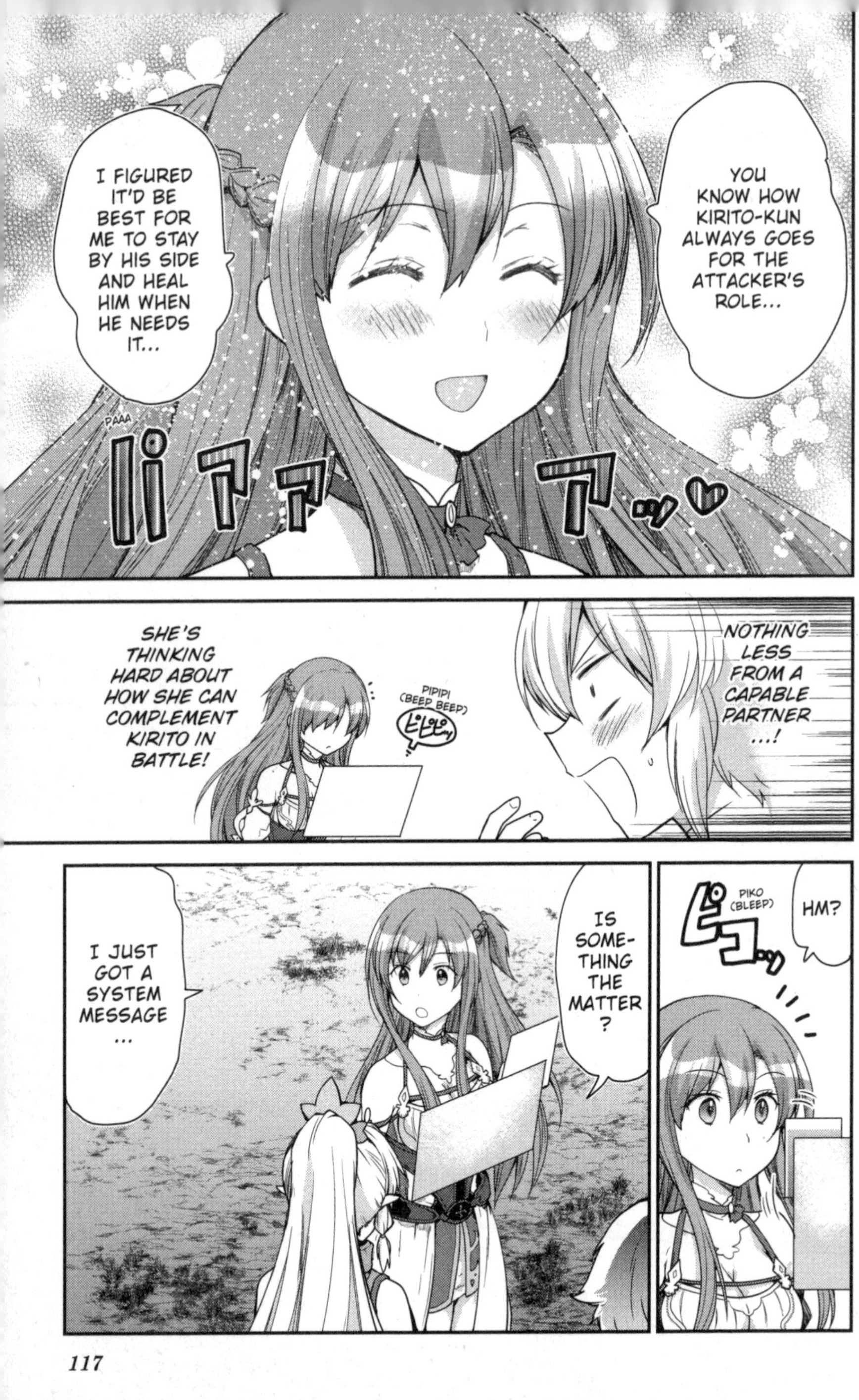
YOU KNOW HOW KIRITO-KUN ALWAYS GOES FOR THE ATTACKER'S ROLE...
I FIGURED IT'D BE BEST FOR ME TO STAY BY HIS SIDE AND HEAL HIM WHEN HE NEEDS IT...
PAAA
パァァァッ
NOTHING LESS FROM A CAPABLE PARTNER ...!
PIPIPI (BEEP BEEP)
SHE'S THINKING HARD ABOUT HOW SHE CAN COMPLEMENT KIRITO IN BATTLE!
PIKO (BLEEP)
HM?
IS SOME-THING THE MATTER?
I JUST GOT A SYSTEM MESSAGE ...

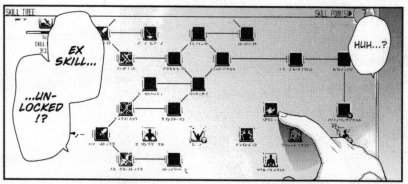

SKILL TREE

SKILL POINTS 7

EX SKILL...

...UN-LOCKED!?

HUH...?

YES. IT SAYS...

YOU MEAN... LIKE KIRITO'S DUAL BLADES SKILL!?

AN EX SKILL...?

"RADIANT HEALING TOUCH"!

...EX SKILL...

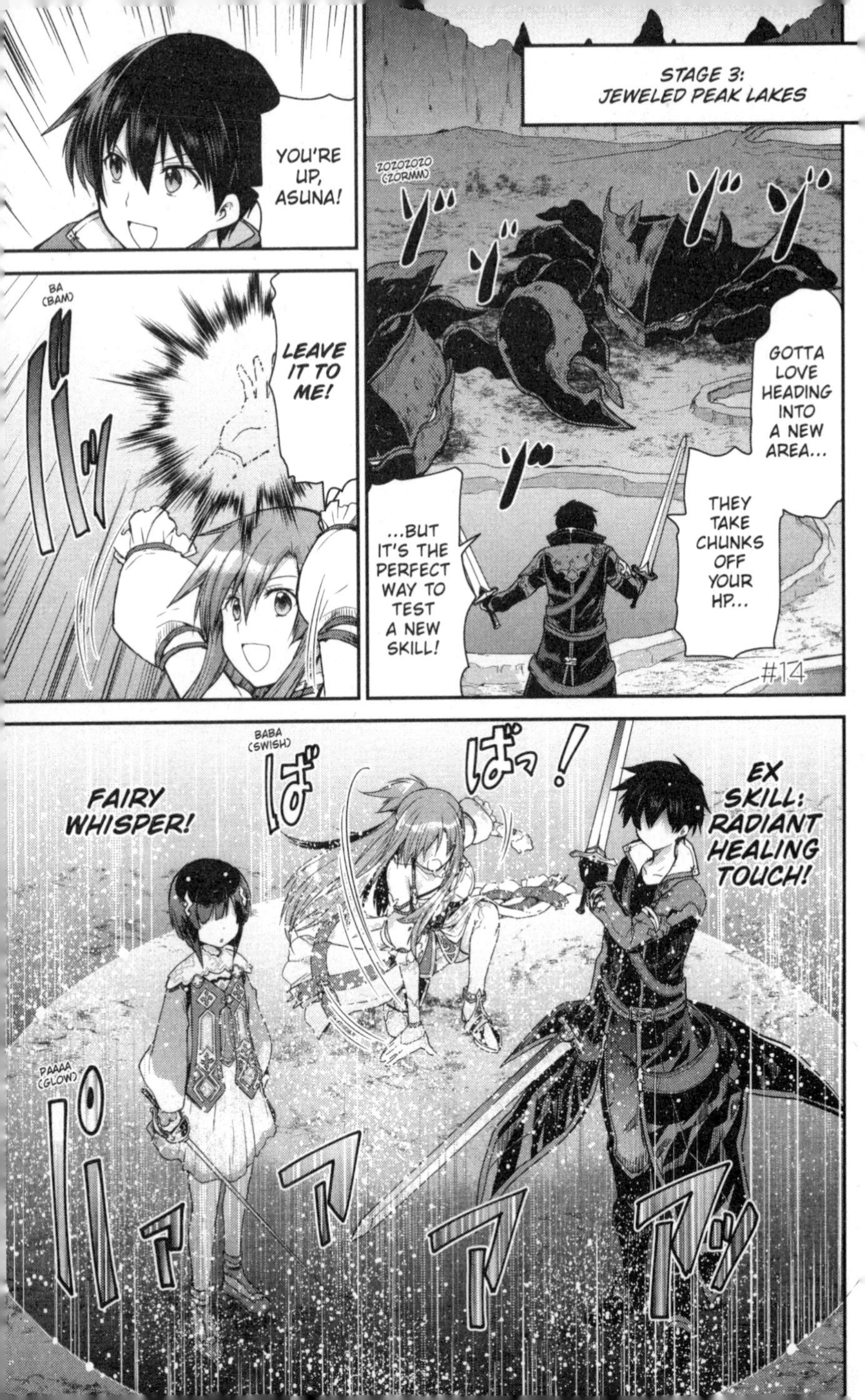
STAGE 3: JEWELED PEAK LAKES
ZOZOZOZO (ZORMM)
GOTTA LOVE HEADING INTO A NEW AREA...
THEY TAKE CHUNKS OFF YOUR HP...
...BUT IT'S THE PERFECT WAY TO TEST A NEW SKILL!
#14
YOU'RE UP, ASUNA!
BA (BAM)
LEAVE IT TO ME!
EX SKILL: RADIANT HEALING TOUCH!
BABA (SWISH)
FAIRY WHISPER!
PAAAA (GLOW)

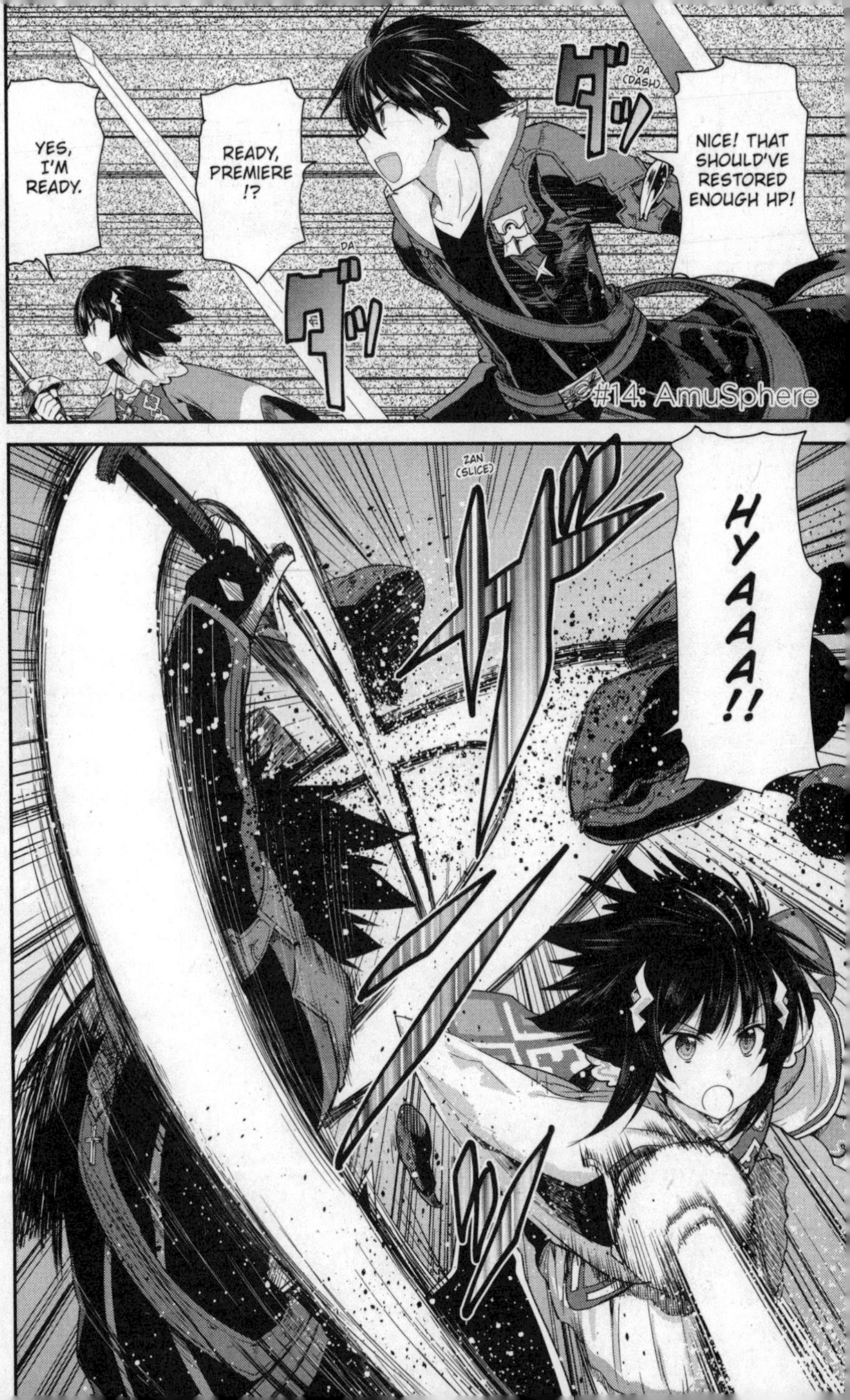

NICE! THAT SHOULD'VE RESTORED ENOUGH HP!
DA (DASH)
READY, PREMIERE !?
DA
YES, I'M READY.
#14: AmuSphere
HYAAAA!!
ZAN (SLICE)

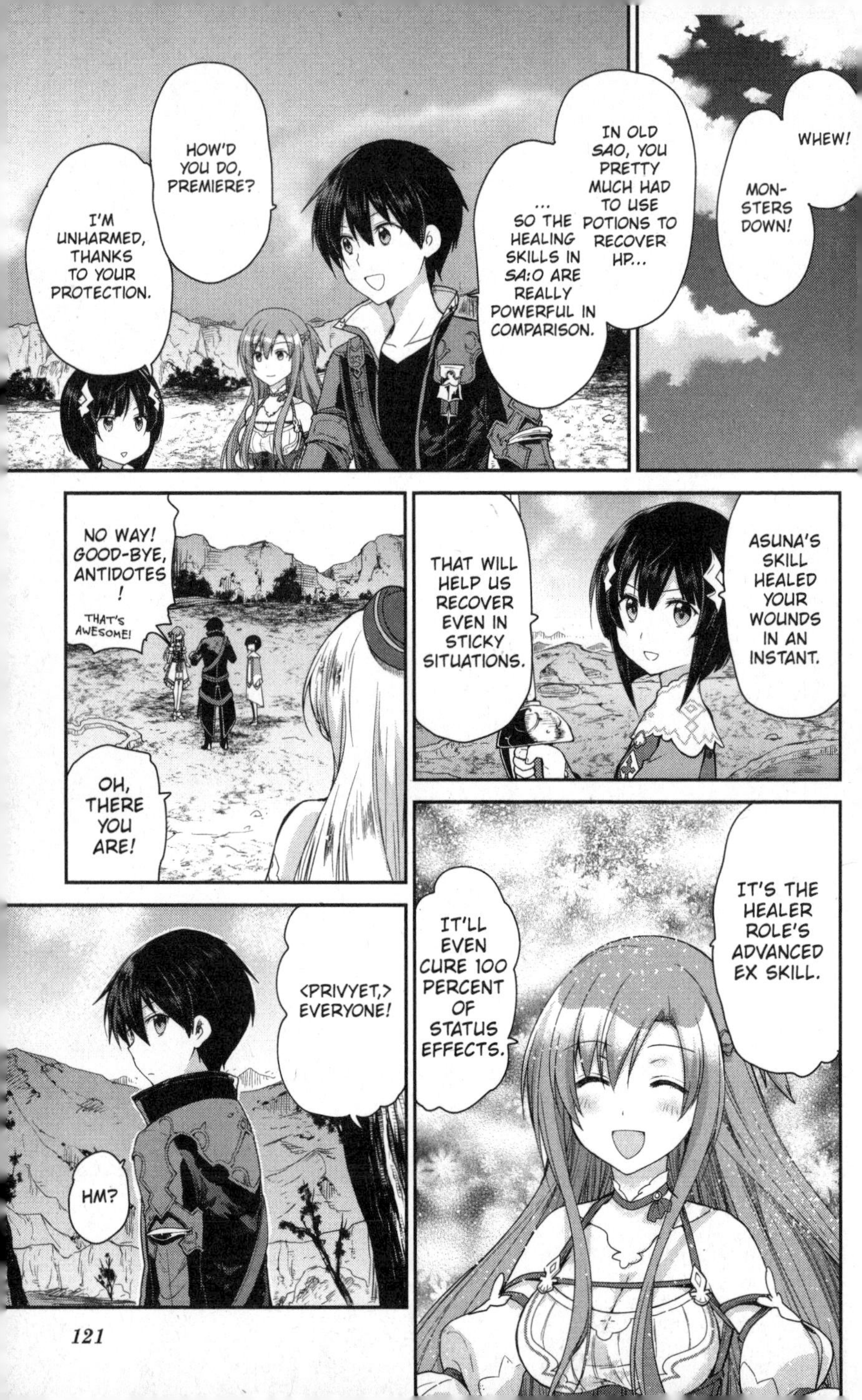
WHEW!
MONSTERS DOWN!
IN OLD SAO, YOU PRETTY MUCH HAD TO USE POTIONS TO RECOVER HP...
... SO THE HEALING SKILLS IN SA:O ARE REALLY POWERFUL IN COMPARISON.
HOW'D YOU DO, PREMIERE?
I'M UNHARMED, THANKS TO YOUR PROTECTION.
ASUNA'S SKILL HEALED YOUR WOUNDS IN AN INSTANT.
THAT WILL HELP US RECOVER EVEN IN STICKY SITUATIONS.
IT'S THE HEALER ROLE'S ADVANCED EX SKILL.
IT'LL EVEN CURE 100 PERCENT OF STATUS EFFECTS.
NO WAY! GOOD-BYE, ANTIDOTES!
THAT'S AWESOME!
OH, THERE YOU ARE!
<PRIVYET,> EVERYONE!
HM?

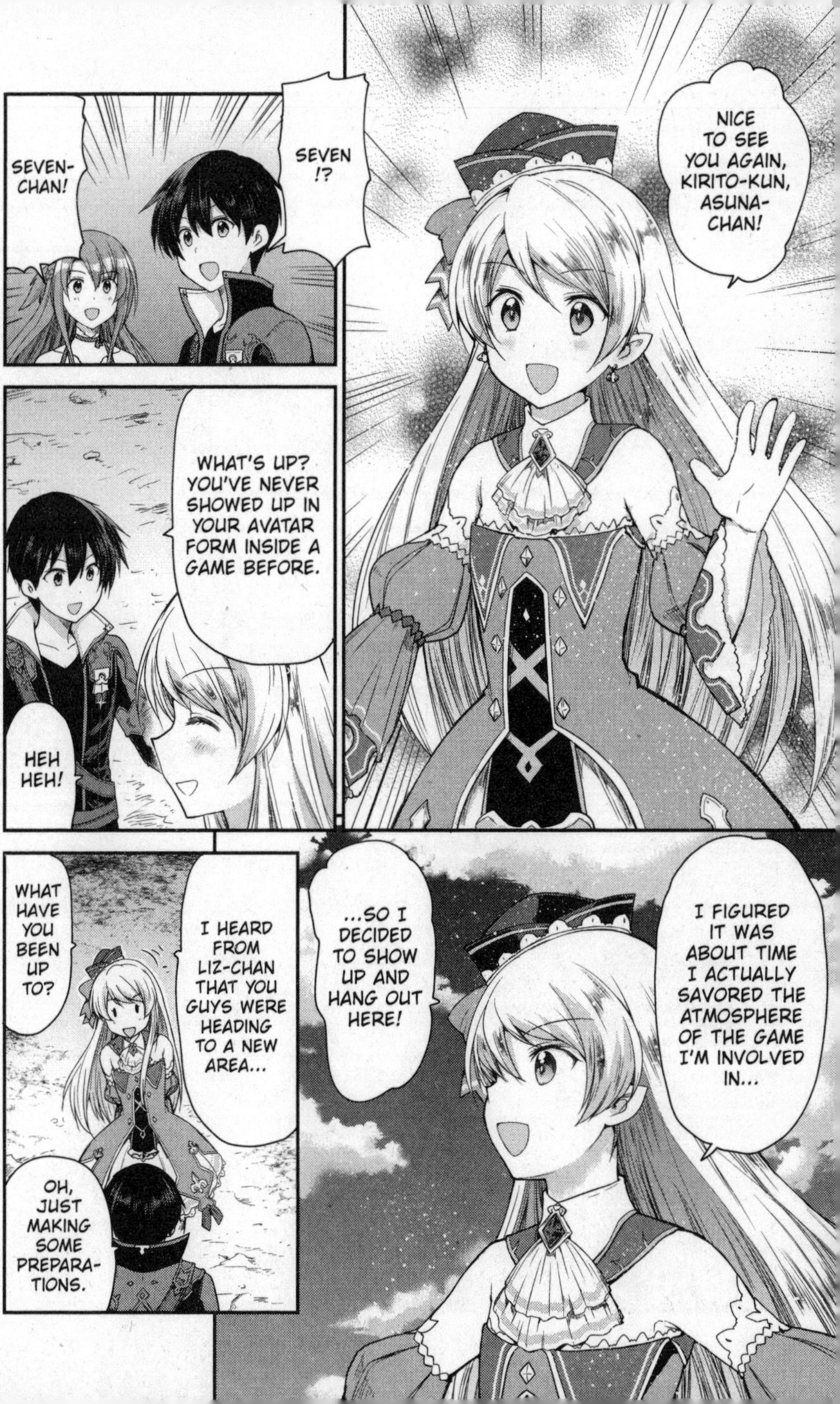
NICE TO SEE YOU AGAIN, KIRITO-KUN, ASUNA-CHAN!
SEVEN !?
SEVEN-CHAN!
WHAT'S UP? YOU'VE NEVER SHOWED UP IN YOUR AVATAR FORM INSIDE A GAME BEFORE.
HEH HEH!
I FIGURED IT WAS ABOUT TIME I ACTUALLY SAVORED THE ATMOSPHERE OF THE GAME I'M INVOLVED IN...
...SO I DECIDED TO SHOW UP AND HANG OUT HERE!
I HEARD FROM LIZ-CHAN THAT YOU GUYS WERE HEADING TO A NEW AREA...
WHAT HAVE YOU BEEN UP TO?
OH, JUST MAKING SOME PREPARATIONS.

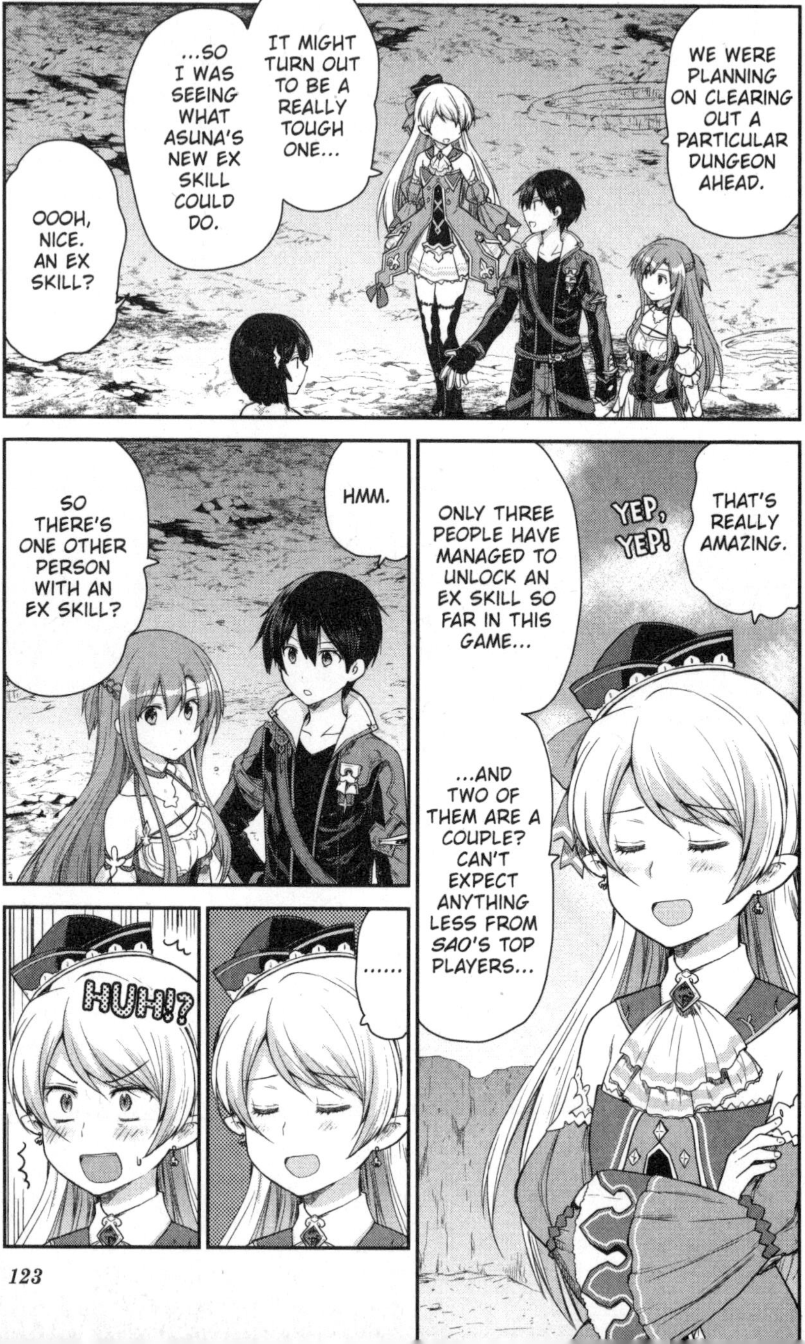
WE WERE PLANNING ON CLEARING OUT A PARTICULAR DUNGEON AHEAD.
IT MIGHT TURN OUT TO BE A REALLY TOUGH ONE...
...SO I WAS SEEING WHAT ASUNA'S NEW EX SKILL COULD DO.
OOOH, NICE. AN EX SKILL?
THAT'S REALLY AMAZING.
YEP, YEP!
ONLY THREE PEOPLE HAVE MANAGED TO UNLOCK AN EX SKILL SO FAR IN THIS GAME...
...AND TWO OF THEM ARE A COUPLE? CAN'T EXPECT ANYTHING LESS FROM SAO'S TOP PLAYERS...
HMM.
SO THERE'S ONE OTHER PERSON WITH AN EX SKILL?
......
HUH!?

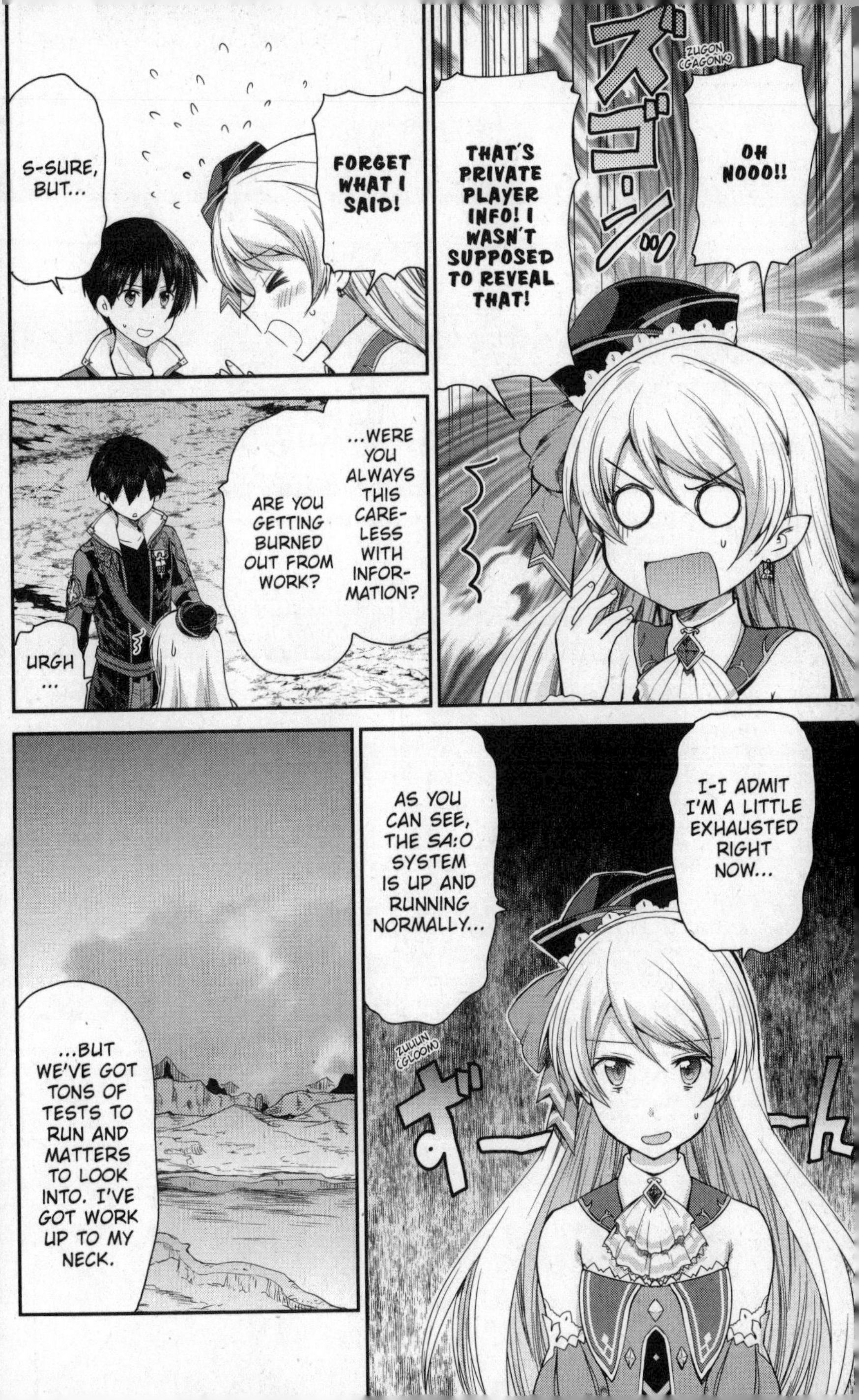
ZUGON (GAGONK)
OH NOOO!!
THAT'S PRIVATE PLAYER INFO! I WASN'T SUPPOSED TO REVEAL THAT!
FORGET WHAT I SAID!
S-SURE, BUT...
...WERE YOU ALWAYS THIS CARELESS WITH INFORMATION?
ARE YOU GETTING BURNED OUT FROM WORK?
URGH...
I-I ADMIT I'M A LITTLE EXHAUSTED RIGHT NOW...
AS YOU CAN SEE, THE SA:O SYSTEM IS UP AND RUNNING NORMALLY...
ZUUUN (GLOOM)
...BUT WE'VE GOT TONS OF TESTS TO RUN AND MATTERS TO LOOK INTO. I'VE GOT WORK UP TO MY NECK.

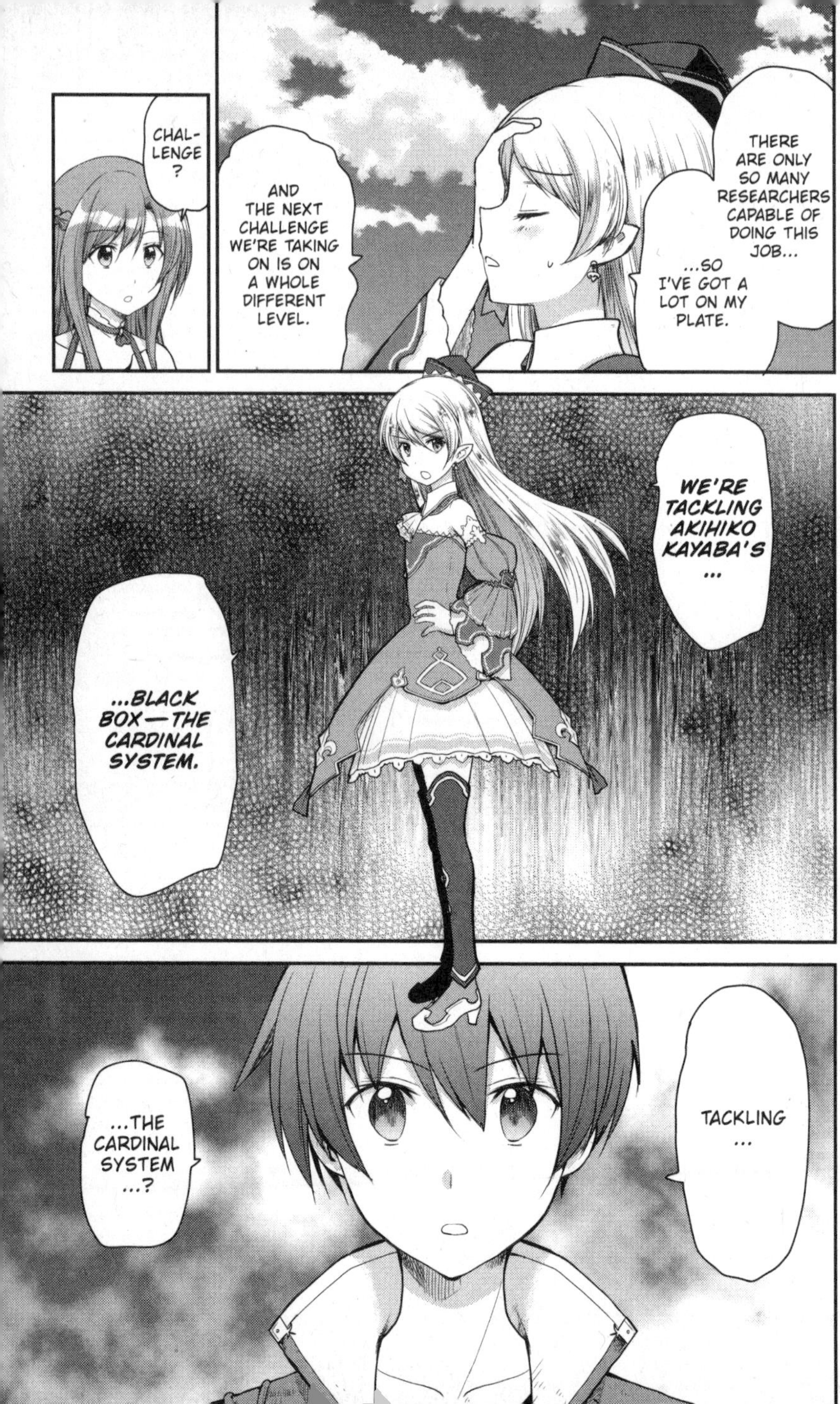
THERE ARE ONLY SO MANY RESEARCHERS CAPABLE OF DOING THIS JOB...
...SO I'VE GOT A LOT ON MY PLATE.
AND THE NEXT CHALLENGE WE'RE TAKING ON IS ON A WHOLE DIFFERENT LEVEL.
CHAL-LENGE?
WE'RE TACKLING AKIHIKO KAYABA'S...
...BLACK BOX—THE CARDINAL SYSTEM.
TACKLING...
...THE CARDINAL SYSTEM...?

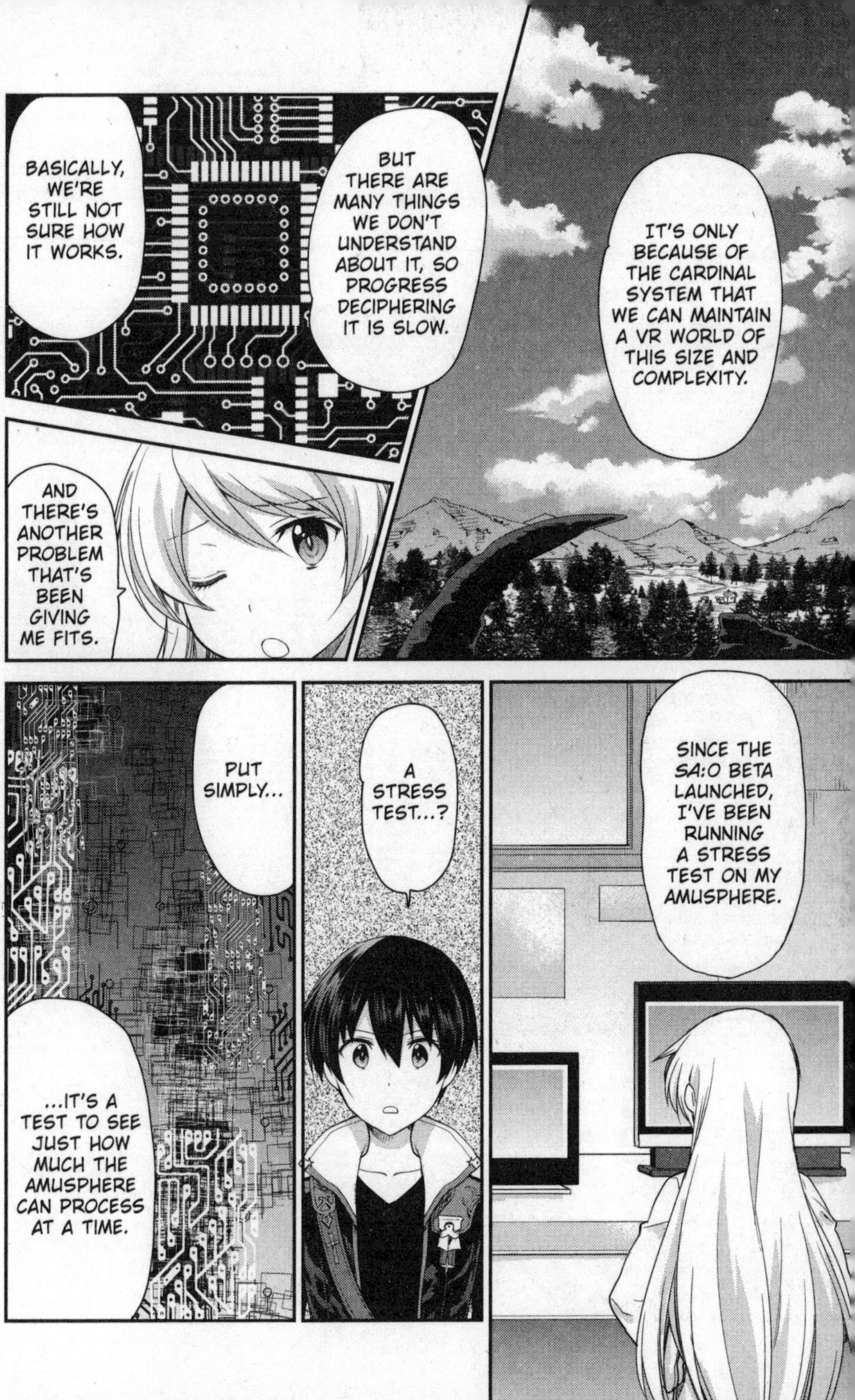
IT'S ONLY BECAUSE OF THE CARDINAL SYSTEM THAT WE CAN MAINTAIN A VR WORLD OF THIS SIZE AND COMPLEXITY.
BUT THERE ARE MANY THINGS WE DON'T UNDERSTAND ABOUT IT, SO PROGRESS DECIPHERING IT IS SLOW.
BASICALLY, WE'RE STILL NOT SURE HOW IT WORKS.
AND THERE'S ANOTHER PROBLEM THAT'S BEEN GIVING ME FITS.
SINCE THE SA:O BETA LAUNCHED, I'VE BEEN RUNNING A STRESS TEST ON MY AMUSPHERE.
A STRESS TEST...?
PUT SIMPLY...
...IT'S A TEST TO SEE JUST HOW MUCH THE AMUSPHERE CAN PROCESS AT A TIME.

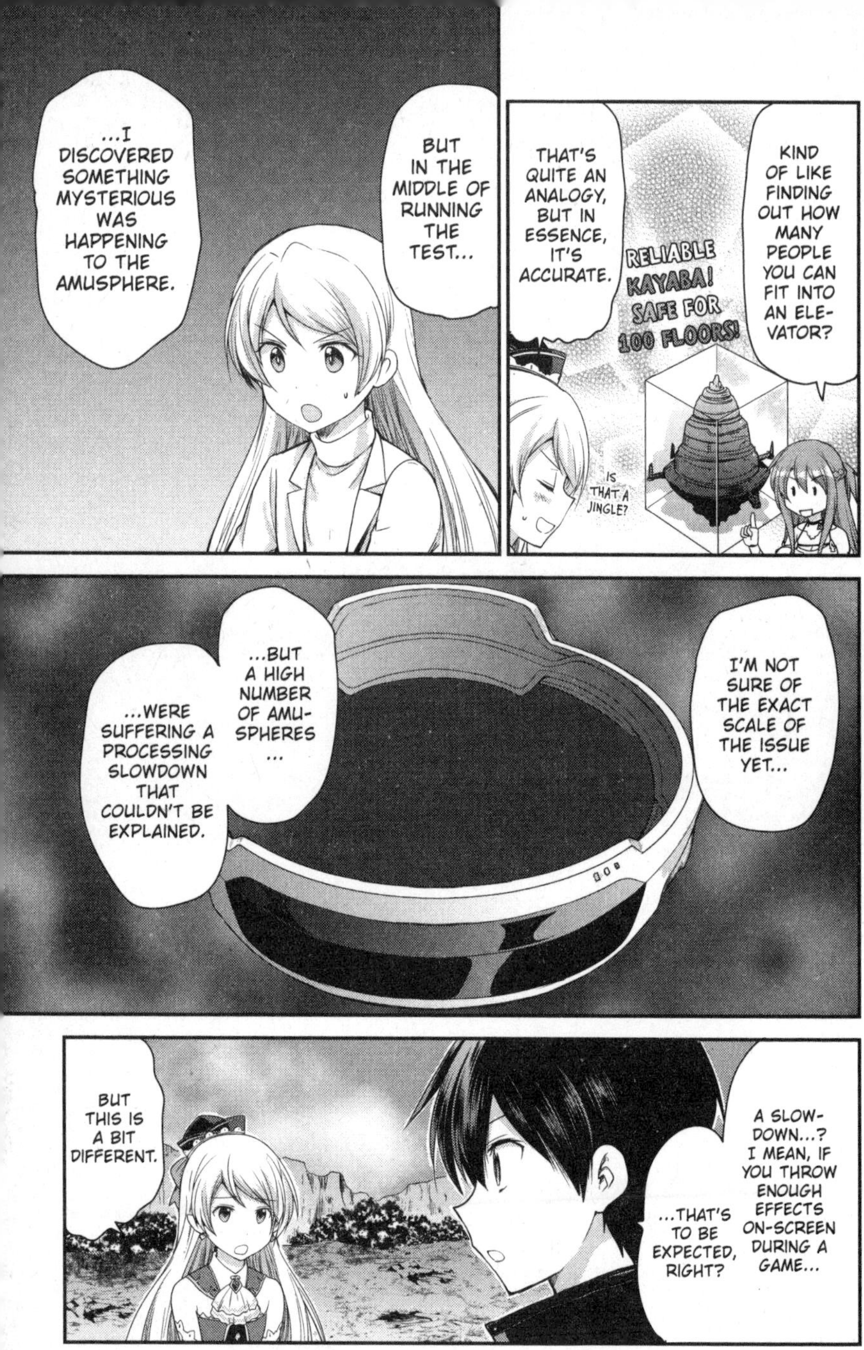
KIND OF LIKE FINDING OUT HOW MANY PEOPLE YOU CAN FIT INTO AN ELE-VATOR?
THAT'S QUITE AN ANALOGY, BUT IN ESSENCE, IT'S ACCURATE.
RELIABLE KAYABA! SAFE FOR 100 FLOORS!
IS THAT A JINGLE?
BUT IN THE MIDDLE OF RUNNING THE TEST...
...I DISCOVERED SOMETHING MYSTERIOUS WAS HAPPENING TO THE AMUSPHERE.
I'M NOT SURE OF THE EXACT SCALE OF THE ISSUE YET...
...BUT A HIGH NUMBER OF AMU-SPHERES...
...WERE SUFFERING A PROCESSING SLOWDOWN THAT COULDN'T BE EXPLAINED.
A SLOW-DOWN...? I MEAN, IF YOU THROW ENOUGH EFFECTS ON-SCREEN DURING A GAME...
...THAT'S TO BE EXPECTED, RIGHT?
BUT THIS IS A BIT DIFFERENT.

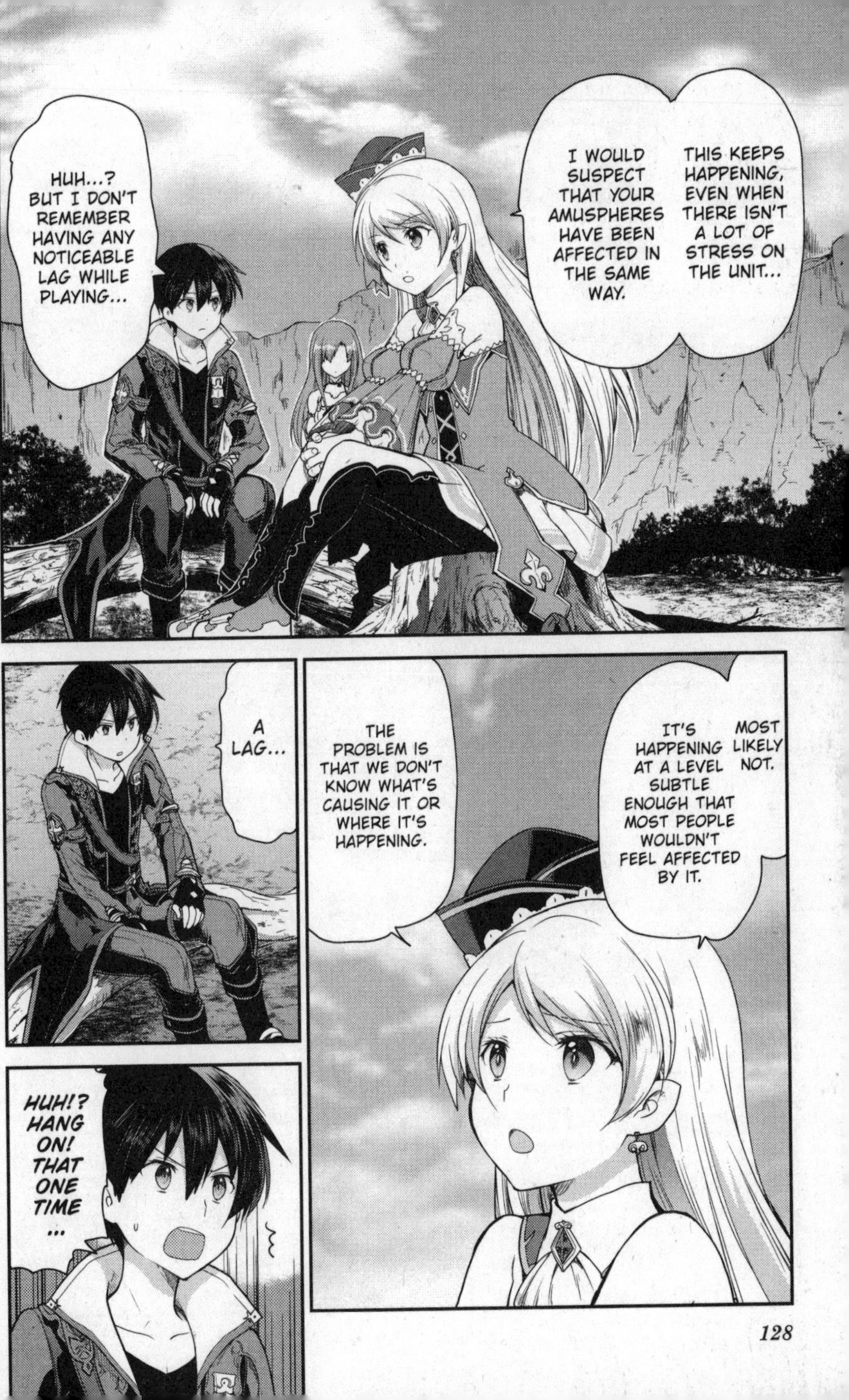
THIS KEEPS HAPPENING, EVEN WHEN THERE ISN'T A LOT OF STRESS ON THE UNIT...
I WOULD SUSPECT THAT YOUR AMUSPHERES HAVE BEEN AFFECTED IN THE SAME WAY.
HUH...? BUT I DON'T REMEMBER HAVING ANY NOTICEABLE LAG WHILE PLAYING...
MOST LIKELY NOT.
IT'S HAPPENING AT A LEVEL SUBTLE ENOUGH THAT MOST PEOPLE WOULDN'T FEEL AFFECTED BY IT.
THE PROBLEM IS THAT WE DON'T KNOW WHAT'S CAUSING IT OR WHERE IT'S HAPPENING.
A LAG...
HUH!? HANG ON! THAT ONE TIME ...

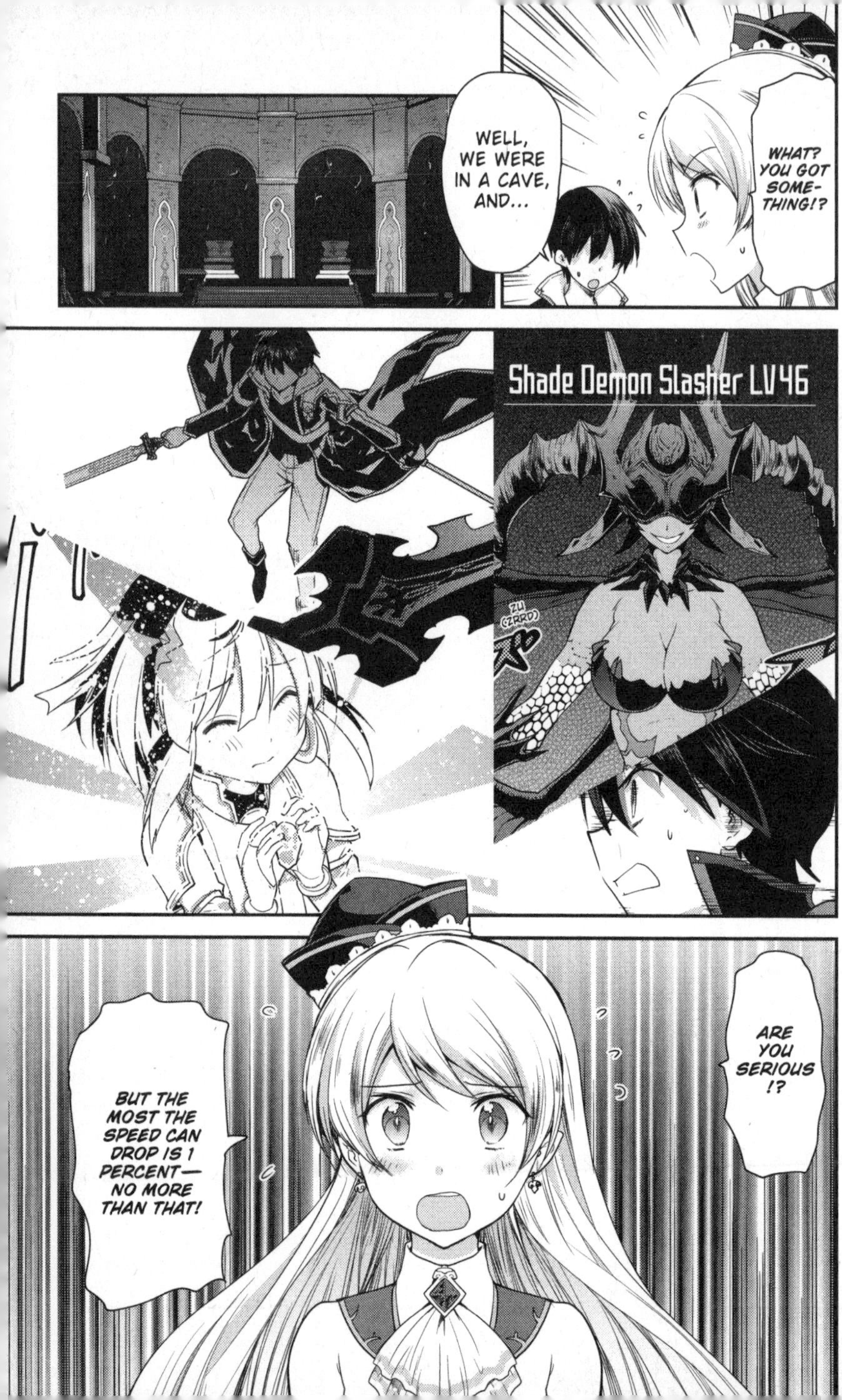
WHAT? YOU GOT SOME-THING!?
WELL, WE WERE IN A CAVE, AND...
Shade Demon Slasher LV46
ZU (ZRRD)
ARE YOU SERIOUS!?
BUT THE MOST THE SPEED CAN DROP IS 1 PERCENT— NO MORE THAN THAT!

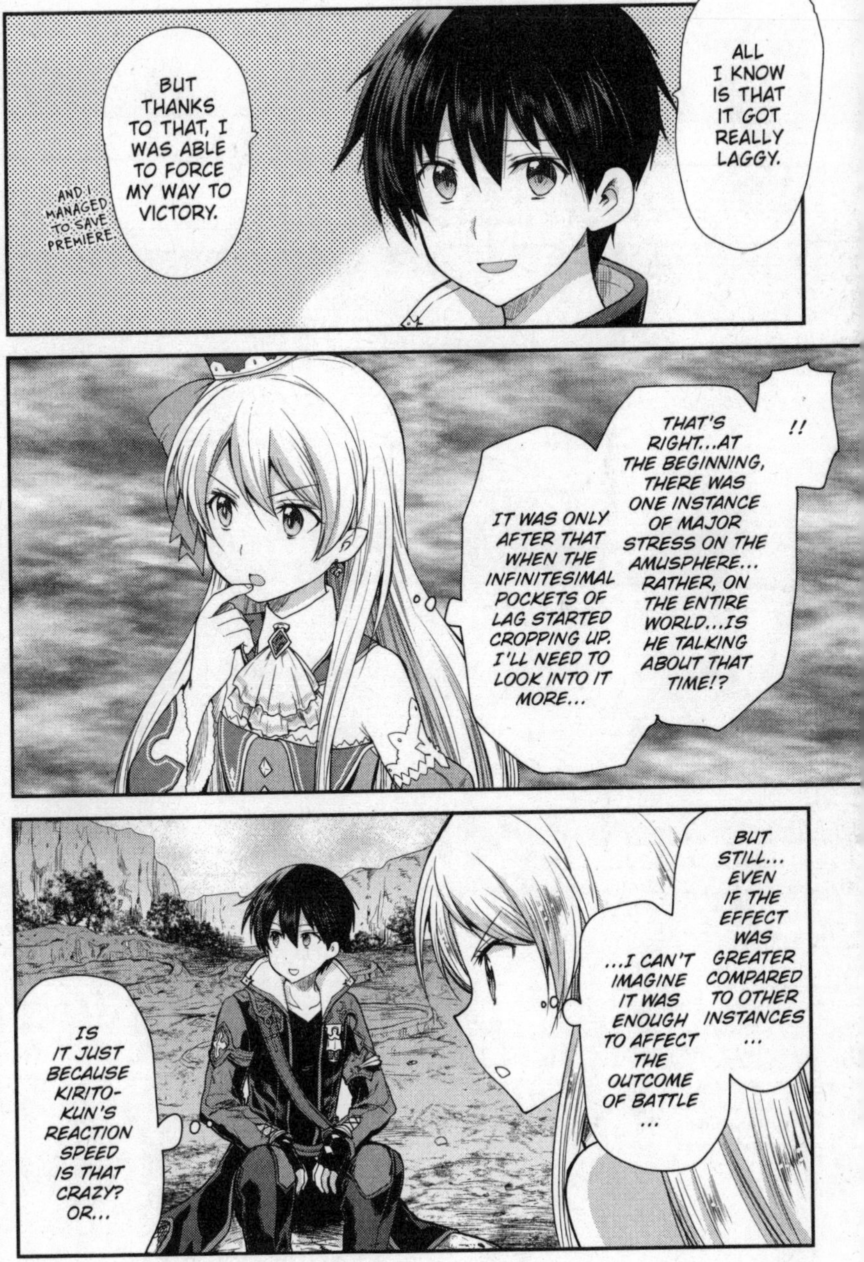
ALL I KNOW IS THAT IT GOT REALLY LAGGY.
BUT THANKS TO THAT, I WAS ABLE TO FORCE MY WAY TO VICTORY.
AND I MANAGED TO SAVE PREMIERE.
!!
THAT'S RIGHT...AT THE BEGINNING, THERE WAS ONE INSTANCE OF MAJOR STRESS ON THE AMUSPHERE... RATHER, ON THE ENTIRE WORLD...IS HE TALKING ABOUT THAT TIME!?
IT WAS ONLY AFTER THAT WHEN THE INFINITESIMAL POCKETS OF LAG STARTED CROPPING UP. I'LL NEED TO LOOK INTO IT MORE...
BUT STILL... EVEN IF THE EFFECT WAS GREATER COMPARED TO OTHER INSTANCES...
...I CAN'T IMAGINE IT WAS ENOUGH TO AFFECT THE OUTCOME OF BATTLE...
IS IT JUST BECAUSE KIRITO-KUN'S REACTION SPEED IS THAT CRAZY? OR...

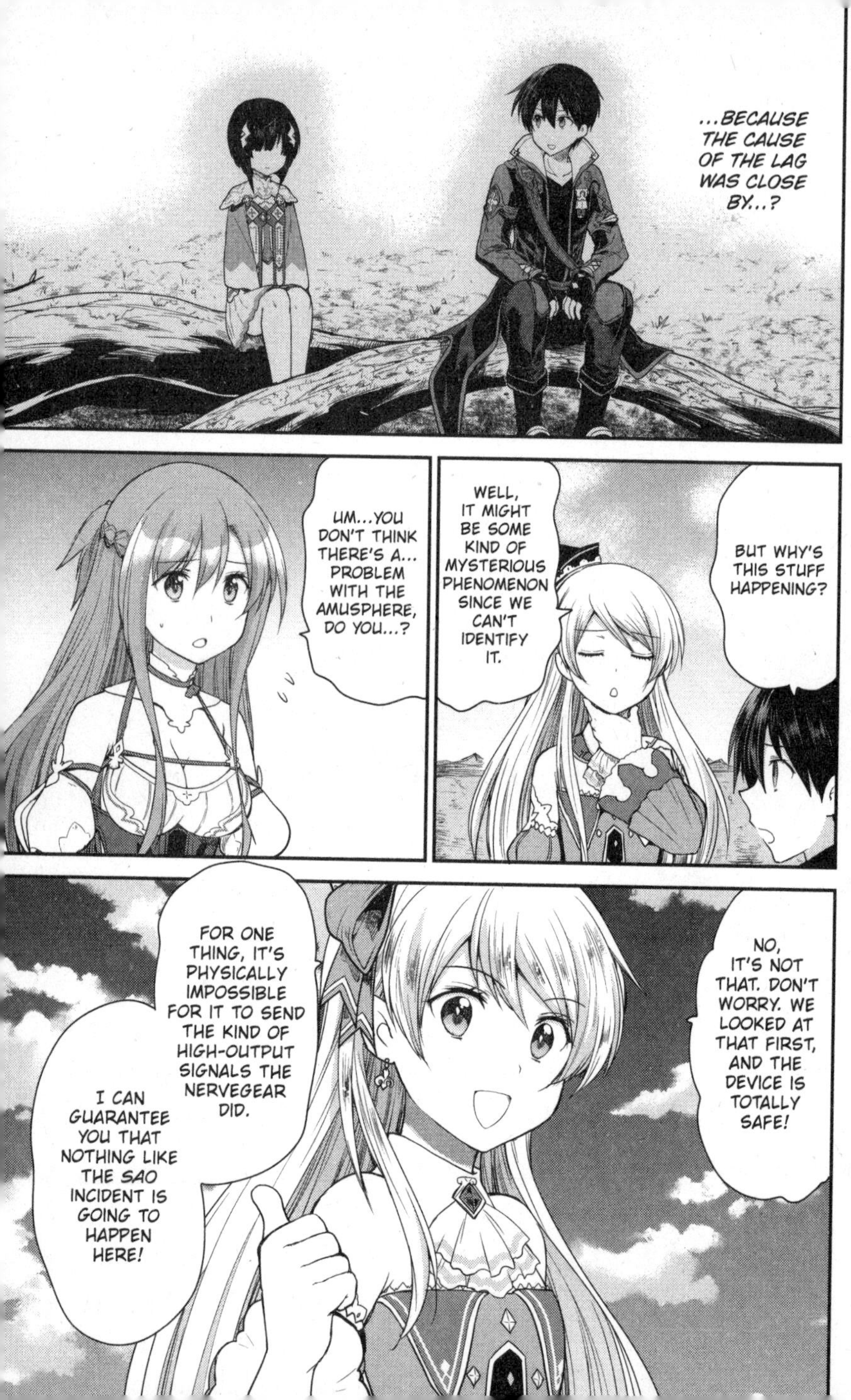
...BECAUSE THE CAUSE OF THE LAG WAS CLOSE BY...?
BUT WHY'S THIS STUFF HAPPENING?
WELL, IT MIGHT BE SOME KIND OF MYSTERIOUS PHENOMENON SINCE WE CAN'T IDENTIFY IT.
UM...YOU DON'T THINK THERE'S A... PROBLEM WITH THE AMUSPHERE, DO YOU...?
NO, IT'S NOT THAT. DON'T WORRY. WE LOOKED AT THAT FIRST, AND THE DEVICE IS TOTALLY SAFE!
FOR ONE THING, IT'S PHYSICALLY IMPOSSIBLE FOR IT TO SEND THE KIND OF HIGH-OUTPUT SIGNALS THE NERVEGEAR DID.
I CAN GUARANTEE YOU THAT NOTHING LIKE THE SAO INCIDENT IS GOING TO HAPPEN HERE!

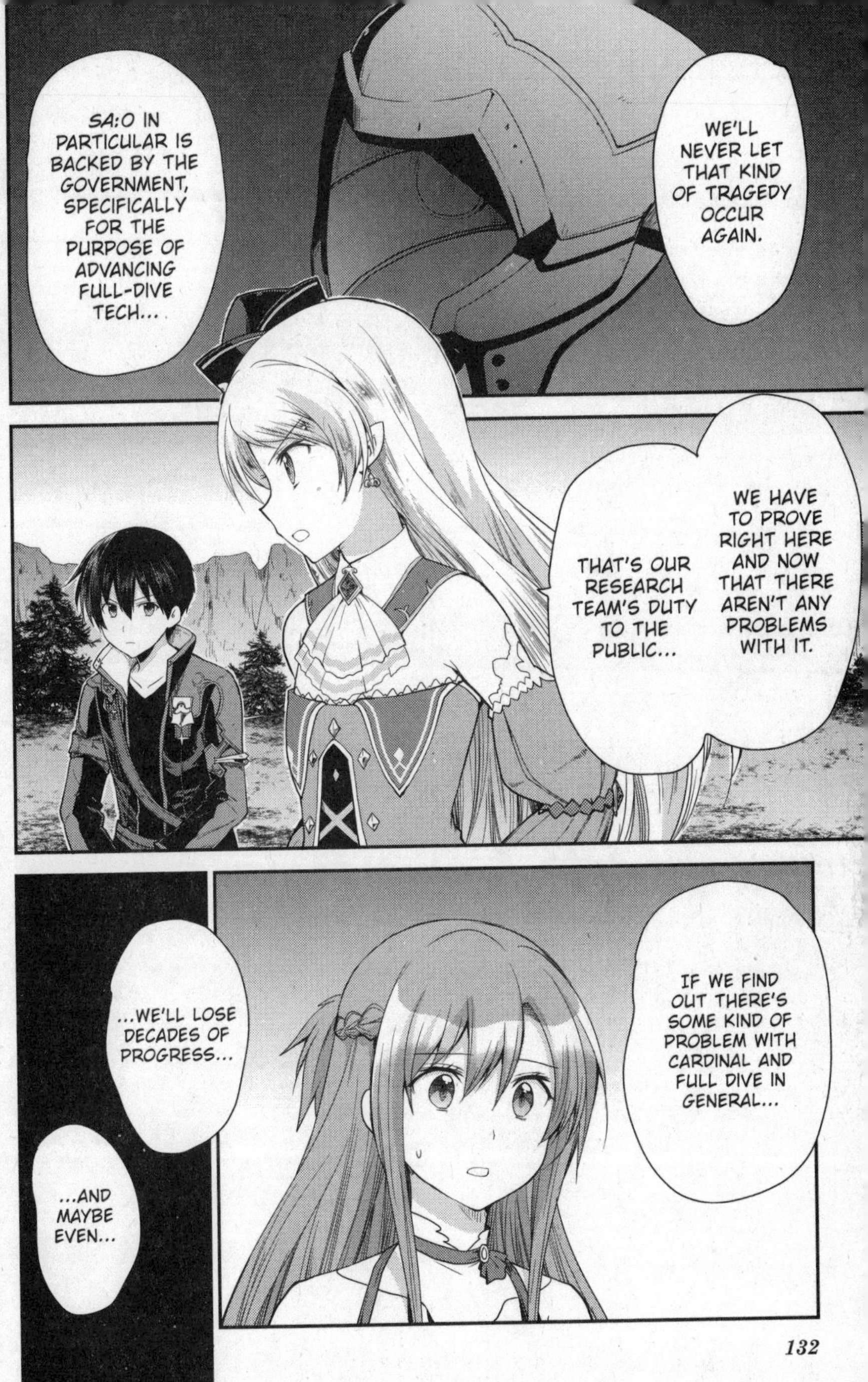
WE'LL NEVER LET THAT KIND OF TRAGEDY OCCUR AGAIN.
SA:O IN PARTICULAR IS BACKED BY THE GOVERNMENT, SPECIFICALLY FOR THE PURPOSE OF ADVANCING FULL-DIVE TECH...
WE HAVE TO PROVE RIGHT HERE AND NOW THAT THERE AREN'T ANY PROBLEMS WITH IT.
THAT'S OUR RESEARCH TEAM'S DUTY TO THE PUBLIC...
IF WE FIND OUT THERE'S SOME KIND OF PROBLEM WITH CARDINAL AND FULL DIVE IN GENERAL...
...WE'LL LOSE DECADES OF PROGRESS...
...AND MAYBE EVEN...

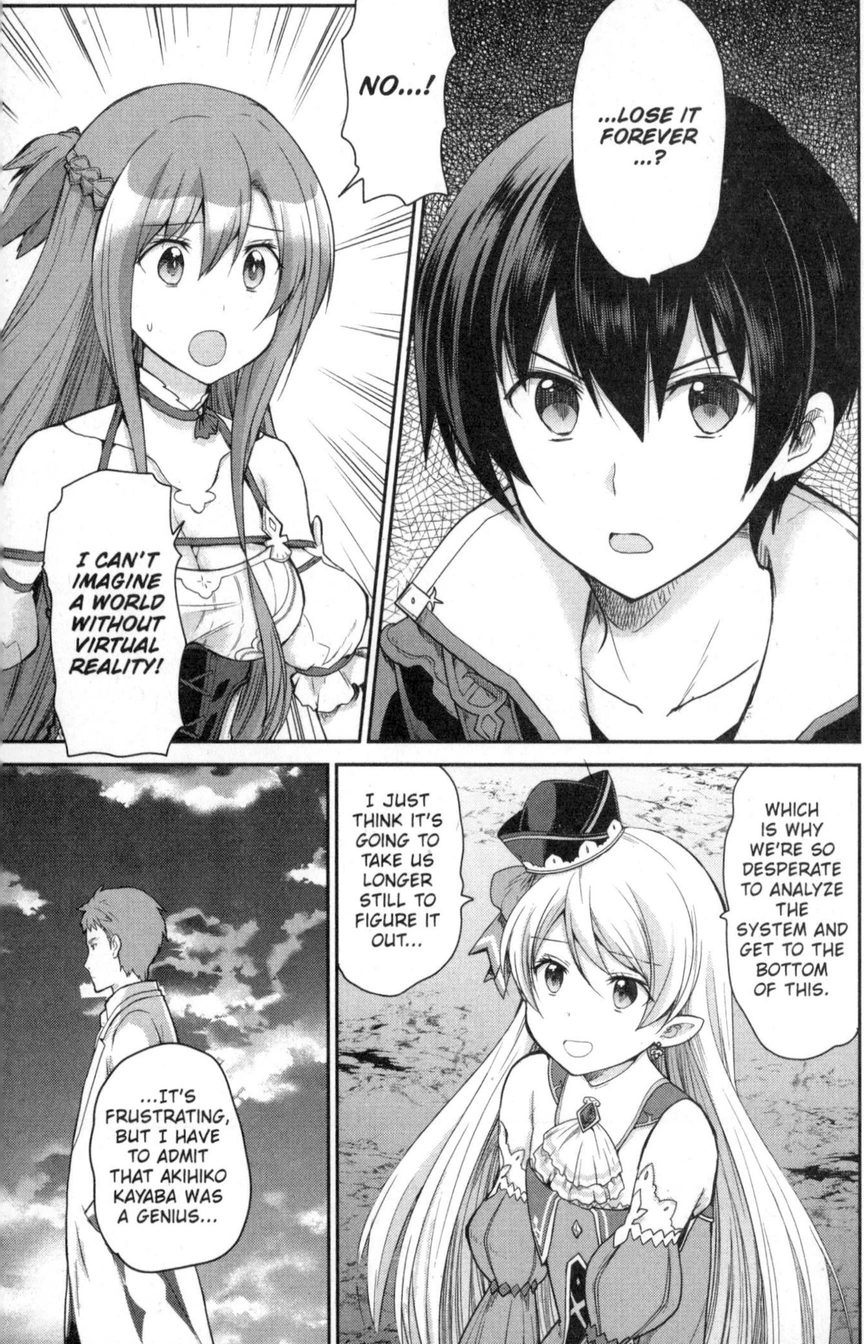
...LOSE IT FOREVER ...?
NO...!
I CAN'T IMAGINE A WORLD WITHOUT VIRTUAL REALITY!
WHICH IS WHY WE'RE SO DESPERATE TO ANALYZE THE SYSTEM AND GET TO THE BOTTOM OF THIS.
I JUST THINK IT'S GOING TO TAKE US LONGER STILL TO FIGURE IT OUT...
...IT'S FRUSTRATING, BUT I HAVE TO ADMIT THAT AKIHIKO KAYABA WAS A GENIUS...

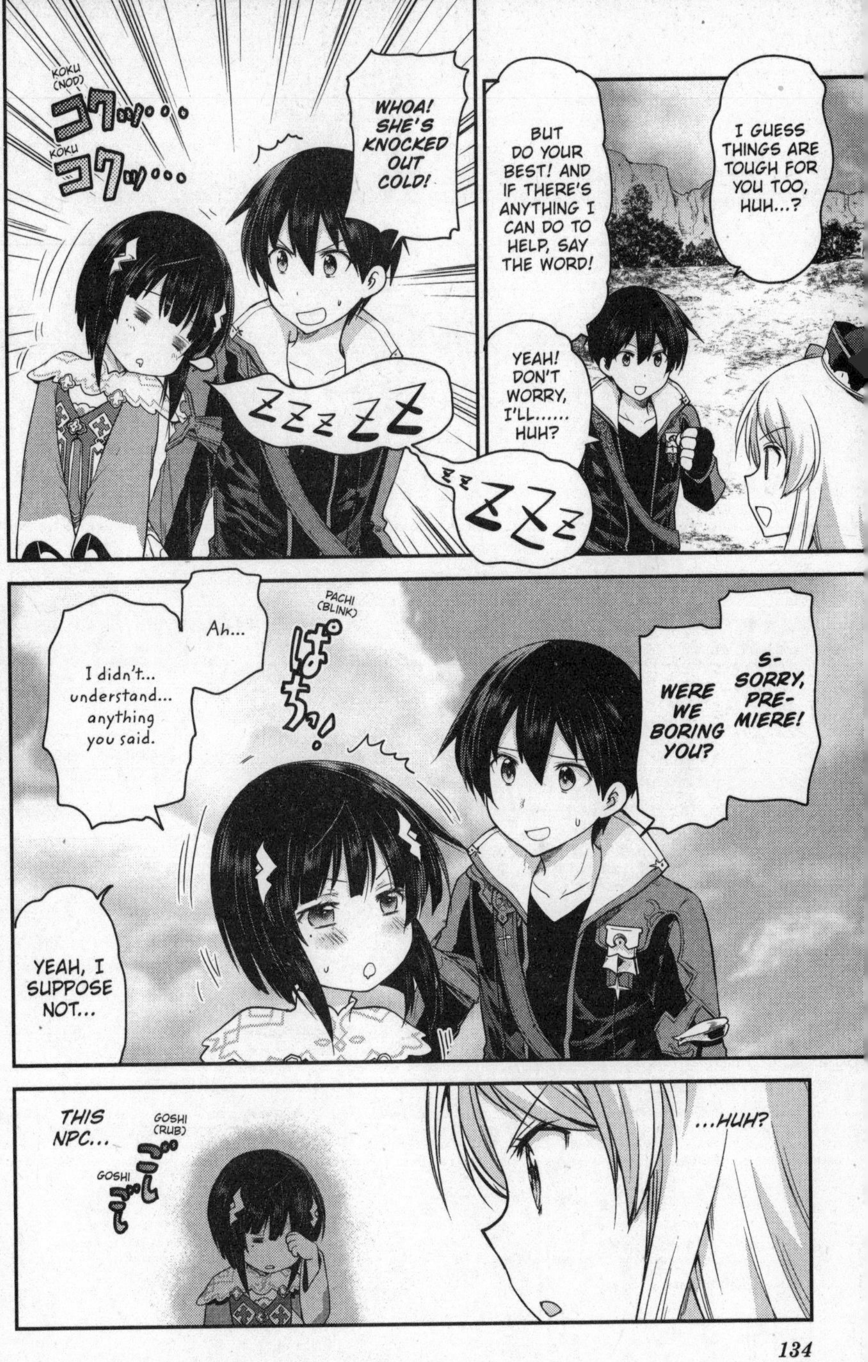
I GUESS THINGS ARE TOUGH FOR YOU TOO, HUH...?
BUT DO YOUR BEST! AND IF THERE'S ANYTHING I CAN DO TO HELP, SAY THE WORD!
YEAH! DON'T WORRY, I'LL...... HUH?
KOKU (NOD)
コクッ...
KOKU
コクッ...
WHOA! SHE'S KNOCKED OUT COLD!
Zzzzzz
zzZZZz
S-SORRY, PREMIERE!
WERE WE BORING YOU?
PACHI (BLINK)
ぱちっ!
Ah...
I didn't... understand... anything you said.
YEAH, I SUPPOSE NOT...
...HUH?
THIS NPC...
GOSHI (RUB)
ごし
GOSHI
ごし

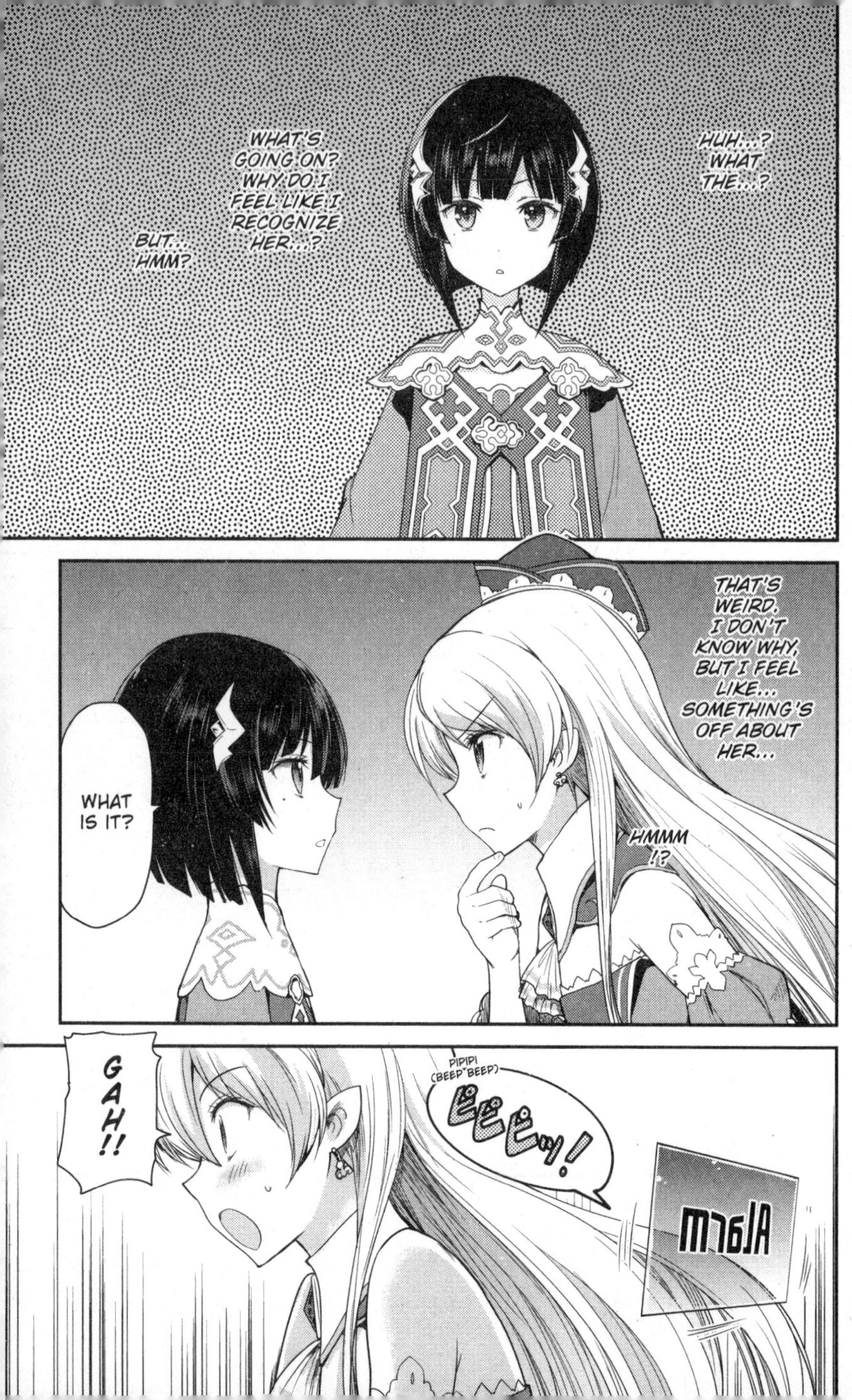
HUH...? WHAT THE...?
WHAT'S GOING ON? WHY DO I FEEL LIKE I RECOGNIZE HER...?
BUT... HMM?
THAT'S WEIRD. I DON'T KNOW WHY, BUT I FEEL LIKE... SOMETHING'S OFF ABOUT HER...
HMMM !?
WHAT IS IT?
PIPIPI (BEEP BEEP)
ピピピッ!
GAH!!

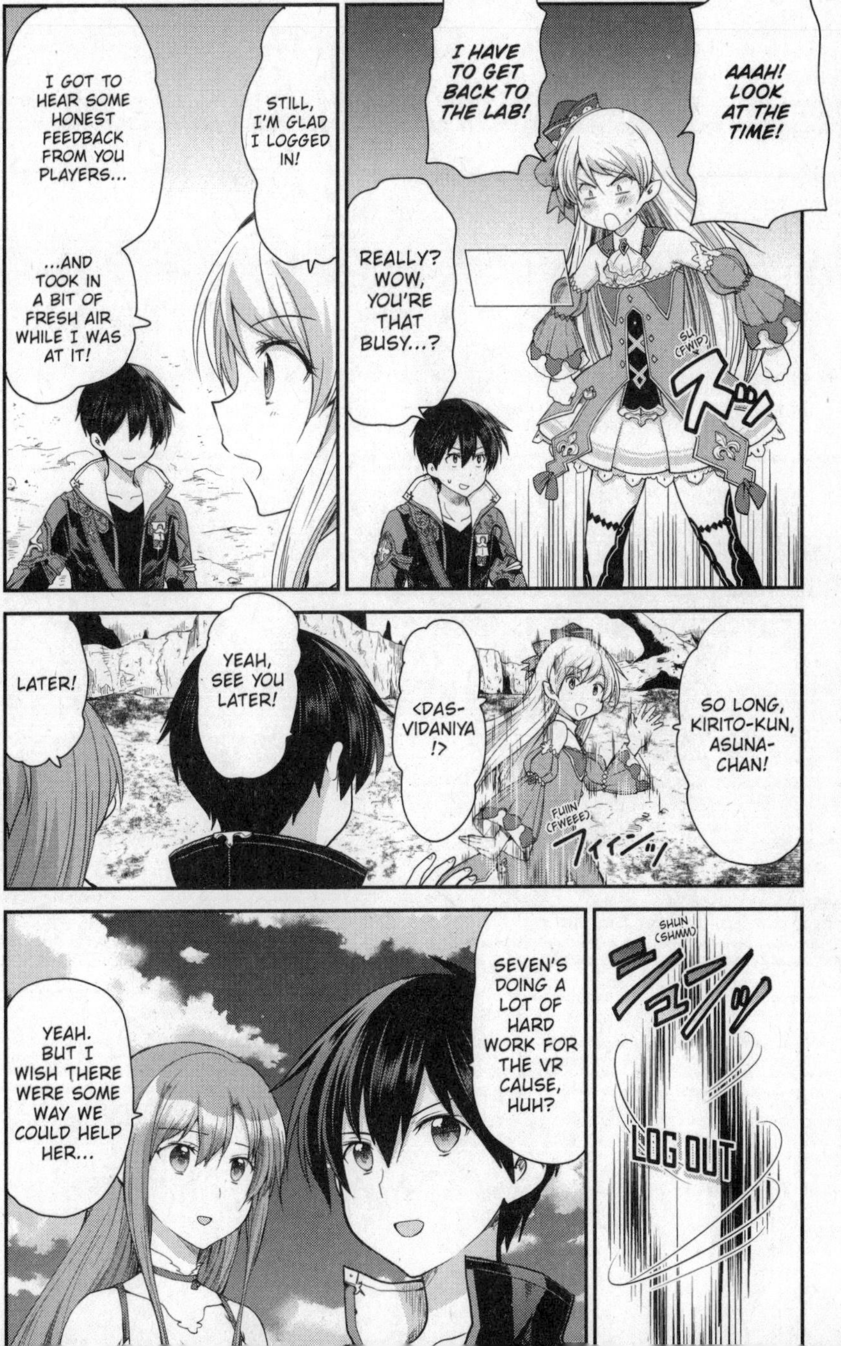
AAAH! LOOK AT THE TIME!
I HAVE TO GET BACK TO THE LAB!
REALLY? WOW, YOU'RE THAT BUSY...?
SU (FWIP)
STILL, I'M GLAD I LOGGED IN!
I GOT TO HEAR SOME HONEST FEEDBACK FROM YOU PLAYERS...
...AND TOOK IN A BIT OF FRESH AIR WHILE I WAS AT IT!
SO LONG, KIRITO-KUN, ASUNA-CHAN!
<DAS-VIDANIYA!>
FUIIN (FWEEE)
YEAH, SEE YOU LATER!
LATER!
SHUN (SHMM)
LOG OUT
SEVEN'S DOING A LOT OF HARD WORK FOR THE VR CAUSE, HUH?
YEAH. BUT I WISH THERE WERE SOME WAY WE COULD HELP HER...

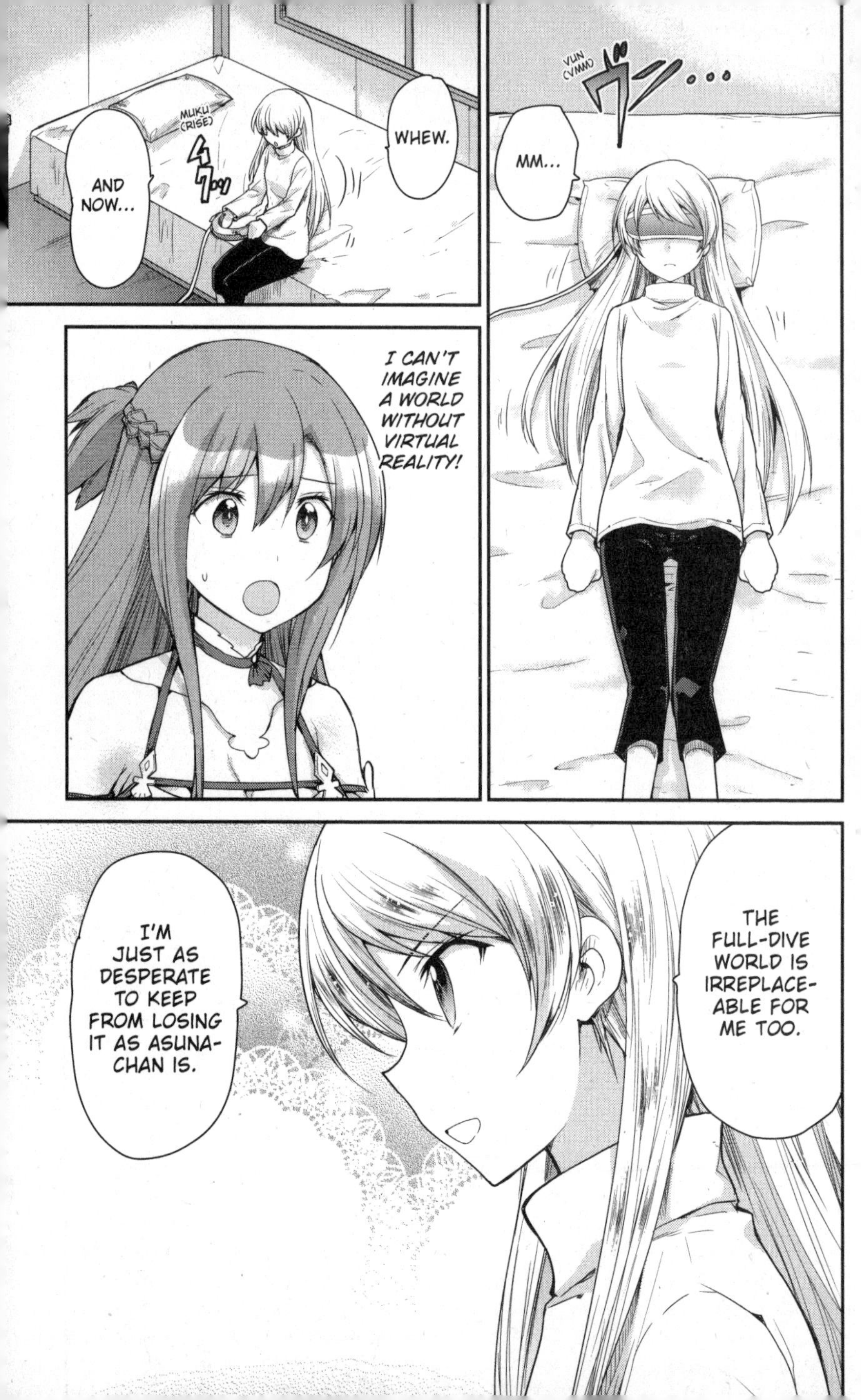
VUN (VMM)
MM...
WHEW.
MUKU (RISE)
AND NOW...
I CAN'T IMAGINE A WORLD WITHOUT VIRTUAL REALITY!
THE FULL-DIVE WORLD IS IRREPLACE-ABLE FOR ME TOO.
I'M JUST AS DESPERATE TO KEEP FROM LOSING IT AS ASUNA-CHAN IS.

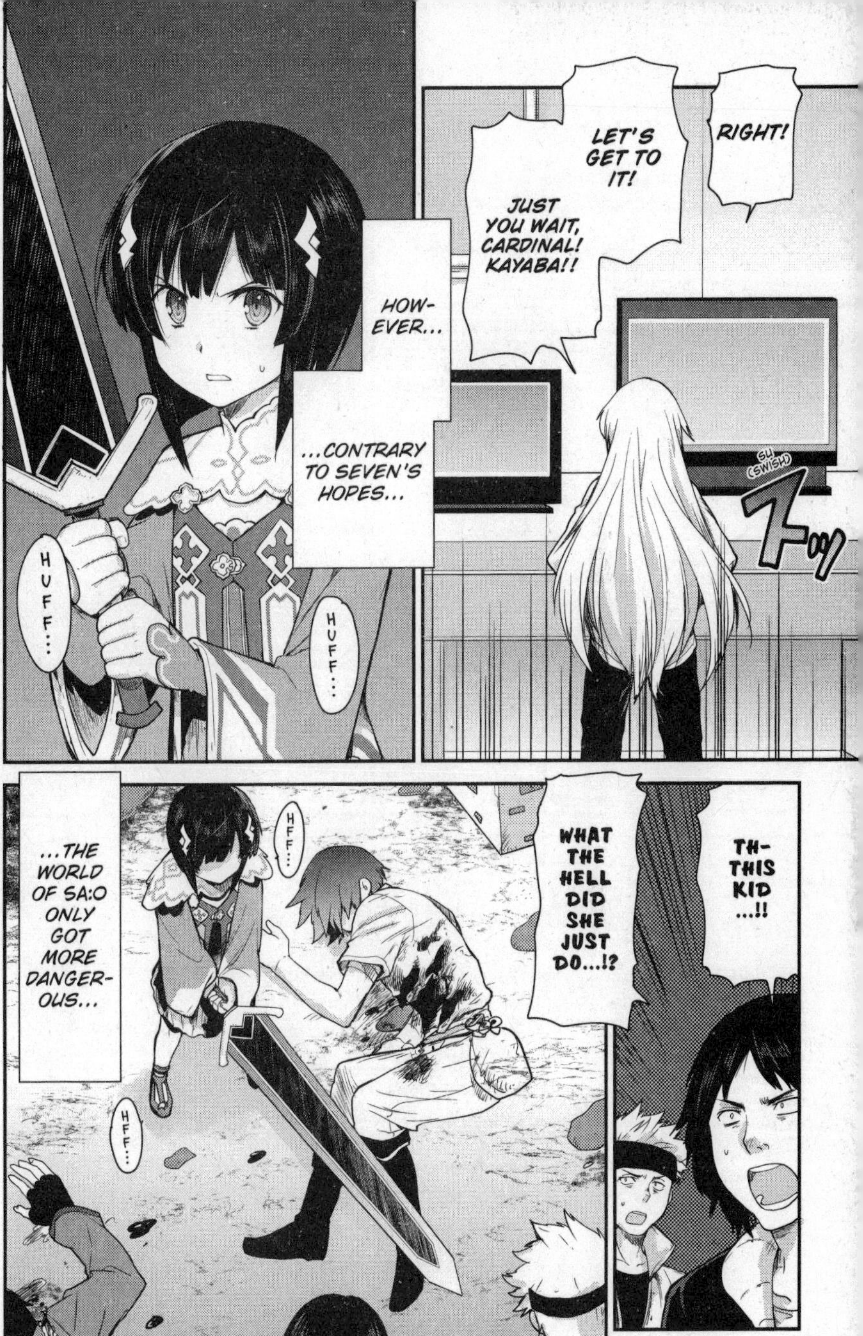
RIGHT!
LET'S GET TO IT!
JUST YOU WAIT, CARDINAL! KAYABA!!
SU (SWISH)
HOW-EVER...
...CONTRARY TO SEVEN'S HOPES...
HUFF...
HUFF...
TH-THIS KID...!!
WHAT THE HELL DID SHE JUST DO...!?
HFF...
...THE WORLD OF SA:O ONLY GOT MORE DANGEROUS...
HFF...

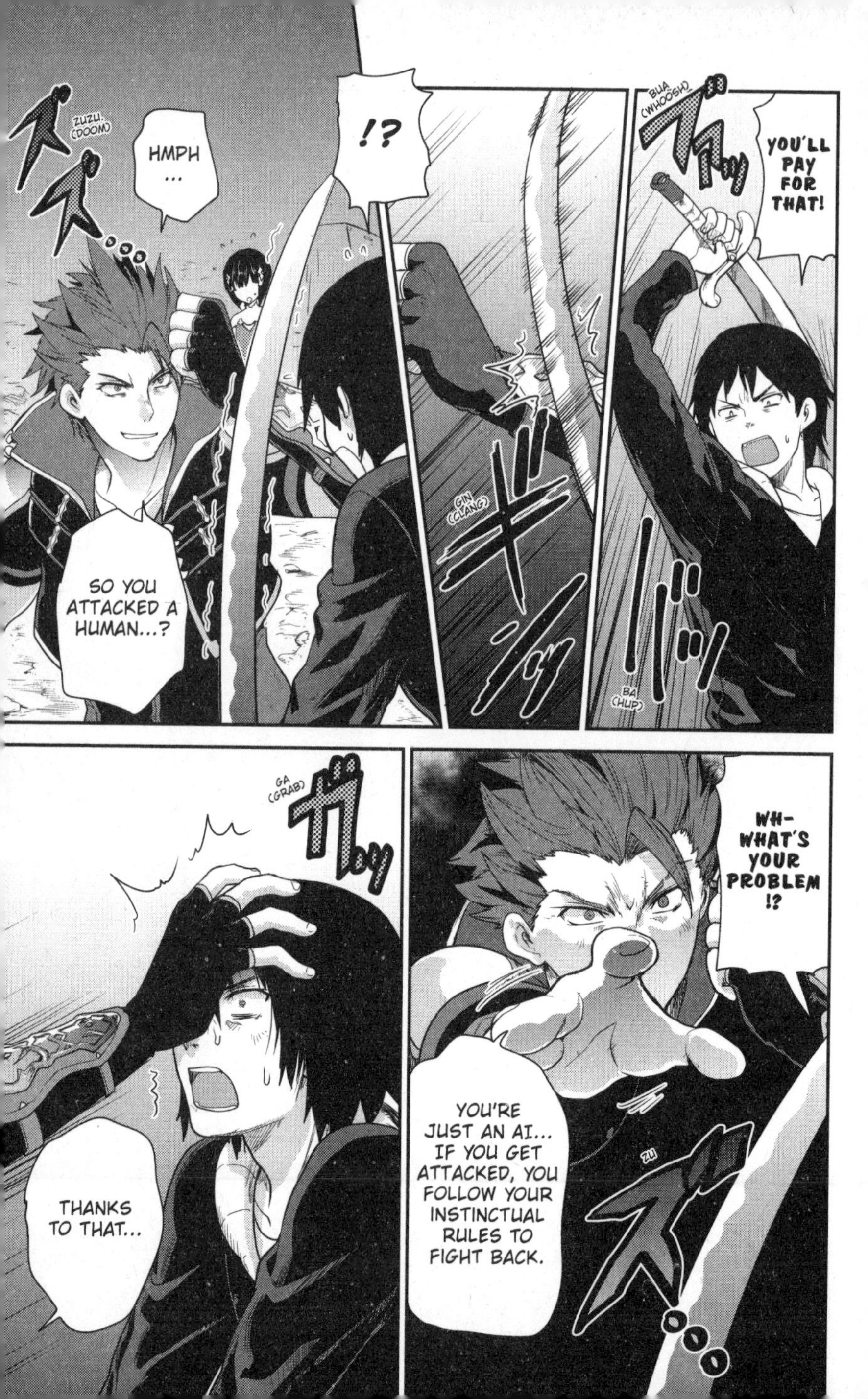
BUA (WHOOSH)
YOU'LL PAY FOR THAT!
BA (HUP)
!?
GIN (CLANG)
ZUZU. (DOOM)
HMPH ...
SO YOU ATTACKED A HUMAN...?
WH-WHAT'S YOUR PROBLEM !?
YOU'RE JUST AN AI... IF YOU GET ATTACKED, YOU FOLLOW YOUR INSTINCTUAL RULES TO FIGHT BACK.
ZU
GA (GRAB)
THANKS TO THAT...

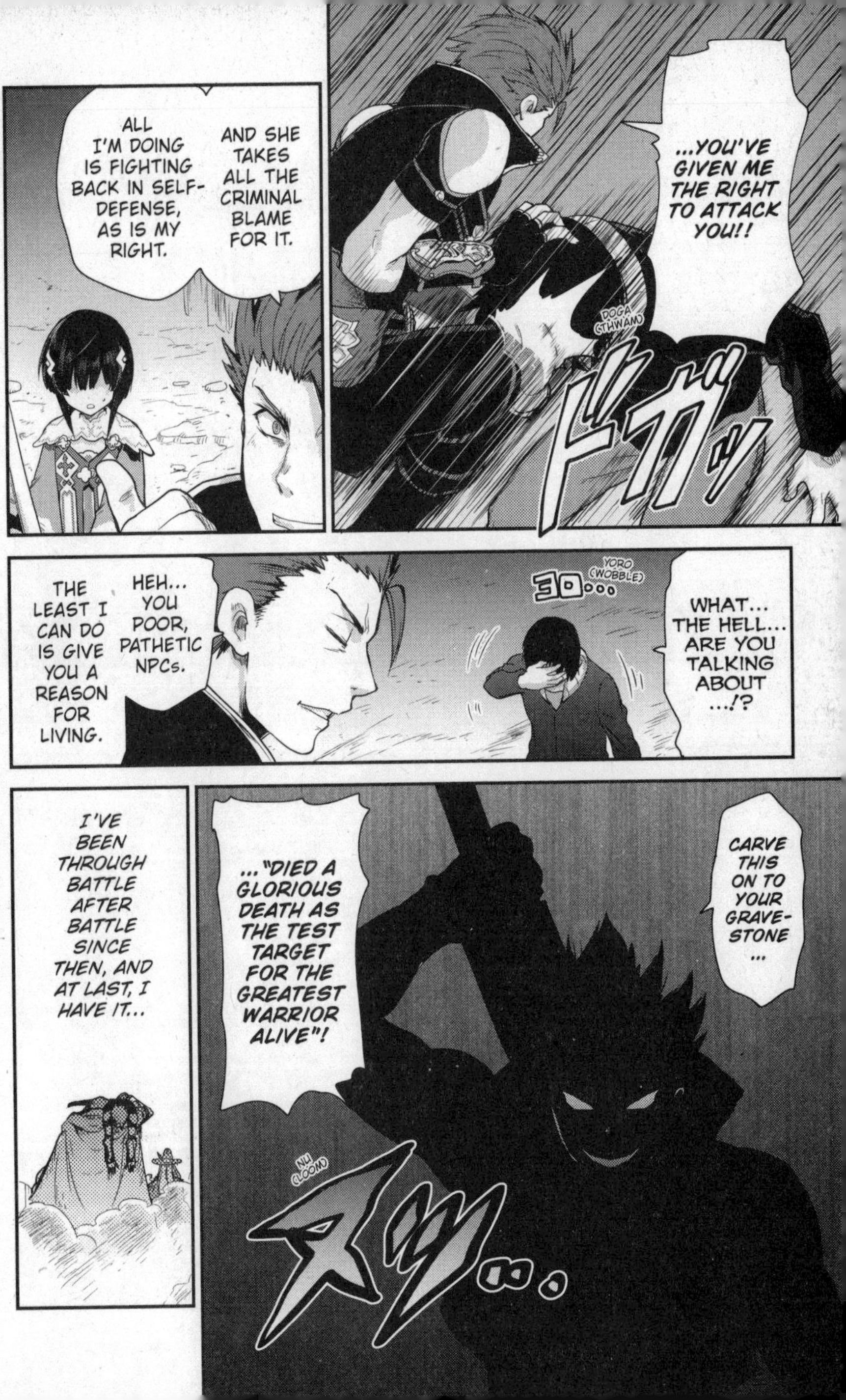
...YOU'VE GIVEN ME THE RIGHT TO ATTACK YOU!!
DOGA (THWAM)
ドガッ
ALL I'M DOING IS FIGHTING BACK IN SELF-DEFENSE, AS IS MY RIGHT.
AND SHE TAKES ALL THE CRIMINAL BLAME FOR IT.
WHAT... THE HELL... ARE YOU TALKING ABOUT...!?
YORO (WOBBLE)
ヨロ...
HEH... YOU POOR, PATHETIC NPCs.
THE LEAST I CAN DO IS GIVE YOU A REASON FOR LIVING.
CARVE THIS ON TO YOUR GRAVE-STONE...
..."DIED A GLORIOUS DEATH AS THE TEST TARGET FOR THE GREATEST WARRIOR ALIVE"!
NU (LOOM)
ヌッ...
I'VE BEEN THROUGH BATTLE AFTER BATTLE SINCE THEN, AND AT LAST, I HAVE IT...

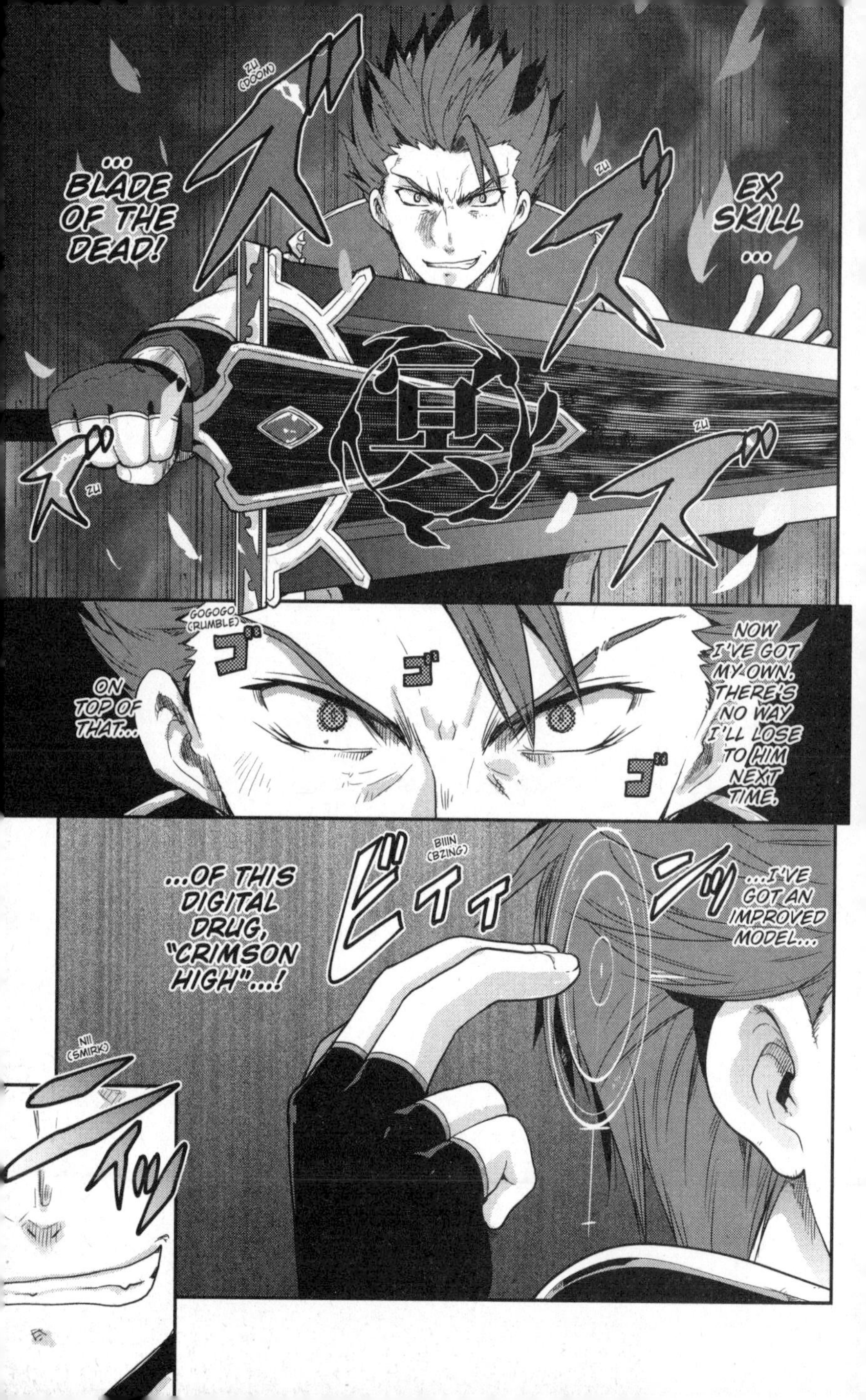
ZU (DOOM)
ZU
EX SKILL...
...BLÄDE OF THE DEAD!
ZU
ZU
GOGOGO (RUMBLE)
NOW I'VE GOT MY OWN. THERE'S NO WAY I'LL LOSE TO HIM NEXT TIME.
ON TOP OF THAT...
BIIIN (BZING)
...I'VE GOT AN IMPROVED MODEL...
...OF THIS DIGITAL DRUG, "CRIMSON HIGH"...!
NII (SMIRK)

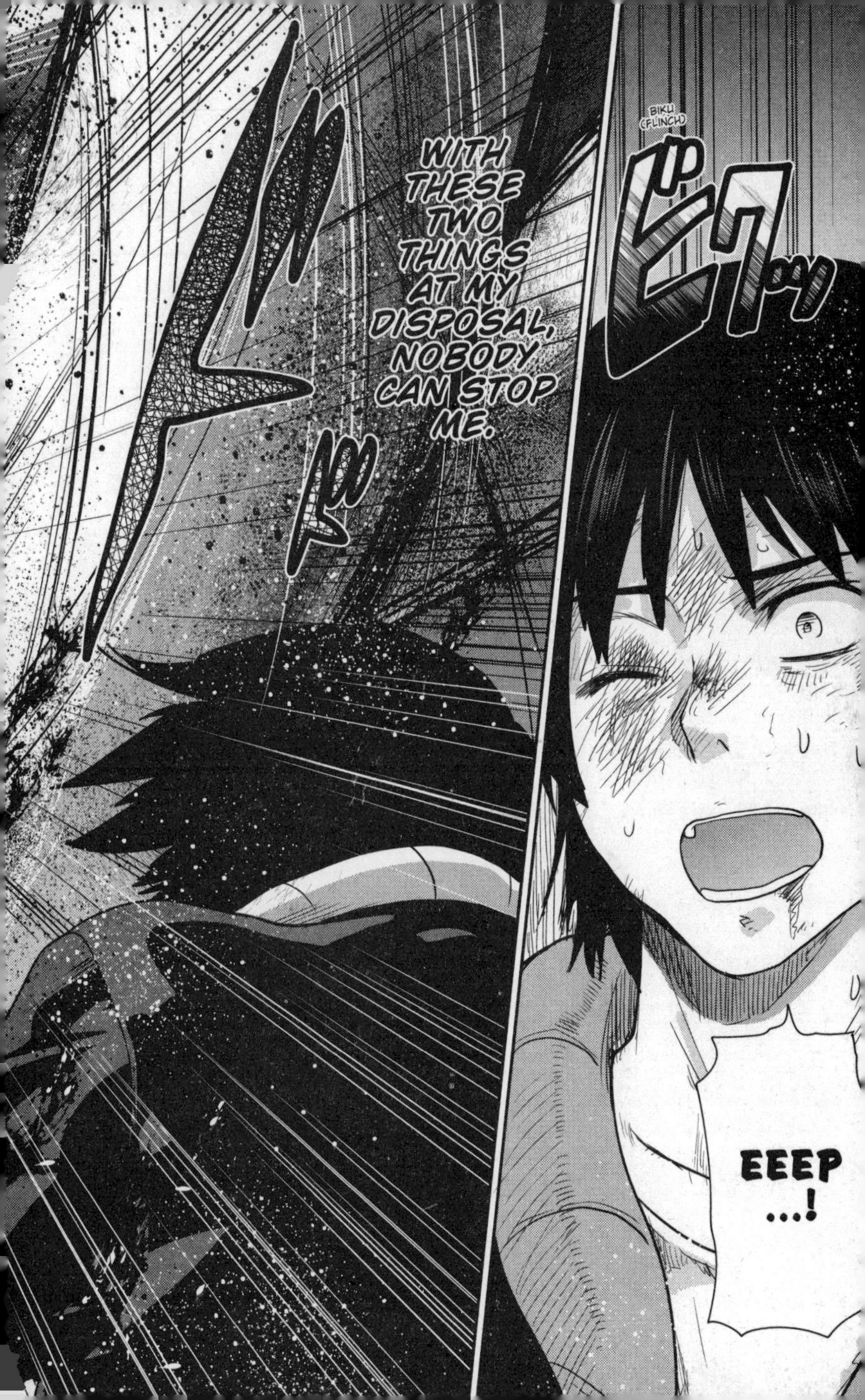
BIKU (FLINCH)
EEEP ...!
WITH THESE TWO THINGS AT MY DISPOSAL, NOBODY CAN STOP ME.

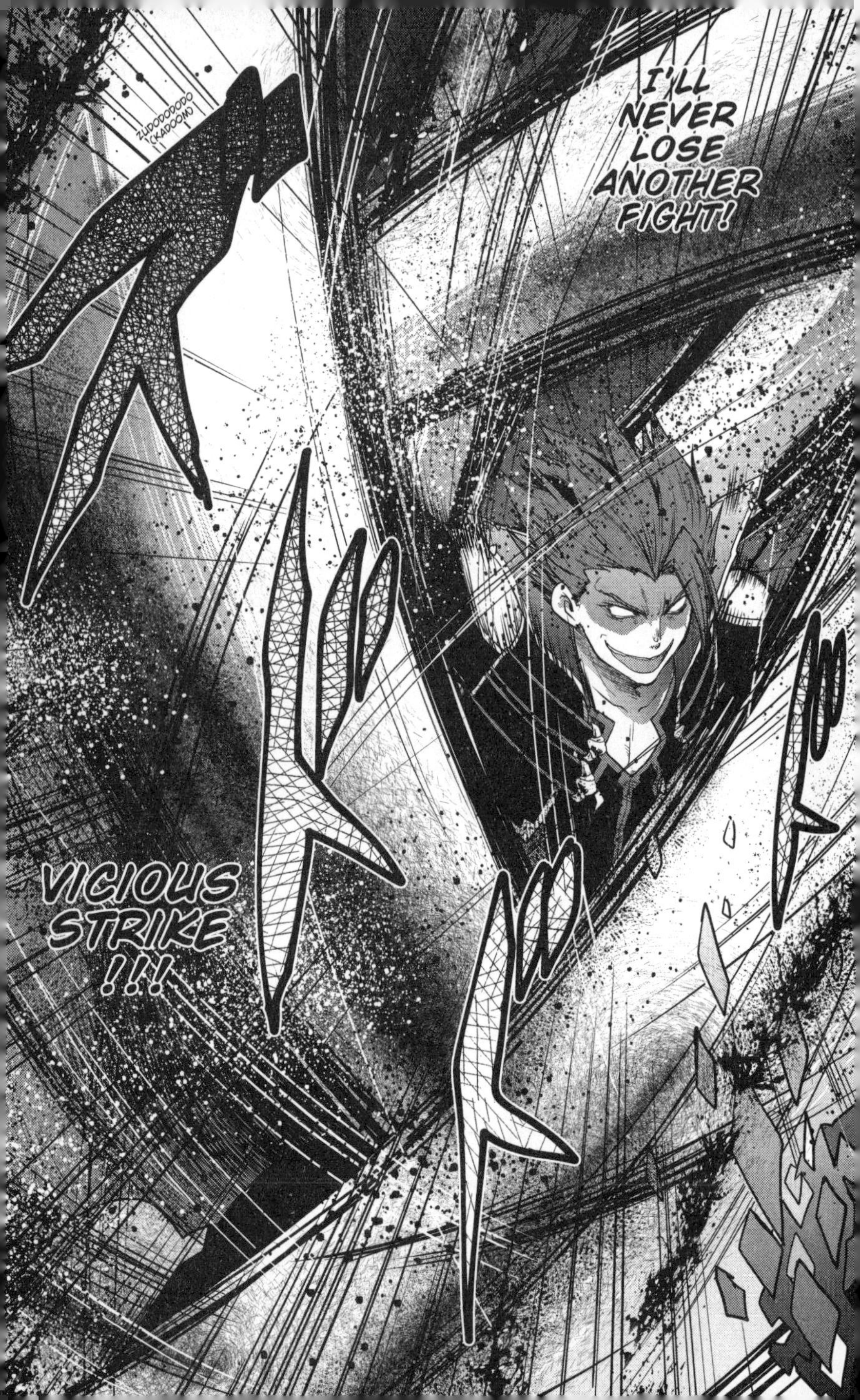
I'LL NEVER LOSE ANOTHER FIGHT!
ZUDODODODO (KADOOM)
VICIOUS STRIKE !!!

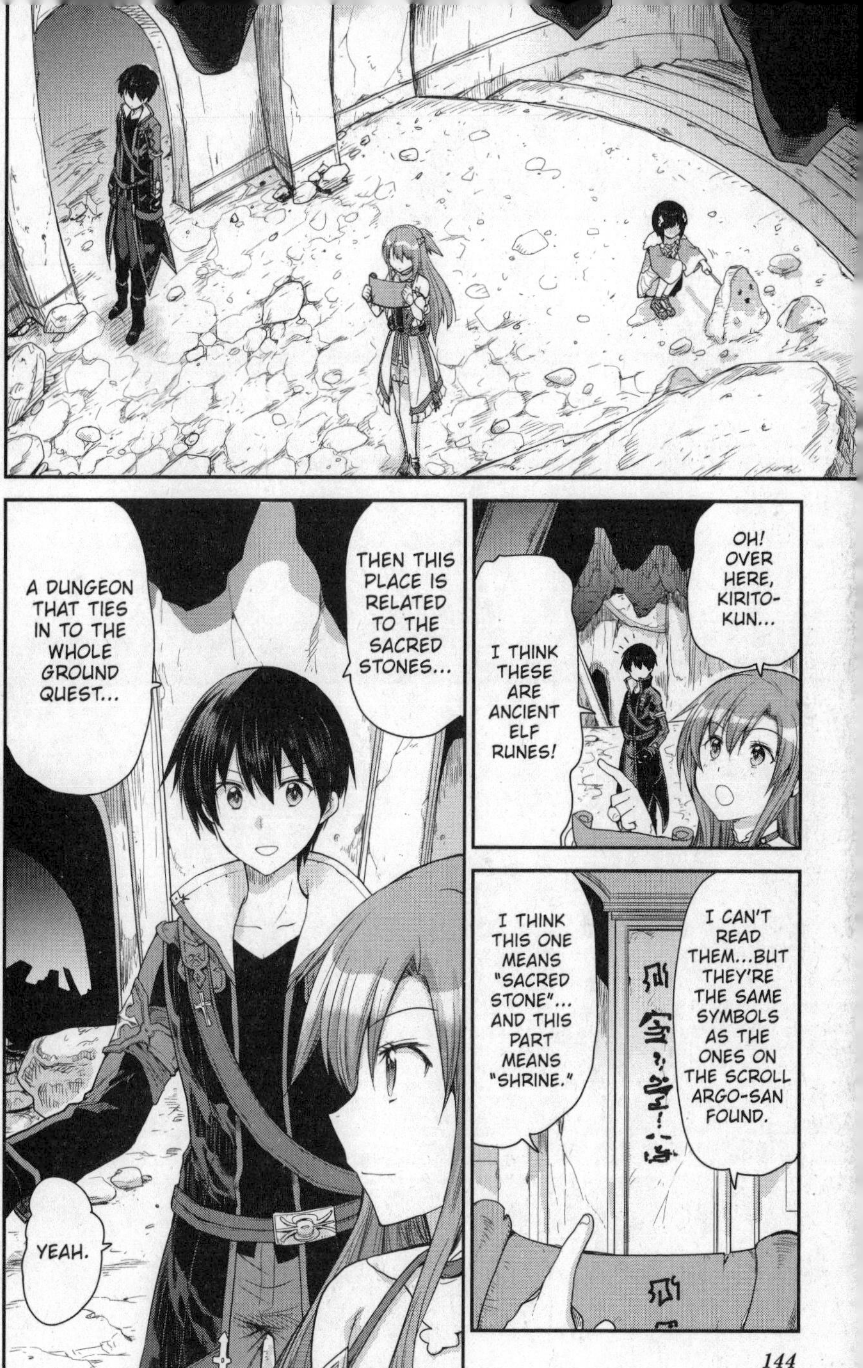
OH! OVER HERE, KIRITO-KUN...
I THINK THESE ARE ANCIENT ELF RUNES!
I CAN'T READ THEM...BUT THEY'RE THE SAME SYMBOLS AS THE ONES ON THE SCROLL ARGO-SAN FOUND.
I THINK THIS ONE MEANS "SACRED STONE"... AND THIS PART MEANS "SHRINE."
THEN THIS PLACE IS RELATED TO THE SACRED STONES...
A DUNGEON THAT TIES IN TO THE WHOLE GROUND QUEST...
YEAH.

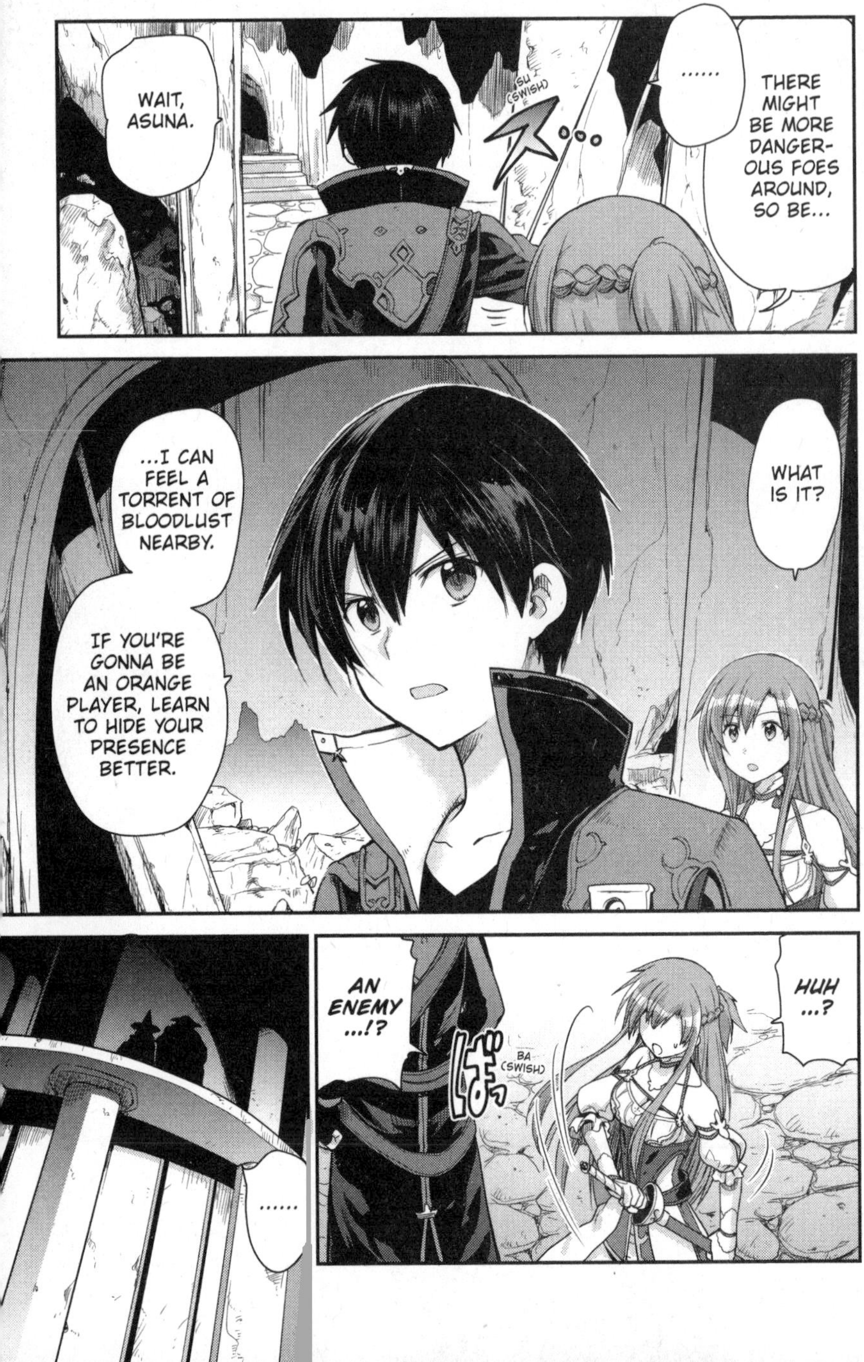
THERE MIGHT BE MORE DANGEROUS FOES AROUND, SO BE...
......
SU (SWISH)
WAIT, ASUNA.
WHAT IS IT?
...I CAN FEEL A TORRENT OF BLOODLUST NEARBY.
IF YOU'RE GONNA BE AN ORANGE PLAYER, LEARN TO HIDE YOUR PRESENCE BETTER.
HUH ...?
BA (SWISH)
ばっ
AN ENEMY ...!?
......

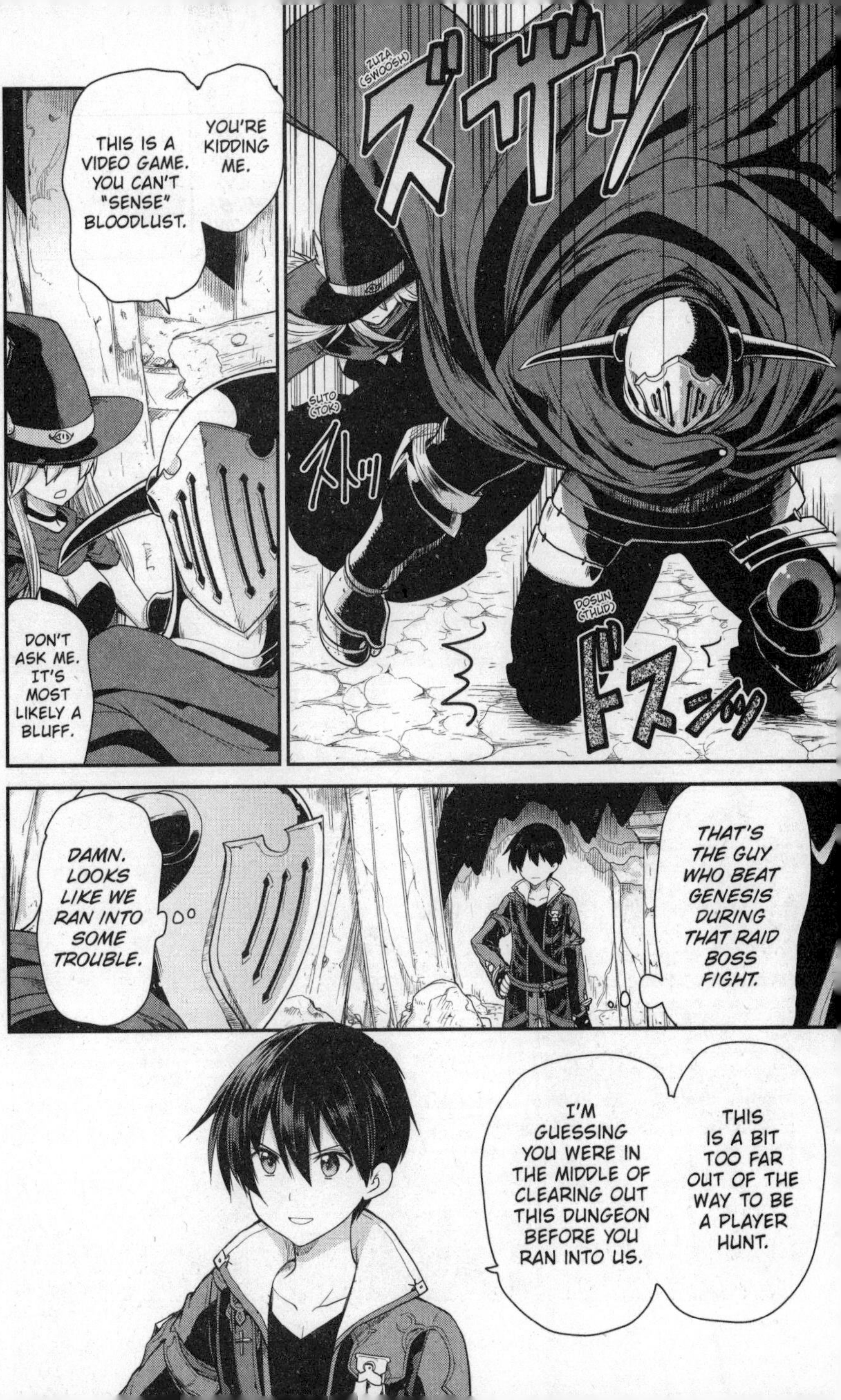
ZUZA (SWOOSH)
SUTO (STOK)
DOSUN (THUD)
YOU'RE KIDDING ME.
THIS IS A VIDEO GAME. YOU CAN'T "SENSE" BLOODLUST.
DON'T ASK ME. IT'S MOST LIKELY A BLUFF.
THAT'S THE GUY WHO BEAT GENESIS DURING THAT RAID BOSS FIGHT.
DAMN. LOOKS LIKE WE RAN INTO SOME TROUBLE.
THIS IS A BIT TOO FAR OUT OF THE WAY TO BE A PLAYER HUNT.
I'M GUESSING YOU WERE IN THE MIDDLE OF CLEARING OUT THIS DUNGEON BEFORE YOU RAN INTO US.

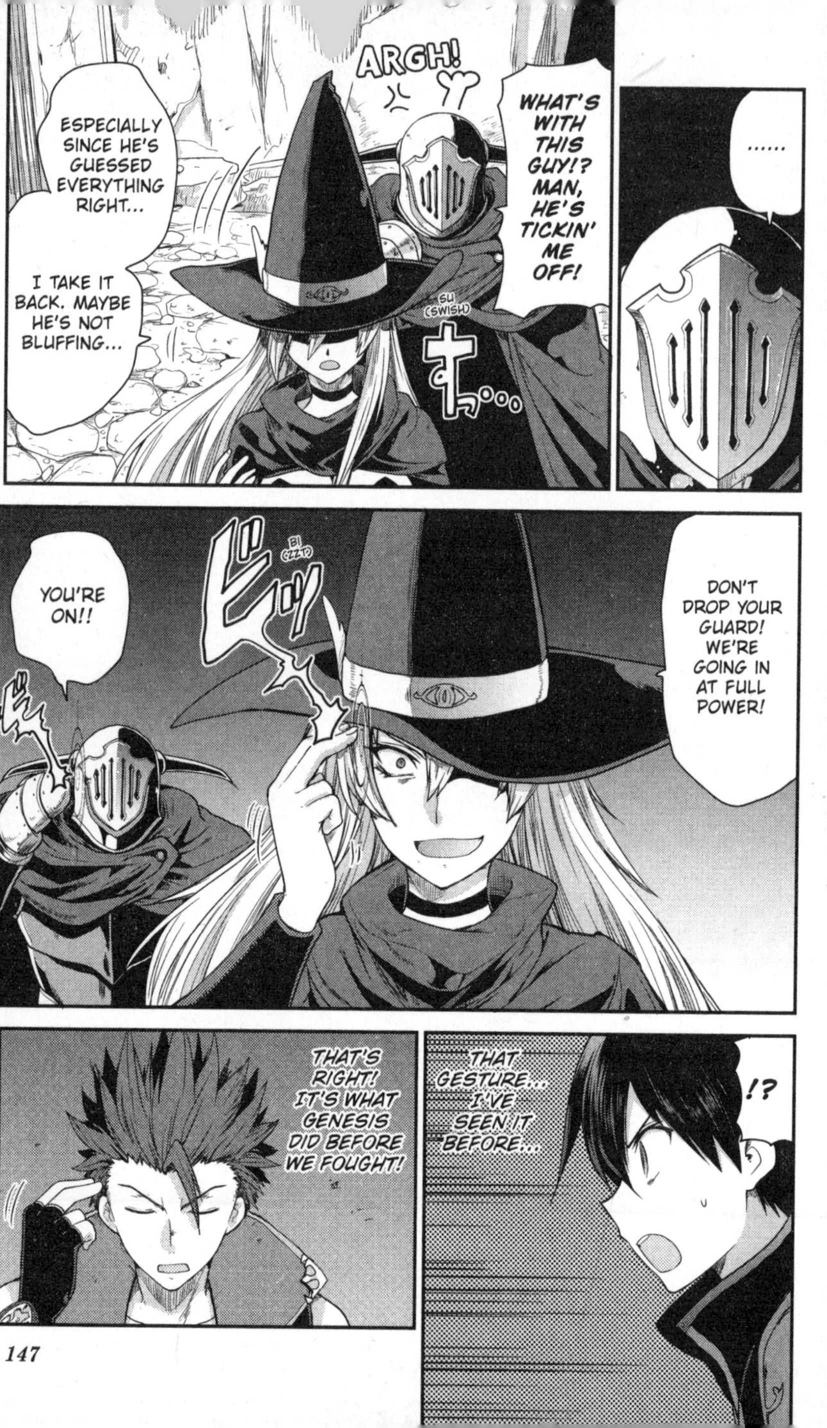
......
ARGH!
WHAT'S WITH THIS GUY!? MAN, HE'S TICKIN' ME OFF!
SU (SWISH)
ESPECIALLY SINCE HE'S GUESSED EVERYTHING RIGHT...
I TAKE IT BACK. MAYBE HE'S NOT BLUFFING...
DON'T DROP YOUR GUARD! WE'RE GOING IN AT FULL POWER!
BI (ZZZT)
YOU'RE ON!!
BIBI
!?
THAT GESTURE... I'VE SEEN IT BEFORE...
THAT'S RIGHT! IT'S WHAT GENESIS DID BEFORE WE FOUGHT!

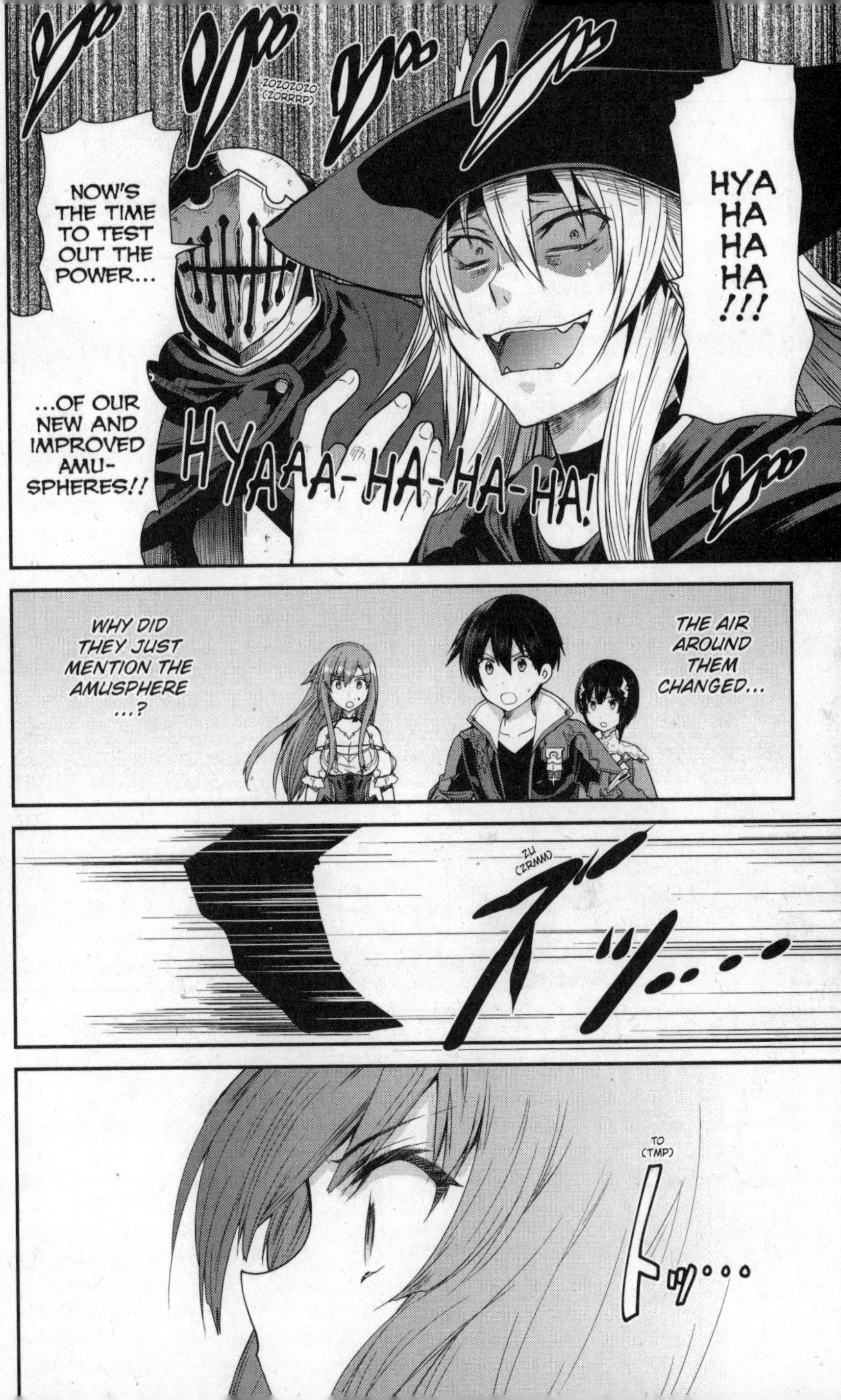
ZOZOZOZO (ZORRRP)
HYA HA HA HA!!!
NOW'S THE TIME TO TEST OUT THE POWER...
...OF OUR NEW AND IMPROVED AMUSPHERES!!
HYAAA-HA-HA-HA!
THE AIR AROUND THEM CHANGED...
WHY DID THEY JUST MENTION THE AMUSPHERE...?
ZU (ZRMM)
TO (TMP)

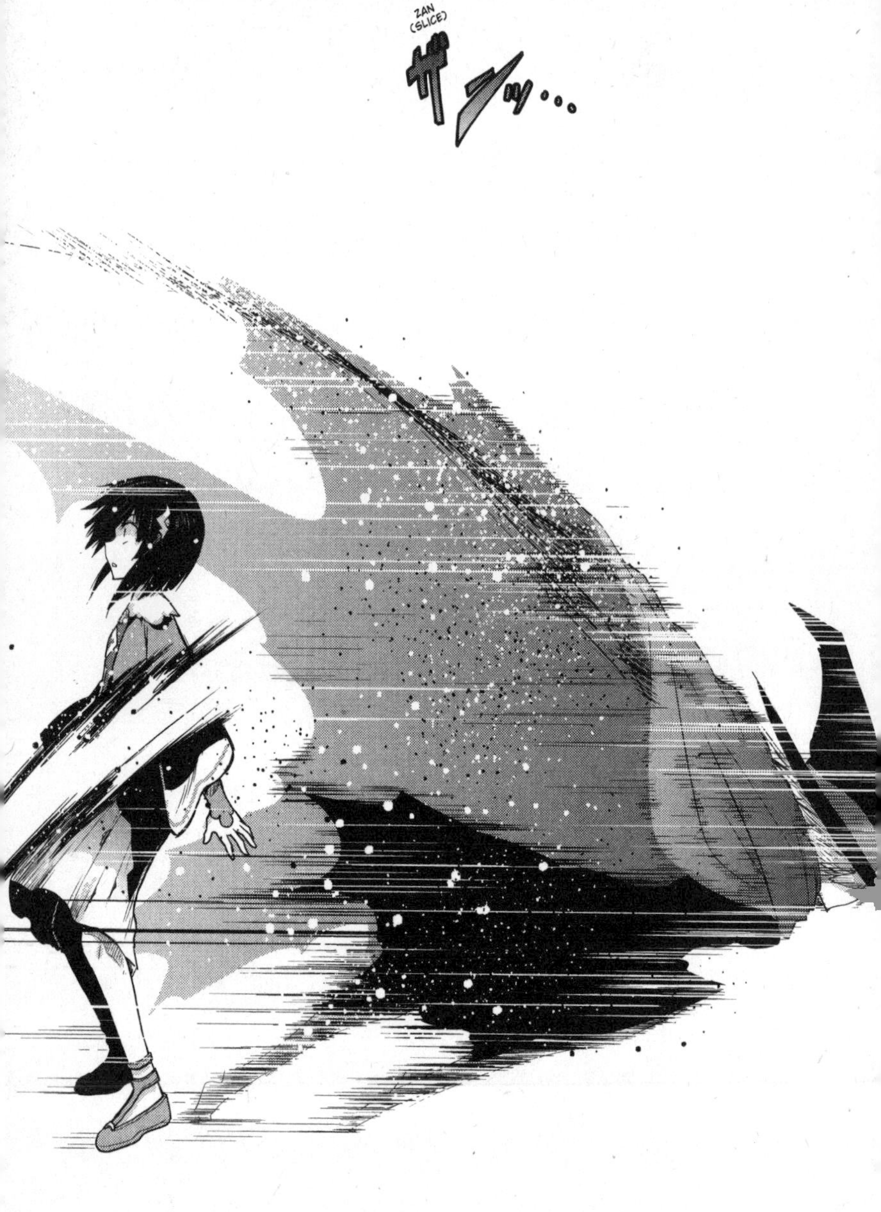
ZAN (SLICE)
ザンッ…

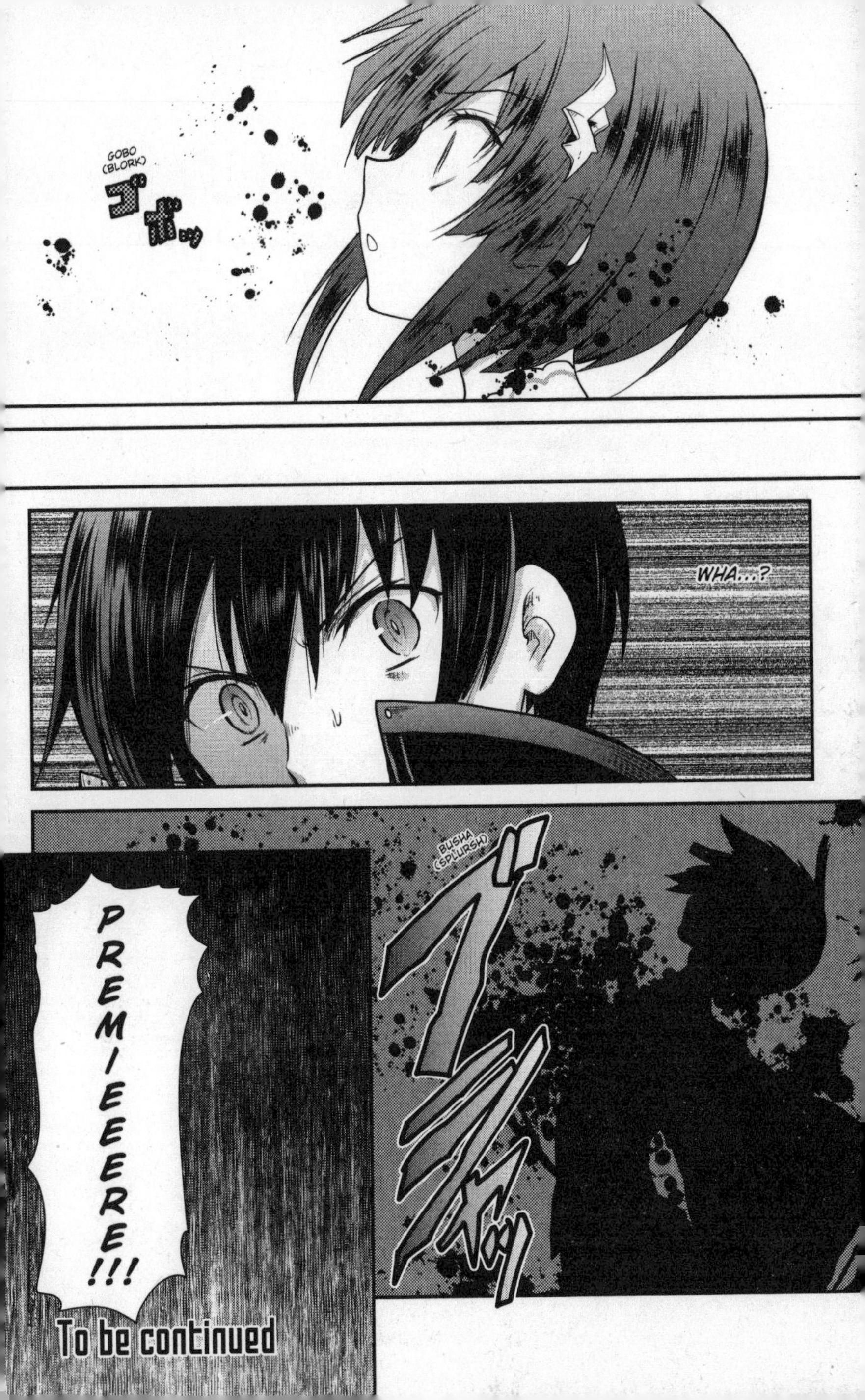
GOBO (BLORK)
ゴボッ
WHA...?
BUSHA (SPLURSH)
PREMIEEEERE!!!
To be continued

Side Story #1: A Written Love (Re)quest, Part I

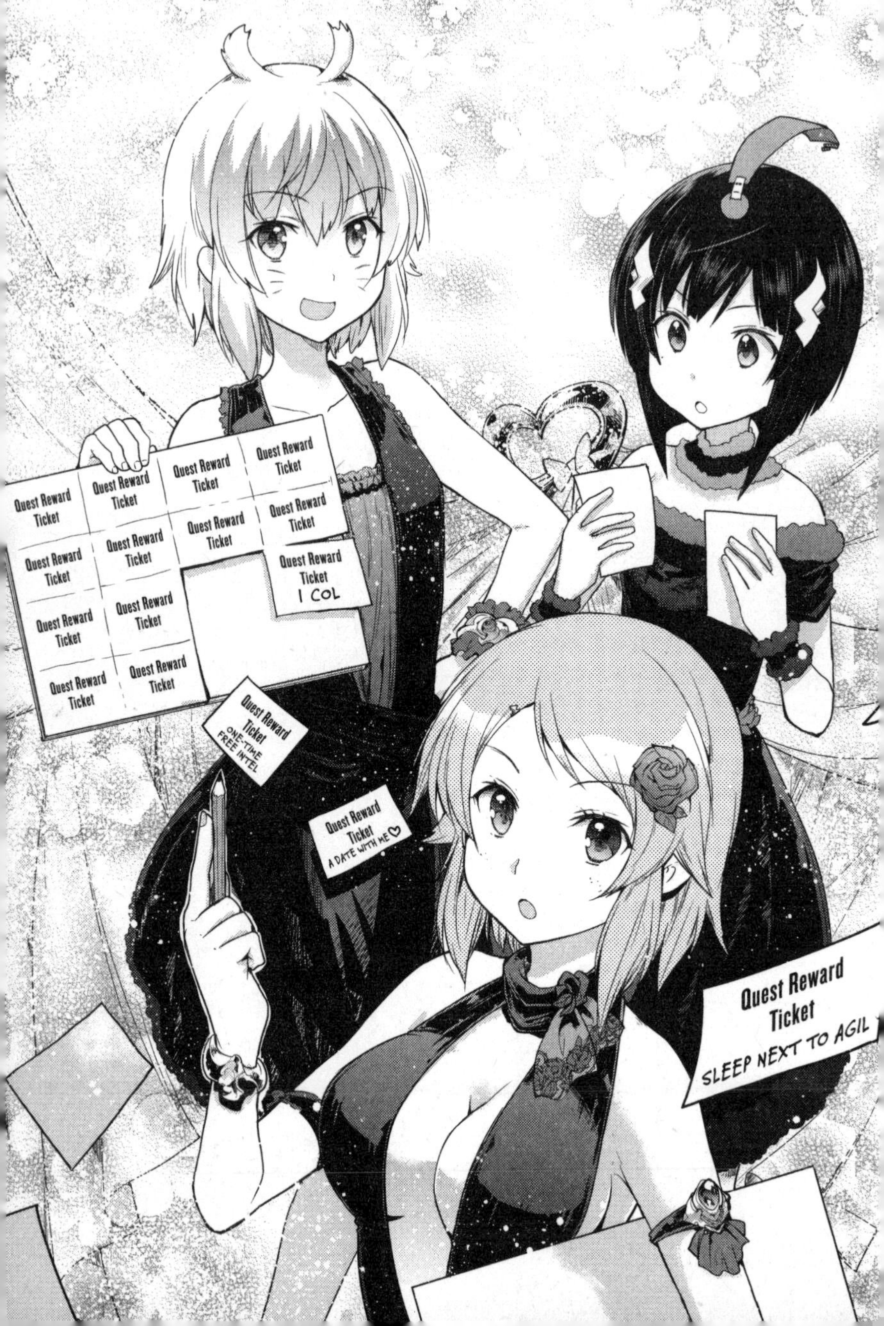
Quest Reward Ticket SLEEP NEXT TO AGIL
Quest Reward Ticket
Quest Reward Ticket
Quest Reward Ticket
Quest Reward Ticket
Quest Reward Ticket I COL
Quest Reward Ticket
Quest Reward Ticket
Quest Reward Ticket
Quest Reward Ticket
Quest Reward Ticket
Quest Reward Ticket
Quest Reward Ticket
Quest Reward Ticket
Quest Reward Ticket ONE-TIME FREE INTEL
Quest Reward Ticket A DATE WITH ME ♡

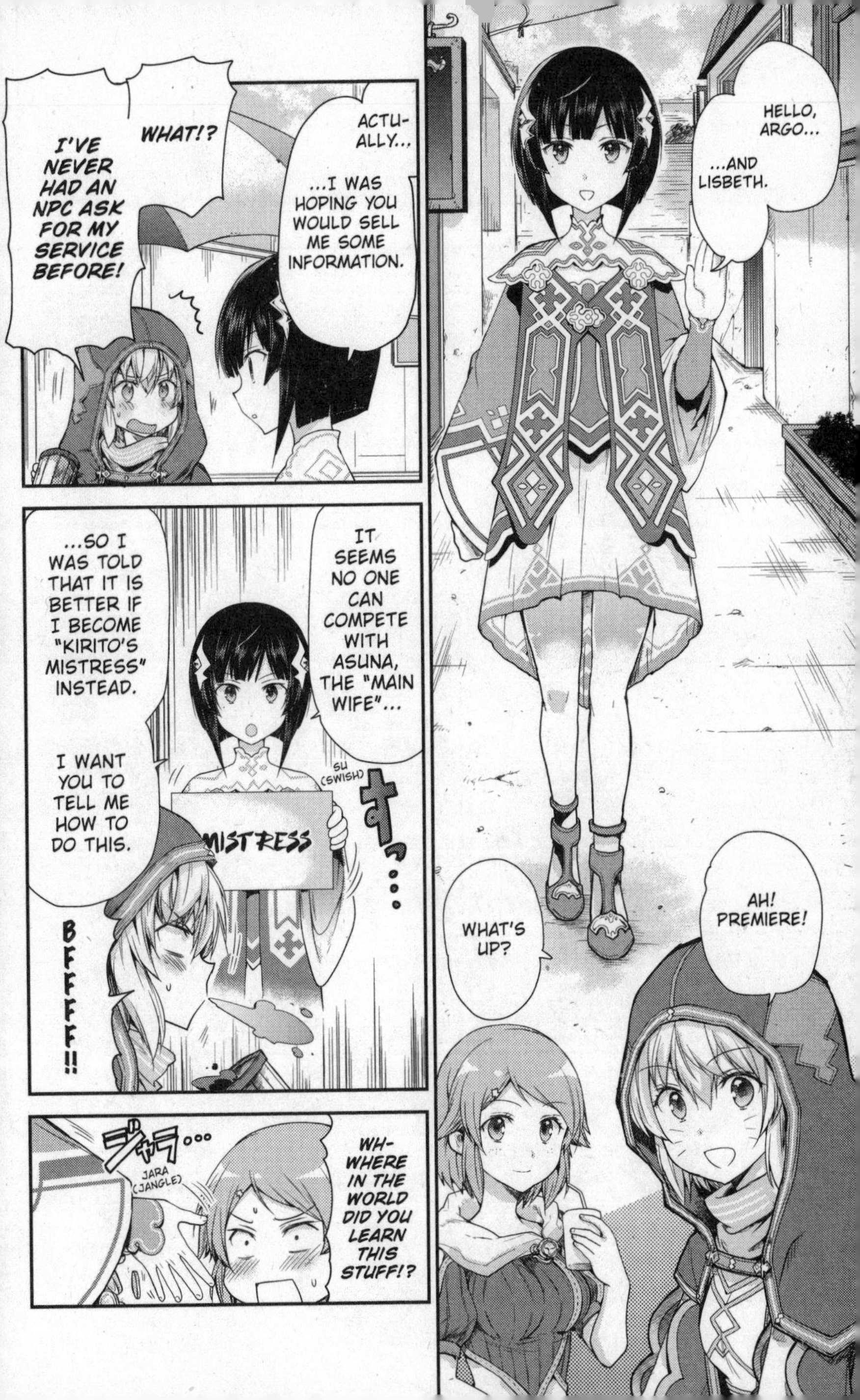
HELLO, ARGO...
...AND LISBETH.
AH! PREMIERE!
WHAT'S UP?
ACTU-ALLY...
...I WAS HOPING YOU WOULD SELL ME SOME INFORMATION.
WHAT!?
I'VE NEVER HAD AN NPC ASK FOR MY SERVICE BEFORE!
IT SEEMS NO ONE CAN COMPETE WITH ASUNA, THE "MAIN WIFE"...
...SO I WAS TOLD THAT IT IS BETTER IF I BECOME "KIRITO'S MISTRESS" INSTEAD.
SU (SWISH)
I WANT YOU TO TELL ME HOW TO DO THIS.
MISTRESS
BFFFF!!
WH-WHERE IN THE WORLD DID YOU LEARN THIS STUFF!?
JARA (JANGLE)

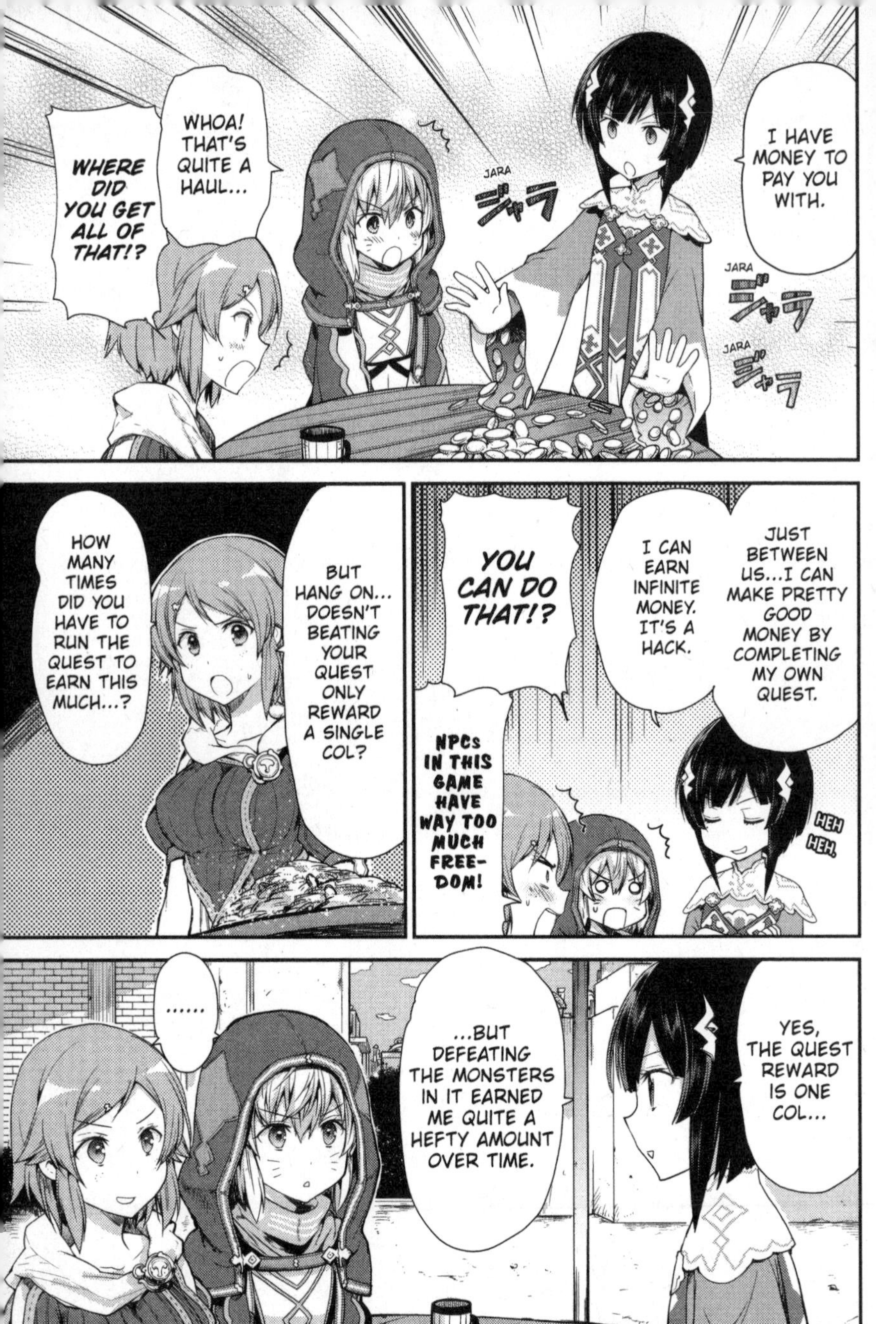
I HAVE MONEY TO PAY YOU WITH.
JARA
ジャラ
JARA
ジャラ
JARA
ジャラ
WHOA! THAT'S QUITE A HAUL...
WHERE DID YOU GET ALL OF THAT!?
JUST BETWEEN US...I CAN MAKE PRETTY GOOD MONEY BY COMPLETING MY OWN QUEST.
I CAN EARN INFINITE MONEY. IT'S A HACK.
HEH HEH.
YOU CAN DO THAT!?
NPCs IN THIS GAME HAVE WAY TOO MUCH FREE-DOM!
BUT HANG ON... DOESN'T BEATING YOUR QUEST ONLY REWARD A SINGLE COL?
HOW MANY TIMES DID YOU HAVE TO RUN THE QUEST TO EARN THIS MUCH...?
YES, THE QUEST REWARD IS ONE COL...
...BUT DEFEATING THE MONSTERS IN IT EARNED ME QUITE A HEFTY AMOUNT OVER TIME.
......

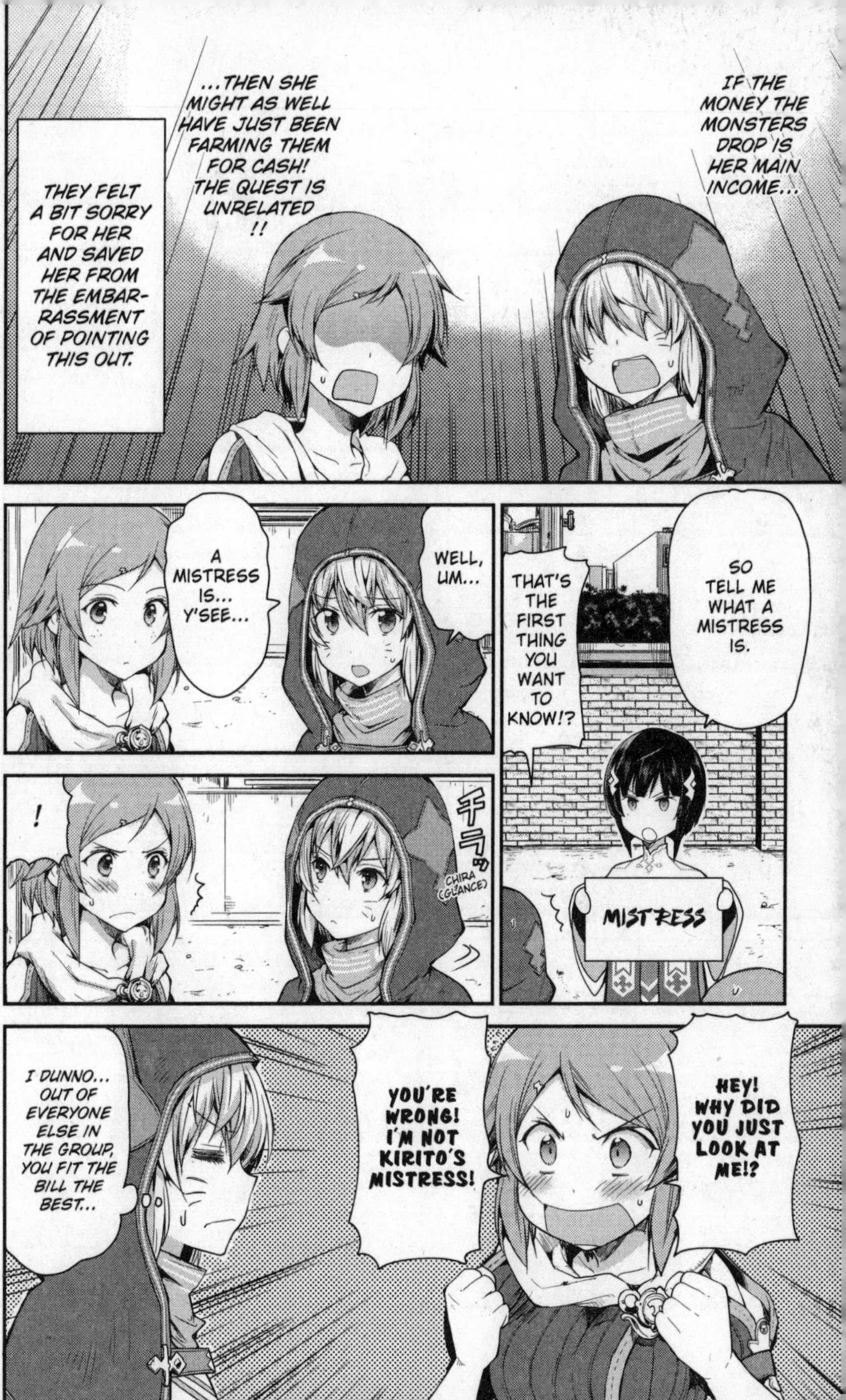
IF THE MONEY THE MONSTERS DROP IS HER MAIN INCOME...
...THEN SHE MIGHT AS WELL HAVE JUST BEEN FARMING THEM FOR CASH! THE QUEST IS UNRELATED!!
THEY FELT A BIT SORRY FOR HER AND SAVED HER FROM THE EMBARRASSMENT OF POINTING THIS OUT.
SO TELL ME WHAT A MISTRESS IS.
THAT'S THE FIRST THING YOU WANT TO KNOW!?
MISTRESS
WELL, UM...
A MISTRESS IS... Y'SEE...
!
チラッ
CHIRA (GLANCE)
HEY! WHY DID YOU JUST LOOK AT ME!?
YOU'RE WRONG! I'M NOT KIRITO'S MISTRESS!
I DUNNO... OUT OF EVERYONE ELSE IN THE GROUP, YOU FIT THE BILL THE BEST...

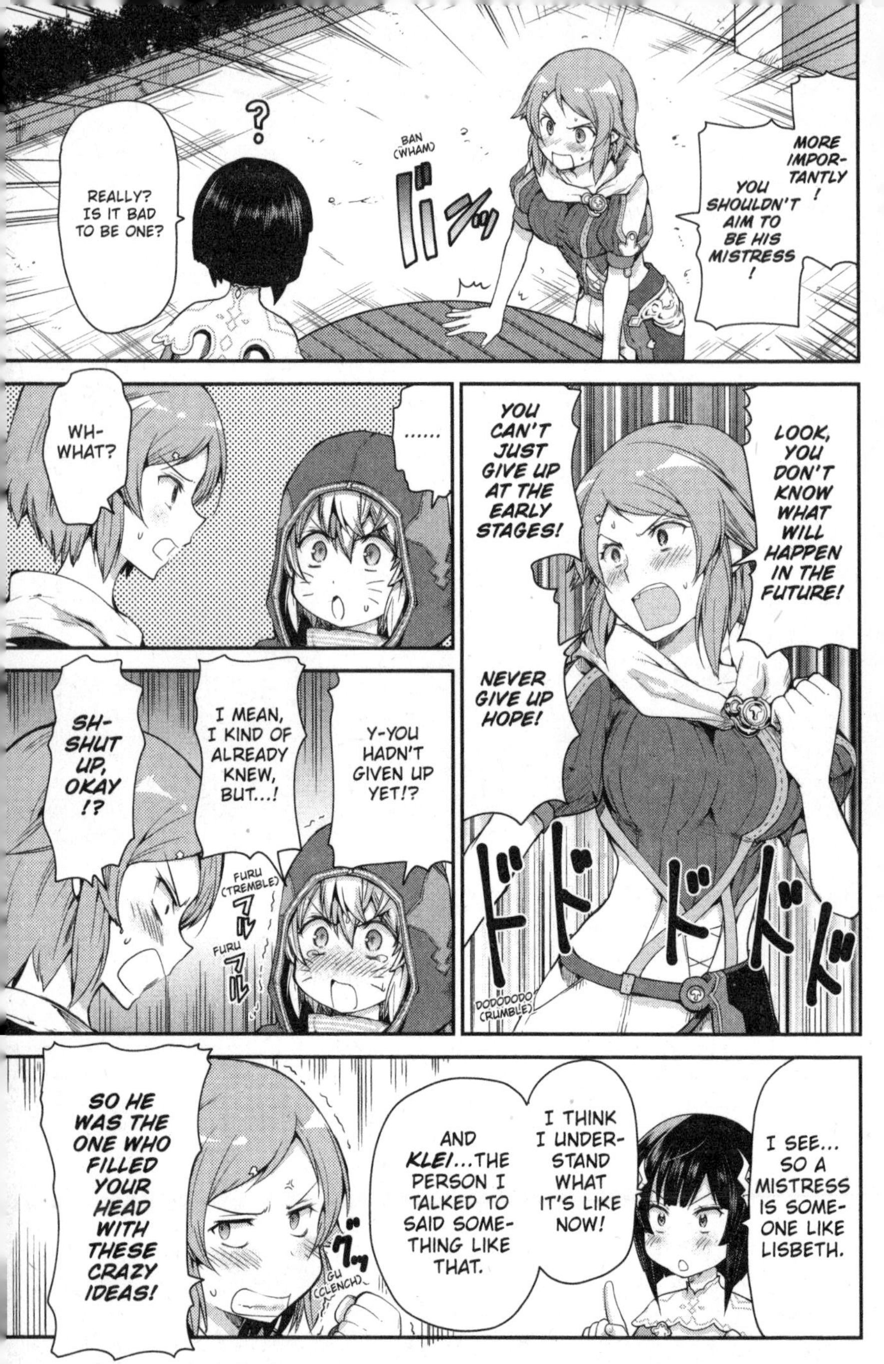
MORE IMPORTANTLY! YOU SHOULDN'T AIM TO BE HIS MISTRESS!
BAN (WHAM)
?
REALLY? IS IT BAD TO BE ONE?
LOOK, YOU DON'T KNOW WHAT WILL HAPPEN IN THE FUTURE!
YOU CAN'T JUST GIVE UP AT THE EARLY STAGES!
NEVER GIVE UP HOPE!
DODODODO (RUMBLE)
......
WH-WHAT?
Y-YOU HADN'T GIVEN UP YET!?
I MEAN, I KIND OF ALREADY KNEW, BUT...!
FURU (TREMBLE)
FURU
SH-SHUT UP, OKAY!?
I SEE... SO A MISTRESS IS SOMEONE LIKE LISBETH.
I THINK I UNDERSTAND WHAT IT'S LIKE NOW!
AND KLEI...THE PERSON I TALKED TO SAID SOMETHING LIKE THAT.
GU (CLENCH)
SO HE WAS THE ONE WHO FILLED YOUR HEAD WITH THESE CRAZY IDEAS!

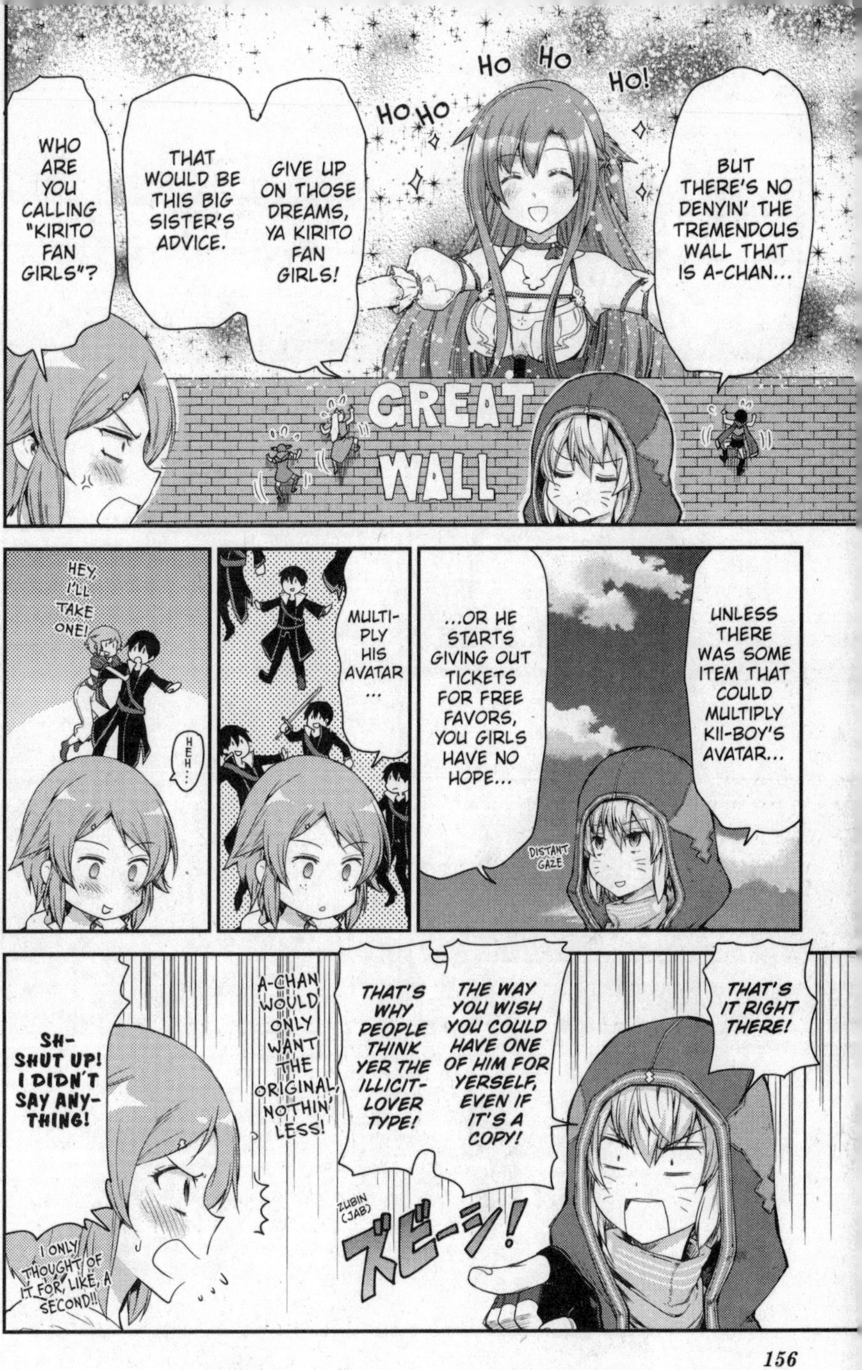
HO HO HO!
HO HO
BUT THERE'S NO DENYIN' THE TREMENDOUS WALL THAT IS A-CHAN...
GIVE UP ON THOSE DREAMS, YA KIRITO FAN GIRLS!
THAT WOULD BE THIS BIG SISTER'S ADVICE.
WHO ARE YOU CALLING "KIRITO FAN GIRLS"?
GREAT WALL
UNLESS THERE WAS SOME ITEM THAT COULD MULTIPLY KII-BOY'S AVATAR...
...OR HE STARTS GIVING OUT TICKETS FOR FREE FAVORS, YOU GIRLS HAVE NO HOPE...
DISTANT GAZE
MULTI-PLY HIS AVATAR...
HEY, I'LL TAKE ONE!
HEH...
THAT'S IT RIGHT THERE!
THE WAY YOU WISH YOU COULD HAVE ONE OF HIM FOR YERSELF, EVEN IF IT'S A COPY!
THAT'S WHY PEOPLE THINK YER THE ILLICIT-LOVER TYPE!
ZUBIN (JAB)
ズビーン!
A-CHAN WOULD ONLY WANT THE ORIGINAL, NOTHIN' LESS!
SH-SHUT UP! I DIDN'T SAY ANY-THING!
I ONLY THOUGHT OF IT FOR, LIKE, A SECOND!!

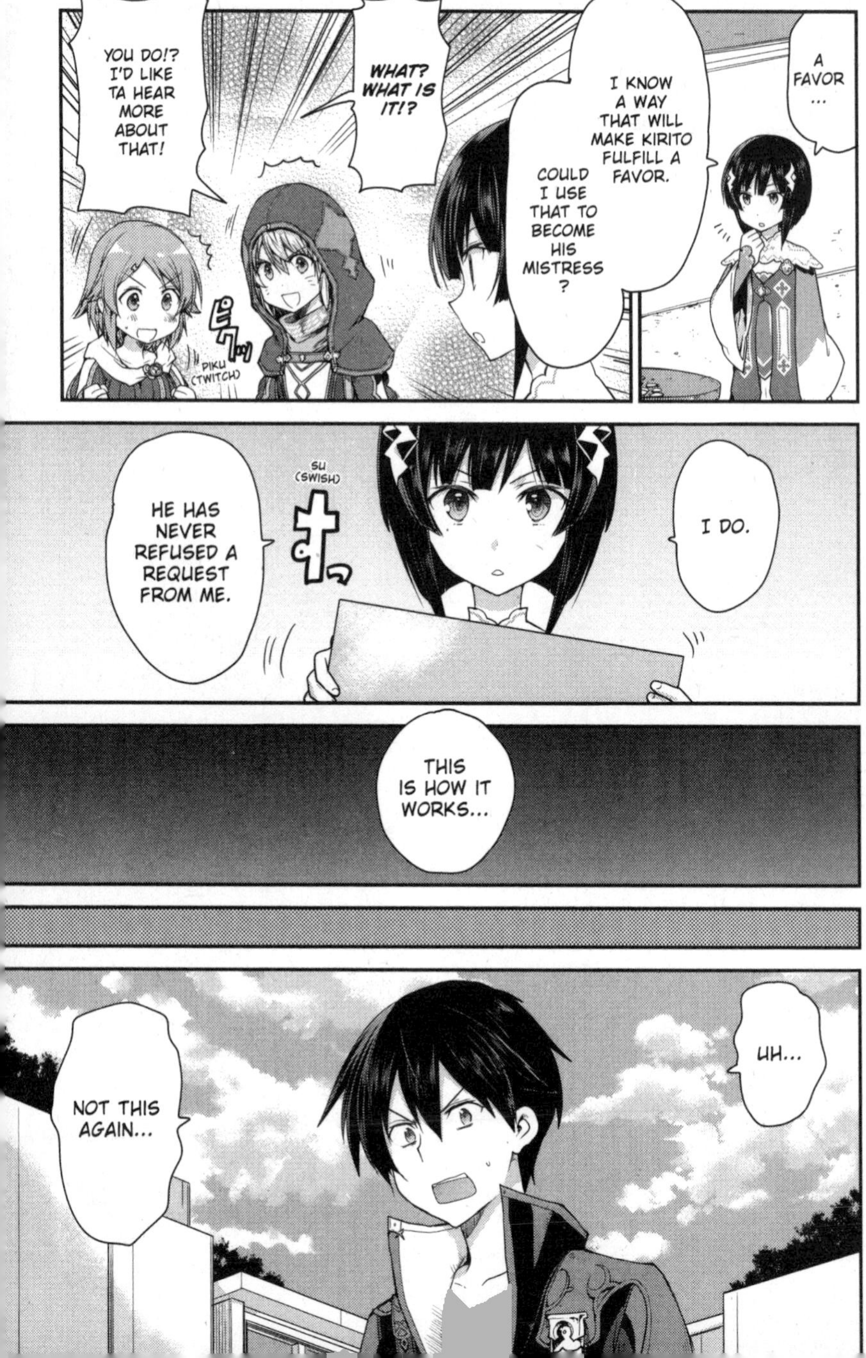
A FAVOR...
I KNOW A WAY THAT WILL MAKE KIRITO FULFILL A FAVOR.
COULD I USE THAT TO BECOME HIS MISTRESS?
WHAT? WHAT IS IT!?
YOU DO!? I'D LIKE TA HEAR MORE ABOUT THAT!
ピクッ
PIKU (TWITCH)
I DO.
すっ
SU (SWISH)
HE HAS NEVER REFUSED A REQUEST FROM ME.
THIS IS HOW IT WORKS...
UH...
NOT THIS AGAIN...

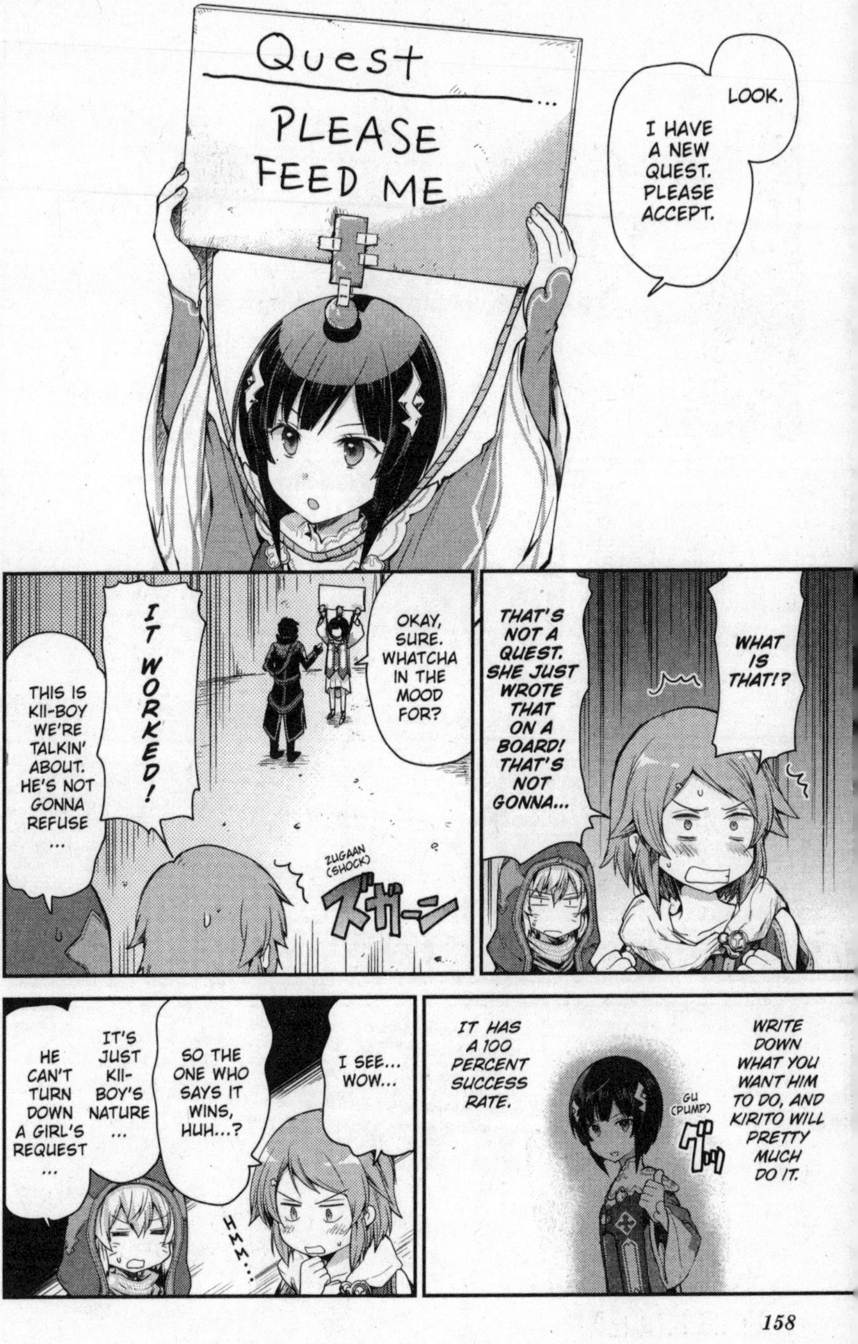
LOOK. I HAVE A NEW QUEST. PLEASE ACCEPT.
Quest ...
PLEASE FEED ME
WHAT IS THAT!?
THAT'S NOT A QUEST. SHE JUST WROTE THAT ON A BOARD! THAT'S NOT GONNA...
OKAY, SURE. WHATCHA IN THE MOOD FOR?
IT WORKED!
ZUGAAN (SHOCK)
THIS IS KII-BOY WE'RE TALKIN' ABOUT. HE'S NOT GONNA REFUSE ...
WRITE DOWN WHAT YOU WANT HIM TO DO, AND KIRITO WILL PRETTY MUCH DO IT.
GU (PUMP)
IT HAS A 100 PERCENT SUCCESS RATE.
I SEE... WOW...
SO THE ONE WHO SAYS IT WINS, HUH...?
IT'S JUST KII-BOY'S NATURE ...
HE CAN'T TURN DOWN A GIRL'S REQUEST ...
HMM...

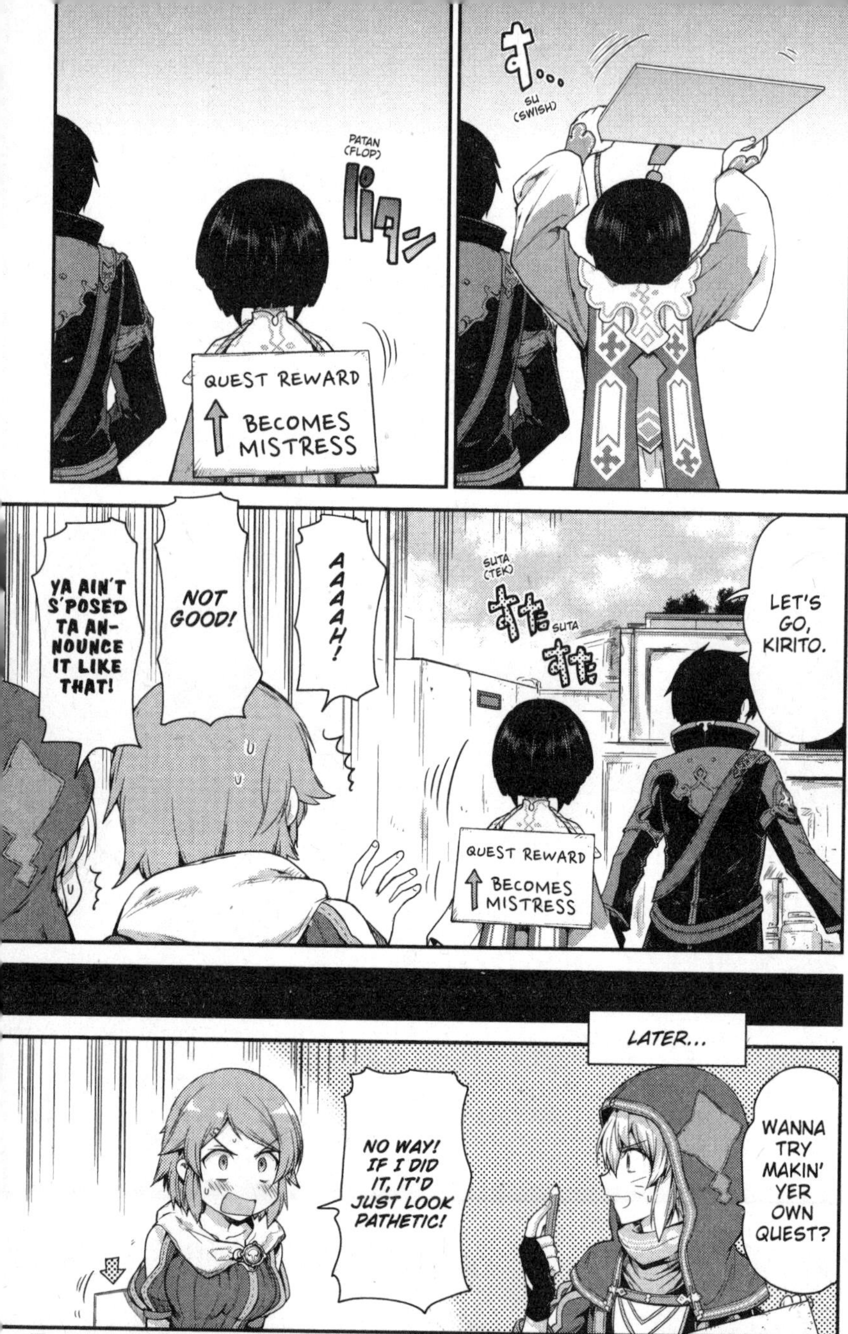
す…
SU (SWISH)
PATAN (FLOP)
パタン
QUEST REWARD
BECOMES MISTRESS
LET'S GO, KIRITO.
SUTA (TEK)
すた
SUTA
すた
QUEST REWARD
BECOMES MISTRESS
AAAAH!
NOT GOOD!
YA AIN'T S'POSED TA AN-NOUNCE IT LIKE THAT!
LATER...
WANNA TRY MAKIN' YER OWN QUEST?
NO WAY! IF I DID IT, IT'D JUST LOOK PATHETIC!

To be continued?

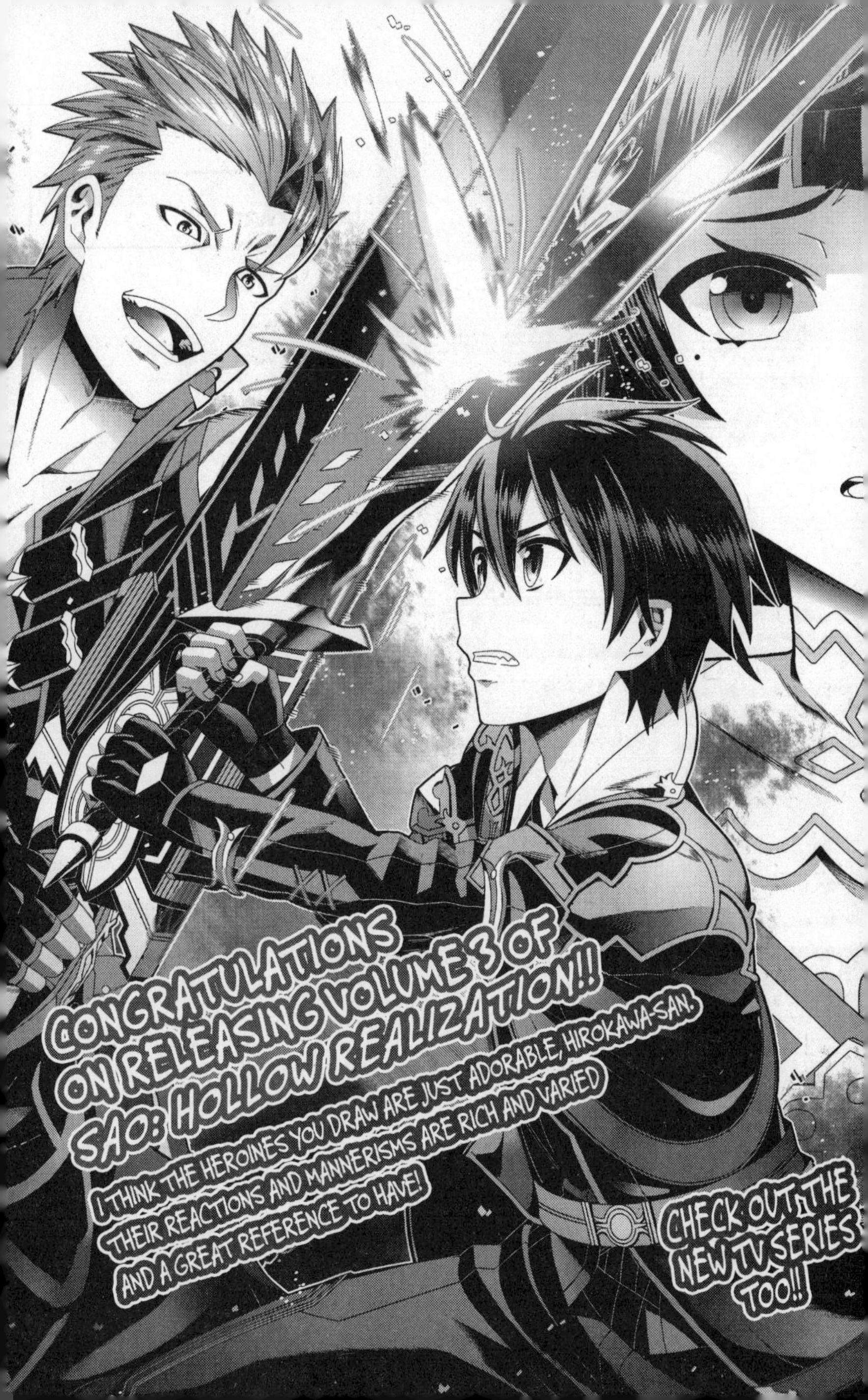
CONGRATULATIONS ON RELEASING VOLUME 3 OF SAO: HOLLOW REALIZATION!!
I THINK THE HEROINES YOU DRAW ARE JUST ADORABLE, HIROKAWA-SAN. THEIR REACTIONS AND MANNERISMS ARE RICH AND VARIED AND A GREAT REFERENCE TO HAVE!
CHECK OUT THE NEW TV SERIES TOO!!

VOLUME 3 AFTERWORD

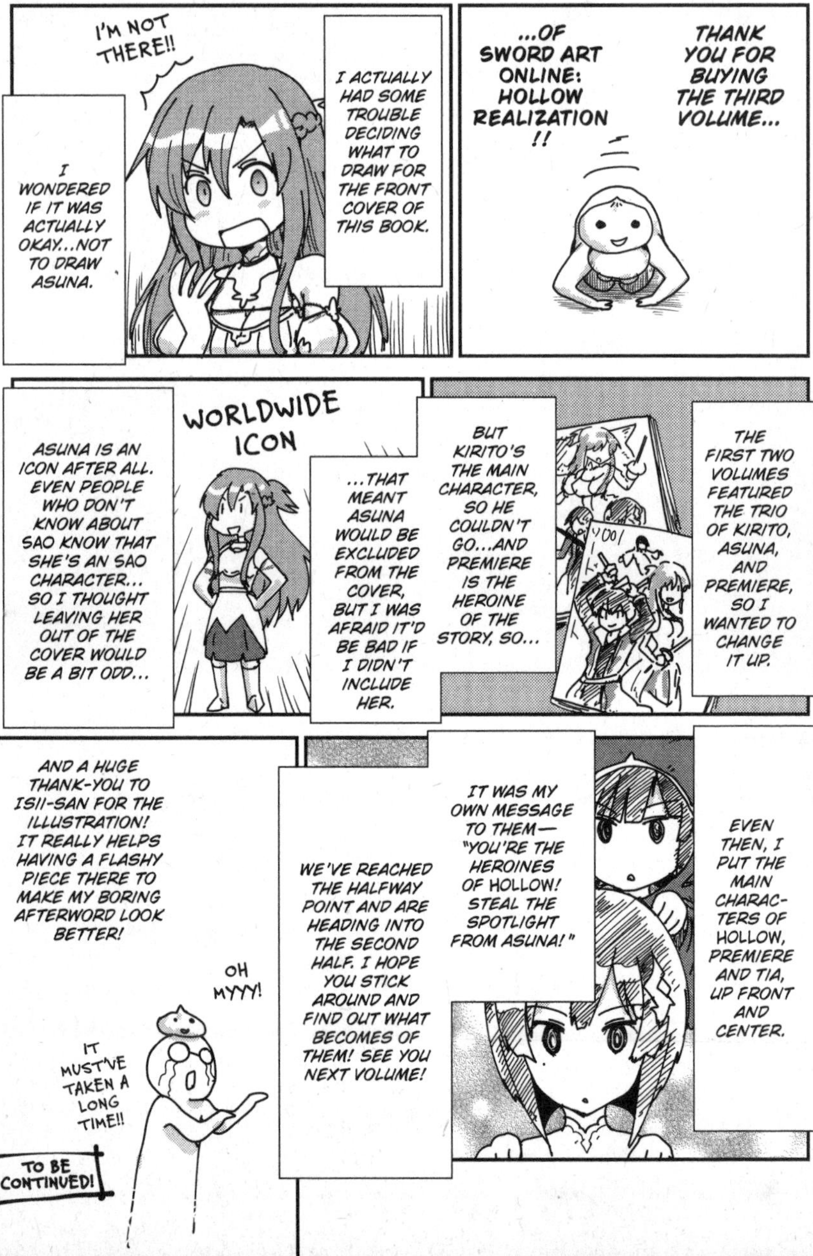
THANK YOU FOR BUYING THE THIRD VOLUME...
...OF SWORD ART ONLINE: HOLLOW REALIZATION!!
I ACTUALLY HAD SOME TROUBLE DECIDING WHAT TO DRAW FOR THE FRONT COVER OF THIS BOOK.
I'M NOT THERE!!
I WONDERED IF IT WAS ACTUALLY OKAY...NOT TO DRAW ASUNA.
THE FIRST TWO VOLUMES FEATURED THE TRIO OF KIRITO, ASUNA, AND PREMIERE, SO I WANTED TO CHANGE IT UP.
BUT KIRITO'S THE MAIN CHARACTER, SO HE COULDN'T GO...AND PREMIERE IS THE HEROINE OF THE STORY, SO...
...THAT MEANT ASUNA WOULD BE EXCLUDED FROM THE COVER, BUT I WAS AFRAID IT'D BE BAD IF I DIDN'T INCLUDE HER.
WORLDWIDE ICON
ASUNA IS AN ICON AFTER ALL. EVEN PEOPLE WHO DON'T KNOW ABOUT SAO KNOW THAT SHE'S AN SAO CHARACTER... SO I THOUGHT LEAVING HER OUT OF THE COVER WOULD BE A BIT ODD...
EVEN THEN, I PUT THE MAIN CHARAC-TERS OF HOLLOW, PREMIERE AND TIA, UP FRONT AND CENTER.
IT WAS MY OWN MESSAGE TO THEM—"YOU'RE THE HEROINES OF HOLLOW! STEAL THE SPOTLIGHT FROM ASUNA!"
WE'VE REACHED THE HALFWAY POINT AND ARE HEADING INTO THE SECOND HALF. I HOPE YOU STICK AROUND AND FIND OUT WHAT BECOMES OF THEM! SEE YOU NEXT VOLUME!
AND A HUGE THANK-YOU TO ISII-SAN FOR THE ILLUSTRATION! IT REALLY HELPS HAVING A FLASHY PIECE THERE TO MAKE MY BORING AFTERWORD LOOK BETTER!
OH MYYY!
IT MUST'VE TAKEN A LONG TIME!!
TO BE CONTINUED!

S0-CAE-483

SWORD ART ONLINE: HOLLOW REALIZATION 3

ART: TOMO HIROKAWA
ORIGINAL STORY: REKI KAWAHARA
CHARACTER DESIGN: abec
STORY SUPERVISION: BANDAI NAMCO ENTERTAINMENT

Translation: Stephen Paul   **Lettering: Phil Christie**

SWORD ART ONLINE -HOLLOW REALIZATION- Vol. 3
© REKI KAWAHARA 2018
© TOMO HIROKAWA 2018
© 2016 REKI KAWAHARA/PUBLISHED BY KADOKAWA CORPORATION
ASCII MEDIA WORKS/SAO MOVIE Project
© 2014 REKI KAWAHARA/PUBLISHED BY KADOKAWA CORPORATION
ASCII MEDIA WORKS/SAOII Project
© BANDAI NAMCO Entertainment Inc.
First published in Japan in 2018 by KADOKAWA CORPORATION, Tokyo.
English publication rights arranged with KADOKAWA CORPORATION, Tokyo,
through Tuttle-Mori Agency, Inc., Tokyo.

English translation © 2019 by Yen Press, LLC

Yen Press
1290 Avenue of the Americas
New York, NY 10104

Visit us at yenpress.com
facebook.com/yenpress
twitter.com/yenpress
yenpress.tumblr.com
instagram.com/yenpress

First Yen Press Edition: May 2019

Yen Press is an imprint of Yen Press, LLC.
The Yen Press name and logo are trademarks of Yen Press, LLC.

Library of Congress Control Number: 2018950180

ISBNs: 978-1-9753-2791-0 (paperback)
        978-1-9753-2792-7 (ebook)

10 9 8 7 6 5 4 3 2 1

WOR

Printed in the United States of America